# FINAL TERM

Also by Harold Wilson

NEW DEAL FOR COAL (1945)

IN PLACE OF DOLLARS (1952)

THE WAR ON WORLD POVERTY (1953)

THE RELEVANCE OF BRITISH SOCIALISM (1964)

PURPOSE IN POLITICS (1964)

THE LABOUR GOVERNMENT 1964–1970 (1971)

THE GOVERNANCE OF BRITAIN (1976)

A PRIME MINISTER ON PRIME MINISTERS (1977)

# FINAL TERM

## THE LABOUR GOVERNMENT
### 1974–1976

## Harold Wilson

Weidenfeld and Nicolson
and
Michael Joseph

First published in Great Britain by
Weidenfeld and Nicolson
91 Clapham High Street
London SW4 7TA

and

Michael Joseph Ltd
52 Bedford Square
London WC1B 3EF
1979

ISBN 0 7181 1860 X

Printed in Great Britain by
Ebenezer Baylis and Son Limited
The Trinity Press, Worcester, and London

# *Contents*

Appendices—*continued*

# Illustrations

*Between pages 150 and 151*

There is one important problem facing representative Parliamentary Government in the whole of the world where it exists. It is being asked to solve a problem which so far it has failed to solve: that is, how to reconcile Parliamentary popularity with sound economic planning. So far, nobody on either side of this House has succeeded, and it is a problem which has to be solved if we are to meet the challenge that comes to us from other parts of the world and if we are to grout and to buttress the institutions of Parliamentary Government in the affections of the population. . . .

I would describe the central problem falling upon representative government in the Western world as how to persuade the people to forego immediate satisfactions in order to build up the economic resources of the country. . . . How can we persuade the ordinary man and woman that it is worthwhile making sacrifices in their immediate standards or foregoing substantial rising standards to extend fixed capital equipment throughout the country?[1]

—Aneurin Bevan, in his last speech
in the House of Commons,
3 November 1959.

[1] This quotation appeared in *The Labour Government 1964-1970.* It seems as apt now as it did then.

# Foreword

My volume *The Labour Government 1964–1970* ended with the declaration of the results of the 1970 General Election, giving the Conservatives a comfortable working majority, and my televised benediction on the Government's history, prior to submitting my resignation to the Queen.

> The improvement in our economic position, as in other ways, had not erased all the scars from the tough things we had to do to get that strong position. . . .
>
> No incoming Prime Minister, if Mr. Heath takes over, in living memory has taken over a stronger economic situation. I wanted to use that as we have never been able to, in the past five or six years, to use the economic situation for building on what we have done, for example in the social services, health and education . . . and housing – to accelerate what we have been doing, to intensify and develop it. Now we hand over the means to do that, to somebody else.[1]

Mr Heath's Government had an overall majority in the House of Commons of 31, the last effective working majority any Government has possessed up to the time of writing.[2]

This present book does not aim to summarize the three years and eight months of that Government, up to the date of its resignation on 4 March 1974, except to highlight events relevant to the tasks faced by its successor in 1974–76, and to draw attention to one or two developments in the Labour Opposition which in some way conditioned – or were thought at the time to condition – the approach of the incoming Labour Government in and after March 1974.

Mr Heath was hardly in the saddle when tragedy befell him, and indeed Parliament and the nation, with the sudden death of Iain Macleod on 20 July 1970. He had been appointed Chancellor and would without doubt have been the most powerful member of the Cabinet, Mr Heath alone excepted. One cannot imagine his making some of the errors which his successor, Anthony Barber, contrived, but he would certainly have used the tremendous power of the Treasury machine to dominate the Government. As a shrewd politician, with imagination and a deep knowledge of his party, in which he had advanced from a Central Office official to Cabinet rank and the party Chairmanship, in a very few years, he would undoubtedly have introduced a subtle strategy which would have made Labour's internal problems, after six

[1] *The Labour Government 1964–1970*, London, 1971, p. 790.
[2] Since these words were written, Mrs Thatcher has secured a still larger majority (see page 241).

1

years of office, even greater than they proved to be. We shall never know whether the events of November 1973 to February 1974 which brought Labour back into office by the narrowest of margins would have been differently handled had Iain Macleod been there, with possibly a re-endorsement of the Conservative Government in a general election.

Anthony Barber was moved to the Treasury from the new monster department of Trade and Industry, and was replaced by a newcomer to Parliament, the late John Davies, former director-general of the Confederation of British Industry. A good manager, he was for a considerable time a fish out of water in Parliament, and was baited with the same relish as the Conservatives had used on Frank Cousins a few years earlier. Writing in 1978 it is good to see how effective and respected, as Shadow Foreign Secretary, he has become.[1]

In seeking to introduce 'a new economic order deliberately based on the disciplines of a market economy', Mr Heath's enthusiasm led to a number of mistakes which he later clearly regretted. High among these was the decision to scrap the Industrial Reorganization Corporation,[2] set up in 1967, which, operating in an entirely unideological way under the direction of a board consisting mainly of senior industrialists, saved a number of ailing firms by making them efficient and competitive, and embarked on a pragmatic policy of industrial mergers. It was incontinently dismissed when the Conservatives came into power; later, when Mr Heath was reported as regretting his error, he tried to set up a substitute based on the City, which never really worked.

In 1971 the Government embarked enthusiastically on 'Competition and Credit Control', based on freedom in the City – an enforced freedom in fact – which required the clearing banks and other institutions to compete more vigorously, while seeking to control the economy by strict management of the money supply. It is only fair to say that despite all Mr Healey's many changes, some of the main features of CCC still operate in the City, and are working – subject to the occasional operations of the Threadneedle Street corsetière. Mr Heath, in common with his predecessors and successors, was intent on increasing the amount of new investment in manufacturing and expanding industries. A somewhat frenetic boomlet in investment ran out of steam – and investment began to turn down in the second quarter of 1973, six months before the oil crisis shattered the world economy. Little is now remembered of the dash for freedom except the wild property boom and bust, exaggerated by the activities of the ephemeral 'fringe banks', most of whom perished in the crisis.[3]

[1] He was forced to resign from Parliament through ill health; and the regrets expressed and the tributes paid to him from all quarters of the House showed the esteem in which he was held.

[2] See *The Labour Government 1964–1970*, pp. 202, 224, 269, 446, 710.

[3] See the evidence by the Bank of England to the Committee to Review the Functioning of the Financial Institutions, second submission, *The Lifeboat Operation*, FI(78)55 of 2 May 1978, published by the Bank of England, as was their paper FI(78)67 setting out the Bank's oral evidence to the Commons Select Committee on Nationalized Industry, 18 and 25 January 1978.

Mr Heath, even more perhaps than some of his colleagues who would have preferred a quiet life, was dedicated to rationalizing the system of industrial relations by placing it under a tight and tidy framework of law. Conservative Ministers of Labour – with the exception of Sir Walter Monckton and Iain Macleod – tend to be as uninformed on trade union realities as some Labour MPs, ministers even, are on financial institutions. His ignorance of the human side and the loyalties of trade unionism was compounded by his employing the most arid of lawyers to draft a Bill which reflected all the finer points of obsessive legalism.

The Government's dedication to the free market led it at first to believe that wages would find their own level as a result of tight monetary control. Disillusionment came with the humiliating outcome of the mineworkers' imposition of their own terms following the Wilberforce report.

1971 was the worst year for loss of working-days through disputes since the year of the General Strike, 1926. Nearly 24 million man-days were lost, more than all those lost in the years 1964 to 1969. By September 1972 the Government had moved to a statutory system of pay and prices control.

Stage I ran from 6 November 1972 to 31 March 1973[1] and Stage II to 6 November 1973: they achieved a remarkable degree of success and apparent acceptability. Strike losses fell to tolerable levels, earnings rose by 2.9 and 9.3 per cent respectively over the two stages, and prices by 4.3 and 5.7 per cent respectively. But all experience shows that Stage III is critical. So it proved.

The period of the Heath Government was significant for important changes in world finance, with the breakdown of the post-war Bretton Woods system, which had lasted a surprising quarter of a century. Faced with a major sterling crisis, Britain went on to a régime of floating exchange rates on 23 June 1972. The US-dominated International Monetary Fund had relaxed its strict régime. The Conservative Government was therefore able to meet a crisis by devaluing without having to face all the misery which the Labour Government had known in the mid-1960s until – and indeed after – the cataclysm of the 1967 devaluation. The Conservatives devalued at will, and not a dog barked.

The Sterling Area was dismantled at a stroke, with such nonchalance that Commonwealth sentimentalists in the Labour Opposition suspected the action as being influenced by a more compelling doctrinal loyalty to the EEC.

For one of the most significant enterprises of Mr Heath's Government was the negotiation for entry into the European Common Market.

President de Gaulle had vetoed two previous applications, that of Mr Macmillan's Government in 1963, and that of the Labour Government in 1967. His successor, President Pompidou, had finally withdrawn from an opposition based on principle, and after difficult negotiations Britain entered

[1] For pay: the prices freeze lasted until 28 April 1973.

the EEC on 1 January 1973. The arguments surrounding this decision and the position of the (divided) Labour Opposition are dealt with in Chapter 3.

One thing which shocked Labour members, going beyond the ranks of the dedicated anti-marketeers, was the character of the consequent legislation. The Labour Government had warned Parliament in the sixties that a Bill of several hundred clauses would most probably be needed. Sir Geoffrey Howe produced one of twelve clauses, so tightly drawn that amendment was virtually impossible. In any case the Government were determined to rail-road it through under the guillotine procedure, which left a large number of valid amendments undebated. The official Labour Opposition was critical not only of the terms on which Britain entered but also of the fact that they were presented, alike for the major and minor issues, on a 'take it or leave it' basis.

There were also differences on foreign and Commonwealth affairs. Early in the lifetime of the Government the Conservatives decided to end the ban we had introduced the day after taking office in 1964 on the supply of arms to South Africa, and went so far as to sign a contract for the supply of military aircraft. Passions were raised, too, about Chile, where the socialist President Allende was murdered by the Fascist right wing.

In the autumn of 1973 things turned sour for Mr Heath and his colleagues. His free market had been no more successful than our policies had been for stimulating investment. A stronger tone entered his speeches when addressing or talking about industrialists. At an industrial lunch convened by the Institute of Directors he spoke right out:

> The curse of British industry is that it has never anticipated demand. When we came in we were told there weren't sufficient inducements to invest. So we provided the inducements. Then we were told people were scared of balance-of-payments difficulties leading to stop–go. So we floated the pound. Then we were told of fears of inflation: and now we're dealing with that. And still you aren't investing enough. . . .

> We have given people the incentives – both corporate and individual – which we promised them, and we let Rolls-Royce and Mersey Docks go bust, and their shareholders lost their money. Certainly we put Government money into the Clyde – but you cannot do the same things regardless with one million unemployed – just as we picked up the pieces of Rolls-Royce because we could not leave 82 air forces (including our own) in the lurch . . . And what was the effect? Did other managements say 'well, the Government hasn't paid out to them, so we are on our own'? Not at all: they said 'the time for risk-taking is over'.

When certain activities of Lonrho became public knowledge, he made his celebrated and obviously prepared statement describing the affair as 'the unacceptable face of capitalism'.

Even before the onset of the oil crisis he was running into difficulties on pay policy. Shortly after Stage III was launched on 7 November 1973, it became clear that the test case would be the pay settlement for the coal industry. Mr Heath had taken great care to avoid a repetition of the Wilber-force situation. The Stage III rules went to great lengths to accommodate the miners, for example by making special provision for those working 'unsocial hours'. Mr Heath, it was widely understood, conferred with Mr Joe Gormley and was confident that there would be no crisis with the miners. Whether it was that Mr Heath was too optimistic in his interpretation of Joe Gormley's advice, or whether Joe Gormley himself was over-optimistic about what the miners would accept, as has been suggested, is not clear. But Mr Heath, deciding to stand firm on the Gormley assessment, had underrated the strength of Jim Daly and Mick McGahey. Once again it was confrontation.

It was not a confrontation desired by the Labour Opposition, particularly when Government press-briefing suggested that Cabinet hawks were pressing for a General Election on the issue 'Who governs the nation?'. Britain had no recent experience of a single-issue electoral confrontation of such a kind, where the rights and wrongs of the miners' case would be thrown into the election scales, and where three and a half years of Conservative Govern-ment policy might take a minor place at the hustings. Throughout the three months ending with Mr Heath's decision to go to the country, I did all I could to avoid it, including meetings with the NUM, and attempts to find a formula which Mr Heath could accept. But, we now know, Mr Heath was surrounded by advisers who were urging an election on what they saw, or hoped they would present to the country, as a major constitutional issue. As a precaution I converted a joint meeting of the Shadow Cabinet and the NEC at the turn of the year into a joint committee to prepare a manifesto in readi-ness. When Mr Heath finally proclaimed the election we were ready. Against 'Who governs Britain?', we were prepared to argue for conciliation and a social contract between Government and industry.

When the Election began Mr Heath appealed to the country on the straight constitutional issue. My first broadcast, platform speech and press conference responded in kind. My second speech was on the cost of living, my third on the Common Market. He sought to narrow the issue; we sought to follow the traditional election approach of fighting on the whole record of the Government, and our alternative policies on every issue of importance to the electorate. Not until the votes were counted would anyone be able to say which approach was right. But it was significant that the question was being asked, 'Is Britain ungovernable?'[1] And if any voter thought it was, how would he vote – for Conservative confrontation to settle the issue once and for all, or for Labour's programme of conciliation and healing?

We had one uncovenanted advantage. The three-day week meant that a significant proportion of the working population was at home on polling-day. Never have we seen so high a vote before midday. Instead of waiting until the last hour for Labour voters to go to the polling-station, we had accounts

[1] See David Butler and Dennis Kavanagh, *The British General Election of 1974*, p. 5. See also an assessment by Peter Jenkins in March 1976, p. 233 below.

of a massive vote before noon. One ward in a neighbouring constituency of mine had registered more votes by noon than they would normally have seen by 7.30 p.m. It was clear, too, that the Liberal vote would include the contribution of a number of worried, traditional Conservative voters. The Election was on a razor-edge, as the counting was to show.

# PART I

*The Short Parliament*

# *Chapter 1*

## FORMING THE GOVERNMENT

IT was clear that no party would have anything like a majority in the House of Commons. The morning's press and news bulletins of Friday 1 March, including all the overnight results, showed that the Conservatives had so far lost 11 seats net to Labour, with nearly two hundred results to declare. The Liberals were doing well, with many results in Scotland and Wales, where the respective Nationalist parties were on the march, still to be declared.

I returned to London on the Friday morning, and found crowds outside my home and outside the Labour Party headquarters all claiming a victory of which I was anything but confident. *The Times*, commenting on the reception, said, very perceptively:

> While overtly registering a quiet confidence, there seems little doubt that he was as perplexed at the possible outcome as the party workers and journalists who pressed around him.

In the afternoon, as we had arranged, the Parliamentary Committee, the so-called 'Shadow Cabinet', met at Transport House. We decided to make a simple statement.

While, we emphasized, there was a need for Government to deal decisively with the economic and industrial crisis facing the nation, 'in these circumstances the Labour Party is prepared to form a government and to submit its programmes for the endorsement of Parliament'. In other words, we were available.

We further resolved that none of us would make any news comment, claim or forecast over the week-end. The Conservatives still formed the Government. They had to decide whether to resign or seek to carry on. They were clearly trailing but by one of the most infinitesimal margins in election history. Neither major party could hope for anything like an overall majority in Parliament because of the gains made by the smaller parties. Mr Heath was still Prime Minister, and there was no vacancy. We agreed to meet – in the Leader of the Opposition's room at the House of Commons – the following Monday afternoon.

The week-end, when we heard of mysterious doings between Mr Heath and the Liberal leader, Mr Thorpe, at least enabled us to catch up with our sleep. One of the unsung disadvantages of our system is that an incoming Prime

Minister usually goes to the Palace to kiss hands on a Friday afternoon, desperately short of sleep as he will have been sitting up for the results, to say nothing of the wear and tear of at least three weeks' campaigning, and he has to proceed at once to form an administration, and take a series of decisions which can dog him and his Government for months – even longer. But for us that week-end was a time for rest – and for planning.

Meanwhile Saturday saw the final results. Labour held 301 seats, a net gain of 14 compared with 1970; the Conservatives held 297 (including the retiring Speaker), a net loss of 33; the Liberals had raised their total from 6 to 14, and 'Others', mainly Nationalists, had gone up from 7 to 23. (Discrepancies in the totals are explained by the redistribution of constituency boundaries, increasing the total seats from 630 to 635.)

It was going to be a minority Parliament. The Liberals could well hold the key.

Mr Heath saw this as clearly as anyone. Mr Thorpe and he were in colloquy almost before the rest of us had caught up with our sleep. It was a temptation for the Liberal Party. The smell of power, or of partial power, or at least of a qualified influence with office for one or two, was in their nostrils, for the first time since the 'Wee Frees', the Samuelite Liberals, had left the 1931 Coalition Government, forty-two years before. But Mr Thorpe's Liberals were not of one mind, and the Young Liberals were on the rampage. Mr Heath's last hope of remaining in office faded as the last Liberal coat-tail went out through the No. 10 doorway.

On the Monday the Shadow Cabinet met, more rather than less available than on the previous Friday. The tone was more than a little impatient, and Shirley Williams and Tony Benn were despatched upstairs to prepare a press statement. Just before 7.0 p.m., while they were still at work, messages reached us that the Cabinet meeting had broken up, and that ministers were 'clearing their cupboards' in their departments. The Shadow Cabinet adjourned. The Private Secretary at No. 10 telephoned my office – as he had, contingently, on the previous Friday – to ask where I might be found. I returned to my home in Lord North Street, and changed into more formal wear.

I was summoned to Buckingham Palace, after Mr Heath's formal resignation, and the Queen asked me the usual question: could I form an administration?

To this question, sanctified by a century and a half of constitutional practice, two answers are possible. The first is, 'Yes, Ma'am'; the second is, 'I will enter into consultation to see whether I can report to you that an administration can be formed.' Although Labour's representation in Parliament was 34 less than a putative coalition of all the other parties, I was confident that a Government could be formed, and that on its first major Parliamentary test, the adoption of the Queen's Speech setting out the

Government's programme for the coming session, we should be sustained by the vote of the Commons.

The position traditionally taken by Buckingham Palace in this kind of a situation following an unclear election result, or a vacancy occurring during the lifetime of an elected Parliament, is not always understood. There were suggestions in March 1974, that as Labour had more seats than any other party, though not a plurality in the Commons, the Sovereign should have sent at once for the Labour leader. This is not so. A Government was in existence, and until it resigns, following the election results, or a defeat on the Queen's Speech, the Palace can only observe the classical doctrine, 'We have a Government'.[1]

My immediate problems were: to form a Government; to prepare and agree with unprecedented speed the Queen's Speech for a Parliamentary session due to begin the following week; to end the coal industry dispute, and confrontation generally; and to get the country back on a full working week.

On reaching No. 10, greeted as is usual by the staff, I spent a few minutes with Robert Armstrong, who had been Principal Private Secretary to Mr Heath, and whom I intended to keep on in Downing Street. He briefly brought me up to date on matters pressing for decision. For my part I contented myself with asking that the Napoleonic War pictures in the main dining room at No. 10 be brought back to their traditional position without delay. These portraits of Nelson, Wellington, Pitt and Fox had been there for Prime Ministerial generations, though it had been widely reported that they had given affront to M. Pompidou, the French Prime Minister, during an official visit in July 1966.[2] Mr Heath had had them removed and replaced by pictures of a more classical art form. I wanted them back, and also, restored to the lobby outside the Cabinet Room from some upstairs posting, the wartime portrait of Winston Churchill in his boilersuit. Immediately afterwards I met Sir John Hunt, the Cabinet Secretary.

I asked Private Office to invite the TUC and CBI to meet colleagues and myself at noon and 2.30 p.m. respectively, the following day, to clear the way for ending the coal confrontation and the three-day week. From then on the priority was on forming the Government. Between 9.30 and midnight I had seen – and recommended to the Palace – Sir Elwyn Jones as Lord Chancellor, the Minister of Agriculture, and Secretaries of State for Industry, Energy, Employment and Defence. The appointment of James Callaghan as Foreign Secretary, Denis Healey as Chancellor, and Roy Jenkins as Home Secretary

[1] See my *The Governance of Britain*, pp. 24–6. In this connection it should be noted that Sir Alec Douglas-Home, when the question was put to him in 1963, took the other line and asked that he might go away and see *whether* he could form an administration. In any such situation the test is the acceptance by Parliament at the conclusion of the debate on the Address in Reply to the Gracious Speech – see *op. cit.* p. 25, on the different responses given by Baldwin in 1923 and 1929.

[2] On this visit, see my *The Labour Government 1964–1970*, pp. 249–51.

and one or two others I had settled in the afternoon while we were awaiting events. In addition to those who were previously members of the Shadow Cabinet, and my ministerial appointments in the Lords, Barbara Castle entered the Cabinet.

In making these appointments I was in a much happier position than in 1964. An incoming Labour Prime Minister must have regard to the membership of the Parliamentary Committee (the so-called 'Shadow Cabinet') of the previous Parliament, for its 15 Commons members have been elected by the whole Parliamentary Labour Party. On this occasion the PLP had elected the very ones I would have chosen; indeed I had voted for them in the secret ballot. This was very different from the 1963–64 Shadow Cabinet. I had voted for only a minority of them, and only a minority had voted for me. (Most of them were appointed in 1964, but some did not remain long.)

From 10 a.m. to midday on the Tuesday I saw further Cabinet appointees, and began to discuss with some of them my suggestions for their Ministers of State and Parliamentary Under-Secretaries.

At noon the TUC deputation arrived. No. 10 had asked me whom I wanted to see – the General Council or the Economic Committee? I said, 'Leave it to them,' and the full General Council arrived. I began by saying that while they knew all the colleagues on my side of the table, they would not know their new roles. There was considerable satisfaction as I introduced them in their ministerial capacities, not least Michael Foot as Employment Secretary. We told the TUC that, subject to Cabinet approval that afternoon, we proposed to move to bring the coal dispute to an end, and that we counted on their support in securing a speedy and effective return to normal working in industry. They, and the CBI in the afternoon, undertook full co-operation in this task, and the Cabinet at 5.0 p.m. authorized the Employment and Energy Secretaries to sanction a pit settlement on the basis we had advocated during the General Election, within an overall cost limit accepted by the Chancellor – slightly increased with his authority the following day, when the Coal Board and NUM were nearing an agreement. By the Wednesday evening, fifty hours after I had returned from the Palace, the settlement was announced. By the Thursday, less than three days after Labour took office, it was announced that the State of Emergency which had ruled for nearly three months was to be abrogated. On the Friday, 8 March, Anthony Crosland, Secretary of State for the Environment, announced the implementation of another election pledge, the freezing of the Council house rent increases which the previous Government had announced would come into force on 1 April. His freeze covered two and a half million local authority houses. It extended also to 2.8 million privately owned rented houses and three quarters of a million private furnished dwellings.

It had been a breathless week. The Emergency over, we then settled down, with greater speed than is usual for an incoming Government, to plan the legislative programme for the following session, for our predecessors had announced the date for the Queen's Speech opening the new session, allowing an unusually short interval after the General Election. They clearly had not based their planning on the arrival of a new Government. Less than two days after taking office we were in the House to elect the new Speaker – in fact to re-elect Selwyn Lloyd – and to take the oath.

The Queen's Speech had been timed for 12 March, only eight days after our taking office: the manoeuvrings of the previous week-end had accounted for part of the allotted time. Not only that: a Budget was due only two weeks later and Britain was facing an unparalleled economic crisis, the worse in that we were confronted by fourfold oil-price increases and by balance-of-payments problems unprecedented in our history.

The usual period of gestation for even a normal Budget covers anything from three to six months. The Chancellor's Budget strategy is usually formulated within the recesses of the Treasury and discussed in general terms with the Prime Minister and First Lord of the Treasury before Christmas. Some tax options have to be accepted or discarded before Christmas, since changes in certain direct, and more particularly indirect taxes, need three months' preparation, or much longer in the case of complex fiscal innovations. The incoming 1974 Government had less than three weeks between its appointment and Cabinet approval of the Budget proposals on the eve of Budget day.

We met to prepare the Queen's Speech the day after the Cabinet was formed. As usual, the Cabinet Office had a draft ready, embodying our principal manifesto commitments. As I have previously noted,[1] this activity is not based on any cynical attitudes. The Civil Service machine has little to do during a general election, except to keep its head down, and stay out of political controversy: it therefore prepares, against any possible election verdict, two draft Queen's Speeches, ready to discard the one which is inappropriate when the results are known. As had happened in 1964, we found that the draft before us covered our commitments for a full Parliament. But, even more than in 1964, when we had had a small overall majority, no one could possibly believe that our minority Government would last anything like five years. Few expected it to survive, unless confirmed by a further general election, to the end of the year. What would have been impossible, however, would have been a brief speech containing just those measures appropriate to a Parliament of a few months' duration. For one thing, it was impossible to plan a timetable related to an election date which was unknown, and could not even be forecast with any confidence.

There was another consideration. We wanted to have on the Parliamentary agenda some of the major legislation which we had put to the country. Even if much of it could not pass into law before an election, it was important to present it to Parliament and the nation in clear legislative form, to minimize misrepresentation on the hustings. Moreover, it would spur Whitehall to constructive activity. Beyond that, in any case where legislation was not even

[1] *The Governance of Britain*, p. 47.

theoretically possible, it was my intention to ensure that Ministers put the election commitments into clear administrative form in a series of White Papers. This meant that the Cabinet and Whitehall would have to work very hard to prepare what was in fact likely to be post-election legislation.

Hardly a member of the Cabinet doubted that, if the Queen agreed to a Prime Ministerial request, we should have to go to the country at some time in 1974. Not all of them, however, were of one mind about the right date. Before Easter, after the endorsement of the Queen's Speech and the Budget Resolutions, we had an informal discussion about electoral plans. Michael Foot and some others were in favour of an early appeal, in order to secure an adequate majority to put through the manifesto programme. I was very much against this. The country had elected us by a hair's breadth – indeed on total votes in the constituencies we were some way behind the Conservatives. The electorate had a right to see what we could do, and in particular to see our election pledges turned into clear legislative and administrative form. Having regard to the nature of the February election it was more than arguable that they had voted *against* Mr Heath and confrontation, rather than *for* Labour, still less for Labour legislation which had not even been clearly formulated.

In the event the issue was quickly settled when I asked Michael whether he was prepared to risk the passage of the Bill he was preparing to repeal the Conservatives' Industrial Relations Act. It was quite impossible to get it through by May or early June: after that, holidays in different parts of the country would rule out any election. With regret he agreed, and that was that. But it was clear that the deferment could not be beyond the autumn. In the event, even then – though we came back with a substantial majority of votes, and with a clear lead of 42 seats over the Conservatives – our effective overall majority was only 4 seats, certain to be eroded, sooner or later, by by-elections.

The Queen's Speech noted the end of the State of Emergency, occasioned by the coal mining dispute, which had existed since 13 November 1973 and which had been renewed by Proclamation on 6 March 1974 before the dispute was settled.

The part of the Speech relating to the domestic programme began with a reference to 'rising prices, the balance-of-payments deficit and the recent dislocation of production', and promised 'measures to establish price limits for certain key foods, with the use of subsidies where appropriate . . .'.

Legislation was promised to extend the law relating to consumer credit, and – an important though contested election pledge – a measure 'to require goods, where appropriate, to be labelled with the price at which they are to be sold, and to provide for Unit pricing'. Parallel measures were promised to halt the rent increases immediately due to take effect, and to reform the law relating to rents and housing subsidies. There was to be a Bill to increase pensions and other social security benefits, and proposals for the redistribution of wealth, the protection of the lower paid and the disadvantaged, and for better methods of meeting the needs of the disabled. Discussions would take place with the TUC, the CBI and 'others concerned', about 'methods of securing the orderly growth of incomes on a voluntary basis'.

Legislation would be introduced to promote the modernization and re-equipment of industry, and priority given to regional development, and to legislation on health and safety for people in their places of work.

On the oil crisis, we promised

urgent action to improve energy supplies, to secure their efficient use and to ensure that oil and gas from the Continental Shelf are exploited in ways and on terms which will confer maximum benefit on the community, and particularly in Scotland and the regions elsewhere in need of development. An urgent examination will be carried out on the future of the coal industry.

The repeal of the Industrial Relations Act was promised, as was the establishment of a new conciliation and arbitration service, to be known as ACAS, the Advisory Conciliation and Arbitration Service.

The changes made by the previous Government in the organization of the National Health Service would be reviewed. So would 'certain major development projects' – we had in mind the Maplin Airport scheme and the Channel Tunnel, both subsequently abandoned. The Concorde project was also to be reviewed.

The museum charges introduced by the previous Government would be abolished; the Government would make proposals for securing equal status for women, and would also 'consider the provision of financial assistance to enable Opposition parties more effectively to fulfil their Parliamentary functions'.

But Mr Heath was not content to assume that the normal procedures of Queen's Speech, debate, and Parliamentary approval would be allowed to follow. On 8 March, four days before the date set for the Opening of Parliament, he queried Labour's mandate with a perfectly constitutional warning that his party, plus allies, might seek to defeat us at the end of the debate on the Speech, thus forcing our resignation.

This warning naturally immediately hit the headlines. It happened that the following day I had a speaking engagement in High Wycombe, not far from Chequers. This had been arranged long before the election had been announced, but I had told the local party that I would keep the engagement. My speech, widely reported in the headlines and on the screen, warned Mr Heath to pursue this 'at his electoral peril'. The implication was that if we were defeated on the Gracious Speech, I should seek a mandate to hold an election on the contents of the Speech, and, more broadly, on 'Who governs Britain?'. Neither Mr Heath nor I had, or could have had, any idea what the Sovereign's response would have been to so quick a request for a second election. But Mr Heath, under pressure from his colleagues, hastened to withdraw his threat, and even to say that his remarks had been misinterpreted. In the event, the official Opposition decided not to divide the House on the amendment they moved in the debate on the economic situation on 18 March, but the Liberals and the two Nationalist parties pressed the Conservative amendment to a vote, and were defeated, with the Conservatives abstaining, by 295 to 21. On the main motion on the Queen's Speech, only a handful of Nationalists voted, and it was carried by 294 to 7. The minority Government had survived its first Parliamentary challenge, and was now set to go ahead with as much legislation as it could get ready in the weeks ahead.

The debate on the Gracious Speech ended on 18 March. A week later the Budget was presented by Denis Healey. Ignoring the crisis statement made by Mr Barber the previous December, it was the first since the world economy had been overturned by the oil crisis and the devastating effect on Britain, already in massive payments deficit, by the then four-fold increase in our oil import bill. Internally, the increase in oil prices, and in those of most foodstuffs and commodities, was bound to give domestic prices a sharp upward twist. The *Economist* index of world primary prices, food and raw materials, for Budget week showed an increase over the previous year of 43.5 per cent in dollar terms, 52.3 per cent in sterling. In sterling terms food prices were up by 55.2 per cent, industrial materials by 39.5 per cent (fibres showing an increase of 5.5 per cent and metals 73.0 per cent).

North Sea oil, we knew, would one day bring our balance of payments into surplus. But not yet; it was not in fact until more than eighteen months later, in November 1975, that the Queen pressed the button which started the first flow of oil from the Forties Field by underwater pipeline to Aberdeen, then on by underground pipe to the Grangemouth refinery. It was not to be until almost three years even after that event that oil began significantly to turn our overseas payments into surplus. For years, in fact, Government and Opposition had played a macabre game of musical chairs, in the hope of being in possession of the chair when the oil began to flow in quantity. This lent urgency to the Outs, now led by Mr Heath, to force us to vacate the chair, and to us, the Ins, to remain seated.

But other crises were pressing on us, quite apart from the economic situation. Foremost among these was Northern Ireland, the subject of a separate chapter below. We had to move quickly, too, on our promised 're-negotiations' on the terms of entry into the EEC.

Meanwhile we were picking up the strings of government in every sphere of responsibility at home and abroad.

In 1964 hardly a single member of the Cabinet had sat in a previous Cabinet. Apart from myself there were just two, Patrick Gordon-Walker and James Griffiths. Patrick Gordon-Walker had been Commonwealth Secretary for a year and a half in the last period of Clement Attlee's administration. James Griffiths for a short time had been Colonial Secretary. I had brought him back at the age of seventy-four as the first Secretary of State for Wales, something between a charter-Mayor and an arch-Druid figure. Lord Paken-ham had been a senior minister previously, and George Brown, James Callaghan and Michael Stewart junior ministers.

In 1974 the Cabinet was richer in previous experience than perhaps any incoming Government this century. Fourteen members had sat in the out-going 1970 Cabinet.[1]

This meant that I could enjoy a different role, as I explained to the Parliamentary Party soon after the Government was formed. In the 1964 Government, I reminded them, I had to occupy almost every position on the field, goalkeeper, defence, attack – I had to take the corner-kicks and penalties, administer to the wounded and bring on the lemons at half-time. Now, I said, I would be no more than what used to be called a deep-lying centre-half – I instanced Roberts of the pre-war Arsenal team – concentrating on defence, initiating attacks, distributing the ball and moving up-field only for set-piece occasions (witness, as I had done, Roberts's famous winning goal in the sixth round of the FA Cup against Huddersfield in 1927). The *Liverpool Daily Post* went further and described my role as that of team manager, sitting on a bench near the touch-line – quite a compliment as Liverpool was Shankly country. But they failed to point out, as I reminded the Party meeting, that, seated there, he also decides the time to pull a player off the field and send on a substitute.

Moreover, the fact that, in office, most heads of departments held responsibilities in the areas they had shadowed in Opposition, meant that they knew most of the details they needed to know, and many of the personalities with whom they would have to deal. Thus, not only had Denis Healey been our spokesman on economic affairs, but James Callaghan had been responsible for handling foreign and Commonwealth affairs for two years; Merlyn Rees for Northern Ireland; Roy Jenkins had been Home Secretary in 1964–67; William Ross had been Scottish Secretary, and carried out the shadow role in 1970–74.

Among the others, Barbara Castle had had the health and social services responsibility in Opposition; Edward Short, now Leader of the House, had been Chief Whip in 1964–66, and had had in all nine years as an Opposition Whip; Shirley Williams had shadowed work on Prices and Incomes; Eric Varley on Energy; and Anthony Crosland the Department of the Environment, having earlier been Secretary of State in 1969–70. Tony Benn had shadowed Industry, and, for a few months, had been virtually minister for industry when Minister of Technology. Fred Peart had had a near six-year stint as Minister of Agriculture; Roy Mason had been a senior Defence Minister. Peter Shore and Harold Lever had had lengthy ministerial experience, and had also been in the Cabinet.

We had the advantage of knowing how to work with one another. So,

[1] See the Postscript on p. 21.

despite the daunting problems we were facing, we were able quickly to create a viable system of government, formal and informal. For one thing, for chairing those important Cabinet Committees not normally taken by the Prime Minister, I had a good number of experienced ministers from whom to select. We were able also to deploy our extremely able team of junior ministers, most of whom had pre-1970 experience.

I naturally retained the positions of Minister for the Arts and Minister for Sport, first created on our taking office in 1964. They had contributed greatly to the quality of life in Britain. Expenditure on the arts had almost trebled from 1963–64 to 1970–71. As Minister for the Arts, Jennie Lee had saved two of the four London orchestras, both virtually doomed until she acted. In that position she had also created the Open University.[1] Equally, Denis Howell, responsible for sport, was able to spend twice as much in 1970–71 as in 1963–64, and had revolutionized the provision of sports facilities for young people in general and particularly for competitive sports, swimming, athletics and cycling.[2] Hugh Jenkins was appointed Minister for the Arts, and Denis Howell re-appointed Minister for Sport.

In October 1974 a further new appointment was made. Alf Morris, who as a back-bencher had been dedicated to the welfare of the disabled, became under-secretary of State in the Department of Health and Social Services, to work full time on problems of disablement. Although necessarily constrained by public expenditure allocations, it is no exaggeration to say that he has changed the lives of millions of people. In January 1977, after I had left the Government, he suggested to me that I should table a written Parliamentary Question asking for a progress report on his work: he had in fact prepared a 'check-list'. His reply covered four columns of *Hansard*, in very small print.[3] Unfortunately, hardly a word appeared in the press, despite the large number of readers and their families who had benefited or stood to benefit from his infinite care and application. Something similar had occurred during the General Election in the autumn of 1974. At our morning press conference I was usually accompanied by one or more Cabinet ministers who spoke and answered questions on the work of their departments, and on relevant issues in the election. Alf Morris's very full report received hardly a mention, yet its relevance to the condition of the people was probably greater than most of the other issues which won headlines.

During Edward Heath's Administration the central direction of government had been further modernized, including the creation of the Central Policy Review Staff, the so-called 'Think Tank'. In my *The Governance of Britain*[4] I have referred to the great improvements in Cabinet Office

[1] See *The Labour Government 1964–1970*, pp. 534, 685–6, 719.
[2] See *The Labour Government 1964–1970*, p. 10.
[3] *Hansard*, vol. 924, cols 471–5 (written). A shortened version of the check-list is printed as Appendix I.
[4] Page 64.

organization and methods under Lord Trend. This had gone further under both Lord Trend and his successor, Sir John Hunt, between 1970 and 1974.

One useful addition was the Friday morning meetings at 9.30. Each week there was an informal meeting in the Downing Street study, attended by the Leader of the House, the Foreign Secretary and usually the Chancellor and the Chief Whip, as well as the Cabinet Secretary and my Principal Private Secretary. Its main function was to review the principal issues coming up for decision, and to plan meetings both of Cabinet Committees and of Cabinet itself to handle them expeditiously. Inevitably it turned into a wider discussion, covering for example matters coming before Parliament – and, occasionally, issues coming before the National Executive Committee of the Party.

Another development affecting both departmental administration and Downing Street co-ordination of the Government machine was the appointment of political advisers. In itself this is nothing new. Harold Macmillan even appointed a party political outsider to private office itself, a practice previously followed only in wartime by Lloyd George and Winston Churchill. Both Edward Heath and I brought in economic advisers into the Cabinet office, who of course left Government service with the end of the Government. But political advisers are a new development.

The idea was recommended in the 1960s by the Fulton Committee on the Civil Service.[1] A political adviser comes with his chief and goes with him. Each has direct access to his minister, and the intention is that he or she also attends inter-departmental committees considering matters important to his department. They should be capable, intellectually, of holding their own with experienced civil servants – most of them were – and of reporting to their ministers. They are *not* expected to act as a kind of political cell, but they can and do assist their chiefs with political speeches, whether dealing with departmental or general political matters. A unit was set up in No. 10 under Dr Bernard Donoughue, and as it had a major co-ordinating role it extended to seven members. Other departments had one or two, though one department spread itself to four. A full description of the system, asked for by the 1975 Commonwealth Conference in Jamaica, and submitted to it as a Conference document, is to be found as Appendix V to *The Governance of Britain.*[2] This was in fact prepared by the Cabinet Office at official level, and it warmly expressed on behalf of the Permanent Civil Service approval of the scheme as it was actually working.

All these improvements in the central machinery of government were going to be tested to the full. The transformation of the economic situation through the oil crisis and world inflation persisted throughout the Short Parliament and beyond, indeed up to the present time. But the same six or seven months, which included the autumn election, saw the sharpening of negotiations with

[1] *The Civil Service*, Cmnd. 3638, para. 129.
[2] Pages 202–5.

our partners in the European Economic Community; the breakdown of power-sharing in Northern Ireland; the problem of relations with Chile and South Africa, conflict and crisis in Cyprus, with at more than one stage the immediate danger of hostilities with Turkey; all these factors were to lead to a quickening of the pace of government, and of diplomatic activity. And all of them had to be dealt with against the background of a minority situation in a Parliament whose life was uncertain, though inevitably of short duration, with the thoughts of front-benchers and back-benchers alike never far from the impending General Election.

Moreover, these momentous events did not emerge in orderly sequence; any two of them or all three could erupt and reach critical proportions simultaneously. Crises are not in the habit of forming queues. So, although the immediately following chapters for convenience deal with them separately, the processes of decision-making they evoked meant that ministers and civil servants, particularly the Foreign Secretary, Chancellor, Northern Ireland Secretary, Defence Minister, with the Prime Minister, were having to deal with them at the same time, while formulating the policies of the new Government on longer-term issues such as South Africa, Rhodesia and Chile abroad, and at home, economic, industrial and oil policy, together with the reform of the social services, the health services, local government and our proposals for devolution in Scotland and Wales.

# POSTSCRIPT

## *The Labour Cabinet, March 1974*

| | |
|---|---|
| Prime Minister and First Lord of the Treasury | Harold Wilson* |
| Lord President of the Council and Leader of the House of Commons | Edward Short* |
| Secretary of State for Foreign and Commonwealth Affairs | James Callaghan*† |
| Lord Chancellor | The Lord Elwyn-Jones† |
| Secretary of State for the Home Department | Roy Jenkins* |
| Chancellor of the Exchequer | Denis Healey*† |
| Secretary of State for the Environment | Anthony Crosland*† |
| Secretary of State for Employment | Michael Foot† |
| Secretary of State for Energy | Eric Varley*† |
| Secretary of State for Prices and Consumer Protection | Shirley Williams† |
| Secretary of State for Social Services | Barbara Castle* |
| Secretary of State for Industry and Minister of Posts and Telecommunications | Anthony Wedgwood Benn*† |
| Secretary of State for Trade and President of the Board of Trade | Peter Shore*† |
| Secretary of State for Defence | Roy Mason*† |
| Secretary of State for Education and Science | Reginald Prentice† |
| Secretary of State for Scotland | William Ross* |
| Secretary of State for Wales | John Morris† |
| Secretary of State for Northern Ireland | Merlyn Rees† |
| Minister of Agriculture, Fisheries and Food | Frederick Peart*† |
| Chancellor of the Duchy of Lancaster | Harold Lever*† |
| Lord Privy Seal | The Lord Shepherd |

Robert Mellish joined the Cabinet as Chief Whip and John Silkin† as Minister for Planning and Local Government later in the year.

* Members of the outgoing Cabinet, June 1970
† Members of the Cabinet formed by James Callaghan following his appointment on 5 April 1976

# *Chapter 2*

## ECONOMICS AND INSTITUTIONS

I T seems to be almost a law of British politics that when Labour becomes the Government, we inherit a record balance-of-payments deficit, and, equally, that we bequeath a record surplus when we go out of office.

In 1964 the out-turn for the year was a deficit of £356 million, the fourth quarter running at a rate close to £600 million. When we left office in 1970, we left a surplus for the year of £695 million which rose to £1,058 million in 1971, an all-time record. In the concluding months of 1973 the worsening of the overseas trade and payments figures had already led to emergency measures by the then Conservative Chancellor of the Exchequer. The final figure for the year was a deficit of £909 million, which rose to £3,537 million in 1974. But the underlying trend, influenced of course by monetary movements, some of them speculative, was already disastrous before the end of 1973. Calculations by the Treasury showed that in the fourth quarter of 1973 the deficit was running at a rate of £4,000 million: of this only £90 million were accounted for by payments on high-priced oil. Thus the basic figures, disregarding oil, were by far the worst since trade and payments figures were first officially collected in 1822.

On this grim situation was imposed the increase in oil prices. It was a tragedy for Britain; still more it was a tragedy for a large part of the world.

At the Commonwealth Conference in Kingston, Jamaica, in May 1975, introducing my proposals for commodity planning, I referred to the blitz which had hit the world economy in the winter of 1973–74:

> We have all been affected. But by far the hardest hit of all are those developing countries whose pattern of exports denies them any chance of profiting by the boom in commodity prices, while at the same time they have had to pay a lot more for all their essential imports, especially oil and food, fertilisers and feeding stuffs. Most tragic of all has been the effect on nations already facing starvation – starvation aggravated in some cases by drought and others by flood – who have then found their resources strained beyond endurance to pay the increased cost of the things they need.[1]

In fact, the leading financial powers reacted in the wrong way. Few saw this at the time: an exception was Harold Lever, Chancellor of the Duchy of Lancaster and a kind of ministerial general economic adviser in No. 10. He

---

[1] Published as an unnumbered Departmental Paper.

would have sought, by borrowing, to raise our reserves to a level high enough to cover any losses due to our payments deficit and at the same time to repel any speculative attacks on sterling, while working for international action to spread reserves. But the forces of Treasury orthodoxy all over the world were too strong, and despite his instinctive reaction even he had not fully rationalized the situation as clearly as he has done since, after the agonies of 1975 and 1976.

In an article in the *Sunday Times* on 5 March 1978, summarizing two of his lectures to bankers, he has examined in world terms the situation which overwhelmed Governments in all five continents in 1973–74:

*BRITAIN cannot prosper unless the world prospers. But the world recession is worse than anything known since 1933. We have mass unemployment and currency instability greater than anything known in the post-war world.* A remarkable period of advance in prosperity and world trade, which marked the first decades of the post-war system, has clearly ended . . .

We can understand how we have got into our difficulties by first examining the impact of the five-fold increase in the price of oil from 1973 exacted by the Opec countries. It meant that their customers had to surrender five times the amount of buying power previously given up. The British economy – and other economies – would have been unaffected by this siphoning of buying power if the whole of the extra money Opec had taken from us could have been spent in Britain. The standard of life of the British people would have been marginally diminished perhaps but the total demand would not have changed. The factory wheels would have been kept spinning. But the Opec countries, as we well know, replaced only part of the demand they had taken away by spending more here. Part of the effective demand of all Opec's customers was sterilised, becoming a financial asset in Opec reserves.

Deficit countries like Britain faced two problems. First, they needed foreign currency to cover the deficits. Secondly, they had a shortfall of demand producing unemployment and bankruptcies.

The foreign currency problem was met by recycling . . .

The second problem of the loss of demand has been more troublesome. Far from being met, it has been aggravated. This is because the conventional response to a balance of payments deficit is to deflate the home economy, i.e. to reduce demand still further . . .

Instead of coping with the price-inflation effect of the oil-price explosion we often added to it by the tax increases involved in deflation. Whipped by the Opec debt, we chastised ourselves with scorpions.

The Opec oil-price rise was thus allowed to depress world demand – creating the phenomenon of an inflationary recession which plagued us from 1973 on . . .

The basic understanding must be that demand has been lost in the deficit countries and accumulated in the surpluses of Germany, Japan, Switzerland and Opec, and that this lost demand must be replaced by equivalent demand by use of the financial asset acquired by the surplus country.

For their part, deficit countries must recognise that deficit represents a receipt of resources over and above national production. It is an investment by the surplus countries in the economies of the deficit countries and it can only be repaid – at some future date – when the deficit countries move into surplus and

2

the surplus countries move into deficit. *Any period of deficit is not a time for the infliction of self-injury. It is a period of opportunity.*

If deficit countries will respond to the receipt of the surplus country investment by organising the restoration of demand lost as the deficit is created, they will strengthen their economies, help to revive world trade, and they, too, will in turn become surplus countries. Of course, deficit countries have to combat inflation as they seek to end the deficit. All their policies, including the exchange rate, should relate to this. This is where the temptation to deflate has arisen. It has been seen as a way of avoiding inflation and correcting the deficit. But deflation for the sake of short-term gains on the balance of payments is self-defeating because it injures future long-term competitiveness. It wastes the surplus countries' investment. The current account may be balanced but at the cost of further unemployment with dangerous political tensions and with future lurches into world-impoverishing nationalism and protectionism as new deficits are inevitably bred on the reduced competitiveness . . .

It is doubtful whether Harold Lever's analysis would be accepted even today by the Treasuries of the leading industrial powers. Manifestly it was not accepted by any of them in 1973–74.

It was against this financial background that Denis Healey prepared his Budget, which he opened on 26 March. Setting out the basic facts, in addition to the balance of payments current account deficit, then estimated at £1,470 million, he spoke of the record three years of stagnation in investment in manufacturing industry. Had he then known it, he would have had to make clear that manufacturing investment had reached its peak in the second quarter of the previous year, and was by this time falling.

But this was not all. The internal situation was dominated by inflation and rising unemployment at one and the same time. The *Economist* main headline on 30 March was 'Slumpflation'.

Despite the three-stage statutory control of wages and prices, the retail price index had risen 10.6 per cent during 1973, and by February, the year-on-year increase was 13.1 per cent up, and as the increase in world oil and commodity prices escalated, price increases shot higher and higher.[1] Money supply had risen by 27 per cent over the year, mainly as a result of the free-for-all announced in the Competition and Credit Control White Paper, and a frenzied property boom, aided and abetted by the so-called fringe banks, by this time either submerged in deficit, or in course of being hauled aboard the Bank of England's 'lifeboat'.[2]

Apart from the problems created by having to prepare a Budget in a very few days, the Chancellor was having to propose legislation for dealing not only with an unprecedented but also with a totally unpredictable situation.

[1] The official index of prices of all items except items of food, the prices of which show significant seasonal variations, taking January 1974 as 100, showed 102.8 for March 1974, 108.6 for June, 111.8 for September, 117.4 for December. In 1975 it was 124.8 for March, 137.1 for June, 140.9 for September, and 146.1 for December. In 1976 it was 149.5 for March, 155.4 for June, 160.0 for September, and 166.8 for December.

[2] See p. 2 above.

His predecessor had contented himself with cuts in public expenditure and new restrictions on hire-purchase dealings. But the major problem was the effect of oil on both the balance of payments and on the price-level. Oil, the Chancellor told the House, which had cost £100 million in the month of September 1973, cost £275 million in February 1974. He estimated that the higher oil price would add £2,000 million a year to an already serious balance-of-payments deficit. The 1973 deficit had been over £900 million, though no accurate figures were available by Budget time. But the trade deficit in January and February was £800 million, representing an annual rate of £4,800 million. In the event, though the final figures were not available until a long time after the end of 1974, the final deficit was just about three-quarters of that figure. Again, estimates for the loss of industrial production due to the imposition of the three-day week were difficult to make. Before long it became clear that industry's ingenuity in planning production had led to a smaller fall than had been expected, and once full working was restored, production recovered quickly.

The effect on the balance of payments was partly cushioned by the success of the clearing banks in arranging a ten-year loan of $2½ million, and by an increase from $2 billion to $3 billion in the 'swap' arrangements made available to the Bank of England by the Federal Reserve Bank of New York. As a further safeguard, the Chancellor tightened the rules on foreign investment, both on capital investment in overseas industry and trade, and on portfolio investment in the non-sterling area. This applied also to the EEC, and within so short a time after our entry we were therefore forced to break its rules about capital movements.

On the balance of his Budget the Chancellor noted that the pressure on real resources caused by the inflation in oil and commodity prices, together with the rise in wages due to the automatic 'threshold' payments introduced by the previous Government, would require offsetting action. He therefore decided to aim at a reduction in the public sector borrowing requirement of some £1,500 million compared with 1973–74, a formidable undertaking.

The Government was committed to increasing pensions. This was the first and priority provision in the 'Social Contract' of February 1973. But there was now an additional urgency, due to the need to protect pensioners from the worst effects of the increase in the cost of living brought about by oil prices and other instruments of inflation. Pensions were therefore to be increased by £2.25 and £3.50 to £10 and £16 for single persons and married couples respectively. Short-term benefits – for the unemployed, the sick and those on supplementary benefit – were to be raised by £1.25 and £2.00. The cost of this would be £860 million in the current financial year, and £1,240 million in a full year – to be met in the main by increased graduated pension contributions, falling mainly on the employers; these amounted in all to £615 million of the £860 million in 1974–75.

Food subsidies were to be increased by £500 million, to assist the ordinary family. Housing subsidies, following the promise in the Queen's Speech, were to be raised by £70 million, and plans introduced for a substantial increase in house building. Public utilities were asked, case by case, to moderate their increases in prices and charges, indeed where possible to hold them steady. Defence expenditure, already reduced by £178 million in the Barber cuts, was to be further cut by £50 million, all at 1973 prices. There was an ominous repetition of the hints previously given that the expensive projects favoured by the previous Government – the Maplin Airport and the Channel Tunnel – were to be 'reviewed', as was Concorde. In the event, the Maplin and Tunnel projects were scrapped; Concorde, after a searching re-examination, went on.

The need to cut the public sector borrowing requirement, particularly after the pensions increase, inevitably meant a massive increase in taxation. The oil situation had in fact created a fiscal problem not very different in character from the requirements of a war budget, and measurably similar in extent.

The Chancellor extended VAT to cover confectionery, soft drinks, ice-cream and similar products, and to petrol and other road fuels; increased the taxes on wines, spirits, beer, tobacco and cigarettes, raising indirect taxes to the amount of £680 million.

On direct taxation on individuals, he announced his intention to bring forward proposals for a wealth tax. (The proposals were torn apart by a Select Committee and up to the time of writing no such tax has since been put before the House.) To end avoidance of death duties by gifts *inter vivos*, he proposed the introduction of a tax on lifetime gifts – now the Capital Transfers Tax, which also replaced death duties except as between a husband and his widow, or a wife and her widower: death duties were abolished on the demise of one of a married couple. He also picked up Mr Barber's proposals for charging as income certain capital gains arising from the disposals of land and buildings with development value or potential – which later became law as the Property Development Tax. He tightened up the taxes on foreign income, and ended a system of tax avoidance which had been operated through insurance life offices and Friendly Societies. Share option and incentive payments to management were to come under the full rigour of income tax, and he blocked lucrative loopholes in the law relating to certificates of deposit and to the use of 'depreciatory transactions' under the Capital Gains Tax provisions. The law was tightened up, pending more far-reaching legislation, on the payment of building sub-contractors – the so-called 'lump' system.

On the rates of direct taxation, he began by raising the personal allowance for income tax by £30 for single people and £90 for married couples and also the child allowance by £40 for each of the three rates. The result would be to take one-and-a-half million people out of tax, and at the same time reduce the burden on those hardest hit by rising prices. For similar reasons he proposed improvements in age exemption. These reductions in tax would cost the revenue some £684 million in a full year, and other taxes would have to be raised to find the revenue – and a good deal more besides.

The basic rate of income tax was raised by 3 pence in the £. This, combined with the new rate structure, raised the maximum rate on the higher earned income from 75 pence to 83 pence in the £, and on the higher investment incomes to 98 per cent.

Surtax was to be increased by legislating for the 'surcharge' announced by Mr Barber three months earlier. The whole structure of income tax was to be changed. The £5,000 'band' charged at the basic rate was to be reduced to £4,500, though the investment income surcharge (the so-called 'unearned income' supplement) was to begin at £1,000 in place of the previous £2,000, with a small concession for those over sixty-five. Tax relief on interest for private borrowing was removed, though retained for businesses, and the tax relief on mortgage interest on house purchase would be limited to only one place of residence, and then only in respect of mortgages up to £25,000.

The changes in income tax would yield £954 million in a full year. So the Budget increased net social expenditure, particularly pensions, food and housing subsidies, by some £700 million, while increasing taxation, net, by nearly £1,400 million. The result of changes taking effect at different times in the financial year 1974–75 would be to reduce the public sector borrowing requirement by the Chancellor's target figure of £1,500 million from the £4,250 million recorded for 1973–74.

The Finance Bill came to the House for Second Reading on 9 May. It closely followed the Budget proposals, but it also contained a clause designed to reverse the previous Government's legislation on trade union finances. Since 1893 the trade unions had enjoyed relief from taxation on that part of their resources used for provident fund purposes for the benefit of their members. But the Industrial Relations Act, 1971, had the effect of preventing unions who chose to de-register under that Act from enjoying that eighty-year-old relief. The Chancellor made the relief retrospective to cover the period of over two years when the tax had been levied.

The Bill, one of the longest in modern times, had its Second Reading on 1 April, and its Third Reading on 22 July. The Committee and Report stages occupied seven days on the floor of the House and nine days in Committee upstairs. Over most of our history all stages had been on the floor of the House, but one of Mr Heath's Parliamentary reforms had led to part of the Committee stage being taken away from the House and into a committee room on the Ways and Means corridor. The Bill passed quickly through the Lords, as the custom has been since the constitutional crisis which followed the Lloyd George Budget in 1910, and received the Royal Assent on 31 July.

But by that time, in what was an unprecedentedly obscure world economic situation, the Chancellor was forced to advise the Cabinet that further measures were needed. The oil-generated inflation, the turn-down in investment and industrial activity which had begun even before the action of the oil producers, a world-wide loss of confidence; all these were combining to threaten employment. Men were being laid off.

Accordingly, just before Parliament rose for the summer recess, the Chancellor announced a series of policy changes, which he himself described as a 'mini-Budget'. The Heath wage thresholds were still operating to force up prices. New wage settlements were inevitably reflecting the increase in retail prices, which had risen by some 17 per cent over the same dates in 1973. In the modern world, inflation is father to unemployment, and there were serious signs that this process was adding to the down-turn which had begun in the early summer of 1973. The Chancellor stressed 'recession' rather than inflation as the immediate danger. The balance-of-payments consequence of the oil increase was being contained by the dollar loan negotiated in March, now reinforced by a further line of credit of $1,200 million made available by Iran, to hoots of derision from the Opposition.

The Chancellor decided to take action to reduce the pressure on the cost of living and at the same time to stem the resultant rise in unemployment. He reduced the VAT rate from 10 per cent to 8 per cent, which of itself would reduce the cost of living by about 1 per cent, and because of its effect on the price-inflationary threshold increase, might lead to a further offset of about a half of one per cent.

Second, he attacked the alarming rise in the householders' domestic rate burden. This was due in part to the increased cost of everything a local authority had to buy, including of course the threshold-inflated wage increases. But even more it was a reflection on the so-called 'reform' of local government carried through the House by the Conservatives in 1972–73, and which took effect within a month of our taking office. In the 1960s Labour had accepted the reforms proposed by the Royal Commission on Local Government under Lord Redcliffe-Maud, which aimed at streamlining rather than inflating local government bureaucracy. The Conservatives, however, set up an indefensible two-tier system based on counties and 'district councils', which simply led to double-staffing at each level. Employment in local government service rose from $1\frac{1}{2}$ million in 1960 to $2\frac{1}{2}$ million in 1975, an increase of 67 per cent, or 65,000 per annum, equal *each year* to the population of a fair-sized town. The Chancellor therefore proposed that in all cases where domestic rates rose by more than 20 per cent, the householder would be given relief to the extent of three-fifths of the excess over 20 per cent. The cost to the Revenue would be £150 million, to which had to be added £60 million to cover the increase in the 'needs allowance' used for calculating rent and rate rebates and rent allowances.

Third, he announced a further release of £50 million from the amount allocated in the Budget statement for food subsidies, to help keep down the cost of household flour – bringing the saving to the retail price index to $1\frac{1}{2}$ per cent.

Fourth, to help counter the rise in unemployment in hard-hit regions, the old depressed areas and certain others, he doubled the regional employment premium, which the Labour Government had introduced in 1967, from £1.50 per male employee to £3. This would cost £118 million in a full year.

Further, to help industry to raise funds for the new investment which was urgently needed to help exports and employment, he raised to $12\frac{1}{2}$ per cent the dividend limit of 5 per cent introduced by the previous Government early in 1973 as part of their statutory policy to restrain wages and prices.

The Chancellor announced these changes in a statement ahead of the two-day economic debate due to begin the following day. In that debate the Government and all its works were roundly denounced by the Opposition – who in fact were denouncing the world economic situation caused by the oil and commodity inflation – but, surprisingly, they did not vote against the Government's policy, including the new Healey proposals, at the end of the debate.

The following day the Leader of the House, in his weekly business statement, announced that Parliament would adjourn on Wednesday 31 July for the summer recess, until 15 October. In the event, the General Election was announced in September, and it was a new Parliament which assembled on 22 October.

The review so far of financial and major economic strategy has ignored one of the major developments of the Government which came into office on 4 March, the industrial strategy.

Our experience in 1964–70 and, no less, the debates and controversies of the 1970–74 Parliament had confirmed the need for major changes in industry. Our Opposition speeches in Parliament, the work of the National Executive Committee of the Labour Party, our annual Party Conferences, and the day-to-day activities of the Shadow Cabinet, were directed more to this issue than to any other, with the possible exception of the European Common Market.

The leftward swing in the National Executive Committee had led to prolonged debates about the industrial policy an incoming Labour Government should follow. Sub-Committees and Sub-Sub-Committees had produced grandiose proposals for nationalizing anything and pretty nearly everything. In the more difficult political conditions in which a Labour leader has to operate when in Opposition, appeals for restraint were less likely to be effective, though the policies of the Heath Government enabled the party to sublimate a great deal of its naturally self-destructive capacity into attacks on the Conservatives. When agreement was reached in 1973 on our policy about renegotiating the terms on which Britain had joined the EEC this also facilitated a release of energies in a constructive direction.

Industrial policy had been directed mainly from further nationalization, to the concept of the National Enterprise Board (NEB) and to 'planning agreements'.

The NEC, and more particularly its Home Policy Sub-Committee (constitutionally only a sub-committee but one which from time to time seemed then – and even more in recent times – to arrogate to itself the right to be Labour's main policy-making body, Cabinet or no Cabinet) were obsessed with a determination to use our period in Opposition to commit the party to a wide-ranging policy of nationalizing major companies, with particular reference to the British component of (mainly American) multi-nationals. There was much talk of nationalizing the hundred biggest companies.

At an all-day meeting of the NEC during the Whitsun recess of 1973, the opportunity was taken late in the evening, when many members had left, to force a snap vote on an outlandish proposal to commit the party to nationalize 25 of the 100 biggest companies. It was carried by 7 votes to 6. The following morning I issued a statement indicating that the decision was inoperative. It would meet a 'veto'. In saying this I was relying on the constitution of the party as drafted by Sidney Webb in 1918, and still in force. Referring to the election manifesto for any general election, it states in Clause V:

> 1. The Party Conference shall decide from time to time what specific proposals of legislative, financial or administrative reform shall be included in the Party Programme.
>
>   No proposal shall be included in the Party programme unless it has been adopted by the Party Conference by a majority of not less than two-thirds of the votes recorded on a card vote.
>
> 2. The National Executive Committee and the Parliamentary Committee of the Parliamentary Labour Party shall decide which issues from the Party Programme shall be included in the Manifesto which shall be issued by the National Executive Committee prior to every General Election.

I had no doubt that the assent of the Parliamentary Committee would not be forthcoming.

In the event little more was heard of the proposal. As David Butler and Dennis Kavanagh comment in *The British General Election of February 1974*,

> After much debate and pressure from Harold Wilson, this was modified in principle to a broad extension of public ownership under a National Enterprise Board.[1]

The 25-companies proposal was not even put to the October conference of the party by the NEC. A farouche and long-winded resolution by the Brighton (Kemptown) and Walton Constituency Parties to Conference advocating the nationalization not of 25 but 250 major companies was defeated by 5,600,000 votes to 291,000, after Anthony Wedgwood Benn, on behalf of the NEC, had advised Conference to reject it.

In the election manifesto for February 1974, which had in fact been pre-

[1] 1974, p. 19.

pared as a statement in advance of the announcement of the General Election, we said,

... we shall:

Sustain and expand industrial development and exports and bring about the re-equipment necessary for this purpose through the powers we shall take in a new INDUSTRY ACT and through the Planning Agreement system which will allow Government to plan with industry more effectively.

Wherever we give direct aid to a company out of public funds we shall in return reserve the right to take a share of the ownership of the company.

In addition to our plans set out in point 5 above for taking into common ownership land required for development, we shall substantially extend PUBLIC ENTERPRISE by taking mineral rights. We shall also take shipbuilding, ship-repairing and marine engineering, ports, the manufacture of airframes and aeroengines into public ownership and control. But we shall not confine the extension of the public sector to loss-making and subsidised industries. We shall also take over profitable sections or individual firms in those industries where a public holding is essential to enable the Government to control prices, stimulate investment, encourage exports, create employment, protect workers and consumers from the activities of irresponsible multi-national companies, and to plan the national economy in the national interest. We shall therefore include in this operation, sections of pharmaceuticals, road haulage, construction, machine tools, in addition to our proposals for North Sea and Celtic Sea oil and gas. Our decision in the field of banking, insurance and building societies is still under consideration. We shall return to public ownership assets and licences hived-off by the present government, and we shall create a powerful National Enterprise Board with the structure and functions set out in *Labour's Programme 1973*.

We intend to socialise existing nationalised industries. In consultation with the unions, we shall take steps to make the management of existing nationalised industries more responsible to the workers in the industry and more responsive to their consumers' needs.

Regional development will be further encouraged by new public enterprise, assistance to private industry on a selective basis, and new REGIONAL PLANNING MACHINERY, along the lines set out in *Labour's Programme 1973*. We will retain and improve the Regional Employment Premium. Revenues from North Sea oil will be used wherever possible to improve employment conditions in Scotland and the regions elsewhere in need of development.

We began to carry through our manifesto policy for industry on three main fronts: the repeal of our predecessors' legislation on labour and trade unions, legislation to set up the National Enterprise Board and Planning Agreements, and North Sea oil.

Michael Foot's Trade Union and Labour Relations Bill was introduced on 30 April and was debated on Second Reading on 7 May. Its main purpose was to repeal the Conservatives' Industrial Relations Act – indeed Michael Foot, introducing it, said he would have preferred to call it the 'Repeal Bill'. Subsidiary to repeal were clauses relating to 'unfair dismissals', largely following our predecessors' legislation which in turn had been based on Labour's 1970 Act. Questions relating to picketing would also be included, though he foreshadowed further legislation in due course, to legalize *peaceful* picketing. This, and a third point, the question of arbitrary exclusion from a trade union, had been aired in a consultative document the Government had issued, recommending an approach through conciliation, as proposed in the Donovan Commission Report, rather than seeking to incorporate sanctions enforceable by law. Again, there was no statutory proposal for a conciliation and arbitration service, though that ranked high in Labour priorities and in trade union thinking. What came to be known as the Advisory Conciliation and Arbitration Service, ACAS, was therefore left for further consultation with – and between – the TUC and the CBI.

Another question which plagued the Secretary of State was the means of repealing the provisions which had set up the Industrial Relations Court. This had provoked sharp reactions by the very fact of its establishment, and a near-crisis situation on the rare occasions on which it had acted against particular groups of workers.

Almost on the eve of the debate the Court, which was still busily functioning, had proceeded against the AUEW, in a dispute case, and punished it by sequestration of over £60,000 of its funds, based on an award to the employers concerned of £2,350 per week, enforcing this by sending the law into the offices of a small local authority in the north-east to seize the union's investment in its funds. A major crisis, including a nation-wide engineering strike, was averted by a donation of £65,000 assembled by a small group of private individuals.[1] Some Labour members were urging swift action to prevent a recurrence by a simple one-clause Bill repealing the powers under which Sir John Donaldson's Court had acted. But, as the Secretary of State pointed out, such a Bill would destroy not only the powers of the Court, but also other pre-existing labour legislation, such as the industrial relations reforms passed by the Liberal Government in 1906, and even the pioneering legislation of Disraeli in 1875. For this reason, Michael Foot felt it right to deal with this problem in the main Bill, so that in dismantling the controversial 1971 legislation, which embodied previous acts of Parliament, specific action could be taken to retain on the statute-book the reforms of past years.

When his Bill came up for Second Reading the Conservatives moved a reasoned amendment praising the 1971 Act and seeking to keep it in being. At the end of the debate the Conservative amendment was defeated by 299 to 264, and the Bill was launched into Committee. After eighteen days in Committee, it reappeared on the floor of the House on 10 July, and took three days on Report and Third Reading. Even then a further hiccup occurred.

After the Bill had received its Third Reading and gone to the Lords, it was found that an irregularity had occurred in the voting, which had resulted in a tie. Under our unofficial voting procedures it is accepted that *if a member is in the building,* but too unfit to be asked to tramp through the division lobby, he can be 'nodded through' by one of his party's Whips, on which his vote is

[1] See *Hansard,* vol. 873, cols 582–6.

counted. Soon after the Bill had gone to the Lords on receiving its Third Reading, it came to light that Harold Lever, who is regularly nodded through on health grounds, had not been in the building. This was confirmed by him and the Speaker ruled the vote invalid. As the Bill was by this time in the Lords, the Commons passed a procedural motion requesting their Lordships to send it back.

When it went back to the Upper House, their Lordships sustained the amendments which had led to the trouble, and made further changes on their own account. On the return of the Bill to the Commons on 30 July, the Conservatives had the edge in successive votes and kept in the Bill both what had now become known as the 'Lever amendments' and also others made by the Lords on their own account. In that form it became law on 31 July, on the very eve of the adjournment for the summer recess, an adjournment, as it proved, until after the year's second general election.

Work had been proceeding in the Department of Industry on the manifesto commitments referring to the NEB and 'planning agreements'. Since there was no possibility of getting legislation through in the Short Parliament I had been pressing for a White Paper setting out exactly what we proposed to do, and, no less important, what we were not going to do. It was vital that no vague statements or half-veiled threats should be left around for use as a scare by the Opposition in the autumn election on which I had decided. Equally, it was essential that both sides of industry should know exactly where they stood, within what it was vital to emphasize was to continue to be a mixed economy.

It was not until late July that the Department of Industry's draft White Paper emerged. As I had feared, it proved to be a sloppy and half-baked document, polemical, indeed menacing, in tone, redolent more of an NEC Home Policy Committee document than a Command Paper. One basic weakness was that it appeared to place more emphasis on the somewhat amorphous proposals for planning agreements than on the NEB.

A special committee of senior ministers was set up under my chairmanship to mastermind its re-drafting, which quickly decided that the document should be re-written. The final draft owed a great deal to Michael Foot,  writing within the parameters we laid down. The section on planning agreements was cut down to size: in the event, at the time of writing, four years later, only one planning agreement with a public company has come into force.[1] The role and powers of the NEB were strictly defined; above all it was to have no marauding role. It should act specifically within guidelines announced by the Secretary of State, which were to be made public. These provided, *inter alia*, that it could not go secretly into the market, whether directly or through nominees, buying the shares of a company with a view to acquiring control, but had to follow normal Stock Exchange procedures.

[1] This planning agreement is with the coal industry, see p. 141 below.

Subject to these limitations, the White Paper defined its role in these terms:

a. It will be a new source of investment capital for manufacturing industry; in providing finance it will normally take a corresponding share in the equity capital. In this it will set out to supplement and not to displace the supply of investment from existing financial institutions and from companies' own resources . . .

b. It will have the former Industrial Reorganisation Corporation's entrepreneurial role in promoting industrial efficiency and profitability by promoting or assisting the reorganisation or development of an industry but, unlike the IRC, the NEB will in general retain the shareholdings it acquires. In discharging these functions it may take financial interests in companies or act in a purely advisory role . . .

c. It will act as a holding company to control and exercise central management of:

i. certain existing Government shareholdings vested in it;

ii. interests taken into public ownership under powers in the Industry Act 1972, which it is proposed to consolidate and extend;

iii. new acquisitions under the arrangements described in paragraphs 30–33.

d. It will be a channel through which the Government will assist sound companies which are in short-term financial or managerial difficulties (see para. 32).

e. It will be an instrument through which the Government operate directly to create employment in areas of high unemployment . . .

f. Government Departments, the nationalised industries and private firms will be able to seek the advice of the NEB on financial and managerial issues.

g. Its main strength in manufacturing will come through the extension of public ownership into profitable manufacturing industry by acquisitions of individual firms in accordance with paragraphs 30–33 below.

h. It will have power to start new ventures and participate in joint ventures with companies in the private sector.[1]

In deciding which projects the NEB was to support within its financial allocation, it was

expected to give priority to the promotion of industrial efficiency; to the creation of employment opportunities in assisted areas; to increasing exports or reducing undue dependence on imports; to cooperation with the Offshore Supplies Office in promoting development in the offshore oil supplies industry; and to sponsoring investment that will offset the effect of monopoly.

It was expected to take an equity share in any assisted organization adequate to reflect the extent of its financial participation.

In addition it was to take over pre-existing Government shareholdings in industry acquired under successive governments mainly to save firms from

---

[1] The document was published as a White Paper, Cmnd. 5710 on 15 August. The 'guidelines' referred to in it were promulgated by the Secretary of State in the *Department of Trade Journal*, see p. 142 and Appendix VIII below.

going under and to preserve employment. These included the investments made by the previous Conservative Government in Rolls Royce (Engines), and in International Computers, George Kent Ltd, Dunford and Elliott, and Norton-Villiers-Triumph and others, but not those of British Petroleum, Cable and Wireless, and the Suez Finance Company. It was intended that holdings in companies whether of 100 per cent or less should be acquired by agreement: NEB could participate in partnerships, and go up to 100 per cent purchase where this was necessary to avoid conflict between its defined objectives and the interests of private shareholders. The White Paper emphasized that suitable criteria for such action would include 'the danger of a company's passing into unacceptable foreign control, and stimulation of competition in a sector where that is weak'.

The provision that the NEB would become the holding company for shares previously acquired, or later acquired by the Government as a deliberate action, e.g. to save a company from bankruptcy, has in the event proved an incubus for the NEB. Its preoccupation with Leyland, for example, has crippled its finances and to some extent depreciated its other achievements.

The White Paper, however, not without a great deal of controversy at the drafting stage, went beyond the mere definition of the NEB's powers, function and limitations. It asserted the Government's belief in a mixed economy. Paragraph 1 stated:

> Britain's prosperity and welfare depend on the wealth generated by its industry and all who work in it. It matters vitally to all of us that British industry should be strong and successful. *We need both efficient publicly owned industries, and a vigorous, alert, responsible and profitable private sector, working together with the Government in a framework which brings together the interests of all concerned:*[1] those who work in industry, whether in management or on the shop floor, those who own its assets, and those who use its products and depend upon its success.

But there was more than that. Paragraph 5 set out the Government's proposals for extending public ownership as listed in the manifesto on which the Labour Party had fought the previous election – community ownership of development land, the establishment of the British National Oil Corporation, the nationalization of the shipbuilding and aircraft industries, the extension of public ownership in the road haulage and construction industries, and schemes for bringing commercial ports and cargo handling activities under public ownership and control.

Paragraph 33 went on to be specific about the future:

> *Together with the separate proposals in paragraph 5, the preceding paragraphs represent the whole of the Government's policy towards public ownership for the next Parliament.*[2] If in any case compulsory acquisition proved to be necessary,

[1] Author's italics.
[2] Author's italics.

this would normally be authorised by a specific Act of Parliament. If unforeseen development of compelling urgency were to arise – for example, the imminent failure or loss to unacceptable foreign control of an important company in a key sector of manufacturing industry – the Government would bring the issue before Parliament, and any action would require specific parliamentary approval. Compulsory acquisition would be subject to prompt and fair compensation to existing shareholders.

The White Paper was published on 15 August, and for this reason could not be debated during the life of that Parliament. It had put the entire policy for further public ownership for the next General Election and indeed the next Parliament firmly on the record – thus, as I intended, limiting the possibility of election scares on the issue. It had proclaimed the doctrine of the mixed economy in industry. And in so doing, it could have been assumed, it pre-empted the whole process of joint agreement with the National Executive Committee on the content of the Autumn Election manifesto. But in fact it was re-asserting the terms of the Spring Election manifesto, drawn up for a full Parliament, as the basis for the election we would have to call to secure a full-length Parliament.[1]

But while we were thrashing out the post-election policy, the Conservatives had acted with a fine bravado. In the early spring they had been circumspect. Their Front Bench had feared that any Parliamentary action on their part to frustrate the progress of the measures foreshadowed in the Queen's Speech would be met by an appeal to the country. In fact I was as loth as they were to see a Spring Election. We had come into office with the smallest possible lead over them, in a minority position in the House as a whole. I judged that an election called over a Parliamentary defeat might evoke nothing in the country more significant than a prolonged yawn. There would be a low vote, and no one could forecast what that would mean in terms of Parliamentary seats. The country had installed a Labour Government in office, though not in power: they had the right to see what we could do, and what programmes we were working out for their approval.

The Conservatives were not risking an electoral confrontation before the summer holidays. They knew as well as we did the holidays timetable, wakes weeks, feast weeks and the rest. The slow progress of the Trade Union and Labour Relations Bill helped to reassure them that there would be no appeal to the country before it became law. Holidays had begun before the Bill went to the Lords, hence no doubt their Lordships' sudden and successful attacks by way of amendment in late June. Once the Conservatives were convinced that their safe period had set in they attacked on a broader front.

---

[1] See also *The Governance of Britain*, p. 66, for an analysis of this operation as an example of an 'assertion by Cabinet, on prime ministerial initiative, of its collective authority', partly to endorse a timetable, but also to act in a situation where 'there seemed to be some departure from the precise manifesto language, in favour of an earlier National Executive Committee document, which had not been adopted as an election programme, and which in fact had not been approved by the Labour Party Conference in 1973'.

The allocation of Supply Days, when the Opposition can choose their subject for debate, gave them the Parliamentary initiative. For the Supply Day on 20 June they chose as their subject 'Labour's Plans for Industry', in part an attack on the Budget they had allowed through without a vote, and in part an attack on a report to a sub-committee of a sub-committee of the National Executive Committee of the Labour Party, but in general a repudiation of planning agreements and the National Enterprise Board. In reality it was an attack on the manifesto on which we had successfully fought the February election which was the main theme for Mr Heath's opening speech of censure.

Safe on seasonal grounds in the knowledge that they could defeat the Government without having to face the consequences in an immediate disso- lution and general election, they challenged us on the final vote. By eleven votes they defeated our amendment to their motion, and by the same margin carried their own motion.

It was a humiliating position for the Government, defeated but with no opportunity of appealing to the country. When the figures were announced Mr Heath, as is customary on such occasions, demanded a statement from me, in particular asking me to abandon the whole of our industrial policy now repudiated in the House. He knew I could not appeal immediately to the electorate. But equally he knew that an appeal would be made at the earliest opportunity, that is, after the peak holiday period. He therefore cannot have been surprised to hear my response:

> No, Sir. The Government will, of course, consider the implications of these two important votes. We shall also consider the implications of the fact that the Right Hon. Gentleman the Leader of the Opposition, has taken a vital part of the manifesto on which we were elected, submitted it to a vote and collected his Hon. Friends in the Lobby. That raises important political and constitutional implications following the speech of the Right Hon. Gentleman seeking to tell Europe what a minority Government could and would not do in negotiations with Europe,[1] and following four defeats in Standing Committee. The Right Hon. Gentleman can be fully assured that we shall consider all the implications following what he has succeeded in doing today, and that in due course our decision will be made known.[2]

None hearing that statement, certainly not Mr Heath, could be in any doubt that a general election would be called in September, once the holidays were over.

Despite our economic travails, there was ground for optimism about the long-hoped-for, now certain, yield of oil from the bed of the North Sea. For

---

[1] Mr Heath had caused some little offence in our party, particularly to James Callaghan, by appearing to go over the Government's heads in our EEC negotiations, and implying that Europe should not take the negotiating position of a minority government very seriously.

[2] *Hansard*, 20 June 1974, col. 769.

years politicians and commentators had proclaimed that twice blest would be that government which held office when the intake of North Sea oil was progressing from a trickle to a flood.[1] Labour had been in office in the 1960s when North Sea gas began to take over from the product of inland gasworks, and when the first smear of oil was discovered under the sea-bed. In 1970–74 the companies granted search and production concessions were setting up their drilling rigs, and before long oil was being pumped into tankers moored near the rigs, the first oil flowing by pipeline, as recorded above, in November 1975.

Even had there been no general election in prospect, a decision on North Sea oil policy would have been urgent. Labour's pre-election policy was as clear as anything produced by the broadest of brushes could be, though Butler and Kavanagh[2] were close to the mark when they said our policy had not been worked out before the February election. It had not gone much beyond a pledge of 'full government control with majority participation' in exploiting and distributing the resources.

Before we came into office there had been great concern in the House – not only on the Labour benches – about the position of companies who had been granted concessions to bring the oil up from the sea-bed. The anxieties had been confirmed during the Heath Government by a devastating report from the Public Accounts Committee of the House of Commons, masterminded by the acting Chairman, Edmund Dell. The Committee was particularly concerned about the terms granted to international companies which would enable them to shift tax liabilities, which North Sea profits would normally have attracted, to other areas of their world operations. The Committee summarized its main conclusions in these terms:[3]

(1) We regard it as unsatisfactory that UK tax revenue from continental shelf operations should be pre-empted by the tax demands of administrations elsewhere in the world; and that for tax purposes capital allowances on extraneous activities, such as tanker operations elsewhere, should be used to offset profits on continental shelf operations.

(2) Under the present arrangements the UK will not obtain either for the Exchequer or the balance of payments anything like the share of the 'take' of oil operations on the continental shelf that other countries are obtaining for oil within their territories.

(3) We consider that it is unsatisfactory that the Department should not have access to licensees' costs: this is an area where equality of information between the government and the licensee would be equitable.

[1] Compare Butler and Kavanagh, *The General Election of October 1974*, p. 42, quoting the Conservative Central Office's *Contact Brief* in April, 'Mr Wilson has long indicated his ambition to make his party the permanent party of government and his calculation must take into account the fact that the party taking office after the next election will have a big economic boost from North Sea oil and gas.'
[2] *The General Election of February 1974*, p. 48.
[3] *Parliamentary Papers*, HC 122 of 1972–73, paras. xxxii–xxxiii.

(4) We consider that, even disregarding the taxation points referred to in sub-paragraph (1) of this paragraph, there are grounds for considering that the UK terms have tended to lag behind those of other countries right from the start.

(5) We consider that by the time invitations were issued for the fourth round of licensing in June 1971 the fear of repercussions from OPEC countries, whatever value might have been put on this consideration in earlier rounds, need not in any way have inhibited the Department from offering blocks on more appropriate terms.

(6) The second and third rounds of licensing had been framed on the initial expectation that offshore petroleum would be in the form of natural gas, but the position was materially altered before the fourth round by the discovery of oil which would be handled and distributed by private companies and not by a nationalised industry.

(7) In our view, before matters of such importance as the timing, size and terms of the fourth round were decided there should have been full inter-departmental consideration.

(8) While we accept that to scale up the £37 million receipts from the tender experiment in proportion to the total number of blocks allocated in the fourth round would be misleading for the purpose of judging what additional premia might have been received if they had all been put out to tender, it is obvious that the additional receipts might have been substantial, even without extending the use of the tender system, if a different approach to the administration of the round had been adopted in the light of the tender results.

(9) We are not convinced that it is impossible to combine the advantages of the discretionary system (eg. the imposition of an obligation on the licensee to perform a satisfactory work programme) with the obtaining of premia by auction.

(10) We consider that, as the object of the tender experiment was to learn lessons, it should have been conducted before and not simultaneously with a major fourth round of licensing; and we think it could have been completed during 1971 before applications were invited for the bulk of the fourth round blocks without resulting in any significant loss of time.

(11) We are surprised that when the results of the tender competition (resulting in successful bids totalling £37 million) were known on 20th August 1971, the questions of reconsidering or withdrawing the invitation for the discretionary allocation were not discussed interdepartmentally or put to Ministers for a policy decision.

(12) We consider that quite apart from the tender experiment and making due allowances for the advantages of hindsight, the Department should have considered tougher terms in the light of improving prospects of the North Sea, the hardening of terms elsewhere and the growing realisation of the implications of the taxation regime.

(13) We are concerned that so many production licences have now been granted with the result that the most promising areas of the North Sea have already been allocated on the original terms.

(14) The most striking fact to emerge from our review of the four rounds of licensing is that the terms for each, apart from the limited tender experiment, have remained virtually unchanged since they were fixed in 1964, before any

discoveries had been made and when the potentialities of the shelf were unknown.

(15) We are concerned that the licences granted remain valid, without a break clause exercisable by the Department, for 46 years; and that there is no provision for variation or renegotiation of the financial terms, however large the finds, or for obtaining a degree of government participation.

(16) We were surprised that a thorough examination of the opportunities for British industry and employment had not taken place much earlier than 1972 . . . as the full opportunities of the discoveries became apparent.

### RECOMMENDATIONS

(1) The government should take action substantially to improve the effective tax yield from operations on the continental shelf; and should consider among other methods the possibility of imposing a system of quantity taxation.

(2) Before any further licences are issued all aspects of the regime for licensing, especially as regards oil, should be reviewed in the light of this Report and the conclusions in paragraph 97 in order to secure for the Exchequer and the economy a better share of the take from continental shelf operations.

In the debate on the Queen's Speech in March 1974 speeches from the Government Front Bench added little to our election statements. There was at that time little to add. On the first day of the debate, after referring to the PAC Report, I indicated that we were considering the practice already followed in Norway, based on majority public participation.

We shall also consider whether the oil, once landed, should be purchased by a public authority, as is already the case for North Sea Gas.[1]

The following day Eric Varley made clear that he was examining different means of achieving our manifesto objectives, but went to some lengths to repudiate suggestions that our policy of public participation was likely to drive international oil companies from our shores. He effectively quoted the *Daily Mail*:

North Sea oilmen are not worried by Labour's plans to take a bigger share of their profits. 'We stay' was yesterday's firm message from the international companies drilling in the area. And they revealed that the massive investment of private enterprise money will, in fact, be increased . . .

The *Mail* went on to quote a statement by a BP director:

We are in partnership with Governments of all political complexions all over the world. We are unlikely to be frightened off by anything the Labour Government has in mind. In any case our investment is now too big. It would be too late to stop even if we wanted to.[1]

A week later there was a further brief debate. Replying for the Govern-

---

[1] *Hansard*, vol. 870, col. 82.
[2] *Ibid.*, col. 343.

ment, Gavin Strang, the Under-Secretary, made it clear that in formulating our policy we should be dealing in particular with taxation, and the wider question of licensing:

It is important to introduce legislation as soon as possible to rectify the present disturbing position regarding the inadequate take that the Government get from the operation and the amount of public participation and control.[1]

It was four months before any clear statement of policy could be made. The Department of Energy was hard at work, together with the Scottish and Welsh Offices and reporting regularly to a committee meeting at No. 10.

Eric Varley was not in fact considering oil in isolation. He was working towards a co-ordinated energy policy, the dream of every Minister of Fuel and Power or Energy since the appointment of Major Gwilym Lloyd George as the first minister a third of a century earlier, and indeed he came much nearer to success than any of his predecessors. It included a major drive to develop coal production, with a £600 million investment programme, and the sinking of new pits.[2] The fact that in 1977 his decision about the choice of the right nuclear reactor to back was changed by his successor is no derogation from his achievement – much had happened in those three years.

In a statement on 11 July[3] he set out his policy in six brief points:

first, an additional tax on profits from the Continental Shelf, and the closing of a number of loopholes in the rules governing existing taxation of oil companies' profits;

second, a decision to make it a condition of future licences that the licensees should, if the Government so required, grant majority participation to the State in all fields discovered under those licences;

third, an invitation to the relevant companies to enter into discussions with the Government about majority State participation in existing licences for commercial fields;

fourth, the establishment of a British National Oil Corporation through which the Government would exercise its rights of participation;

fifth, an extension of Government powers of physical control over offshore operations, including production, and also over pipeline developments;

sixth, the establishment of a Scottish Development Agency, with similar arrangements for Wales as oil exploration developed in the Celtic Sea.

At the same time the Secretary of State tabled a White Paper, Cmnd. 5696, which spelt out his oral statement in further detail. This statement was to guide the Government's policy for the next three years and more.

In the election campaign of September–October 1974 this was the policy put forward by the Government north and south of the border, and east and

[1] *Hansard*, vol. 870, col. 1221.
[2] See p. 116 below.
[3] *Hansard*, vol. 876, cols 1558–9.

west of the Welsh marches. But it was to require a great deal of negotiation and the passage of two major Bills in the Parliamentary session 1974–75, the Petroleum and Submarine Pipelines Bill and the Oil Taxation Bill, before it was in operation. And it was not until a Sunday evening meeting at Chequers, with Eric Varley's successor, Tony Wedgwood Benn, and the Chairman of BP and a colleague, on 25 January 1976, that the detailed working of the partnership was clinched.[1]

In the months during which we were working out policies for manufacturing industry and for North Sea oil we were engaged in discussions with the TUC and the CBI on anti-inflation policy, pay and prices.

It was a sombre prospect. Taking what it is now fashionable to use, the monthly retail price index on a 'year on year' basis, the increase in the cost of living had reached 13.1 per cent in February 1974, and was rising rapidly. Quite apart from the increase in world prices, the 'threshold' formula for wages provided a built-in accelerator. Under this formula, additional increases beyond the weekly permitted increases were to be allowed – first an addition of 40 pence a week if the Retail Price Index rose above 7 per cent beyond that ruling in October 1973, and a further 40 pence for each one per cent rise beyond that figure. These threshold payments were not to be reckoned as part of the basic rate for the calculation of overtime and similar payments.

We decided on taking office not to repeal the Conservative pay and prices measure, which had reached the always difficult Stage III. Our decision to retain it provided something of a face-saver for the Conservatives, and it was for this reason, it was reported, that they decided not to vote in force against us at the end of the Queen's Speech debate. But this meant retaining thresholds, which in the event generated no less than three threshold payments with the publication of the retail price index on 24 May 1974: £1.20 per week automatic increase – a savage inflationary inheritance.

Viewed with hindsight the thresholds were a disastrous mistake. That does not in fact mean that Mr Heath had been wrong to introduce them in October 1973; indeed despite our reservations about his statutory policy we ourselves had supported his threshold proposals. Denis Healey put it very fairly in the debate on his July 1974 'budget', when he said that Mr Heath could not have known that we were now seeing the world price explosion which began *after* he had introduced thresholds. Had he known, the Chancellor said, 'he would never have made these agreements a central feature of his compulsory wage control'.[2] But in the situation where world prices

---

[1] See p. 217 below.

[2] In a public speech on 30 June I had referred to Mr Heath and the threshold payments. 'I, for one, am not going to criticize them, because in an earlier period I had pressed the adoption of a threshold policy on the then Conservative Government. I will stand my corner on that.'

were rocketing, thresholds provided a major internal reinforcement to add to the already damaging external forces putting up prices.

What the Government wanted to persuade the House to recognize was that in any wage settlements to be negotiated, account should be taken of any threshold payments received. If that concept were rejected, workers would receive a threshold, perhaps monthly, which would push up prices. If they then pressed for higher wages to compensate for those higher prices, we should be driven into a vicious spiral caused by internal pressures super-imposed on those caused by external factors.

In saying this the Chancellor was speaking with TUC support. On 24 June the General Council had unanimously accepted a proposal that negotiators should seek rises only to keep up with the cost of living, after tax, and should take account of threshold payments. This decision was endorsed at the subsequent TU Congress in September.

The TUC were in fact acting in accordance with an agreement made with the Labour Party in February 1973. In the years of opposition the party and the TUC had come much closer together, following an agreement to set up regular meetings with the NEC and the Parliamentary Party. The agreed document *Economic Policy and the Cost of Living*, which came to be known as the 'Social Contract'[1], was published on 28 February 1973. After setting out the record of the then Government in terms of prices and unemployment, together with criticism of their new and increased social charges and rents, and the uncontrolled financial and property boom, the parties agreed on a comprehensive alternative strategy, covering a wide area of the social and economic life of the nation. This included food subsidies, price controls, housing and rents, transport and a redistribution of income and wealth, combined with a policy for increasing investment in industry. Together with the repeal of the Conservatives' Industrial Relations Act, this would 'engender the strong feeling of mutual confidence which alone will make it possible to reach the wide-ranging agreement which is necessary to control inflation and achieve sustained growth in the standard of living'.

This was widely interpreted as a voluntary agreement to accept restraint in pay demands as part of a wider social agreement. Indeed Mr Len Murray in a television programme in which he and I appeared together confirmed this interpretation in answer to a question by the interviewer.

In the February 1974 election we put forward proposals on these lines as an alternative to the policy of confrontation. At Nottingham on 17 February

[1] There has been much argument, some of it not altogether literate, about the authorship of the phrase. It would seem reasonable to ascribe it to Rousseau, in default of any earlier claimant being proposed. In recent years it has been ascribed to, among others, Tony Wedgwood Benn and myself, as both have used it in particular contexts specifically related to the trade union movement's relationship with the Government. In my own case it was used at a 26–nation conference on industrial relations in the public sector convened by the then Governor Nelson Rockefeller, of New York, in April 1971. My own proposals were picked up by the *Guardian* and called the 'Social Compact' in a leading article (5 May 1971), reproduced together with the report of the speech as Appendix II.

I referred to the need for a 'social contract' between government, industry and the trade unions, on the basis of mutual sacrifices to reach agreement on a strategy to curb rising prices, and went on, 'We have agreed such a new contract with the TUC.' Doubt was thrown on this by Mr Hugh Scanlon when he told his BBC interviewer, 'We are not agreed on any specific policy as of now,' but other union leaders, including Mr Murray, rallied to confirm the reality of the agreement.[1]

The trade union response signified by the decision of 24 June 1974 could not of itself reduce inflation to tolerable levels, but it was of vital importance in preventing inflation compounding inflation. It required great courage to seek to relate wage increases, including thresholds, to the price level. But it soon became clear that we should have to run very fast even to stand still and maintain living standards, a warning I gave to fellow Socialist leaders at a conference held at Chequers shortly afterwards.

Addressing 170 Labour Parliamentary candidates in July, I told them, 'As a nation we cannot look for any substantial improvement in the standard of living in the years immediately ahead. Indeed, it will require the utmost statesmanship and a united national effort to preserve it.'

At the TUC Conference at Brighton on 5 September I repeated the warning:

> ... because of the crisis we face, including the oil surcharge, we cannot expect any significant increase in living standards over-all in the next year or two, indeed it will be a tremendous challenge to our statesmanship even to maintain average living standards.

In this speech to the TUC there was a series of anything but oblique references to 'the coming General Election'. Few who heard it or read it were in any doubt that, in Parliamentary terms, there was an odour of dissolution about.

Reference has been made earlier to my desire, on issues where there was no hope of legislating during the probable life of the Parliament, to make crystal clear by Parliamentary announcements or, better, White Papers, the exact nature of each item where legislation had been promised.

Our timetable was urgent. On 30 July we announced our proposals for the public ownership of the shipbuilding industry; on 8 August for the wealth tax and gift tax; on 15 August our industry White Paper was published; on 11 September that on pensions; on 12 September that on land; on 17 September the White Paper on devolution. On 18 September the General Election was announced.

Two important subjects where we were determined to finalize and publish our proposals were development land and devolution.

[1] Butler and Kavanagh, *The General Election of February 1974*, pp. 98–9.

Ever since the war Labour had been concerned to ensure that, so far as possible, any increase in land values – for example by the community granting permission for low-priced farm land to be sold as high-priced building land – should accrue to the community which created it. Indeed, this had been a Liberal demand from the nineteenth century. In the 1910 Election the Liberals had a battle song, to the tune of 'Marching through Georgia', each verse ending with 'God gave the land to the people'.

In Clement Attlee's 1945 Government, Lewis Silkin, Minister of Town and Country Planning – and the creator of New Towns – carried legislation, later repealed by the Conservatives, to transfer to the community any increments in land values. In the 1964–70 Government similar legislation was prepared by Fred Willey and Tony Crosland, and a Land Commission established – only to be scrapped by Mr Heath's Government. We were committed in our manifesto and by long-standing Party policy to yet another attempt. The February manifesto had said,

> Land required for development will be taken into public ownership, so that land is freely and cheaply available for new houses, schools, hospitals and other purposes. Public ownership of land will stop profiteering. It will emphatically *not* apply to owner-occupiers.

Moving forward from a quotation by Lloyd George in 1909, it dealt with Lewis Silkin's 1947 Act, following the wartime Uthwatt Report which had recommended the transfer to the state of all development rights in land, repealed by the Conservatives in 1959. It then referred to the 40 per cent betterment levy of the Land Commission Act, 1967, again repealed following the change of Government in 1970.

The legislation foreshadowed in Cmnd. 5730 was to be based on two principles:

(a) to enable the community to control the development of land in accordance with its needs and priorities; and
(b) to restore to the community the increase in value of land arising from its efforts.

Unlike the 1947 and 1967 proposals where special national agencies were set up, the White Paper recommended that the acquisition and disposal of development land in England and Scotland should be the charge of local authorities: in Wales it should be by an all-Wales body. The proposals, which excluded land to be used for agriculture and forestry, provided that local authorities should work to a ten-year rolling programme as they built up their 'land banks'. The local authorities would have a duty to acquire all land required for private development: 'no development will be allowed to begin save on land owned by a public authority, or made available by them for this purpose.'

The basis of compensation laid down in an act of 1958 was to be changed.

Under this act the price paid by an acquiring authority for land purchased had not been limited to the value of the land based on its current use, but could reflect any value due to the prospect of carrying out development, including the value for the development which the acquiring authority intended to carry out.

Under our proposals land prices were to be ultimately based on what would be the current use value. Where land had little or no market value in its current use, a special basis of compensation might be needed.

The meetings I chaired were only too well aware that our opponents would act – indeed in February had not scrupled – to scare individual householders into believing that their back garden or their house could be taken over at will, and without any real compensation. A special section of the White Paper made it clear that the scheme would exclude the building of a house for owner-occupation on a single plot owned by the prospective owner-occupier on the date of publication of the White Paper, 12 September 1974. Other exceptions related to alterations and extensions to existing houses; the building within the curtilage of an owner-occupied dwelling of a single house for his occupation or that of a member of his family; buildings for use in agriculture and forestry or the extraction of minerals.

The White Paper had further sections dealing with transitional arrangements; financial hardship tribunals, and encouragement to local authorities to help would-be owner-occupiers; the position of statutory undertakers. The final sections dealt with disposal procedures, financial implications and empty office blocks.

Devolution[1] is a boring word, a boring and soporific subject so far as legislation is concerned, but potentially a most powerful means of achieving one of the highest aims of democracy, bringing the process of decision-making as close as possible to the people affected by it.

In 1968 the then Labour Government had set up a Royal Commission under Lord Crowther to enquire into constitutional matters with particular reference to devolution for Scotland and Wales. Lord Crowther died before the work was completed, and he was followed by Lord Kilbrandon, a Scottish Law Lord. The Commission reported in October 1973, rejecting separatism and federalism, but divided on issues of administrative and legislative devolution.

The February 1974 Labour manifesto was cautious. Not a great deal was made of the subject in a heated campaign related to more immediate and controversial issues.

In the Queen's Speech the only reference was in the last few sentences:

---

[1] 'The British people do not like four-syllable words, like devolution and metrication' – speech (strongly supporting the Government's Devolution proposals) on the Second Reading of the Bill to legislate devolution for Scotland, 13 December 1976, *Hansard*, vol. 922, col. 1008. Or, as a Tory wit interrupted, 'Harold Wilson'.

My Ministers will initiate discussions in Scotland and Wales on the Report of the Royal Commission on the Constitution, and will bring forward proposals for consideration.

Edward Short, Lord President and Leader of the House of Commons, was given direct charge of the subject, working in close contact with the Secretaries of State for Scotland and Wales. A Parliamentary Under-Secretary was attached to him (later a Minister of State), and Lord Crowther-Hunt was appointed constitutional adviser to the Government.[1]

The Government proceeded cautiously, and rightly decided to concern itself in the first few months primarily with consultations.

Meanwhile the crudities of party in-fighting took charge. The Scottish Labour Party was notoriously cool on devolution, and earlier in the summer had rejected any substantial move in that direction. At this point – July 1974 – the National Executive met, not particularly well attended by those of its members who were ministers. Mr Alex Kitson was the man who turned the tide of history. He had been General Secretary of the Scottish Horse and Motormen's Union, later the Scottish Commercial Motormen's organization. On its absorption into the Transport and General Workers' Union he became their Scottish chieftain, and as he was not in the running for nomination to the General Council of the TUC, he was proposed for election to the trade union section of the NEC, to which he was elected.

At the July Executive he proposed that the NEC should support Scottish devolution. This was carried. Now there was a clash between the NEC and the Scottish Conference decision. An emergency re-assembly of the Scottish Party conference was requisitioned, where devolution was carried, another illustration of the fact that the Party, above all its NEC, moves in a mysterious way its wonders to perform. The *volte-face* would certainly be ratified by Conference, but first there would be a General Election. In the Cabinet there was a measured degree of rejoicing, since the work of the Lord President and the Secretaries of State for Scotland and Wales had been engaged in this direction.

In Scotland sixty organizations, including the political parties, submitted written views, but only 170 individuals sent in their comments. In July and August Scottish Ministers, with Lord Crowther-Hunt, spent weeks on end in discussions with representative Scottish organizations. The consultations showed sharp divisions in opinion. Many favoured a substantial measure of devolution, involving a directly elected Scottish assembly with real powers. A minority opposed any radical changes, apart from possible measures of administrative devolution. The overwhelming view of those consulted, however, as a White Paper published later was to record, was that 'the essential political and economic unity of the United Kingdom should be preserved'. In Wales the Secretary of State toured the entire principality. In addition he

---

[1] After the October Election he became Minister of State in charge of higher education, and was later transferred to the Privy Council Office as Minister on devolution questions.

received written comments from thirty organizations. About a third were in favour of legislative devolution, nearly half preferred executive devolution, the remainder favouring other solutions or the maintenance of the status quo. Written views from individuals showed a majority for, at the least, some scheme of legislative devolution.

The Cabinet Committee under the Lord President worked through the late summer, finally reporting to meetings held at No. 10 and to the Cabinet. Their draft was not too well received, but it was noted that an ad hoc sub-committee of the NEC, chaired by Shirley Williams, had produced an excellent draft. Sections of this were therefore grafted on to the document before us, issued as a White Paper, *Democracy and Devolution Proposals for Scotland and Wales* (Cmnd. 5732). This first recited the history, going back to the report of the Kilbrandon Commission, and reported on the consultations in Wales and Scotland, commenting that there would have to be further consultations with representative bodies in England. (It was already becoming clear that there were anxieties in some of the English regions, particularly the North-West and the North-East, where there were fears that the assemblies proposed for Scotland and Wales would be endowed with strong powers to attract new industry, especially 'footloose' firms, whether British or multi-national, considering where to locate a branch establishment. The opposition of a number of Members of Parliament representing these areas to any meaningful proposals for devolution was to persist right through the progress of the legislation in the Parliamentary sessions of 1976–77 and 1977–78.)

For Scotland and Wales the Government said flatly in the White Paper that they proposed the creation of directly elected assemblies. The Scottish assembly was to have a legislative role, including legislative powers within areas where separate Westminster-enacted Scottish legislation already existed as, for example, in housing, health and education. Partly because of the different legal structures in Scotland and Wales the proposed Welsh Assembly's powers were to be limited to exercising certain powers of the Secretary of State for delegated legislation, as well as taking responsibility for many of the executive functions exercised by nominated bodies, statutory or otherwise, in Wales, and certain functions by the Secretary of State. Neither in Scotland nor in Wales would the new assemblies take over powers currently exercised by local authorities.

The assemblies would consist of constituency members, one for each area. The most revolutionary change – certainly as seen by the Treasury – related to finance. The financial allocation at the disposal of the assemblies was to be based on a block grant voted by the Westminster Parliament from the United Kingdom tax revenues, related to local needs and the maintenance of comparable standards in the United Kingdom as a whole. But

It will be for the assemblies to judge among competing priorities within Scotland and Wales in the light of their own assessment of their communities' needs: as between, for example, hospitals and roads or schools and houses.

The White Paper went on to reiterate the Government's determination to remain fully responsible for the overall interests of the United Kingdom. For this reason it was regarded as essential that both Scotland and Wales should retain their existing number of MPs in the United Kingdom Parliament, which would, of course, have the duty of allocating resources as between Scotland, Wales and the English regions. Moreover, the two Secretaries of State would continue within the Cabinet to speak for Scotland and Wales, and to speak for their decisions in an undiminished Westminster Parliament.

Another important decision set out in the White Paper related to the North Sea oil industry. The Offshore Supplies Office for stimulating the development of native industry to provide the equipment for drilling and raising the oil was transferred to Glasgow, and the new British National Oil Corporation[1] was also to have its headquarters there.

The new development was the establishment of a Scottish Development Agency responsible to the Secretary of State, to stimulate new industrial expansion. It would also carry out in Scotland the appropriate functions of the National Enterprise Board. Its establishment was followed by the creation of a Welsh Development Agency. These decisions naturally enhanced the anxieties of English MPs in hard-hit regions. They would have been still more worried had they heard – or since read – the evidence of the SDA given in Edinburgh to the *Committee of Inquiry into Financial Institutions* in December 1977, and that of the WDA in February 1978, recording the extent of their activities.[2] Another act in administrative devolution was the decision to set up within the British Airports Authority a separate organization to be known as Scottish Airports.

Appended to the White Paper was a ten-page Appendix setting out the proposals in a form suitable for legislation, or, let us say, instructions to Parliamentary Draftsmen.

The White Paper on Devolution was published on 17 September. The following day the widely expected Autumn General Election was announced. The Government's devolution policy, in common with all the other September White Papers and the Government's entire six months' record, was before the people for endorsement or rejection.

[1] See p. 41 above.
[2] See p. 143 below.

# Chapter 3

## EUROPE AND THE WORLD

JAMES CALLAGHAN moved into the Foreign Office on the evening of 4 March. While it was clear that one of his major tasks would be the renegotiation of the terms on which Britain had entered the European Economic Community, this was not his only immediate task. The problems facing a Foreign Secretary and the Government for which he acts as spokesman and negotiator can be very roughly divided into two groups. The first covers those where he takes the initiative in pursuit of a clear objective; the second those where he has to react to world events, few of which he has initiated, and many of which he could wish had not occurred, but which require action, alone or in concert with our allies or partners. Again, many of the issues, in both categories, are liable to stimulate reaction amongst party activists, whether, in our case, in the Parliamentary Labour Party or in the National Executive Committee – or, usually, in both.

Action had to be taken at once on the EEC.

On 1 January 1973 Britain had become a member of the European Economic Community, on the terms negotiated by Mr Heath once President Pompidou had withdrawn the Gaullist veto exercised in 1963 and 1967.[1]

The Labour Party did not accept the terms which had been agreed. As a party we were sharply divided, as indeed the country was. In 1967 Conference had accepted by 4,147,000 votes to 2,032,000 a motion submitted by the National Executive which ended with the words:

> We believe that the British Government has sought membership of the EEC in a manner fully in accord with the principles and objectives of the Labour Party. That is why the Labour Party fully supports Britain's application to enter the EEC.

I had much more difficulty keeping the Party on the right lines in Opposition. Labour MPs in the 1970–74 Parliament were against entry, many of them regardless of the terms, a smaller number opposed simply to the terms. But in the minority of Labour members who supported membership was a considerable number of 'marketeers' to whom adherence to the EEC was not so much a policy as a way of life. A good number believed more strongly in British membership than in any other tenet of policy, and would, if the choice

---

[1] See *The Labour Government 1964–1970*, p. 468, and pp. 3-4 above.

had to be made, reject the Party in favour of what was to them the wider aim, Europe.

But we were concerned also by the fact that Mr Heath had no mandate to take Britain in. During the 1970 General Election, his manifesto had said, 'Our mandate is to negotiate; no more, . . . no less.'

In all my thirteen years as Leader of the Party I had no more difficult task than keeping the Party together on this issue, particularly in our Opposition years, 1970–74. On the Sunday before Conference in October 1973 I had to lay my leadership on the line, and make it clear that I would resign and face the Party with the election of a new leader if the NEC recommended Conference to bind us to a policy of withdrawal. We had reached this situation after a process which had lasted several months.

Mr Heath had put the issue of entry to Parliament with the terms he had negotiated.[1] Following his signing of the Treaty of Accession on 22 January 1972, he published the text of the European Communities Bill four days later. The Bill outraged anti-marketeers, and indeed a good number of others, by its terse style, leaving nothing open for amendment. It infuriated many Labour members just as the Industrial Relations Bill had done. Both were the product of Sir Geoffrey Howe's draconic drafting, a characteristic exercise in legislation by reference, covering just twelve clauses and four schedules.

Labour was on a three-line whip, the most mandatory of Parliamentary voting procedures, to oppose the Bill. Something like a third of the Labour MPs were dedicated pro-marketeers: 69 voted *for* the Second Reading; 20 more abstained. Pro-marketeers defied the whip in division after division. The Conservatives, too, were divided, and the Second Reading was carried by 8 votes, as was the key (Accession) clause. Roy Jenkins, the elected Deputy Leader of the Party, had resigned his post, and with it membership of the Shadow Cabinet, on the Party's decisions to support a referendum to allow the people to decide. The Third Reading was carried on 13 July. 296 Conservatives and 5 Liberals voted for; 264 Labour members, 4 independents, 16 Conservatives (including 5 Ulster Unionists), against. Three Conservatives, 1 Ulster Unionist and 13 Labour members abstained. The Bill received the Royal Assent on 17 October.

It was a miserably unhappy period. There was the further worry that Conference might very well reject our membership of the EEC in a way which could preclude any hope of leaving the issue open in a general election and in the Parliament that was to follow.

The decisive meeting of the NEC was in the last week of June 1973, which began in the morning at Transport House, continued over lunch, was adjourned to a Committee room at the Commons, and finally when that was required for Parliamentary purposes to my own very crowded room behind the Speaker's Chair. The NEC was deeply divided. We began to work towards

[1] Cmnd. 5109. This was followed by the Treaty of Accession, Cmnd. 5179.

a compromise but finally reached agreement on the one outstanding problem – a single sentence – thanks to a formula proposed by Judith Hart. This formula was included in *Labour's Programme 1973* which was submitted to the autumn Conference:

> Britain is a European nation, and a Labour Britain would always seek a wider cooperation between the European peoples. But a profound political mistake made by the Heath Government was to accept the terms of entry to the Common Market, and to take us in without the consent of the British people. This has involved the imposition of food taxes on top of rising world prices, crippling fresh burdens on our balance of payments, and a draconian curtailment of the power of the British Parliament to settle questions affecting vital British interests. This is why a Labour Government will immediately seek a fundamental renegotiation of the terms of entry.

> We have spelled out in *Labour's Programme for Britain* our objectives in the new negotiations which must take place:

> The Labour Party *opposes* British membership of the European Communities on the terms negotiated by the Conservative Government.
> We have said that we are ready to renegotiate.
> In preparing to renegotiate the entry terms, our main objectives are these:

> Major changes in the COMMON AGRICULTURAL POLICY, so that it ceases to be a threat to world trade in food products, and so that low-cost producers outside Europe can continue to have access to the British food market.

> New and fairer methods of financing the COMMUNITY BUDGET. Neither the taxes that form the so-called 'own resources' of the Communities, nor the purposes, mainly agricultural support, on which the funds are mainly to be spent, are acceptable to us. We would be ready to contribute to Community finances only such sums as were fair in relation to what is paid and what is received by other member countries.

> As stated earlier, we would reject any kind of international agreement which compelled us to accept increased unemployment for the sake of maintaining a fixed parity, as is required by current proposals for a European ECONOMIC AND MONETARY UNION. We believe that the monetary problems of the European countries can be resolved only in a world-wide framework.

> The retention by PARLIAMENT of those powers over the British economy needed to pursue effective regional, industrial and fiscal policies. Equally we need an agreement on capital movements which protects our balance of payments and full employment policies. The economic interests of the COMMONWEALTH and the DEVELOPING COUNTRIES must be better safeguarded. This involves securing continued access to the British market and, more generally, the adoption by an enlarged Community of trade and aid policies designed to benefit not just 'associated overseas territories' in Africa, but developing countries throughout the world.

> No harmonisation of VALUE ADDED TAX which would require us to tax necessities.

If renegotiations are successful, it is the policy of the Labour Party that, in view of the unique importance of the decision, the people should have the right to decide the issue through a General Election or a Consultative Referendum. If these two tests are passed, a successful renegotiation and the expressed approval of the majority of the British people, then we shall be ready to play our full part in developing a new and wider Europe.

If renegotiations do not succeed, we shall not regard the Treaty obligations as binding upon us. We shall then put to the British people the reasons why we find the new terms unacceptable, and consult them on the advisability of negotiating our withdrawal from the Communities.

An incoming Labour Government will immediately set in train the procedures designed to achieve an early result and whilst the negotiations proceed and until the British people have voted, we shall stop further processes of integration, particularly as they affect food taxes. The Government will be free to take decisions, subject to the authority of Parliament, in cases where decisions of the Common Market prejudge the negotiations. Thus the right to decide the final issue of British entry into the Market will be restored to the British people.

If that formula held we would be through our troubles. The Party would be saved from polarization, and ultimate control would pass to the incoming Labour Government if we were successful at the General Election. We breathed again.

But in September the issue was brutally and dangerously re-opened. The TUC, in their annual Congress at the beginning of the month, contrived to end the week facing both ways. Their Annual Report was endorsed by Congress, and this contained a clear commitment to remain in the EEC but to go for better terms. But a resolution calling for withdrawal was moved from the floor and carried.

Immediately the anti-marketeers who were powerfully placed on the NEC saw their chance. At two separate sub-committees, Home Policy and International, the decision was taken to back the TUC's negative vote, but the final outcome remained with the meeting of the NEC itself during the week-end preceding the opening of Conference. On the Friday morning before Conference we began to take up our stance on major resolutions on the EEC which would come before Conference. It was clear that a majority of the NEC would vote in favour of recommending Conference to oppose membership. I tried to get this reversed, but the majority decided to leave it over until our Sunday meeting, by which time we should have the final wording of the resolutions – particularly the 'composited' ones drafted by agreement between those constituency and trade union delegates who were content to merge their drafts into a single form of wording to put to Conference.

It was a week-end of button-holing, cajoling and fierce argument, a process in which I clearly could not take a direct part. By late Saturday evening it was clear that the vote could not be better than 13–12 *against*, perhaps worse. Persuasion became more urgent. At the Sunday afternoon meeting I had no alternative but to play the ace. I made it clear that if the NEC were to recommend withdrawal they and the Party would have a leadership crisis on their hands, and that what was presumably the last conference before the General Election would be dominated by speculation and direct canvassing over the new leadership. Two members changed their votes, Barbara Castle and Joan

Lester, and the line the Party had taken in Parliament was upheld by 14 votes to 11.

On the following Thursday, when the issue was debated, there was no resolution from the NEC. An entirely helpful motion by the (anti-Market) Transport and General Workers' Union mainly calling for the referendum, which was accepted Party policy, was overwhelmingly carried, and a violently-worded resolution rejecting British membership was defeated on a card vote – in fact by 3,316,000 to 2,800,000. A narrow verdict, but, as Winston Churchill once said, 'One is enough.'

When the manifesto was drafted and agreed early in January, the words used were exactly those which had been agreed in the previous June.

Labour fought the election on that formula: renegotiation of the terms of entry to be followed by a referendum. The referendum proposal had been made by Tony Benn earlier in the year in the context of the Parliamentary debates on the Heath Government's Bill. It was accepted by the Shadow Cabinet – and it had been this, on top of the imposition of a three-line whip, which had led to Roy Jenkins' resignation.

On coming into office the Cabinet moved quickly to prepare for the negotiations in the Council of Ministers. In the first week I had a series of meetings with the Foreign Secretary. On the machinery of government for handling the negotiations we set up a strategic committee of the Cabinet under my chairmanship, which included the Foreign Secretary, the departmental minister principally concerned. It was also sufficiently representative of Cabinet feeling as a whole to include Peter Shore (who as Trade minister would be involved in some of the negotiations), Michael Foot and one or two other committed anti-marketeers. For the tactical handling of the negotiations and supervision of briefing material, the Foreign Secretary was put in the chair of an operating committee, reporting to my committee as necessary.

I was concerned that if all the official work were concentrated on the Foreign Office, we should run into serious difficulties with ministers, since it was widely suspected that the Foreign Office was so committed to membership of the EEC that they would tend to use their position to override the interests of other departments, for example, Agriculture, Industry, Energy, and Trade. To ensure that renegotiation policy was kept firmly in the centre, rather than in a department, a Second Permanent Secretary was appointed to the Cabinet Office, to be responsible for all inter-departmental co-ordination of the approach, reporting as appropriate to the Foreign Secretary's tactical committee or the No. 10 strategic committee.

The EEC Council of Ministers was due to meet on the 1st and 2nd of April. Following the agreed Cabinet instructions the Foreign Secretary referred briefly to our principal objectives in the renegotiations, and reported to the House on 3 April on the discussions. This was to be the pattern for all future discussions: at the end of each, whether at Foreign Minister level or later at

Head of Government level, a full oral statement was made to Parliament, and followed by sustained questioning. His statement was laid before Parliament on 1 April as a White Paper (Cmnd. 5593).

He began by stating the Government's position substantially as it had been put before the people at the General Election:

> It will come as no surprise to you that the Labour Government opposes membership of the Community on the terms that were negotiated at the time of our entry in January 1973. We do not consider that they provided for a fair balance of advantages in the Community and we are of the opinion that the terms should have been specifically put to the British people for their approval or otherwise. We wish to put these errors right and if we succeed there will then be a firm basis for continuing British membership of a strengthened Community . . .
>
> We should negotiate in good faith and if we are successful in achieving the right terms we shall put them to our people for approval. But if we fail, we shall submit to the British people the reason why we find the terms unacceptable and consult them on the advisability of negotiating the withdrawal of the United Kingdom from the Community. I am confident that no one in the Community would wish to argue that it would be in the interests of the Community to seek to retain my country as a member against its will.

But he went on to make clear that he was not hoping for a negotiation about withdrawal. He would prefer an outcome which meant continued membership. This would depend both on Britain and her partners.

He then went on to quote the exact words of Labour's election manifesto as set out above,[1] making clear that we should meanwhile halt further processes of integration, particularly measures affecting taxes on food.

Setting out the issues with which the Government was mainly concerned, he listed the resolutions confirmed at the October 1972 summit which laid down a programme for achieving an Economic and Monetary Union, with permanently fixed parities by 1980; the statement in the Paris Summit Communiqué outlining the intention to form a European Union by the same date; and the Common Agricultural Policy, with its butter mountains, which accounted for 80 per cent of the Community budget, of which Britain would have to pay an undue proportion. He went on to stress the special problem of Britain's trade with the Commonwealth and developing countries (including New Zealand butter), the need for aid to poorer countries to cover areas where Britain had a special interest. On the question of domestic economic régimes he feared interference with British regional, industrial, fiscal and counter-inflationary policies. Finally, on the Community budget, Britain's income per head and her rate of economic growth were lower than that of many of her partners, yet her financial contribution would be out of all proportion to her resources. While in the transitional period we were paying only 8.5 per cent of the Community budget, we were already the second largest net contributor, and in the post-transitional period we should have to

[1] See pp. 52–3.

3

provide 19 per cent. He undertook to bring forward proposals on the more important issues.

Finally stressing that 'the image of the Community in the United Kingdom is not good', he emphasized the importance of the Atlantic Alliance and regretted the degree of disagreement between the Community and the United States.

His statement was – and was regarded as – an opening bid. But it soon became clear that there was little prospect of meaningful negotiations while the Government was in a minority situation in Parliament, with the real prospect of being ousted in the forthcoming General Election, which was expected to be early.

During the Short Parliament Britain was represented at meetings of the Council of Ministers of the EEC on twenty-five occasions involving thirty-nine ministers in all. The Foreign Secretary attended six of these, which were held at Foreign Minister level, usually accompanied by Peter Shore and Roy Hattersley, Minister of State in charge of European affairs. When the Council of Ministers was dealing with agriculture and food, Fred Peart went, while meetings on overseas development were attended by Judith Hart.

In October 1974 the Foreign Secretary tabled the first of a series of six-monthly reports on transactions in the EEC,[1] following a resolution of the Parliamentary Select Committee on European Community Secondary Legislation as far back as the 1972–73 session. The report dealt with development in all three European Communities – EEC, the European Coal and Steel Community (ECSC), and the European Atomic Energy Community (Euratom).

Some of the meetings covered questions relevant to the renegotiations, such as the Community budget, the Common Agricultural Policy (CAP), Community policy towards Commonwealth and developing countries on trade and aid, and regional and industrial policy, but little was attempted in terms of meaningful renegotiation. British ministers were concerned mainly to avoid commitments which would make it more difficult to produce a satisfactory outcome on the major issues. On subjects such as agriculture, Fred Peart, a long-committed opponent of the EEC but by now a convert, was anxious to see that the CAP did not develop still further in the direction of a high-priced, protectionist cartel.

Meanwhile ministers, particularly the Foreign Secretary, were engaged on a large number of bilateral visits to EEC capitals, explaining our position and seeking support. I paid only five visits to the capitals – three of them to Paris, of which one was for the memorial service to President Pompidou. The other two were to Bonn and Brussels, though I visited Luxembourg for a Heads of Government meeting to celebrate the twenty-fifth anniversary of NATO. Naturally on all these visits we sought to advance our cause in the renegotiations.

[1] Cmnd. 5790.

The twenty-fifth anniversary of NATO was a notable occasion. Every Government except Canada was represented at Head of Government level – Pierre Trudeau was fighting an election. We endorsed the Ottawa declaration on NATO's achievements and the need for maintaining our collective strength in the future. Though no notice had been given, each of us was asked to make a five-minute speech. As the only Head of Government present who had been a member of one of the founding Cabinets I naturally paid a tribute to Ernest Bevin, the prime mover in the creation of NATO, and simply asked who of the founders could have forecast with confidence that we should be meeting a quarter of a century later. Above all, who among them could have had any confidence that above all Italy, and perhaps France, would not have gone Communist within a few years, but for the military and political solidarity provided by NATO?

On 8 April I had a visit from the Polish Foreign Minister, Mr Stefan Olszowski, to discuss negotiations then proceeding for a tractor contract with Massey Ferguson/Perkins. This contract, worth £155 million, was agreed in August, and formally signed in September. At that time it was the largest single contract Britain had secured in Eastern Europe. On 12 September I met the Polish Ministers of Trade and of Machine Industry, who had come to London for the signing ceremony.

It was at this time that I became again involved in the question of the Panovs. These distinguished members of a Soviet *corps de ballet* had some time before applied for exit visas in the hope of coming to the West and ultimately to Israel. In 1972 the Soviet authorities had granted a visa to Valery Panov, but he had refused to leave without his wife, Galina, who had been denied a visa. Over many years I had been concerned with the release of Soviet Jews, and – because it was done quietly without demonstrations and denunciations – some dozens, including such well-known names as those of Ruth Alessandrovich and others, had come out in consequence. I had been approached many times about the Panovs.

On 20 May 1974 Academician Kirillin, Deputy Premier of the Soviet Union and Chairman of the State Committee on Science and Technology, came to London to take charge of discussions on an import–export deal, and on technological exchanges. Half-way through his talks with the Trade and Industry Secretaries I asked him to dinner. After getting through our agenda I turned to him and, saying I wanted him to take this very seriously and transmit it to top level in Moscow, I raised the question of the Panovs. The Bolshoi ballet were due to visit London. I had first proposed such a visit twenty-seven years earlier during my trade discussion with Deputy Premier (later President) Mikoyan, at 2 a.m. when my real motive was to give time for a London telegram to be deciphered for me to make the next bid in the trade talks. Mikoyan had dismissed the idea on the ground that our stage was not big enough, nor in all probability was the orchestra.

To Kirillin I said I hoped to see the Bolshoi, but I could not in all conscience do so if the Panovs were still held against their will. Turning to one of his two aides, a KGB man if I have ever seen one, I charged him to take down my exact words, which I repeated for him. Kirillin promised to do all he could. HM Embassy were asked to ensure that the matter was being pressed.

On 5 June I involuntarily made a great mistake. I was recording a BBC 'Analysis' interview at Downing Street with Ian McIntyre, one of the BBC's best and most searching interviewers. Commenting on my attitude to South Africa he suddenly asked me why I was not applying the same standards in respect of Soviet attitudes to human rights; why, for example, was I not pressing the question of the Panovs. One thing you cannot do in a broadcast is to cover up on a question, still less try to waffle away. The reaction must be instant: I simply said that I had made this personal approach and hoped it would succeed. There was no alternative, though at once I regretted what I had said, and asked my office to telephone the Embassy asking them to report it and hoping it would not prejudice the decision. Two days later I heard that the Panovs were out.

On their arrival there was a great reception at the Israeli Embassy residence. I did not attend, but the Israeli Ambassador spent several minutes attributing this happy release to my intervention. I could only hope that it would not prejudice the release of others. Nor did I attend the Bolshoi first night at Covent Garden, to the obvious annoyance of the Russians.

The reason was that weeks before, No. 10 had booked the evening for a farewell dinner to Sir William Armstrong, now Lord Armstrong, who in my time had been Permanent Secretary first of the Treasury, then, on its creation, of the Civil Service Department.

Foreign affairs are not simply a question of conferences and bilateral negotiations. During the Short Parliament the Foreign Secretary particularly, but also No. 10, was seriously preoccupied with South Africa, with Chile, and with decisions we had to take about a grave crisis that arose in Cyprus, inevitably involving Greece and Turkey.

One question relating to South Africa was urgent. On taking office in October 1964 I had announced an immediate ban on arms shipments to that country, on the Saturday following the Election, before indeed the Cabinet had met for the first time. It came into force at once. Dockers were unloading an arms cargo the next morning.

In 1974 the situation was more complicated. Mr Heath's Government had cancelled the arms ban. I called a meeting of the Ministers concerned and we took certain immediate decisions, including the cancellation of a helicopter still on order. But a number of items nearly ready for shipment included highly technological equipment which could have either a military or a purely civil use. We went through them, deciding on each item, and it was laid down that the Secretaries for Defence and Trade would meet to draw up lists of permitted and banned items for the future, any disagreement to be reported to my Committee for settlement. In the event definition presented little difficulty.

Both the Foreign Secretary and I made clear in the Commons that our attitude to Chile involved a reversal of that taken up by our predecessors. On 27 March James Callaghan said,

> Chile has a strong tradition of democratic government, and our policy towards the military junta will be governed by our desire to see democracy restored and human rights fully respected there. To this end, we shall take part in any future representations to be made to the United Nations on human rights in Chile, and our ambassador has been instructed to represent strongly to the military junta our concern at the treatment of prisoners.[1]

Aid was suspended. A projected naval training exercise arranged by our predecessors was cancelled. A review of existing contracts was in progress, but we said 'We shall not grant new export licences for arms.'

Ships they had ordered had already been handed over, and were engaged in trials. International law would have forbidden us to take them back, or to instruct the Royal Navy to force them into port or sink them.

On 9 April I was asked whether I would pay an official visit to Chile, the last thing the questioner (Dennis Skinner) would have wanted, but an accepted Parliamentary means of opening up the way to more detailed supplementary questions. My reply was 'No, Sir,' and I went on to attack Chilean repression, saying that we had interceded in the matter of certain political death sentences, adding, 'Anyone who wants to go to Chile would probably want to see who were in the Chilean gaols and what kind of democracy they stood for.'

On 21 May I made a statement on arms supplies to Chile and South Africa.[2]

The Chilean Air Force had a contract with Rolls Royce Engines for the overhaul of aero-engines and the supply of spares, with a provision for three months' notice of termination. At the Government's request, notice was given to be end the contract, and obligations to supply spares would also come to an end.

Referring to the last remaining Westland Wasp helicopter ordered by South Africa, under a contract signed during the period of office of our predecessors, I said 'the export licence for the remaining one aircraft, delivery of which was outstanding when we came to office, is to be revoked.' The Conservatives attacked these decisions in unmeasured language, and were supported by a hostile Labour member who asked me to take similar action with the Soviet Union, to loud Conservative cheers. I replied that there were no arms contracts with the Soviets – there had been none since the winding up of wartime supplies:

[1] *Hansard*, vol. 871, col. 424.
[2] *Ibid.*, vol 874, cols 186–93.

So far as the Soviet Union is concerned, I was myself involved[1] with negotiating the Comecon agreements for stopping on a NATO basis the supply of arms to the Soviet Union and to members of the Warsaw Pact. Therefore, my hon. Friend's oratory is beside the point and so is the cheering of hon. Members opposite . . .

Such cheering would have implied that they had tolerated supplies by our Conservative predecessors, which was not the case.

It was in subsequent questions that I nearly put myself out of order. At a serious point in one of my answers, a Conservative back-bencher, objecting to my announcement, interjected, 'Where is the Foreign Secretary?', to which I replied, invoking a favourite phrase of Aneurin Bevan, 'He is in Washington, fathead . . .,' and rapidly recalling that all Parliamentary remarks are addressed to the Chair, I added, 'through you, Mr Speaker'.

On relations with South Africa we later announced the abrogation of the Simonstown agreement. The dire Opposition warnings of the certain consequences have not, to this day, materialized.

Chile and South Africa proved to be the subject of problems involving the collective responsibility of ministers. At a meeting of a sub-committee of the National Executive Committee in May three ministers dissociated themselves from Government policy by voting for a critical motion about the Chilean ships. I circulated to the Cabinet a memorandum I had originally issued, and published to the Press, in 1969 when a minister attending the NEC dissociated himself from Cabinet policy on Barbara Castle's *In Place of Strife* proposals.

The problem was to come up again just after the October General Election, when three ministers voted in favour of a National Executive resolution criticizing the Government over a routine naval visit to Simonstown. As it happened, two days earlier, at the Eve of Session reception which the Prime Minister always gives for all ministers, to hear the Queen's Speech read, I had specifically reminded them of their collective obligation to support the Government wherever they might be. Two days later three ministers, Tony Wedgwood Benn, Judith Hart and Joan Lestor, broke ranks at the NEC.

My personal minute to each of them[2] was more than a reminder of good conduct – or else. The doctrine of collective responsibility I took as read, by reference to previously circulated démarches. It went on:

> Your vote in support of the Simonstown resolution at yesterday's meeting of the National Executive Committee was clearly inconsistent with the principle of collective responsibility. You will be aware of the embarrassment which this has created for your colleagues.
>
> I must ask you to send me in reply to this minute an unqualified assurance that you accept the principle of collective responsibility and that you will from

[1] In the 1940s.

[2] Reproduced in full, together with the other texts referred to above, in *The Governance of Britain*, pp. 192–3.

now on comply with its requirements and the rules that follow from it, in the National Executive Committee and in all other circumstances. I must warn you that I should have to regard your failure to give me such an assurance, or any subsequent breach of it, as a decision on your part that you did not wish to continue as a member of this administration. I should of course much regret such a decision, but I should accept it.

I doubt if so strong and unequivocal a minute as this has been issued before – certainly not since – for it differed from usual warnings in treating a refusal to accept the doctrine in full as constituting resignation. There were one or two unsatisfactory and equivocal drafts sent in reply, but I insisted on the exact words of my demand, which in each of the three cases was finally met.

On a different aspect of the subject, I had to intervene again some time later. When Tony Wedgwood Benn was elected Chairman of the Home Policy Sub-Committee he decided to do the news briefing after each meeting. It was made clear to him that whatever decision the Sub-Committee took, he would not be allowed to be the purveyor of any announcement which was not totally consistent with Government policy and collective Cabinet responsibility. He also surprised me by deciding that in that capacity he would follow my precedent in Opposition days of attending the TUC Economic Committee. I told him he was not to do so, and secured Len Murray's confirmation that he would not be welcome – the Home Policy Sub-Committee regularly considers the line of any approach the TUC is to make to ministers.

Soon after the questioning on Chile died down, the Government was faced with a serious crisis over Cyprus, which at one point looked like escalating into a military confrontation with Turkey.

Cyprus had been an independent Commonwealth country since 1960. Its President, Archbishop Makarios, had attended Commonwealth Prime Ministers' Conferences from that year onwards. Because its population was divided between Greeks and Turks owing a kind of extra-territorial loyalty to their mother states, Cyprus was a target for Greek and Turkish oratory, diplomatic pressures, threats and subversion.

On 15 July 1974 a fanatical Greek called Sampson started a revolt. The National Guard intervened and the presidential palace was attacked. Indeed in James Callaghan's first statement to Parliament on 15 July he referred to the reputed assassination of President Makarios, and both he and the Conservative spokesman, Sir Alec Douglas-Home, expressed their condolences and tributes.[1]

In fact the President had escaped to a monastery in the western part of the island, but his life was in danger. We arranged to lift him to safety in a helicopter based on Britain's sovereign base at Akrotiri, whence he was flown, via Malta, to Britain.

[1] *Hansard,* vol. 877, cols 27–8.

On arrival he came straight to Downing Street, where I received him at the door, in accordance with the protocol for Heads of State and Governments, which he still was. He was still wearing the clothes he had worn when the crisis began. Prime Minister Mintoff had provided him with a clean shirt and I supplied him with a change, as we had the same collar size, but the cassock he always wore was more than due for a change. I gave orders for a reconnaissance of all the Greek Orthodox Churches in London, in search of a priest who equalled the Archbishop in height, and who might have a spare cassock. This was forthcoming.

James Callaghan's statement referred to the Treaty of Guarantee, signed by the Greek, Turkish and Cyprus Governments, as well as Her Majesty's Government, and announced that he had drawn the attention of the Governments concerned to their undertakings, urging restraint on all concerned. In answer to a question the Foreign Secretary said that we had no responsibility under the independence treaty for internal security, though there was a small United Nations force on the island. But we had the two bases at Akrotiri in the south and Dhekélia in the East.

The first reaction of the Turkish Government was to say that violence would not solve the problems of Cyprus. They were referring, of course, to Greek violence.

On 17 July, the Turkish Prime Minister, Mr Büleat Ecevit, informed us that he was on the way to London for urgent talks. The Foreign Secretary and I cancelled our engagements and entertained him and his ministerial team to dinner at No. 10. The purpose of his visit was to seek our agreement to a Turkish invasion of the island, to protect the Turkish minority there. To this end, he asked us to allow him to use the sovereign base at Akrotiri for the purpose. He received from us a courteous but declaratory 'No'. As the argument developed, our rejection of his plan became still more firm. He and his team returned home but we were sure that we had not heard the last of him.

Parliamentary questioning was still based on fears of aggression by the Greek Government, whose intimidatory approach had already been referred to the United Nations, which President Makarios was due to address. We for our part were becoming increasingly concerned about Turkish intentions.

On Thursday and Friday, 18 and 19 July, the Foreign Secretary and I were in Paris for a series of bilateral discussions with President Giscard and his ministers. We left there in the afternoon. The Foreign Secretary left the aircraft at Gatwick to go to his farm for the week-end. I flew on to Durham where I was due to address the Durham Miners' Gala the following morning. I retired to bed rather late, and at 3 a.m. was awakened by a knock on the door. The No. 10 private secretary in attendance had been aroused by a message from London that a Turkish invasion of the island was thought to be imminent. I replied that if this proved to be so I would return to London in the early morning and asked for RAF transport to be ready. Meanwhile

I asked that the Ministry of Defence should prepare against my return a schedule of the position of all naval vessels and RAF units within the area or within reasonable distance.

At 7 a.m. I was told that the invasion had begun. All my Gala arrangements were cancelled, and I left soon after 8. The Foreign Secretary likewise came up to the Foreign Office from Sussex. We gave orders that our Sovereign base areas should be strengthened with military air support. Back at No. 10 we were in direct operational touch with the Admiralty and other service departments. Naval vessels, those at hand in the Mediterranean, the Atlantic and at United Kingdom bases, were ordered to proceed in the direction of Cyprus. The first arrivals were soon involved in reinforcing arrangements made in Akrotiri to get British residents and holiday-makers to places of safety, whether in the base areas, or on board ships leaving the island. Before long they were engaged in humanitarian work rescuing Greek Cypriots threatened with a campaign of murder and pillage by the advancing Turkish forces, who sought to occupy areas of Cyprus which could not by any stretch of the imagination be regarded as Turkish Cypriot territory. In all, the RAF flew 9,000 people to Britain.

On 22 July a cease-fire was agreed which froze the situation on the basis of the Turkish conquests. It was agreed that meetings directed to a final settlement should be held at Geneva, whither James Callaghan and representatives of the Turks and Greeks were to repair. It was a tragedy at this time that the United States were diplomatically in baulk. Dr Kissinger was later to express his regret that the United States had been so ineffective at a critical time. As Secretary of State he was concerned with the last agonies of the Nixon presidency, since the duties of his office included supervision of the procedures which had to be followed on a Presidential resignation.

Meanwhile a dangerous crisis developed. A United Nations Force was on the island, with units stationed at Nicosia airport, including British, Canadian and other national cadres. In the evening of 24 July, I was in my room at the House of Commons as a division was expected on Denis Healey's mini-Budget statement.[1] At 8 o'clock the Foreign Secretary came to see me urgently. The Turks had informed us that they were going to bomb the airport, and inevitably there would be casualties among the UN forces, of which the biggest component was the British, including the 16th/5th Lancers. He felt I should telephone Prime Minister Ecevit. This I did and warned him strongly against his plan, but he refused to comply with what I asked; later he came back after, no doubt, consulting his military advisers. He had identified the exact location of the British forces, and undertook to avoid bombing the sector where they were. I said his proposal must be resisted. We had a responsibility, as the only UN member nation with forces close at hand, to defend UN troops. Furthermore, there were Canadians in the UN force. I was not entering into any collusion whereby British troops were

[1] See pp. 28–9 above.

3*

safeguarded and the lives of Canadians endangered. He must realize that we must resist. If he proceeded with his design we should not hesitate to order our fighters to shoot down his aircraft. Emergency arrangements were made to reinforce Akrotiri, and to get fighters into position. He persisted in his decision. But an hour and a half later he telephoned again to say that he had cancelled the project. Had he not done so we would undoubtedly have been involved in hostilities which might well have escalated. Apart from the lunacy at Suez, that was probably the nearest that Britain came to war with another nation since 1945.

By the end of the month a cease-fire had been negotiated, and it was agreed that all outstanding questions should be settled at a conference to be held at Geneva, with representatives of Britain, Turkey and Greece. James Callaghan had to spend most of August in Geneva, but on all major substantive issues the Turks refused to move. Once again the intervention of the United States was missed.

In September the last cards were played in the EEC renegotiations before the expected election. President Giscard d'Estaing (France holding pro tem the presidency of the Council of Ministers) telephoned round to ask all his colleagues to attend a Heads-of-Government meeting in Paris on Saturday 14 September. This was not unwelcome news despite my preoccupation with the forthcoming General Election, which I was about to announce. No Prime Minister begrudges time so spent when an election is near.

We were to meet at the Elysée quite informally; the meetings would take place without our Foreign Secretaries, or officials. No minutes would be taken. The subject was to be the further integration of the European Economic Community.

Nothing could have been more informal. We sat in armchairs arranged in a semi-circle in a drawing room at the Elysée. Each of those requiring interpreters had one seated behind his chair whispering the translation. The President welcomed us and asked Helmut Schmidt, the German Federal Chancellor, to open up. To everyone's surprise he said that he felt that the growth in unemployment seemed to him so urgent that he proposed to speak on that subject. This suited me as I had prepared nothing on the subject we had been invited to discuss, feeling that Britain had nothing to contribute while negotiations were proceeding. After Helmut Schmidt, the President took others in turn round the room, anti-clockwise, omitting only, and very pointedly, M. Ortoli, President of the EEC Commission, who sat at one end of the semi-circle. One or two with prepared speeches on European integration read out their set pieces, but most of us tried to get to grips with the growing unemployment problem.

At lunch the conversation was more general, and Valéry Giscard took the opportunity to ask me how seriously we took the EEC in view of our emphasis on renegotiation. I stressed what the Foreign Secretary had said, that we were negotiating from within the Commission in the hope of making enough progress on the issues we had stressed to justify our continuing as members and playing our full part. This was welcomed, but I was in no doubt that they were awaiting the result of the election, which by this time was rightly regarded as imminent.

Europe was awaiting Britain's General Election. So was Britain. No one had long to wait. It was announced four days later, on 18 September.

# Chapter 4

## JOHN BULL'S OTHER IRELAND[1]

THE division of Ireland and its resultant centuries of misery dates back to the 'Plantation of Ulster' in the reign of James I, when the City of London, founding the new city of London, Derry, together with a flood of immigrants from Scotland and other parts of the United Kingdom, created a major and robust Protestant presence in St Patrick's Catholic island.[2] The religious split and Ireland's other problems dominated politics on both sides of the water, caused the resignation of Pitt the Younger in 1801 – he was to return briefly to office in 1804 until his death in 1806 – and can be said to have ended the ministerial careers of Peel, Gladstone and Lloyd George. Winston Churchill was intimately concerned with its problems before the First World War, and played a major part with Lloyd George in the settlement of 1921, which led to King George V opening the first Northern Ireland Parliament in 1921. This endured for forty-five years, but it ended the Lloyd George era, for it was the Irish settlement, rather than the Chanak crisis, which caused the mass desertion of his Conservative majority at the Carlton Club meeting in October 1922.[3]

The Irish Free State was created in 1922, with the separate six Ulster counties remaining under direct rule from Westminster. It was not until 1949 that Clement Attlee's Government carried through the legislation which gave Ireland, outside the six counties, its independent status: the Act formally 'recognized and declared that the part of Ireland heretofore known as Eire ceased to be part of Her Majesty's Dominions'.

Tension in Northern Ireland developed again in the late 1960s. By this time the Irish Republican Army (IRA) was split into two mutually hostile factions. The 'Official' IRA had become left wing, virtually Trotskyist. Its

[1] The heading of this chapter is taken from a *Tribune* pamphlet by the late Geoffrey Byng, MP, published in 1952, after Bernard Shaw.

[2] Loyal Unionists would blame the troubles on St Patrick.

[3] See my *A Prime Minister on Prime Ministers*, London, 1977, pp. 29–30, 57–9, 143 and 160.

As Winston Churchill put it in *The World Crisis: The Aftermath*, London, 1929: 'Yet in so far as Mr Lloyd George can link his political misfortunes with this Irish story, he may be content. In falling through Irish difficulties he may fall with Essex and with Strafford, with Pitt and with Gladstone; and with a line of sovereigns and statesmen, great or small, spread across the English history books of seven hundred years.'

Indeed, for a time it looked as though Ireland might have ended Churchill's own career. He went out, as Lloyd George's closest colleague, with his Prime Minister, lost his seat in Dundee, and did not return to Westminster until October, 1924.

objectives were essentially long-term: convert the North and the South, separately, to the true Trotsky faith and let the two parts of Ireland peacefully coalesce. The 'Provisional' IRA were committed to violence as the only means to ending British rule in the North.

The events of the troubled days from October 1968 onwards have been described elsewhere.[1]

Violence became the order of the day: in 1969 British troops were given the overriding responsibility for public security, and the Downing Street Declaration (Cmnd. 4154) was promulgated, repeating the pledges of successive Governments that Northern Ireland would not cease to be a part of the United Kingdom without the consent of the Parliament of Northern Ireland: 'The border is not an issue.'

Mr Heath took over as Prime Minister in June 1970, but although he introduced many changes of policy in both domestic and overseas affairs, the handling of the Northern Ireland problem was marked by a continuity of policy. Just as he and I had consulted fully in the Prime Minister's room behind the Speaker's chair in the early sixties, so, though our Parliamentary roles were reversed, policy towards the troubles in Ulster remained, in the main, bipartisan.[2] There were pockets of opposition on both sides of the House: some of his supporters gave full backing to the Ulster Unionist parties, some Labour members sought refuge in proposals to withdraw the troops and leave the Irish to murder one another. Both Governments, and Oppositions, went to great lengths to prevent the spread of factional violence in Britain itself.

On one occasion, for example, a Court judgment in Northern Ireland cast doubt on the legal basis for certain security action by HM forces. Mr Heath asked me to call on him and invited our support – which was immediately forthcoming – for getting legislation through the House in a single day to validate action by the troops.[3]

In 1970–71 the murder of British soldiers and of members of the Royal Ulster Constabulary and the Ulster Defence Regiment became the order of the day. The shooting of thirteen demonstrators in Derry on 30 January 1972 greatly exacerbated the situation, and the findings of a one-man inquiry by the Lord Chief Justice, Lord Widgery, while generally welcomed this side of the water, caused resentment in Ulster Catholic circles. Catholic opinion,

[1] For these troubled years, see *The Labour Government 1964–1970*, pp. 671–5, 693–7, 718, and 770–74. Since that was written, the most authoritative book on the period has been published: *A House Divided*, by James Callaghan, London, 1973. As Home Secretary from November 1967 to April 1970, he had been in direct charge of the situation – the separate Northern Ireland Department had not been created until Mr Heath's premiership. Conor Cruise O'Brien's *States of Ireland* (London, 1972) is another valuable book, examining the history of Irish attitudes from the time of Parnell onwards.

[2] Labour did, however, vote against the Government on 29 November 1971, and abstained on the Emergency Provisions Bill, which received its Second Reading on 17 April 1973, its Third Reading on 5 July, and the Royal Assent on 25 July.

[3] 23 February 1972, *Hansard*, vol. 821, cols 1368–449.

North and South, was further aroused by reports of inhumane treatment of men detained for interrogation at an Army barracks. This was denounced by the Labour Opposition, and although two members of a three-man inquiry exonerated those responsible (Lord Gardiner, former Labour Lord Chancellor, dissenting) Mr Heath had the courage to accept the minority report and announce that such practices were to cease. It was a triumph for the doctrine of supererogation that the Irish Government insisted on pursuing the matter before the European Commission and Court of Human Rights for over six years. The Conservative Government instituted internment without trial, and on 24 March 1972 Mr Whitelaw was given the new post of Secretary of State for Northern Ireland. No one could have tried harder to bring peace: there were moments when he appeared to be within reach of success, a situation only to be reversed by new outbreaks of terrorism.

In November 1971, with Mr Heath's approval and help, I had gone to Northern Ireland for meetings with representatives of all the parties, and groups of varying opinions, in Belfast and in Derry, as well as meeting the Government in the South. In a major two-day debate on 25 and 29 November I put forward a fifteen-point programme, which was warmly received by the responsible ministers. The second to seventh points are paraphrased below, the others are taken directly from *Hansard*, some with omissions:

*First*, violence must cease, and be seen to have ceased.

*Second*, I suggested inter-party talks first at Westminster, then with the Northern Ireland parties, leading to tripartite discussions between the United Kingdom, the Irish Republic, and Northern Ireland aimed at establishing a constitutional commission of the three Governments, to examine the implications of a united Ireland with protection for minorities, north and south.

*Third*, an end to internment once the necessary conditions existed – though criminal charges would continue against those responsible before and after the new arrangements came into force.

*Fourth*, any resulting constitutional agreement to be submitted for ratification by all three legislatures, with full legal safeguards for the rights of minorities: the agreement to be based on a study of such possibilities as a Federal constitution, a dual system, or on the four historic Irish provinces, or on a system of meaningful devolution. It would include a blocking vote mechanism to protect minorities.

*Fifth*, the agreement should be enshrined in an international convention entered into by the two sovereign powers, with provision for binding arbitration by the International Court or other agreed appropriate tribunal.

*Sixth*, – given agreement on the above – the Irish Republic would seek, as a Republic, membership of the Commonwealth recognising the Queen as Head of the Commonwealth.[1]

*Seventh*, for a long period of years, the constitutional settlement would pro-

[1] I pointed out that had the Indian precedent occurred before Ireland gained her independence, that might have been the case at the time.

vide for an oath of allegiance to the constitution of the new Ireland, and to the Queen as Head of the Commonwealth.

*Eighth*, from the moment of agreement, if one could be reached on the Irish settlement, the Government of the Irish Republic would give a solemn undertaking, incorporated in the agreement, not when it comes into effect, but now, to use all appropriate powers and all the energy, forces and means at its command to pursue and extirpate terrorist organisations, operating from, located in, or supported from Irish soil. It would further undertake, jointly with the British Armed Forces, and other security services, to engage, as the situation required, in all necessary operations of Border patrols and other means of Border control to prevent terrorist infiltration into the North.

*Ninth*, the Government should give a binding undertaking to maintain, for the whole 15-year period of transition, and thereafter if the Sovereign power so agreed, sufficient military forces to safeguard law and order and eliminate violence. I could see no reason why they should not remain, if the Government of a united Ireland saw fit, for a further five or ten years, that is, for up to a quarter of a century from the date of these negotiations.

To emphasise Britain's determination in this regard, new buildings and facilities of a permanent character should be constructed, not so much a garrison as a military town, including married quarters and training facilities, so that there would be a large force of troops, both for training and available for operations. The idea would be a peacetime establishment similar to Aldershot or Catterick, so as to avoid the drama and sensation of the entry of troops for riot or subversive situations. The building and maintenance would provide much-needed employment.

*Tenth*, during the transitional period the Government should assume full Ministerial responsibility for all aspects of security, military and police, with the maximum devolution I have suggested to the police authority. Arrangements would be made for reports to be made by United Kingdom Ministers to the Parliament of Stormont, whether through a Standing Committee or direct to Parliament itself.

*Eleventh*, in the interim period, the Stormont Government should include representatives of minority views, provided that each such Minister made clear his loyal acceptance of the interim constitution, in addition to his acceptance of the long-term settlement set out in the agreement.

*Twelfth*, the constitution of the new Ireland would include the Human Rights Provision of the Downing Street Declaration, together with adequate machinery for its enforcement.

*Thirteenth*, – and here we come to the theocratic problem – the constitution would further provide for changes in the 1937 Irish Constitution necessary to give assurance that there would be no constitutional impediment to the creation of a National Health Service on the British model; to a social security system not less eligible than that now enjoyed by the citizens of Northern Ireland; that all censorship or prohibition of books or the importation of newspapers would be removed; that the right would be asserted to legislate in the field of personal liberties, for example, in family planning, abortion and other matters, in accordance with British practices, and provision made to place legislation on all these matters on the British model, on the Statute Book during the transitional period.

*Fourteenth,* it should also provide for a dual and equal system of education on the lines of the English and Scottish models, with such limited changes as are required for the needs of a united Ireland.

*Fifteenth,* and finally, social service provisions should be progressively assimilated to the British system to guarantee to Northern Ireland citizens the rights they have enjoyed within the United Kingdom. The task of harmonising the Irish system of social security with the British should begin with the signature of the Constitutional Agreement, having regard to wage levels and other matters affecting the standard of living in both countries. Five years after signature of the Agreement the first of 10 annual increments in Irish social benefits would begin, assisted by an injection of British financial aid, total harmonisation being effective simultaneously with the entry into force of the long-term constitutional provisions of the Agreement and Treaty, and the achievement of a united Ireland.

The fifteenth point, a programme designed to move towards a united Ireland in fifteen years' time was, in our view, an essential component of any lasting settlement. Looking back on it, it was not realistic, for it was a much milder version of the White Paper following the Sunningdale Conference mentioned below.

On 24 March 1972 Mr Heath's Government imposed direct rule on the province, with the support of all three major parties in Parliament.[1] On the same day Mr Whitelaw became Secretary of State, a position he held until 2 December 1973. In September 1972 the Government held a conference at Darlington, County Durham, with the three leading Ulster political parties. In October a discussion paper was issued, and further consultations followed. In March 1973 Northern Ireland voted in a referendum on the border issue: an overwhelming majority voted to remain within the United Kingdom, as opposed to merging with the South. In the same month a White Paper, *Northern Ireland Constitutional Proposals* (Cmnd. 5259), was issued outlining plans for an elected Assembly from which would be drawn a coalition administration – the 'power-sharing Executive'. Legislation followed to establish the Northern Ireland Assembly and to set up the new Constitution. In June 1973 an Assembly was elected.

In early December 1973 ministers again met with representatives of the three Northern Ireland parties who were willing to accept the Government's invitation. This Sunningdale Conference agreed on 9 December on declarations on the constitutional status of Northern Ireland, and also on proposals for setting up a Council for Ireland, North and South, and on the establishment of a British–Irish Commission to deal with cross-border acts of violence. It was a move towards the North–South consultations which led to the crisis of May 1974, which caused the destruction of the Executive. By that time Labour was in office.

On 31 December the power-sharing Administration was sworn in in Belfast, and took over on New Year's Day 1974.

[1] *Hansard,* 24 March 1972, vol. 883, cols 1859–63.

In March 1974 Merlyn Rees became Secretary of State, and at once made it clear that he was following the lines of policy of the outgoing Government. This was made explicit in the first debate in the new Parliament.[1] Nine days later Merlyn Rees was making a statement on the murder of two soldiers of the 14th/20th Hussars, returning from leave. Ten days after that he was reporting to the House on an outbreak of mass violence which wrecked an Army building and Catholic bars in Belfast, together with incendiary and explosive bomb attacks in Armagh, Lisburn and Bangor as well as Belfast: six civilians were killed and sixty-five injured, as were eight soldiers and two members of the RUC.[2] Both groups of extremists were at it.

On 4 April Merlyn Rees opened a major debate on the Ulster situation. He began:

> When we were in Opposition we supported the previous administration in its policies. We had our differences, but on all matters of principle there was all-party support for the Government of the day. It is our aim to maintain this approach towards Northern Ireland in this Parliament. Our policies will be firmly based on those of our predecessors in office . . .[3]

He particularly stressed the Northern Ireland Constitution Act, which we had fully supported, and which provided the Parliamentary basis for the new power-sharing, cross-party, ministerial executive.

Our predecessors had recognized that the Catholic minority in Northern Ireland, mainly peaceable, could not be asked to face another forty years of total exclusion from power. To realize their aspirations, all parties agreed, provided the best hope of removing from the IRA terrorists 'hearts and minds support from the mass of the Catholic population'.

To maintain the fight against terrorism, the Secretary of State announced that while we had reservations about the Conservatives' Emergency Provisions Act of the previous year, and would wish to introduce amendments, the Government were asking for its continuance by Order for a further period.

Again, only six days later, on 10 April, he was reporting a further outbreak of bombings and widespread shooting incidents. In addition he gave Parliament an account of a growing menace: small, home-made incendiary devices, using for instance lipstick cases, left in shops and elsewhere, and capable of destroying whole buildings once they took hold. Clearly the most intensive search operations had little hope of discovering these in time.

After a brief Easter holiday in the Isles of Scilly, I made, on 18 April, my

---

[1] *Hansard*, 12 March, vol. 870, cols 73–4. The Ulster problem was constantly before Parliament: equally it was rarely off the Cabinet Agenda: Mr Heath told *The Listener*, 22 April 1976, that together with EEC questions Irish affairs were regularly included in the first items on the weekly Agenda, in addition to the traditional items 'Parliamentary Business' and 'Foreign and Commonwealth Affairs'.

[2] *Ibid.*, vol. 871, cols 879–82.

[3] *Ibid.*, col. 1463.

first visit to Northern Ireland since returning to office. The following extract from the official No. 10 diary gives some impression of what was involved.

*Thursday 18 April*

7.50    The Prime Minister left St Mary's by helicopter and flew to RAF Culdrose. From there the Prime Minister and his party flew to RAF Aldergrove in an HS 125.

10.05   On arrival, the Prime Minister was met by the Secretary of State, Mr Reid, Mr Gilliland, Group Captain Langston (the Senior RAF Officer, Northern Ireland and Station Commander).
        They all then left for HQ Northern Ireland in two helicopters.

10.20   Arrival at Lisburn and met by Lt-Gen. Sir Frank King.

10.25   Briefing by GOC.

11.20   The Prime Minister and his party left by helicopter for HQ, RUC.

11.30   On arrival at Brooklyn, the Prime Minister was met by the Chief Constable, Mr Flanagan.

11.35   There the Prime Minister was briefed by the Chief Constable.

12.30   The party left for Stormont Castle by helicopter.

12.35   Arrival at the Northern Ireland Office, Stormont Castle, and met by the Minister of State.

12.40   In the First Floor Conference Room the Prime Minister had a meeting with the Northern Ireland Administration.

1.30    A buffet luncheon was served for the Prime Minister's party and guests in the Ministerial Conference Room.

3.00    Briefing for the Press Conference followed.

3.30    The Press Conference was held in the First Floor Conference Room. The Conference was followed by TV interviews.

4.30    The Prime Minister paid an impromptu visit to Mr Orme's meeting with Trade Unionists in the Speaker's House.

5.05    The Prime Minister left Stormont Castle for Girdwood Park Barracks, again by helicopter.

5.30    Arrived Girdwood Park Barracks, and met by Brigadier Richardson (Commander 39 Brigade). The party left by road for North Queen Street Police Station.

5.35    Arrival, and met by ACC Bradley, Chief Supt Faulkner (Commander "B" Division RUC), and Lt-Col. Brewster (QC 42 Commando RM), introduced to the troops and RUC.

6.05    The Prime Minister left the Police Station and returned to Girdwood Park Barracks, from there he and his party flew by helicopter to RAF Aldergrove, arriving at 6.25 p.m. The party then flew by HS 125 back to London.

8.25    The Prime Minister arrived at Chequers.

I returned with very mixed feelings. The reports on violence were extremely depressing, even though there was some feeling that terrorists were no longer finding ready open doors in the homes of their co-religionists when seeking refuge from the forces of law and order. At one time a gunman on the run had been able to go into almost any house in the right kind of street and be given shelter.

On the other hand it was heartening to see Northern Ireland's first power-sharing executive at their job, taking responsible administrative and political decisions with a great deal of willingness to make concessions to representatives of causes they had been brought up to hate.

The administration headed by Brian Faulkner had been in office only fifteen weeks. I could not have guessed that three-quarters of its life was already spent.

Violence was on the increase. On 16 May Stan Orme, Minister of State for Northern Ireland, told Parliament that between 1 January and 30 April, seventy-four people had been killed, and claims for damage to property amounted to £10½ million. In addition to the upsurge of IRA murders, the extreme 'Loyalists' were busy organizing strikes designed to exert pressure to end the power-sharing experiment. But a major putsch was being organized on the other side.

On Monday 13 May I made an emergency report to the House. I had received from the security forces (the RUC and the Army) a number of documents they had seized, the general purport of which I felt should be brought to the attention of Parliament.

> These documents reveal a specific and calculated plan by the IRA, by means of ruthless and indiscriminate violence, to foment inter-sectarian hatred and a degree of chaos with the object of enabling the IRA to achieve a position in which it could proceed to occupy and control certain pre-designated and densely populated areas in the city of Belfast and its suburbs. The plan shows a deliberate intention to manipulate the emotions of large sections of the people by inflicting violence and hardship on them in the hope of creating a situation in which the IRA could present itself as the protector of the Catholic population.
>
> It is also clear that the IRA did not expect, even if it was initially successful, to be able to continue to hold a number of strong-points in parts of Belfast and that its intention would have been to carry out a scorched earth policy of burning the houses of ordinary people as it was compelled to withdraw.
>
> Some of the information in the possession of the RUC may be important in the bringing of potential criminal charges, and the House will understand that there must be some reservation on the disclosure of documents. I can however say that the documents include orders to battalion commanders, and the outline of the general concept, with associated maps and a draft proclamation to the civilian population . . .[1]

The documents, subject to the reservation about criminal proceedings, were published that afternoon in Northern Ireland, and made available to the House. A sequel to this event was a recommendation to the Sovereign that Stan Orme be sworn of the Privy Council. Without such status he could not be allowed access to the more sensitive documents, should he be required to make a further statement to the House, if the Secretary of State were in Northern Ireland, as he had to be on this occasion.

Just a week later he was making an even graver statement for the future of the Province, and for the hopes of the main Westminster parties for tolerance and unity in its governance.

[1] *Hansard*, vol. 873, cols 891–2.

On Sunday 19 May, Merlyn Rees flew over urgently to Chequers. Ulster was in the grip of an undeniably political strike, arguably the first in the history of the United Kingdom. There have been those who have argued that the brief and unsuccessful General Strike of 1926 was political, though its motive was economic – resistance to the cuts in miners' wages. The 'Ulster Workers'' strike was directed to two political ends, indeed constitutional ends – the destruction of the power-sharing executive, and the rejection of the Sunningdale Conference's proposals for an all-Ireland Council to promote contacts on economic and other subjects, on lines which would fall a long way short of constitutional links, still less any move to union in the island as a whole.

The Ulster Workers were not a trade union organization. The Northern Ireland TUC was to the workers of Ulster what the Trades Union Congress is to the trade unionists of Britain. I had met them a number of times, and as shown above, Stan Orme held regular gatherings with both leaders and rank and file. Their interests were specifically industrial. Northern Ireland's congenital pabulum of Unionist versus Catholic shibboleths had no place in their activities.

The course of events following Stan Orme's statement on 13 May was ruthless and remorseless. On Tuesday 14 May a body known as the Ulster Workers' Council, which had no trade union or party standing, but had been brought into being by the para-military organizations, placed an advertisement in the press that they would call a general stoppage of work in the Province if the Northern Ireland Assembly voted on that day to support the Sunningdale Agreement. The Assembly did so vote to support the Agreement and the constitutional settlement laid down in Westminster's 1973 legislation.

The following day the Rev. Ian Paisley and Mr William Craig MP, together with a Unionist member of the Northern Ireland Assembly, led a deputation to Northern Ireland ministers of three members of the Ulster Workers' Council, and three observers directly representing Protestant para-military organizations. Ministers were told flatly that their object was to destroy the Sunningdale Agreement and the Assembly pending new elections. They would enforce their demands by controlling the supply of electricity, themselves determining who should have current and who should be cut off.

On 16 May intimidation became virtually total. Workers seeking to go to the shipyards, textile mills or engineering works were prevented by manned barricades. The following day the Secretary of State agreed to have a meeting with elected political leaders and members of the Ulster Workers' Council, making clear that no recognition was involved. In fact no Council member turned up.

On Saturday 18 May the Ulster Workers' Council called for a total stoppage from Sunday midnight. It slightly qualified this, but called for industrial and commercial closures and sought to dictate the times when shops could open. The Secretary of State, after consultations with the Northern Ireland Executive, proclaimed a State of Emergency. By the time the Minister of State reported to the House on 20 May, most main roads around Belfast were blocked, as were those in other towns, including Larne and Bangor. The TUC, after consulting the Northern Ireland Trades Union Committee, issued a statement condemning the Ulster Workers' action:

they are a body created to pursue a sectarian policy which . . . is rejected by the trade union movement generally, and their objectives and activities have no connection with the protection of working people or the promotion of their common interests . . .

On 22 May Merlyn Rees reported to the House the action taken to keep major roads open, but had to admit the seriousness of the situation. Unblocked roads were soon re-blocked, and few were getting through to work. Not all that many were trying to. Soon supplies of food and fuel were being cut off from certain Catholic areas, and the Ulster Workers were trying to maintain a total blockade on tanker deliveries to petrol filling stations.

The following day Westminster adjourned for the Whitsun recess, though the Government stood ready to recall Parliament should that be necessary. Meanwhile the Northern Ireland Executive bravely stuck to its task, and somewhat quixotically pressed on with the implementation of the Sunningdale Conference's decision that a Council of Ireland be set up, North and South. Merlyn Rees in a constitutional statement endorsed the Executive's decision, but with schools, shops, factories and petrol stations closed, this was becoming a hollow vision. Attention began to be directed to the electric power stations, where workers, including maintenance men, had been turned away, but where high-level power-station engineers sought to keep electricity supplies moving.

The Secretary of State for Defence brought more troops over. One spearhead battalion[1] moved in, another moved up in readiness. Soldiers were soon involved in every kind of activity to keep essential services going. Military establishments at home and overseas were combed for specialists of various kinds, particularly those who could help keep the power stations in operation, for it was clear that the Ulster Workers' blockade, as they had threatened, would be enforced on a discriminatory basis in the power stations. I had brusquely adjourned a meeting called to provide an additional £9 million subsidy to the shipyards, refusing to let ministers even consider the provision of money to help employment when men were not even allowed to get through to the shipyards: indeed many shipyard workers were prominent in the now completely effective picket-lines.

On Friday 24 May leading members of the Northern Ireland Executive

[1] The spearhead battalion is maintained in readiness in Britain, in case instantly needed whether in Northern Ireland or anywhere else in the world. As one moves out another takes its place.

came over to Chequers and spent most of the day there. It was clear that the situation was desperate, and the very existence of the Executive was in grave doubt. Essential services had broken down, shipyards and factories were closed, the writ of government no longer ran, except – and then with difficulty – in the field of law and order.

Mr Brian Faulkner, leader of the Executive, Mr Gerry Fitt and Mr Oliver Napier, leaders of the other two parties, called for maximum help by service personnel, particularly on keeping the roads open, maintaining petrol distribution, and above all keeping the power stations working. We were able to meet him on unblocking major roads, and on providing oil and petrol for essential users, including oil and chemicals for the Derry Gasworks, and the operation of twenty-one strategically-placed petrol stations. But the key, as Mr Faulkner made clear, was electricity. Unless we could find technicians from within the services or elsewhere, Northern Ireland would be at a standstill. Transport to take food to the starving Catholic areas was scarcely less urgently needed. Our search for Army specialists to man the power stations had produced a useful number, but they could not run power stations on their own. Power engineers, that is managers and undermanagers, had remained at their posts, but it became clear that this would not continue. Their lives were being threatened; worse still, they were receiving clear warnings that unless they backed the Ulster Workers' strike, their wives' and children's lives would be at stake. The professional association of power station engineers in Britain made clear that their members would not be allowed to go and help out in the North. As Mr Faulkner and his colleagues left Chequers at 5.0 p.m., there seemed little hope of breaking the strike or of maintaining the Executive in being, but they returned to their beleaguered Province determined to fight on to the last. The British ministers at Chequers returned to London for an urgently summoned Cabinet, less than fully attended because some ministers had left London for the Spring holidays. (Parliament had adjourned for the Spring recess until 10 June.)

On my return to Chequers I began work on my ministerial broadcast due for the Saturday evening. There was little likelihood that mere words would shake the self-appointed, power-drunk but disciplined faction which had taken unchallenged control.

It is arguable that the words I used were provocative and bitter. Certainly there was no hope of appealing to the organizers of the strike. But, rightly or wrongly, I felt it right to underline the fact that while Westminster was taxing the people to find hundreds of millions of pounds to provide work for the men and women of Ulster, a self-appointed group of bigots appointed by no democratic means and responsible to no one, were denying the right to work-for a political objective. And that objective was simply to destroy an Assembly freely elected by the people of Northern Ireland, and the quasi-ministerial Executive created and sustained by that Assembly, at the same time tearing up a Westminster Act of Parliament.

The people on this side of the water, British parents, British taxpayers, have seen their sons vilified and spat upon – and murdered. They have seen the taxes they have poured out almost without regard to cost – over £300 million a year this year with the cost of the army operations on top of that – going into Northern Ireland. They see property destroyed by evil violence and are asked to pick up the bill for rebuilding it. Yet people who benefit from this now viciously defy Westminster, purporting to act as though they were an elected government, spend their lives *sponging* on Westminster and British democracy and then systematically assault democratic methods. Who do these people think they are?

The idea I was seeking to get across was that Ulster was always ready to come to Auntie for spending money, expressing their thanks by kicking her in the teeth. The phrase I used was open to criticism, and was picked up by the extremists. In no time the Rev. Ian Paisley was buying sponges, small pieces of which were in the button-holes of his supporters, no doubt as a badge of pride.

After recording the broadcast at the BBC I flew to the Isles of Scilly for a brief holiday. It turned out to be even briefer than planned. After Sunday morning Church I received a call from the Secretary of State. Things had deteriorated still further. He was flying to the Royal Naval Air Service station at Culdrose, near the Lizard in Cornwall, and wanted to see me urgently. A Culdrose helicopter picked me up and when we met he made it clear that the political situation in Belfast was in a state of total collapse.

By Monday night he reported that all hope had gone. I decided to return the next day, and at the same time propose to Mr Speaker that the House be recalled for the following Monday under the emergency provisions of Standing Order No. 122 ('Earlier meeting of House in certain circumstances'). Under the powers of the Constitution Act the functions of the Executive were discharged, and the Assembly prorogued for four months.

Merlyn Rees opened the debate setting out the sad history of the previous ten days. My own speech the following day was concerned with two main points, one, to emphasize the argument about the vast assistance given by Westminster to help unemployment in the Province, and two, to open up a debate about the future.

On finance, we had provided £70 million for the Harland and Wolff shipyard, 'where the employment is almost 100 per cent from a single religious community'. Yet it was Harland workers who more than any had denied their fellow Ulstermen the right to work. The managing director of the Northern Ireland Finance Corporation had estimated that the stoppage had cost companies £225 million of business. More than that, the Corporation, set up with Government finance to attract and help new firms and industries, would find their task much harder when they sought to persuade new ventures, such as multi-nationals, to establish plants in the Province.

There is one thing our people will not accept and that is power without responsibility . . . we in this country have the right to ask the elected representatives of
Northern Ireland to agree among themselves and to recommend to us. What I
do not believe they have a right to ask of their fellow citizens in the United
Kingdom, is an indefinite, unlimited continuation of responsibility on the
Government, the people and the legislative of this country for security without
power to ensure that political conditions are conducive to better security; or a
responsibility for providing money from the United Kingdom taxpayer when
the purposes for which that money is provided are being frustrated by faction
and violence.[1]

In looking to the future it was necessary to face ineluctable facts. Ugly
external pressures had brought about a defeat for those who had courageously and with great forbearance sought to create a representative form of
government, in the spirit of the Sunningdale agreement. It was an extra-
Parliamentary defeat for the combined efforts of all the major parties at
Westminster, a defeat for law and order, with all this meant for Britain, not
least in our overseas relationships. For centuries no external attack had been
successfully made on the authority of Parliament. Now it had. The bully
boys had won.

While it may have seemed negative, almost defeatist, the Government
inevitably had no new proposal for the future of the Province. The initiatives
taken at Darlington and Sunningdale, the policies of the Heath Government
and of our own had reached a dead end. No solution could be imposed from
across the water. From now on we had to throw the task clearly to the
Northern Ireland people themselves. Let Parliament see what they would
come up with, and we would consider it – a Northern Ireland solution.

Merlyn Rees began almost immediately to consult the different parties and
interests. On 27 June he was able to report that he had had very full discussions with leaders of all political parties represented in the Assembly and
with many other groups and interests. He promised a report to the House.
On 4 July he presented a detailed White Paper, *The Northern Ireland Constitution* (Cmnd. 5675), which was debated on 9 July.

One problem was the need to pass the legislation prepared by the
Executive before its abrogation. The Westminster Parliament could not
carry the burden of passing a number of Northern Ireland bills. Legislation
would therefore be introduced to give the Secretary of State power to give
them the force of law by Orders made under the Act. The replacement of the
Executive would be effected by powers deriving from the 1973 Constitution
Act, enabling the Secretary of State to appoint ministers. Under these powers
the two Ministers of State and the two Parliamentary Under-Secretaries at the
Northern Ireland Department would be designated as political heads of the
various Government Departments and Offices in place of Executive members.
Each one, in fact, had to take over a number of departmental portfolios.

[1] *Hansard*, vol. 874, col. 1053.

In other words, Northern Ireland would come under direct rule from Westminster, with ministers – of course spending most of their time in Northern Ireland – accountable not to Stormont, but to Westminster. At the same time legislation would be introduced for the election of a Constitutional Convention, under an independent Chairman nominated by the Queen, to consider 'what provisions for the government of Northern Ireland would be likely to command the most widespread acceptance throughout the community there'.

The Northern Ireland Bill accordingly was passed through all its Commons stages without a division, on 15 July. It went through the Lords with equal speed, and received the Royal Assent on 17 July. From then to the present time of writing, 'Direct Rule rules.'

Parliament adjourned for the Summer Recess on 31 July, nominally until 15 October. Few MPs expected that the House would assemble again until after a General Election. This was announced on 18 September, and the country voted on Thursday 10 October.

# PART II

*October 1974–August 1975*

# *Chapter 5*

## THE NEW PARLIAMENT AND THE EEC NEGOTIATIONS

THE second General Election of 1974 was relatively quiet and un-
eventful. Public opinion polls and press comment seemed to give
Labour the edge, though in the concluding days a substantial section
of the press and other media gave a great deal of emphasis to a new line
taken by Mr Heath. Inevitably in the second election within a few months
public opinion was more than a little bored, and the case for a national
government, a coalition, an administration of all the talents, was being
assiduously argued. Mr Heath did not go as far as this but in the last three
or four days he spoke of a national government, not as between the parties
– though he no doubt had not given up all hope of the Liberals – but one
which would include an unspecified number of national, unaligned figures.
Such suggestions always have an appeal, both among the uncommitted and
among disaffected voters who want to vote for their party, but would
welcome a little outside recruitment from the great and the good, or from
Woolton-type industrialists. It was a difficult argument to repudiate, and
it was the harder to seek to counter it by sticking to the main election
themes.

Another diversion was successfully launched by a pressman at our daily
press conference. Each morning, as I sat there flanked by a succession of
senior ministers, questions were directed to one after another – particularly
dedicated pro-marketeers – asking them if they would remain in a Labour
Government if the referendum went against their cherished beliefs. The
questioner unfortunately drew blood with Shirley Williams, who declared
that in such an event she would retire from public life. Immediately television and press reporters were pursuing Roy Jenkins round Birmingham:
he did not go so far as to forecast retirement, only an unwillingness to
remain in the Cabinet. These replies undoubtedly drove a number of committed marketeers into abstention, or into voting for the Conservatives – or
Liberals.

Most of the pundits forecast a Labour victory with a viable majority. The
wildest estimate was flashed on the screens by BBC television just before the
first constituency results were declared. Their tallymen had manned the
exits from polling stations in some 70 representative constituencies, asking a
sample in each how they had voted. The computer gave Labour an overall

majority of 150, beyond our wildest dreams. This figure headed the election night screens, until the 'swingometer' working on the first declarations rapidly moved into a much more moderate posture.

I was worried about the Liberal vote.

The Liberals in the main do very well under a Conservative Government. Any Government, Conservative or Labour, becomes unpopular over a period of time, particularly if it is trying to follow a long-term strategy in the short term. So in by-elections, and to a lesser extent in a General Election, people who had voted for the Government party tend to stay at home or to switch their vote. In by-elections, particularly, but also in General Elections, there are many Conservatives who would rather be found dead than vote Labour, but who have a sense of duty that they must vote, and who therefore find themselves in the Liberal camp. This certainly happened in the first election of 1974; the political consequence was not so much the number of Liberals elected, fourteen, but the number of seats where Labour came in on a minority vote, through Conservative votes going Liberal. But when Labour is in power many Conservatives return to the fold.

These anxieties were confirmed. The first dozen or so results which I saw on TV in my Liverpool hotel were mainly safe Conservative or Labour seats, showing no gains or losses. But as I left by car for the count in my own constituency it was clear that the Liberal vote was seriously down. Final figures were to show that while the Liberals had lost only one seat, their overall vote fell by nearly 200,000, and their proportion of the total vote from 19.3 per cent to 18.3 per cent, on a total poll which had fallen by over 2 million, from a 78.1 per cent turn-out to one of 72.8 per cent. The Conservative vote was down by 1,400,000 and their share of the poll from 37.8 per cent to 35.8 per cent. Labour's vote fell by 190,000 but our share of the total vote rose from 37.1 per cent to 39.2 per cent.

But as the night went on, slowly Labour gains began to appear on the screen, notably in Lancashire and the Home Counties. Highly marginal Lancashire seats, which had failed to come over in February, such as Bolton West, Nelson and Colne, Bury and Radcliffe, and Rossendale now showed mainly small Labour majorities, as did Peterborough, Hemel Hempstead and Welwyn and Hatfield. By 2.0 a.m., when I returned from the count to my Committee rooms, it was clear that we should have a substantially bigger lead over the Conservatives, though it was very doubtful whether we should have an overall majority in the House of Commons. Hence my somewhat muted claim when I addressed our supporters: 'Well, they can't take it away from us.'

The final result was as follows (February results in brackets)

| | | |
|---|---|---|
| Labour | 319 | (301) |
| Conservative | 276 | (297) |
| Liberal | 13 | (14) |
| Scottish National Party | 11 | (7) |
| Plaid Cymru | 3 | (2) |
| Others (GB) | — | (1) |
| Ulster Unionists | 10 | (10) |
| Social Democratic & Labour Party (Northern Ireland) | 1 | (1) |
| Others (Irish Republican) | 1 | (1) |
| Mr Speaker's seat | 1 | (1) |
| | 635 | 635 |

Labour's overall majority, allowing for the Speaker, was thus 4. Eighteen seats had been gained from the Conservatives, the main factor in Labour's majority over them of 43.

But the overall majority would clearly not long survive the erosion of by-elections, and of possible defections. It was for this reason that I pressed the Cabinet at our first post-election meeting to push on fast with our declared legislative programme, particularly with Bills likely to prove controversial, and/or complicated and lengthy. The strategy was to get on with the major legislation in the first two sessions, and after that to pursue a policy – good for the Government and certainly good for the country – of concentration on governing. This is what has largely happened.[1]

In this we were fortunate in having forced the pace during the short session in preparing detailed White Papers, or even 'Heads of the Bill', or instructions to Parliamentary draughtsmen, on a variety of important subjects, so that new major legislation was soon ready for introduction.

The pressure on Government, and on individual ministers, from the October 1974 Election to the Summer Recess, beginning on 7 August 1975, was the most hectic and demanding of any I have known in over thirty years in

[1] The number of Government Bills becoming law during the Short Parliament was 35. In the first session of the new Parliament, ending in November 1975, the number was 73. In 1975–76 the total was 76. In the 1976–77 session, 73 Bills became law, one or two, such as Shipbuilding and Aircraft and Dock Labour, being badly mauled on the way. For a comparison of legislative productivity, a table in *The Economist*, 5 August 1978, shows the following numbers of Government Bills becoming law in recent years: 1966–67, 103; 1967–68, 63; 1968–69, 51; 1969–70, 38; 1970–71, 76; 1971–72, 59; 1972–73, 57; 1973–74, 15; the 1974 Short Parliament, 35. The sessions of 1969–70, 1973–74, and 1974 were foreshortened by General Elections. Correspondingly, 1966–67, running over from the March 1966 Election to the autumn of 1967, and to a smaller extent, 1970–71 from June 1970 to the autumn of 1971, were abnormally long because of election timing.

Parliament. This was due not so much to the Parliamentary programme, though our small majority meant more constant attendance in the House, nor to Cabinet work on legislation. It was due far more to the intensity of the economic problems Britain was facing, through the, now, five-fold rise in oil prices, its effects on the balance of payments of Britain and our trading partners, world inflation and the ever-increasing threat of world unemployment.

But transcending even domestic problems, the work load of many ministers was greatly increased by the intensity of overseas relationships, particularly at Head-of-Government level. The number of conferences, incoming and outgoing bilateral meetings, though greatly increased, is itself no real measure. There were far more urgent problems than there had been before 1973, many of them requiring decisions in one or other international forum, rather than the attempts to achieve 'a mutual understanding of one another's positions' of more easy-going days.

So far as bilateral Heads-of-Government meetings were concerned, in the five years eight months of the 1964–70 Government, there had been nine official meetings between the President of the United States and Britain's Prime Minister, most being informal contacts at the fringe, or as the diplomatic phrase is, 'in the margin' of international conferences, and 'working funerals'[1] much more attended by Heads of Government than in the pre-jet age. In the twenty-five months from March 1974, there were six meetings with the US President, even though President Nixon began to cut down his overseas engagements before the end, and President Ford had to work himself in before undertaking much travelling.

The speeding up of the process of top-level bilateral and multi-national contacts was, of course, due in part to the development of the EEC, and President Giscard d'Estaing's institution of regular summit meetings. In the ten months from October 1974 to August 1975 there were three EEC summits, the NATO Summit of 1975, the Commonwealth Prime Ministers' Conference at Kingston, Jamaica, in May 1975, and the European Conference on Security and Co-operation at Helsinki. It was not only the time spent there, and the intensity of formal meetings, group meetings such as EEC Heads of Government, but the days and weeks of preparation, involving usually three or more massive files of briefs, including all those needed for bilaterals, and a number of oral briefings with all the departments concerned. But often the briefing was as voluminous before a bilateral meeting, whether in London or abroad. In the period of just over two years from March 1974 to April 1976, there were thirteen official Head-of-Government visits abroad, and fifty-nine incoming visits. These were Head-of-Government meetings only; they did not include the visits of, for example, Dr Kissinger, Mr Gromyko, and

---

[1] The phrase is owed to Robert Carvel of the London *Evening Standard*: its development from the ubiquitous 'working dinner' dates from the funeral of Dr Adenauer. See *The Governance of Britain*, p. 87.

French Foreign Minister Sauvagnargues, all of which required very full briefing.

In the period from the second 1974 Election to the adjournment of the House on 7 August 1975 there were well over forty major visits, including in date order the Prime Ministers of the Maldives, the Irish Republic, the German Federal Republic, Mauritius, Australia, New Zealand, Egypt, Canada, Turkey, Malaya, Ceylon, Iceland, Belgium and Trinidad; the Sultan of Oman, the President of Malawi, the King of Jordan, and the Vice-President of the United States; in addition, the Foreign Ministers of Somalia, Japan, Zambia, Yugoslavia, Israel (three times), Romania, the United States, Liberia, Egypt, Portugal; the Premier of British Columbia, the Governing Mayor of Berlin, the Hungarian Trade Minister, the President's *Chef de Cabinet* from Romania, Mr Gvishiani (Prime Minister Kosygin's son-in-law and technology chief), the Deputy Prime Minister of Cuba, the Speaker of the French Assembly, the President of the Radical Party of Chile, the President of Western European Union, the Secretary-General of the OECD, and the two successive Secretaries of the Commonwealth. In addition there was a succession of US Senators, including four Presidential aspirants on their world tour, all of whom had to be received if one were received, and State Governors (including Henry Wallace).

All the conferences and meetings had to be fitted in with the domestic programme, also increased to a great extent because of economic problems and the EEC negotiation. For example, there were frequent meetings with the CBI and the TUC, as well as the National Economic Development Council (Neddy), with individual unions, such as those held at the time of the threatened rail stoppage, and worried consultations with textile unions about the effects of the world slump and foreign competition. Pay policy meant very difficult meetings with the Government's own employees, the various Civil Service unions, the most serious representations from the nurses and the doctors, as well as deputations on behalf of local government.

Because each week's engagements could cover the whole range of subjects for which the Government had responsibility, this section of the book, like its predecessors, will be divided for the sake of continuity into main subjects, chapter by chapter, even at the risk of giving the false impression that the work of the Government, and the Prime Minister, can be compartmentalized. It is not only that crises at home and abroad can compel immediate attention: developments in one area can powerfully affect decisions and negotiations in another, and Parliamentary developments could affect all of them. That proviso applies to the course of the renegotiations of the terms of entry into the EEC, with which the remainder of this chapter will be concerned.

The theme of President Giscard d'Estaing's evening meeting in the Elysée on 14 September 1974, it has been made clear,[1] was at the last moment switched from European integration to the growth in unemployment. Only

[1] See pp. 64-65 above.

4

over a meal was the question of our negotiations raised, with everyone clear that the British Parliamentary election would be on the agenda first. The President's proposal for a European Council of Heads of Government meeting three or four times a year under the chairmanship of the EEC Presidency for the current six months was adopted. As soon as the election was over, with a Government committed to renegotiations still in West-minster, the pace quickened and concentration grew. The Council of Ministers were meeting, charged with settling the renegotiation question. But it was clear that progress would have to await the Paris Summit on 9–10 December. In theory the preliminary work for it should have been the main preoccupation of the Foreign Ministers' meetings. But no one was going to give away negotiating points before Heads of Government met.

At this point Helmut Schmidt, the German Federal Chancellor, took a hand. He had been invited to attend the last morning of the special Labour Party Conference, held at Central Hall, Westminster, from 27 to 30 November as a substitute for the regular Annual Conference fixed for October, but postponed because of the election timing.

His speech was courageous and clear. He was addressing a Conference which on a vote of the individuals present would probably have rejected membership altogether: a card vote reflecting trade union decisions had laid down tough conditions for staying in. Helmut Schmidt, without condescending to appeal or argue, laid the case for Britain's membership on the line – and received a great ovation.

He came to Chequers for dinner and to stay the night. We met in the study before dinner. He pointed out that Giscard was not only the host and chair-man of the Paris Summit due to convene nine days later, but the one we had most to convince if new terms were to be agreed. Indeed, he mused, he felt Giscard really needed to be persuaded that we were in earnest, not negotiat-ing with a view to an agreement to part. Why did I not go over for a meal with Giscard and discuss it *à deux*? I accepted this idea at once and he suggested that he should telephone the President then and there, which he did in my presence. I knew that they were in continuous touch by telephone, always speaking in English, and I suspected that Giscard had agreed with this proposal before it was put to me. It was simply a question of the date and time. We agreed on dinner the following Tuesday evening.

There were six of us, the Foreign and Commonwealth Secretary and HM Ambassador in Paris, with me, and Giscard, his Foreign Minister, and M. Brossolette, his *Chef de Cabinet*. We went deeply into the main issues, though without in any way negotiating in detail. He clearly wanted – and was sure that his fellow Heads of Government would want – a clear statement from us about our desire to see the negotiations succeed, and, given success, our full acceptance of what the Community meant, without any *arrière-pensées* about destroying it or changing its nature from within.

At the Elysée dinner the President's main preoccupations on the Paris

Summit related to the EEC Regional Fund, on which he was anxious that we should not seek a privileged position. In his view Italy and Ireland should be the principal, indeed the sole, beneficiaries. James Callaghan made the point that regional aid for Ireland had to be for the South only: if any attempt were made to include the North, we should have to press for comparable assistance for hard-hit areas in Great Britain itself: we were not in fact asking for regional assistance.

On renegotiation Giscard was anxious to question us on our concern about the Common budget. We replied by reference to our manifesto, especially in relation to traditional food imports from Australia and New Zealand. We welcomed the advance that had been made on negotiations with African, Asian and Latin American countries, including traditional French suppliers from Africa. 'Harmonization' of VAT was another problem for us: we were opposed to taxing necessities.

Jim pressed for a fair deal on the budget: we wanted a 'self-adjusting mechanism' related to our ability to pay. M. Sauvagnargues, the French Foreign Minister, warned us that the Germans as well as his own team opposed us. The essence of the Market was that it was financed by *ressources propres*, i.e. specific taxes and levies, imposed on a list of commodities and saleable goods, mainly VAT and import duties in each country, the whole of the proceeds going to the EEC budget. There could be no question of relating our contribution or that of the others to GNP calculations.

We pointed out such problems as the fact that our largely mechanized bakeries were used to hard wheat of the Canadian variety: while as individuals we might like French bread, soft wheat was of little use to us. There were long established preferences for New Zealand cheese.

Going on to future EEC procedure, I praised Giscard's September initiative in calling the informal Heads-of-Government meeting, and said we supported the idea that such meetings be held three or four times a year. He proposed the title 'European Council', which we welcomed. (We were as anxious as he was, though for different reasons, to have summit meetings which could inject a political reality often missing from the Council of Ministers, particularly when agricultural ministers dominated the proceedings.) We agreed to support his idea that M. Tindemans, the Belgian Prime Minister, should prepare a report on EEC procedures and institutions. On direct elections we could not commit ourselves until negotiations were complete, but I said Labour MPs, who were not attending the European Assembly, would undoubtedly begin to attend if the renegotiations were successful. On the question of unanimity and the 'Luxembourg Compromise', we were in general agreement. The unanimity rule, involving the possibility of a veto, should be reserved for questions of the highest national interest.

On general policy the President hoped that we should all be able to put pressure on Helmut Schmidt to embark on a real degree of reflation and expansion, and the Americans also. Wider questions were raised, such as the world gold price, and such bilateral issues as the continental shelf, where there were Anglo-French boundary disputes on the possibly oil-rich area of the western approaches, and Concorde and the Channel Tunnel, two projects which our Governments were still examining.

It was a worthwhile meeting, though the major renegotiation issues remained for the Summit meeting and beyond.

In particular, he asked, should the negotiations produce results acceptable to us, would we go out and campaign actively for their endorsement by the British people in the referendum? There was some fear that the referendum was being used as a fall-back position for opponents to invalidate the negotiations.

I decided that I would use a speaking engagement due on the following Saturday to make something approaching a declaratory statement just before the Summit. Accordingly on 7 December, addressing the annual dinner of the London Labour Mayors' Association, I delivered a very carefully prepared speech, which the audience speedily recognized was not directed purely to the edification of their Worships. A statement of the main points was sent in advance to the British and foreign press: it was also telegraphed to all HM Ambassadors to the Common Market capitals, for immediate delivery. In the speech and hand-out[1] I made the following points:

> ... it is imperative that our partners in Europe should know exactly where the British Labour Government stands – where indeed we have always stood.
>
> The position I have put forward on behalf of the Party since the terms of entry into the Community became known in 1971 has been totally consistent, and indeed it is the line we have taken ever since the time when, during the previous Labour Government, we made our first approaches to Europe in 1966.
>
> We said then, we say now, that entry on the right terms would be good for Britain and good for Europe. But at no point over these years have I disguised my conviction that we should reject terms which would cripple Britain's ability to solve her own problems, and prevent Britain from making the contribution to Europe of which she is capable. The kind of terms we proposed in 1967 are precisely the kind of terms for which we are negotiating now ...
>
> The position of the Government is clear.
>
> If re-negotiations are successful, it is the policy of the Labour Party that, in view of the unique importance of the decision, the people should have the right to decide. If these two tests are passed, a successful re-negotiation and the expressed approval of the majority of the British people, then we shall be ready to play our full part in developing a new and wider Europe.
>
> If re-negotiations do not succeed, we shall not regard the Treaty obligations as binding upon us. We shall then put to the British people the reasons why we find the new terms unacceptable, and consult them on the advisability of negotiating our withdrawal from the Communities.
>
> That was what we said in the February Manifesto. That has been the policy of

The text of the press hand-out is printed below as Appendix III.

the Labour Party, endorsed by Conference; it is the policy of the Government, endorsed by the people . . .

It stands to reason that provided we get the right terms – but only if we get the right terms – I shall commend them to the British people, and recommend that we should stay in and play our full part in the development of the Community.

I have made this clear again this week, and I shall repeat it at the meeting of the European Council next week.

Having put the issue twice to the people within this year, I owe it not only to the Party, not only to the British people who endorsed our Manifesto, but also to those with whom we are negotiating, to make it clear that those are the terms and we do not seek to add to them . . .

I believe that the necessary speed and urgency, combined with the thoroughness that is needed, can best be achieved if Ministers, accountable to their own people, now take charge. At the Press Conference which Herr Schmidt and I held at the conclusion of our talks last Sunday, I said: 'I would like to see the negotiations coming under much clearer political direction by politicians who know what is important to their own country, their own electorate, as well as to the countries with whom they are negotiating and their electorates.' This was immediately endorsed by the Federal Chancellor, who said, 'I very much agree with the British Prime Minister, that political questions in the first and in the last instance are to be solved and answered by political animals. They can be prepared, and must be prepared of course, by civil servants of various capacities, but we ought to be aware that what we are facing are political questions that are not very likely to be solved by legal procedures . . .'

There is a famous story about a Welsh Fifteen at Cardiff Arms Park. For twenty minutes, ankle deep in mud, the forwards hardly released the ball from the scrum for a moment. At last it emerged to the scrum half, who passed to the fly half, who then kicked it high over the Grandstand. A search party set off to look for it, and after ten minutes had not returned. One of the Welsh pack – or it may have been the English – was heard to say: 'Never mind the ruddy ball, let's get on with the ruddy game.'

We must take great care that we do not become so obsessed with the game that we lose sight of the ball. So let's get it out of the scrum. It has been there so long that I would like to know if it is in fact oval or oblong or banana-shaped or even flat. I want to get it into the hands of the three-quarters, the politicians, those with authority to move. Then let's see if we are able to score the try or not.

For many years I have been accused of putting Party interests or the requirement of Party unity before all else. I do not think Party unity is necessarily an unworthy aim, particularly for the Leader of the Party.

The fact is, as others have admitted so clearly, that the Labour Party is divided on this issue. So are the Conservative Party, even though they have more ruthless means of suppressing freedom of thought than a democratic party would consider to be right. So are the Liberals . . .

While I do not apologize for doing all in my power to get this Party *united*, what I can claim to have done since 1966 is to keep this Party *consistent*. And this is what our Manifesto means. We will work wholeheartedly for the success of the European venture if we get the terms for which we have asked and the endorsement of the British people. But if we do not, we believe that our national interest would not be served by accepting a situation which would undermine our economic strength, and our capacity to protect our national as well as our wider international interests . . .

The Paris Summit on 9–10 December was important not only for the ground it covered, including 'the British problem', but for its approach to the idea of making the 'European Council' a permanent institution of the Community.

In opening the meeting, President Giscard said we were not there just to ratify decisions taken by the Council of Ministers. The problem was that Heads of Government did not meet often enough. There had been only three meetings in five years, and personal relations between Heads of Government were not close enough. The world was becoming increasingly 'organized'. For example, the Arab oil producers had frequent and regular meetings, as did the non-aligned countries. We had to become more organized. Our task was not to preoccupy ourselves with detail but as Heads of Government to take an overall view and perspective both of the Community itself and of the wider world. He wanted leaders to stand back and forswear bureaucratic problems – certainly not feel that they were there just to rubber-stamp documents produced by subordinate meetings of ministers or officials.

I raised the economic problems: energy, trade, unemployment and inflation, and said we should discuss them at the current meeting. The President suggested that we should begin with institutional matters, 'convergence' of economic policy, regional policy – on which decisions were urgently needed, especially the funding of the programme as between individual member countries – and 'renegotiation'.

Supporting this, I pressed for a communiqué covering what we had said, not the barrage of pre-prepared documents and drafts, amended page by page. The September meeting had gone well because Heads of Government had sparked ideas off each other. I pressed for three or four a year, preferably four summits, each meeting ending with agreement on the timing and preliminary agenda for the next. Some supported this, others favoured twice-yearly meetings. Helmut Schmidt proposed a compromise figure of three a year, one in the capital of each country assuming for the six-month period the Presidency of the EEC, plus a third in Brussels, at the EEC headquarters. We supported Giscard's title 'European Council', but there were some misgivings in other quarters. I pointed out that if it had no baptismal name it would be called the 'summit'. The important thing was that if it became regular, reasonably frequent, and the dates settled well in advance, we could do a serious job free in the main from 'crisis' headlines. Our peoples would get used to it and not expect some dramatic action (or confrontation) from every single meeting. Attempts to create a regular and permanent secretariat were shelved, perhaps through anxieties that France would seek to control it. In the event the host country, meeting by meeting, took over all the preparatory arrangements and provided the secretariat. M. Ortoli, then President of the Commission, would be there in a policy sense. In Paris to a small extent, in Dublin three months later in a very real sense, he in fact acted as a bridge between opposing views, reconciling differences, working out alternative drafts, and acting as the Council's 'wise man'. At Dublin in the last difficult hours of the renegotiation arguments he played a decisive role, and it is more than arguable that we should not have succeeded without him.

Before the meeting moved to the British renegotiations, it was in danger of breaking down over the proposed regional fund. M. Ortoli produced the Commission's plan, based on specific allocations to Italy (40 per cent of the total) and Ireland (6 per cent). But it was clear that the method of financing a total of well over 1,000 million 'units of account' (the Community's 'currency', in fact a euphemism for dollars at the then rate of exchange) over three years would mean that an overwhelming proportion would have to be provided by Germany. Helmut Schmidt, clearly sickened by his role, as he saw it, as the milch-cow of Europe, made a bitter attack. It was not an easy situation for a Finance Minister to stand up in the Bundestag and pledge Germany to pay such large sums across the exchanges for three years ahead. He was not impressed by the fact that the Commission was ready to spend the money for Germany. Salaries had recently been raised by 16 to 17 per cent by the Council of Ministers. At whose expense? It was easy to spend other people's money. In Germany state employees would get an increase of only 8 per cent. Ireland and Italy should recognize that Germany had had to cancel a number of cherished national 'programmes' to keep their own expenditure under control. M. Ortoli replied to the attack on the Commission in kind, and Giscard had to adjourn the meeting, while we all walked up and down, for a short period of buttonholing, clump-forming and informal negotiations.

In the event Helmut Schmidt made some very generous proposals, agreeing to go well over the 1,000 million units. The final figure was 1,300 million. Before the allocation was agreed Britain was again in trouble. James Callaghan thought it might be helpful if Britain were to stay out of the scheme both as contributor and recipient for three years, assuming that the renegotiations led to Britain's remaining a member. But this was rejected: any scheme had to cover all the nine: one after another said you could not have an eight-nation Fund in a nine-nation Community. At this point Helmut Schmidt reminded the meeting that Ireland and Italy had had firm assurances that a Fund would be established. Britain had to be in. James and I were modestly content to go along with the proposals, and to accept a surprising proposal that Britain would receive 28 per cent of the total, against 40 for Italy and 6 for Ireland. The Communiqué[1] set out the figure for each state, with an addendum nevertheless that Ireland would be given another 6 million as a result of passing the hat round to all member states except Italy. Peace reigned. The regional fund has been one of the Community's successes, and in the subsequent referendum campaign we were able to cite generous allocations for Britain's hard-hit industries and regions.

[1] Cmnd. 5830, p. 7.

I was then asked to open up the subject of our renegotiations. I pointed out that there had been delays in making progress because of the many changes in European Governments,[1] and because of the second General Election. But the position of HM Government had been set out in the two elections in a single year: there had not been two elections in a year since 1910. In both elections the Government's position was reinforced by the vote of the people. I quoted my stage-setting speech of the previous Saturday.

The Government believed that entry on the right terms was good for Britain and good for Europe: that had been my position since 1966.[2] If the terms were wrong they would be bad for Britain, and for Europe.

The British Government was negotiating with a real intention to succeed and to achieve what had been set out in the manifesto. Within twelve months of the last General Election the British people would decide through the ballot box. If the terms were satisfactory and were approved by the people then Britain would play its full part in a cohesive Europe.

I then set out the seven main issues in the negotiations, in each case quoting the manifesto demand, together with our assessment following negotiations and developments within the Community during the previous few months:[3]

### 1. *The Common Agricultural Programme (CAP)*

A stock-taking was taking place. Britain did not challenge the main principles but arrangements had to be made for producers outside Europe (a reference to New Zealand and Australia for meat and dairy products, the Caribbean for cane sugar).

### 2. *The Budget*

We hoped that this could be cleared up later in the discussion, as substantially it was.

### 3. *Economic and Monetary Union*

We had already set out our position in the general discussions. Helmut Schmidt had asked whether the UK had a real interest in EMU or whether the British position represented an intellectual objection. James Callaghan replied that it was largely a dislike of intellectual dishonesty. It was wrong to pretend that EMU was going to become a reality in the foreseeable future. Helmut Schmidt dismissed the issue as unimportant. He and Giscard had known in 1972 that EMU was an illusion fostered by idealists who did not understand the problem. The policies of individual countries diverged: until you had a single central bank and a single currency EMU would remain an ideal. All delegations subscribed to the communiqué:

[1] M. Thorn, Prime Minister of Luxembourg, pointed out at one stage that he was the only one of the nine Heads of Government who had been involved in the negotiations for British entry, completed just three and a half years before.

[2] Compare speech to the Council of Europe, Strasbourg: *The Labour Government 1964–1970*, pp. 333–4.

[3] Our host would not allow officials or note-takers to be present, apart from the French who were servicing the Conference. Hence Foreign Ministers had to act as shorthand-writers. This summary is from James Callaghan's notes.

'The Heads of Government having noted that internal and international difficulties have prevented in 1973 and 1974 the accomplishment of expected progress on the road to EMU affirm that in this field their will has not weakened and that their objective has not changed since the Paris Conference.'

The truth is that heads of (European) Governments are kind to animals. The Emu if not an extinct species had long lost the ability to fly and was not likely to recover it.[1] But I was to be attacked in Parliament for accepting this form of words.

### 4. *Parliamentary Sovereignty*

This, I explained, was a matter of great importance to us. Serious problems had not in fact arisen during our membership, but in questions affecting employment such as regional policies, governments must be free to act quickly especially at a time of recession. We had no major industrial problems so far as the Market was concerned except steel: that very weekend the Commission had made pronouncements which had created difficulties. On fiscal matters the European countries were in fact following their own national policies, so this issue might not raise the difficulties we had feared.

### 5. *Capital Transfers*

A 'derogation' from existing rules had been agreed to, following the March Budget. It was clear that a number of EEC countries had made use of Article 104 of the Treaty in respect of policies necessary to protect the balance of payments. Articles 108 and 109 also provided for special measures to be involved for balance-of-payments reasons.

### 6. *Developing Countries*

Here much had happened in recent months, though there remained the problems of food from traditional suppliers, particularly sugar.

### 7. *Value Added Tax*

There was an increasing tendency for EEC Governments to develop and operate divergent systems, and this despite the fact that VAT yields were part of the *ressources propres* for calculating contributions to the common budget. Britain was opposed to taxing food. But I concluded that this was a matter for politicians, not 'technicians' – by which I had in mind Eurocrats and Euro-lawyers.

Helmut Schmidt then welcomed our approach. 'Renegotiation', he said, 'had proved a misleading term.' It did not mean Treaty-revision (it never had). This should be made clear to national Parliaments. What we sought could be fitted into the framework of the Treaty of Rome and the Treaty of Accession. Some issues were on their way to settlement and Heads of Government should express their satisfaction. The CAP issues would have to be settled by those 'fighting-cocks', the Ministers of Agriculture. He clearly

---

[1] *The Economist* had used a better analogy from birdland: if EMU is not a dodo it is at any rate an endangered species. At the Bremen Summit in July 1978, a new bird, the ECU, has emerged with the idea of taking wing within the proposed European Monetary System (EMS), due to come into operation on 1 January 1979. In the event, last-minute reservations by France deferred EMS. As these words are being written it is too early to evaluate its prospects.

4*

welcomed our role as allies in fighting the big spenders, not excluding his own Agriculture Minister, whom he himself was notably unable to control. All in all, our approach, and my speech the previous week-end, were taken in Germany as positive.

It was clear that the share of the Budget would be the most difficult problem. We wanted it to be related to GNP. This was anathema. No, the EEC worked on a basis of the yield of particular taxes, such as VAT and the levies: there was no escape. The formula was sacrosanct. The Belgians said that eight out of the nine rejected our approach.

It was a long and difficult argument. Fortunately the eight had submitted eight different papers. Helmut Schmidt again, while insisting on the purity of past decisions, began to work towards a system based on the rules but with the use of 'parameters' if they produced an 'inequitable situation'. James Callaghan, studying the several drafts, perceived glimmers of enlightenment in a number, which he proceeded to exploit.

The communiqué[1] as agreed was a masterpiece of helpful gobbledegook:

> The Prime Minister of the United Kingdom indicated the basis on which Her Majesty's Government approached the negotiations regarding Britain's continued membership of the Community, and set out the particular issues to which the Government attached the highest importance.
>
> The Heads of Government recall the statement made during the accession negotiations by the Community to the effect that 'If unacceptable situations were to arise, the very life of the Community would make it imperative for the institutions to find equitable solutions.'
>
> They confirm that the system of 'own resources' represents one of the fundamental elements of the economic integration of the Community.
>
> They invite the institutions of the Community (the Council and the Commission) to set up as soon as possible a correcting mechanism of a general application which, in the framework of the system of 'own resources' and in harmony with its normal functioning, based on objective criteria and taking into consideration in particular the suggestions made to this effect by the British Government, could prevent during the period of convergence of the economies of the Member States, the possible development of situations unacceptable for a Member State and incompatible with the smooth working of the Community.

We still had to face a further Heads-of-Government meeting in March, with the inevitable ritual of progress, breakdown, formulae, crisis, confrontation, eyeball-to-eyeball, wheeling and dealing, which are the stock in trade of our multilateral world, EEC or non-EEC. But we were in fact nearer home than we knew.

Giscard's innovation went beyond the formal meetings. After lunch at the Elysée on the first day we adjourned to an adjoining room for coffee. Helmut Schmidt, by arrangement with our host, raised the subject of the Middle East from a strongly anti-Israeli standpoint. Giscard supported him, following de Gaulle's position, from the moment at the outset of the Six-Day

---

[1] Presented to Parliament as Cmnd. 5830.

War in 1967 when he abandoned his unqualified support for Israel for a pro-Arab stance.[1] My intervention expressing the opposite view was, I was glad to see, supported by a majority of our colleagues.

Another subject, initiated by President Giscard, related to the recent revolution in Portugal when Spinola had led the armed forces and driven Caetano out of the country. For some months there were fears that Communist leaders, particularly in the Navy, would succeed in replacing one dictatorship by another. EEC Governments had been active diplomatically in trying to steer Portugal on a democratic course, and we decided to support substantial financial help if, but only if, Portugal accepted a democratic solution. This was made a firm offer at succeeding summits, and when Francoism yielded after forty years to an at first fragile democratic régime in Spain, we made a similar offer.

In my report to the House[2] on 16 December, I dealt with progress on each of the manifesto subjects. On the key budget issue I said:

> Substantial progress was made on the question of Britain's budgetary contribution to the Community and appropriate instructions given to the Community institutions, so that they can now get to work to set up as soon as possible what was called the 'correcting mechanism' referred to in the communiqué. We intend to have a firm proposal and decision on this by the early spring.

The statement was taken by pro- and anti-marketeers equally as suggesting that we were well on the way to agreement. Mr Heath warmly blessed it, indeed with generosity. While he clearly thought that the whole process of renegotiation was an unnecessary and far from edifying charade, nevertheless he took up each of the substantive points, welcoming the progress made. Subsequent questioning, especially from Labour back-benchers, seized on the reference to EMU. My replies sold EMU very short, and when pressed again, I said:

> . . . it was unattainable, or if attainable, utterly damaging to this country. There is not a hope in hell – I mean in the Common Market – as the other Heads of Government have made clear, of EMU taking place in the near future.[3]

Concern was also expressed about the meeting's commitment to direct elections of the European Assembly. I was able to draw attention to a specific reservation in the communiqué, headed *Statement by the United Kingdom Delegation*:

[1] See *The Labour Government 1964–1970*, pp. 403–5.

[2] *Hansard*, vol. 874, cols 1121–4.

[3] *Ibid.*, col. 1139. The quick geographical correction was due to the fact that hell is not a Parliamentary expression, outside strictly germane theological debates, e.g. on a new Prayer Book. My forecast can now be seen to have been falsified to the extent that EMS and ECU became a reality, though the December 1978 discussion was inconclusive and bewildering.

The Prime Minister of the United Kingdom explained that Her Majesty's Government did not wish to prevent the Governments of the other Eight Member States from making progress with the election of the European Assembly by universal suffrage. Her Majesty's Government could not themselves take up a position on the proposal before the process of renegotiation had been completed and the results of renegotiation submitted to the British people.

Though the renegotiations were far from complete, and few final decisions had been taken, anti-marketeers within the Cabinet sensed that the ultimate outcome would be an agreement enabling James Callaghan and myself to recommend first, the Cabinet, and subsequently Parliament and the nation to accept the terms, with the result – subject to the outcome of the referendum – that Britain be a full EEC member without reservations. I knew the strain this would place on some half-dozen or more members of the Cabinet whose opposition was not to the terms of entry but to membership of the EEC on any terms. I did not want to see, nor did I really expect, any resignations, but I knew that the anti-marketeers would be under heavy strain. Michael Foot asked to see me: I knew what it would be about. He was concerned that a majority of the Cabinet would support continued EEC membership, and that under the traditional rules of collective Cabinet responsibility the minority would be required so to vote when we reported to the House, and indeed at least not to dissociate from the Cabinet decision during the referendum campaign. I had given a great deal of thought to this, and had consulted the Foreign Secretary and Edward Short, who as Leader of the House would be charged with preparing the referendum legislation and conducting it through the House. They accepted my view that the minority should not be coerced either into resignation or into commending a course repugnant to them, but that there should be an 'agreement to differ', which would be announced to the House, and would, of course, extend equally to the very considerable number of junior ministers.

This was by no means easy. There was a precedent, the imposition of import duties by the 'National' Government in 1932, when one of the two Liberal wings (the Samuelites as opposed to the Simonites) was granted the right to dissociate. The parallel, however, was by no means exact, and it was further marred by the fact that the Samuelites (or 'wee frees') shortly afterwards resigned from the Government en bloc as did Philip Snowden, the Cobdenite former Labour Chancellor.[1] The main difference lay in the fact that the Government in 1975 was a single-party administration, with an overall majority: the decision to hold a referendum had been put to the electorate in two successive general elections. The 'agreement to differ' in 1932 was in the context of a coalition Government, formed during the 1931 crisis. In the 1931 election there had been no proposal by the Government to

[1] An account of the 1932 partial precedent is set out in *The Governance of Britain*, Appendix III, pp. 194–7.

introduce tariffs: Ramsay MacDonald had simply asked for a 'doctor's mandate'.[1]

On 23 January I made a statement in Parliament on the referendum and the 'agreement to differ' in the period ahead.[2] This was the first time that our decision to hold a referendum was formally announced. During the two elections, and in all statements thereafter, we had stuck to the phrase that the people would make the ultimate decision 'through the ballot-box', leaving it open, technically at least, to call a general election on the issue, or to hold a referendum. The former would in fact have caused major difficulties in both parties, though more in the Labour ranks than in the Conservative. Few doubted that we were planning a referendum, the more so as Roy Jenkins had resigned from the Shadow Cabinet through our decision to vote for this course while the Conservative European legislation was going through Parliament.

I began the statement by saying that the ballot-box pledge would be met by a referendum. After fifteen years of negotiation and discussion, Parliament and the country would want to see the issue decided once for all. The Government had committed itself in the second 1974 Elections to submitting the question for decision within one year, i.e. by 10 October 1975. Pointing out that, as we were learning, a great deal of preparation would be needed – the drafting of the legislation and its passage through Parliament, and the complicated electoral arrangements – I proposed June for the vote. The renegotiations were not yet complete, but at their close the Government would make their own recommendation to Parliament and the electorate, whether for continued Community membership on the basis of the re-negotiated terms, or for withdrawal. This would be followed by a debate in the House. I then came to the position of ministers:

> The circumstances of this referendum are unique, and the issue to be decided is one on which strong views have long been held which cross party lines. The Cabinet has, therefore, decided that, if when the time comes there are members of the Government, including members of the Cabinet, who do not feel able to accept and support the Government's recommendation, whatever it may be, they will, once the recommendation has been announced, be free to support and speak in favour of a different conclusion in the referendum campaign. (Hon. Members: 'Oh!')

On the arrangements for the conduct of the referendum, as I had told the House earlier, the rules for the test of public opinion must be made by Parliament. Accordingly the Government would publish a White Paper on the proposed rules and arrangements, setting out possible alternative courses,

---

[1] During the formation of the 1931 Government, King George V had advised Mac-Donald to secure guarantees that the Cabinet would not be disrupted by either Samuel or Snowden over the issue of protection. MacDonald replied that he would prefer to 'let sleeping dogs lie'.

[2] *Hansard*, vol. **884**, cols 1745–50.

and the Government's proposals on such matters as the information policy of the Government during the campaign, broadcasting arrangements, expenditure by the campaigning organizations, the form in which the question was to be put (a highly important and indeed controversial matter), arrangements for conducting the poll, the counting of the votes and the announcement of the result. Debates would be held on the outcome of the negotiations and on referendum procedure, in time for the Government to hear the views of Parliament before finalizing legislation.

Parts of my statement had a noisy reception, but Mr Heath, who was clearly worried about some of the implications of this innovation, was right on the ball in his questions – 'a unique operation and a major question of our time, the Government are not going to maintain collective responsibility'. On collective responsibility, he asked, how would the Government make their recommendation on voting: would the Government set out the number of Cabinet dissentients, their names indeed? Or would I make 'a recommendation which will include freedom for them to decide to make no recommendation'?

Would I confirm that the referendum, if it took place, would be advisory and consultative and that it 'cannot be binding on Members of the House of Commons'?

Would the details of the referendum be set out in a Green Paper as a consultative document, so that MPs could express their views and influence the Government on methods and procedure?

Would the Government ensure an adjournment of the House to allow Members 'to express their views to constituents and to campaign up and down the country'?

He ended by repeating that a major constitutional issue was at stake – which his Party had always maintained was undesirable. Parliament must decide whether this constitutional innovation should take place.

I agreed with him that it was a major constitutional innovation, a very special situation not to be taken as a precedent. The Government would make their recommendation for a 'Yes' or 'No' vote in the light of the renegotiation, first, of course, making a recommendation to the House itself, who would debate it and vote on it before the nation voted.

On the question whether the vote of the people would be binding, I expressed the view that Members would not vote against a clear statement of the nation's feeling through a referendum. On the question whether the paper would be White (a clear statement of Government views) or Green (a consultative document) I said it would be 'White with Green edges', in that I was prepared to discuss with the Leader of the Opposition the basis on which we would advise the House.

On time for campaigning, I suggested that a lengthened Whitsun recess might meet what he had in mind. He came back on the constitutional issue, and I commented that no one could press Hon. Members on how they should vote, though it is not unknown – I had the Whips on both sides in mind – and therefore the referendum could not be binding or involve compulsion, but I believed not many Members would pit their judgment against a decision by the country. On another issue he raised, I said I would consider his point that the House should be told how many had dissociated and who they were. It did not seem a problem anyway: they would be identified very quickly – as indeed happened.

But before the Government could make a recommendation to Parliament and the country, we had to face one further negotiating hurdle, the meeting of the European Council in Dublin on 10–11 March.

The preparations made by the Irish Government were admirable. Consultations between Governments had rejected the idea of a continuing secretariat for Council meetings, as the French had wanted. Each host country would make all the necessary arrangements.

The meetings took place in Dublin Castle. Much was made of the fact that this was the first time a British Prime Minister had entered the Castle since Asquith in 1914. Our conference room was the home of the Order of St Patrick, and the banners of the last Knights still hung round the walls.

The Irish Prime Minister, Liam Cosgrave, was in complete charge of the proceedings, with his very able Foreign Minister, Garret FitzGerald, alongside him. They devoted themselves exclusively to the conduct of the conference, to the point where they could almost have been criticized for not stating the Irish case on each of the issues before us.

Unlike the procedure followed at the Paris Meeting, the Taoiseach proposed that the first item should be the British renegotiations. A great deal of work had to be done, through bilateral meetings, by Foreign Ministers meeting separately, by officials, and not least by the President of the Commission, who played a leading part in the detailed negotiations, and indeed produced at critical times a series of compromise proposals to get over a problem of substance or a drafting difficulty.

I was therefore asked to lead off with a statement on the progress made, and the outstanding problems we had to solve. My statement raised three issues, the Budget, New Zealand, and a specific problem which had risen on the steel industry. I made clear that apart from these Britain would not raise any other new issues before the referendum. This last remark was widely welcomed.

On the Budget I expressed pleasure at the progress made by the Commission which was moving towards a GDP-related solution.

On New Zealand I stressed our need for reasonably-priced dairy products and lamb. As I later pointed out, our EEC partners' objection to Britain's imports of lamb from New Zealand was not that they wanted to keep their own lamb prices up – they produced very little. They wanted to protect their high-priced beef.

On steel we had the problem that while the Government had to control prices and capacity in our publicly-owned steel industry, the private steel-makers under EEC rules were free of all controls. So when the British Steel Board, in the interests of efficiency, were closing down plants, perhaps in areas of high unemployment, private industry could open up in competition there or elsewhere. There was, in fact, a proposal for a new private steel works which was regarded as highly provocative by the Board and the steel unions. The text of my opening statement is set out in Appendix IV.

The negotiations on these items continued until very late on Tuesday 11 March, particularly on the Budget. But thanks mainly to President Ortoli's indefatigable production of increasingly helpful drafts, agreement was finally reached on terms acceptable to us. Interpreting it in United Kingdom terms, a whole set of criteria was laid down for the assessment of a refund if in any year our Budget contributions were to go significantly beyond what would be fair in relation to our share of the total Community GNP. The criteria covered GNP per head, the real rate of national growth, an assessment under the 'own resources' rule excessive in relation to the share of Community GNP, and a general rule relating to 'net potential foreign exchange liability', that is an excess of contributions over direct receipts, as a result of the operations of the Community's budget mechanism.[1]

On steel, as we had some reason to hope, there has proved in practice to have been no problem; we knew as well as our partners that other countries were taking this problem in their stride without challenge.

On New Zealand a reasonably satisfactory outcome was reached including improved arrangements for continued access for her dairy products after 1977. But in practice what we thought we had gained has since proved illusory. The market has been squeezed, and in fact New Zealand herself soon became more interested in moving up towards EEC prices than in continuing to supply large quantities to Britain at the favourable prices to which we were accustomed.

At the Dublin meeting, as three months earlier in Paris, the Heads of Government and Foreign Ministers dined together and then adjourned for discussions on wider world affairs, until well after midnight. (As midnight struck, James Callaghan, who had been doing some discreet canvassing, struck up 'Happy Birthday to You' for my fifty-ninth birthday. He secured one hundred per cent participation, no one singing with more élan than France's President. At this point our hosts wheeled in a huge iced cake. After we had all sampled it, the remainder went to a Dublin hospital.)

After this diversion we returned to serious discussion. The main theme was the forthcoming Helsinki Conference on Security and Co-operation in Europe, planned for the late summer and due to be attended by all European states, regardless of political alignment, and by the two North American Governments with a stake in Europe's affairs. A preparatory conference at ambassadorial level was still planning the arrangements and procedures,

[1] A detailed description is set out in Cmnd. 6003, paras. 39–45.

and there were still one or two questions outstanding, notably the inclusion of human rights in the agenda, where the USSR was still proving difficult. Further discussion took up the Paris colloquy on Portugal.

On 12 March I reported to Parliament on the Dublin discussions,[1] and – an unusual practice – arranged for Hansard to print the relevant statements agreed by the conference.

Mrs Margaret Thatcher had by this time been elected Leader of the Conservative Party. She asked me if I would use my personal authority 'to recommend we stay in Europe'. I replied that the Government's decision would be made before Easter. James Callaghan and I had not at that time reported to Cabinet, which we did the following day. (On a personal note, that was the only time in nearly eight years that I was ever called out of Cabinet by my wife: it was to inform me that our daughter-in-law had had twin daughters.) Cabinet further met on Monday 17 March to finalize the statement for the House.

The recommendations of the Foreign Secretary and myself were accepted by a substantial proportion of the Cabinet. Since it would be necessary to announce the names of those who would be free to dissociate themselves in the referendum campaign, I counted heads, declared a majority in favour and asked each of the others if he (or she) would wish to dissociate publicly. Seven did – Michael Foot, Barbara Castle, Eric Varley, Willie Ross, Tony Benn, Peter Shore and John Silkin. Sixteen Cabinet ministers were in favour. This was not the result of having packed the Cabinet with a pro-Market majority a year earlier. A quick calculation I made after the decision – which I mentioned to Cabinet – was that on all the facts known to me in 1974, twelve would have been assumed to be anti-Market, nine in favour, with James Callaghan and myself agnostics, depending on the terms we got in the renegotiations. Fred Peart, John Morris, Merlyn Rees, Lord Shepherd and Reg Prentice had clearly changed their view: Reg Prentice had first been elected to the Shadow Cabinet in 1971, and actually topped the poll, on anti-Market votes, many of them from the Tribune Group on that account. But with his work on Overseas Development he had clearly been impressed by Judith Hart's success at the Lomé Conference in playing a leading part in negotiating the most generous EEC assistance to forty-six Third World countries, including twenty-two from the Commonwealth.

The names of those dissociating were made public at once. Similar freedom was given to junior ministers, whom I had met on 17 March at Downing Street to hear their views, and to explain how the 'agreement to differ' was intended to work.

But the following week I made a serious error of tactics. I had arranged to visit Northern Ireland on 25 March, the day on which the Cabinet, meeting under Ted Short's chairmanship, had before them some of the detailed rules about dissociation. It was my fault that I never assumed for a moment that

[1] *Hansard*, vol. 888, cols 509–22.

my colleagues would agree that ministers, junior as well as senior, would be free to vote against the Government's recommendation in the forthcoming debate in Parliament. Abstention would have seemed right, and to me obvious. But the decision was taken, leading to a great deal of embarrassment in the debate on 7 to 9 April. In this connection there was some press criticism that instead of steering the Cabinet in the right direction I had gone to the Savoy Theatre for the D'Oyly Carte centenary celebrations of *Trial by Jury*. I certainly did go there later, but by the time I reached No. 10 from Belfast, the decisions had been taken, and the Cabinet, dealing with other business, was about to break up. The Cabinet had, however, placed a ban on ministers speaking in the debate, other than those appointed to speak. When the debate took place Eric Heffer, Minister of State for Industry, insisted on speaking despite the ruling, and a number of warnings about the consequences. He was clearly determined to go, and on receiving my request for his resignation immediately after the debate, he complied at once. He was the only one to break ranks in this way, but seven Cabinet ministers, and thirty-one ministerial other ranks, exactly half the juniors, voted against the Government motion.

The process of reporting the Cabinet's decision to Parliament began with a very lengthy statement on Tuesday 18 March, and culminated in a three-day debate on 7 to 9 April.

The 18 March statement[1] – beginning with an apology for its length – set out, item by item, all the issues covered in the negotiations, directly quoting the election manifesto and reporting in detail on each. This was followed by a much fuller White Paper, *Membership of the European Community: Report on Renegotiation*, extending to over forty closely-printed pages. Beginning with a brief history of EEC negotiations from May 1967 onwards, the document set out item by item 'Renegotiation Objectives', as set out in the manifesto, followed by a long section headed 'Outcome', itself supplemented by 'Details'. For example, the 'outcome' on 'Food and Agriculture' covered seven paragraphs, and the 'details' a further nineteen – six and a half pages in all. Other sections were about the same length.

The three-day debate on the outcome of the negotiations began on 7 April. It was on the motion:

> That this House approves the recommendations of Her Majesty's Government to continue Britain's Membership of the Community as set out in the White Paper on the Membership of the European Community (Command No. 5999).

On the first day, I opened, and Roy Hattersley wound up for the Government. The following day we did not put in front-benchers, but on the third day, Fred Peart opened and James Callaghan wound up. The principal

---

[1] *Hansard*, vol. 888, cols 1456–67, followed by a further 16 columns of supplementary questions and answers. The statement was published as Cmnd. 5999.

Opposition speakers were Mr Whitelaw, Mrs Thatcher, Mr Peter Kirk and Mr Maudling. Mr Heath spoke from below the gangway on the third day. The vote was 396 for the motion and 170 against. The majority of those against were Labour members, and indeed, taking Labour votes only, 137 voted for and 145 against the motion. Thirty-three did not vote.

The following day Edward Short moved the Second Reading of the Referendum Bill, the drafting of which he had been masterminding since the turn of the year. It was a great achievement: he and his colleagues in the Privy Council office were engaged on a totally unprecedented operation. He was in charge of all the preparation and machinery for the vote itself, and had to consult not only the principal parties, but the spokesmen authorized by the pro-Market and anti-Market organizations to negotiate with him.

Some very difficult decisions had to be taken. Perhaps the hardest related to the count. Should it be a single national count, undifferentiated by areas? If so, it would always be possible to claim without the possibility of refutation that, say, Scotland, or Wales, or Northern Ireland had voted against. Should it be by constituencies? If it were, MPs who had voted one way in the House would be mercilessly attacked if their constituency voted the opposite way. In the event, it was decided that the results should be declared county by county.

In this unprecedented situation the Lord President and Home Secretary, and their advisers, based their planning as far as possible on a political general election. But this meant that the two sides must so order themselves as to create two polling and propaganda organizations. This did not prove difficult. Both sides were to have a free house-to-house distribution of the literature of each side, accompanied by strictly impartial polling instructions. They were told that their equivalent of a candidate's election address, in effect a manifesto, uniform for the whole country, must not exceed 2,000 words. Government grants of £125,000 were available to each side, though in the final financial tally it proved that the pro-marketeers (Britain in Europe) had spent £1,365,583 against £133,629[1] by their opponents.

In addition the Government bore the cost of distributing the statements of both sides to every voter.

The national and provincial press were in favour of a 'Yes' vote almost without exception. Ministers were of course free to campaign for the side of their choice, subject to two rules I laid down. The first was: no personal attacks. At one stage Tony Benn and Roy Jenkins got into a public brawl, and were promptly instructed to stick to issues: no personalities. Second, ministers were told that the 'agreement to differ' ended on 6 June, the day following the poll. From 6 June full collective responsibility would apply on EEC as on all other issues. This was fully observed, and on the day when the

---

[1] Each figure includes the Government subvention, which accounted for 94 per cent of the 'antis' ' expenditure, against 8 per cent of the 'pros' '. In addition, 'Britain in Europe' received £351,006 from the European Movement.

results were declared I was happy to see Tony Benn on TV handsomely accepting the verdict.

James Callaghan and I addressed meetings nearly every evening in the last fortnight, and came together on the eve of the poll at Cardiff. Meetings were well attended, and on the whole quiet and ready to listen, though I had some rough heckling in Glasgow, and barely succeeded in being heard at all in a London meeting packed by shouting demonstrators from the mindless extreme left, mainly Communists.

The broadcasting authorities ran their part of the campaign on general election lines, though with one difference – the Prime Minister and Foreign Secretary, who had been in charge of the negotiations throughout, were not invited to appear. We were somewhat puzzled, but when we met with the BBC and the Chairman of the Independent Broadcasting Authority, we learnt the reason – and it was unassailable. The contest was not between parties but between two identifiable organizations. Balance in the general election sense meant equality of treatment for them, and would be upset if such extraneous characters as James Callaghan and myself were on the screens. The broadcasting authorities were absolutely right.

In the event each of us was invited, but my own BBC interview, with Robin Day, was concentrated almost entirely on the economic situation. That with Julian Haviland of ITV was much more on the referendum issues.

The National Executive Committee of the Labour Party decided to support the 'No' lobby. There was one acrimonious meeting where there was talk of an outright campaign against the Government. For only the second time since 1963 I laid my leadership of the Party on the line, and a formula was produced with the help of the General Secretary. Looking back on that strange period a most interesting constitutional situation would have arisen had I resigned the leadership and yet been elected by the Parliamentary Party. The NEC decided in the event to support the 'No' cause on the basis of all aid short of war. Concretely they resolved to call a special one-day conference in London.

This took place at the Sobell Sports Centre in Islington on Saturday 26 April. The NEC had decided that I should be invited to speak at the beginning, after which the real conference would begin. My speech was in a sober key, concerned principally to show that from Hugh Gaitskell's speech at Conference in 1962 our line had been that great good could come from membership; equally if we were faced with over-onerous terms Britain's interests would be harmed. I gave the simple arguments underlying the Cabinet's decision and recommendations to the House and the country. I was heard politely, with such cheers as there were coming from pro-marketeers. It was not my happiest Conference speech, but it was a chore and it was good to get it over. I left them in no doubt that however they voted – and how they would was never in question – the country would decide.

This message was underlined by the curtain back-drop to the stage, which was behind the speakers' rostrum and so placed that it was on television throughout the proceedings. Its message was 'Conference Advises – the People Decide'. The vote at the end of the afternoon – a card vote – recorded 3,724,000 against the Market, 1,986,000 for, practically 2 to 1. The national verdict less than six weeks later was more than 2 to 1 the other way.

The Conference was, in fact, a non-event. It had had a great build-up in the press, though it was forgotten by the following week. Political occasions are very much like Grand Nationals and Cup Finals. There is feverish speculation and great prophesying in the days before. Once the outcome is known discussion ceases, and all that is remembered is the name of the winner, give or take a few who still cry 'foul'. So it seemed to us, as James Callaghan and I winged our way to the thirty-four-nation Commonwealth Conference at Kingston, Jamaica. The events there are recorded below,[1] but one surprise development there related specifically to the EEC and the referendum. While the final communiqué was being drafted, our Chairman, Prime Minister Michael Manley of the host country, asked me to see him. He said, 'You don't know anything about this, and I'm not consulting you. I'm just telling you that there have been consultations going on between all delegations except the British. We have decided to add a paragraph to the text declaring that the members of the committee regard continued membership of the European Community as in the best interests of the Commonwealth.' I was in no doubt, and he confirmed, that this was in part due to the successful negotiations of the Lomé Convention, with its massive EEC help for forty-six developing countries.

A statement on these lines was made by Mr Manley at the end of the Conference. In addition, the communiqué paid tribute to the Lomé achievement:

> Heads of Government welcomed the conclusion of the Lomé Convention drawn up by the European Economic Community and 46 countries of Africa, the Caribbean and the Pacific. They welcomed the increased cooperation within the Convention between Commonwealth and non-Commonwealth countries in these areas. They expressed the hope that the principles underlying the Lomé Convention could usefully contribute to the further development of relations between the EEC and other industrialised countries, on the one hand, and developing countries, including the Asian and other Commonwealth countries, on the other.[2]

It was to be much quoted in the last weeks before the referendum, and provided an effective reply to those who argued that EEC membership was harmful to the interests of the Commonwealth and a betrayal of developing countries everywhere. Clearly the Commonwealth did not think so.

On Thursday 5 June the country voted. It was a high poll, shown the next day to be 64.5 per cent of the electorate, only 8.3 per cent lower than in the

[1] See Chapter 8.
[2] Cmnd. 6066, para. 38.

October 1974 General Election. Of an electorate of 40,086,677, 25,848,654 voted. The figures, announced from the Albert Hall by Sir Philip Allen (now Lord Allen of Abbeydale), the National Returning Officer, were

|  |  |  |
|---|---|---|
| FOR membership | 17,378,581 | (67.2%) |
| AGAINST | 8,470,073 | (32.8%) |
| Majority | 8,908,508 | |
| (Spoilt papers | 54,540) | |

The figures for individual countries were:

|  | FOR | AGAINST |
|---|---|---|
| England | 14,918,009 | 6,812,052 |
| Wales | 869,135 | 472,071 |
| Scotland | 1,332,186 | 948,039 |
| North Ireland | 259,251 | 237,911 |

The turn-out for England was 64.6 per cent; for Wales 66.7 per cent; for Scotland, 61.7 per cent; and for Northern Ireland, 47.4 per cent. The low figure for Ulster probably reflected the fact that the Republic of Ireland was a member country and might also gain economic advantages in her trade with Britain at Northern Ireland's expense.

What was remarkable, as the results were declared county by county, was the almost uniform pattern shown everywhere. Every county recorded a majority for membership, with the exception of the Western Isles and Orkney and Shetland. (The last two, of course, are much closer geographically to Norway than to the Scottish mainland, and Norway's referendum had led to her failure to enter the EEC.)

I had heard the results at Chequers and returned to Downing Street in the early evening. To quote *The Times*:

At 6.30 p.m. Mr Wilson stood on the steps of 10 Downing Street to make his historic announcement. He said:

'The verdict has been given by a vote with a bigger majority than has been received by any Government in any general election. Nobody in Britain or the wider world should have any doubt about its meaning. It was a free vote, without constraint, following a free democratic campaign conducted constructively and without rancour. It means that fourteen years of national argument are over. It means that all those who have had reservations about Britain's commitment should now join wholeheartedly with our partners in Europe, and our friends everywhere to meet the challenge confronting the whole nation.'

In its leading article *The Times* commented: 'Mr Wilson found in the referendum the answer, perhaps the only answer, to the problems of getting

Labour consent to Britain staying in Europe. He has shown great political skill and insight.'[1]

True or not, it was a matter of some satisfaction that an issue which threatened several times over thirteen years to tear the Labour movement apart had been resolved fairly and finally, despite the anti-EEC vote at the Special Conference and the spread of Labour MPs' votes in the Commons vote, and that from 6 June, as I had asked months before, all that had divided us in that great controversy was put behind us.

---

[1] Philip Goodhart, Conservative MP for Beckenham, in his history of the referendum, *Full-Hearted Consent*, London, 1976, p. 190, quotes an MP, 'who was not an enthusiastic admirer of Harold Wilson's style': 'The whole issue was ideally suited to his approach. He won by delaying a decision as long as possible. Ted Heath on Europe was like one of these magnificent All Black forwards. Give him the ball and he would smash his way over the line by sheer strength of purpose. But Harold Wilson was a Welsh fly-half. He would start and stop and jink and dummy and swerve and, when a gap opened up, he would trot across that line without anyone laying a hand on him.'

Goodhart's own comment is, 'Two unanswerable questions remain. If Tony Benn had not persuaded the Labour Party's National Executive Committee and then the Shadow Cabinet to support Neil Marten's Referendum Amendment to the European Communities Bill on 18 April 1972, would a referendum have been held? The answer is almost certainly yes. With his customary astuteness Harold Wilson would have certainly seen that a decision to press for a referendum would be the only way of neutralizing impossibly tight shackles on his renegotiating position. He needed room for manoeuvre – a referendum was the only device that would give it to him.'

He also quotes the *Daily Telegraph*: 'The result of the referendum is quite frankly a triumph for Wilson. It goes without saying that the campaign will have a lasting effect on British politics. Quite what it will be, well, it is almost certainly too early to discern. Something that is already clear, however, is that British electors have been vouchsafed a glimpse of politicians acting in a way which many of those electors wish they would more often adopt towards the serious questions facing the country. That is bound to have its effect in the future, in possibly subtle ways.'

# Chapter 6

## ECONOMICS AND INFLATION

THE staggering increase in oil prices which was the prompt Arab response to the Yom Kippur War had forced inflation on the world; on the advanced industrial world, on the Third World, and on the starving Fourth World. Only those developing countries with oil resources such as Nigeria, or with raw materials such as tin, phosphates and bauxite sharing in the commodity boom, grew richer: others grew immeasurably poorer. Indeed, as African and Asian countries urged at the Jamaica Commonwealth Conference, their poverty was aggravated by surcharges on the use of oil for tractors and other agricultural machinery, fertilizers and other essential imports, while the world commodity boom passed them by. And few statesmen with perception could brush aside the certainty that in the wake of inflation lay unemployment. There were warnings such as those summarized in Harold Lever's analysis[1] that a massive surplus on the part of the oil-producing countries should not be regarded as a signal for deflation in the importing countries. But wherever the representatives of developed countries met, in the EEC, in the IMF, at the conferences of the World Bank – less so in the OECD – or the monthly meetings of the US–European Central Bankers at Basle, the emphasis was on deflation. When the strong, such as the United States – as they then were – and West Germany, showed no inclination to pursue policies of expansion, the weak were in no position to argue. Deflation ruled. The disciples of Keynes and Galbraith sang small, those of Friedman, and especially the master himself, were canonized. Even two and three years later the surplus countries, such as Japan and Germany, with a better record on anti-inflationary policies than their partners, were still resisting the call to give a lead to economic expansion, because they feared that such obvious boldness would lead to internal inflation. For the rest, including the weaker EEC countries, it was clear that inflation itself, not to mention counter-inflationary measures, appropriate or inappropriate, would lead speedily to widespread unemployment.

What was clear to Her Majesty's Government was that there was no escape route for Britain on a go-it-alone basis. Our balance-of-payments position was too vulnerable. The prospective dividends of North Sea oil were still too far away: even when the oil torrent began, Britain's balance of payments failed to reflect the hopes all parties had cherished of at least a brief respite.

[1] See pp. 23-24 above.

Internally the Government had to work with a trade union movement which had endured three years of statutory pay restraint. 'The fourth year is always the most difficult.'[1] What the Government was going to have to ask very soon was not a fourth year, but the acceptance of a fresh three-year period of restraint, with real living standards already falling, and the perennial problems of differentials and hard cases already acute. The Labour Government had good relations with the unions. The 'Social Contract' was an admitted fact. The problem, not so much for government as for their partners in the Contract, was that of selling eminently reasonable pay restraint proposals to millions of workers and their wives, who could see their standard of living being reduced month by month – even before the pinch of unemployment began to be felt.

In common with most of my colleagues in the economic departments, the Treasury, Industry, Employment, I was regularly meeting industrial leaders, and addressing trade union conferences. During the Short Parliament up to September 1974 I addressed the annual conferences of six major trade unions, the TUC at their Annual Congress, and regional and local bodies, in addition to receiving several deputations from national unions. On 27–28 February 1975 I spent, together with half-a-dozen senior ministers, two days in Scotland with the Scottish Trades Union Congress leaders in general discussions, and specialized group meetings on the problems of inflation and unemployment, the steel programme, coal, and the anxieties of vulnerable local areas in the Scottish economy.

In all these meetings, whether annual trade union delegate conferences, or ad hoc meetings, my colleagues and I stressed at first the fact that existing living standards would be impossible to maintain, and, as time went on, what had become the inevitable truth, that they must fall. The only offset we could hold out was the marked improvement in the provision of the social service 'family bonus'.[2] Above all, we emphasized that every single point in the inflation index would inexorably mean a worsening in unemployment.

In the first half of 1974 the retail price index[3] (RPI) rose by 10.6 per cent, representing an annual rate of well over 20 per cent. But from June to September it rose by only 2.9 points (January 1974 = 100), an annual rate of just over 10 per cent. In the two months from July to September it rose by 1.5 points, or about 1.4 per cent. Multiplying this by six is presumably how Denis Healey got his 8.4 per cent, his battle-cry throughout the autumn General Election. This claim was scorned by the Conservatives and even to the time of writing, three and a half years later, there can be seen on a railway bridge near Chequers, 'Wilson Out – $8\frac{1}{2}\%$'.

In his March Budget and a further financial statement in July, Denis

---

[1] These words were written several months before the events of January 1979.

[2] See pp. 25-27.

[3] The RPI 'for all items except [those] items of food whose prices show significant variations'.

Healey reduced VAT from 10 per cent to 8 per cent, and increased food subsidies, rent subsidies and rate subsidies to an extent which was equivalent to cutting the retail price index by $1\frac{1}{2}$ per cent, moving to $2\frac{1}{2}$ per cent in a full year. The Regional Employment Premium, subsidising jobs in hard-hit areas, was increased from £1.50 per man per week to £3. In addition, the Chancellor was able to claim that the 'social wage' had increased, in the fiscal year 1974–1975, by 34 per cent in cash terms, 12 per cent in real terms. The TUC's pay restraint policy was based on appeals that wage settlements should be 'confined to compensation for the rise in the cost of living since the last settlement', itself of course an inflationary process. But as Denis Healey noted in his Budget speech on 15 April 1975,

> The general rate of pay increases has been well above the increase in the cost of living and much further still above the level in countries which compete with us ... As a result, by February the retail price index stood 19.9 per cent over a year earlier, and the wage rate index was 28.9 per cent ... pay has been running about 8 per cent or 9 per cent ahead of prices. I do not believe that anyone would claim that the TUC guidelines were intended to permit this result.[1]

The wage index for all industries and services (seasonally corrected), rose by 5.9 per cent from March to June 1974; 7.3 per cent from June to September; 9.6 per cent from September to December; 2.1 per cent from December 1974 to March 1975; and 3.9 per cent from March to June 1975.

From March 1974 to March 1975 the wage index had risen by 32.9 per cent, against a rise in the RPI of 21.4 per cent.

There were some prospects, the Chancellor pointed out, that external factors forcing up prices were moderating. Oil prices had ceased to rise, and the prices of most imported foodstuffs – sugar and beef apart – were fairly stable. Sir Arthur Cockfield, Chairman of the Price Commission from 1973 to 1977, had produced an optimistic report the previous autumn indicating an easing of inflationary pressures – provided that price increases were not generated at home.

The part of the Budget speech dealing with pay settlements ended with a grim warning:

> Bitter experience under many post-war Governments has, I think, taught most of us on both sides of the House that a statutory policy for incomes is unlikely to produce better results. Unless, however, the voluntary policy achieves stricter adherence to guidelines laid down by the trade unions of their own free will, the consequence can only be rising unemployment, cuts in public expenditure, lower living standards for the country as a whole, and growing tension throughout society.[2]

More than one of his hearers interpreted this as, first, an appeal for

[1] *Hansard,* vol. 890, cols 281–2.
[2] *Ibid.,* col. 282.

voluntary pay control, with wages keeping pace – but no more – with cost of living increases, but, second, as a warning that if the choice became as stark as he forecast, the Government might have to act.

The RPI (net of seasonal items) began to rise after the brief 8.4 per cent period. From September to December it rose 5.9 points or 5.3 per cent, back to the annual rate in the twenties. From December to March it rose 7.4 points, or 6.3 per cent, more than 25 per cent at annual rate. March to June showed an increase of 12.3 points, or nearly 10 per cent – partly aggravated by the Chancellor's increases in VAT and other indirect taxes designed to reduce the danger of overload on the economy.

Before those last figures were known action in fact had been taken. Meanwhile, sterling had come increasingly under pressure. Gloom and despondency took charge, not least in the United States, whose consistent failure to measure up to their own deep-seated economic and social problems traditionally leads to sanctimonious utterances about their partners. (To be fair to them, the Founding Fathers inflicted upon them an unworkable constitution with which they do the best they can.) Calling in at Washington for a brief meeting with President Ford in May, after the Jamaica Commonwealth Conference, I found HM Embassy in a state of deep depression, following a doom-laden pronouncement on Britain's future by the journalist, Mr Eric Sevareid, who had recently honoured Britain with a visit.[1] At a press conference I found Washington's opinion-formers nearly as prepared to write us off as they had been in 1940, 1941, 1942, 1943, and selective years in the 1950s and 1960s.

I knew, and those of my colleagues most directly concerned knew, that the Government would have to act. Equally we knew that action at half-cock would worsen the situation. We had to play for time, not, as some have suggested, because the EEC referendum lay immediately ahead, but because the key to the situation was the National Union of Mineworkers' annual conference in July.[2] We did not intend to make either of the mistakes that the Conservatives had made in 1972 and 1973: first, the belief that an incomes policy will hold without the miners, or, second, that you can get the agreement of the coal-mining community in discussions with one or two of their national leaders at Chequers or Downing Street. The mineworkers were dedicated democrats long before advanced Conservative leaders such as Baldwin and Churchill steered the Conservative Party into the twentieth

---

[1] In the summer of 1978 Mr Sevareid, on a visit to London, generously confessed that he had been wrong in his diagnosis and warning.

[2] Even before the mineworkers' pay crunch, a dangerous situation developed on the railwaymen's pay claim. On Saturday 14 July, immediately after the Trooping the Colour ceremony, I met the NUR Executive in the Cabinet room. We were prepared to face a national railway strike if need be, rather than prejudice the pay issue, and throughout that week-end it appeared inevitable. By the Sunday evening we laid down a figure which we said must not be exceeded, and left the railwaymen to think this over, and then get into talks with the Minister and the Railway Board. A settlement only minimally above our figure was agreed early the following week.

century.[1] D-day in the battle against inflation was 7 July, nearly two months ahead. The doubt was whether irrevocable decisions, good for confidence, bad for results, would be forced on us by external pressures in the period of waiting. It was a lot to hope for.

Meanwhile not merely prices but the rates at which prices were rising were increasing. A powerful section in the mineworkers' union was pressing for a wage increase to £100 per week, 63.9 per cent over the level then ruling, for face workers, with £85 for other underground workers, and £80 for surface workers on the screens and elsewhere. A month before, on 7 June, I had a scheduled run over the course. I had been invited to address the Nottinghamshire miners at Mansfield. This gave me the opportunity to talk to Len Clarke, their leader, and one of the statesmen of the industry ever since the war. I knew the Nottinghamshire miners well. More than thirty years before I had been involved in negotiations with George Spencer, legendary leader of the breakaway union after the 1926 stoppage, who had come back in an uneasy alliance with those he had deserted, and I had seen the first experiments in modern British mechanization at the coal-face, and had to arbitrate on Notts. claims under the first productivity bonus scheme, as well as on basic rates.

But more important than memories and friends, the Government had the advantage of the plan for the expansion of the coal industry worked out by the Energy Secretary – himself an ex-miner from neighbouring Derbyshire – as part of his integrated fuel and power policy. This envisaged an expansion of production and the sinking of new pits in the fertile East Midlands. That provided a helpful background to my speech to the Notts. miners, a deliberate rehearsal for the grimmer task to be faced at the national Scarborough Conference.

In advance of that we were living on borrowed time. But what of the bailiffs, in the shape of the international financial community, from cautious treasurers of international corporations, multi-nationals, to currency operators and monetary speculators? Would they give us time – to win the support of the miners and take all necessary corrective action? The answer came on 30 June.

I was in Stoneleigh to open the Royal Agricultural Show, which I later toured. (One of the marquees I visited was exhibiting fruit, including the products of local strawberry growers. Naturally I accepted their invitation to partake. Next day the press had photographs of me in an abdicatory posture, eating strawberries while Rome was burning.) My speech, carefully prepared and checked with the Treasury the previous Friday, was on the theme of 'no panic'. It was just as I was leaving to fly to London that grim messages reached me from the Treasury via No. 10 that the foreign exchange markets were in turmoil. As the *Guardian* put it the next day,

---

[1] See the part played by both statesmen in industrial relations in the chapters on Baldwin and Churchill in *A Prime Minister on Prime Ministers*.

The international financial community was stunned yesterday by the biggest slide in the value of the pound against major world currencies to take place on one day within living memory.

Strangely, the 'no panic' speech, when reported, stabilized the situation for an hour or two, until it was realized that it had been made in ignorance of the market convulsions. Then the reverse interpretation took charge: 'no panic' was interpreted as 'no action'. Sterling fell sharply against all major currencies, from a depreciation of 27.6 per cent against the 'currency-basket' as measured by the Smithsonian parities, to 28.9 per cent, from \$2.2245–2.2255 to \$2.1910–2.1930 on the dollar.

On the Monday afternoon and evening I held a number of anxious meetings with the Chancellor and other ministers. We were particularly concerned about a fall in the value of sterling which would cause Middle East oil money held in London to move out of sterling. It was widely believed that if the sterling–dollar rate fell markedly below \$2.20, this would happen. Already there were rumours that this was about to occur. To quote the *Guardian* again, reporting on Monday's events,

Selling pressure was relentless, coming from virtually every international financial centre. Selling was heaviest from Swiss and West German banks, some of whom were reported to be operating on behalf of Middle East interests.

The Treasury that Monday night was utterly depressed, and when depressed it tends to go fetishist. Their fetish on this occasion, not for the first time, and not unnaturally, reflected international market demands for statutory controls over pay. The Treasury, of course, can hardly ignore market prejudice. No matter that all experience – including that of Mr Heath's final months – taught us that statutory sanctions would not dig coal. It was the Biblical case of the perverse generation seeking after a sign. Or, in the words of the poet,

> Somebody's got to be summonsed,
> So that was decided upon.

Without a legal framework, indeed one backed by criminal sanctions, we were told, sterling would go. At 1.0 a.m. ministers emerging from the Cabinet room were so advised. In this respect Mr Joe Haines's book reproducing his note to me on the midnight Treasury démarche is accurate.

On the Tuesday sterling fell from the overnight depreciation of 28.9 per cent to 29.2 per cent, picking up slightly on the dollar. Denis Healey made an announcement which we had authorized the previous evening. He and other ministers had been conducting talks with the TUC. He said that the TUC would be given another *week* to produce 'results' or the Government would take action on its own. By results he meant the setting of a 10 per cent limit on pay increases, effective in each case for a year. That week would cover the

opening of the mineworkers' conference, which we had recognized all along
would prove decisive.

I was pressed at question-time on the Tuesday about legal sanctions. The
reply was that there would be 'no criminal sanctions against workers'.

The markets suspended judgment for 'Healey's week'. Increasingly attention was directed to Scarborough, where at the end of the week the mineworkers were gathering. Their NEC was sharply divided: the delegates who
controlled the ultimate decision by their votes were even more so. The issue
was the demand made by Yorkshire, Scotland and other militant coalfields,
for the £100 a week wage for coal-face workers.

Tallies of how the districts, whose total on a full vote would come to 267,
would vote gave the militants one vote short of a majority. Lobbying and
arm-twisting went on through the week-end. Derbyshire, with eleven votes,
was believed likely to abstain.

It was against that background that I began to prepare my speech over the
week-end. Never, in thirty years in Parliament, had I prepared a speech with
such care – dictating, writing, amending, inserting, discarding and drafting
again. On the Government's main approach to the future of the industry I
drew in detail on the Varley Plan. Substantially, I outlined the specific
proposals for the sinking of new pits, and referred to the unprecedented
decision of the Government to provide £100 million of new money for the
relief of between 40,000 and 50,000 old pneumoconiosis ('black lung') cases
who had been omitted from previous schemes.

The work went on – according to the No. 10 diary – until just before
Sunday midnight. In that last hour I re-wrote the final appeal, stressing how
much was at stake, for the industry, for the mineworkers and for Britain.
At 10 a.m. next morning I left for Northolt airport, flew to Leconfield in East
Yorkshire, then on to Scarborough.

I was not lacking advisers – nor prophets of doom – to apprise me of the
latest voting assessments. The odds were that the £100 minimum would
carry by a very small majority. As I had expected, the key lay in the eleven
Derbyshire votes, and the three from the West Midlands, which I had known
as Cannock Chase, Shropshire, North and South Staffordshire, and Warwick-
shire. Pit closures had reduced those coalfields almost to extinction: they now
had just 3 out of 267 votes. In the days I had dealt with them they had
accounted for 8.5 per cent of the national output of coal.[1]

The general atmosphere was one of gloom, but the Government did not
lack friends, determined friends, led by Joe Gormley. The mood at lunchtime
was to offer me the best of British.

Mineworkers are amongst the warmest-hearted of Her Majesty's subjects.
But mineworkers' delegates at conferences, unlike their summer galas, are
dour, immovable. The more they agree with you, the less they show it. I had

[1] See the writer's *New Deal for Coal*, London, 1945, p. 4. A North Staffordshire pit was
the first I had ever gone down, thirty-four years before.

found this, as a political apprentice, in my own constituency. Anyone not knowing them would misinterpret their silence as sullenness. But they are listening. They will decide. Better get on with it, and no pauses for applause.

The key extracts from this speech are set out in Appendix V, partly because of its effects in moving the mineworkers to the pay policy which was essential, partly because it clearly highlights the relations between a Labour Prime Minister and the unions – especially the mineworkers.

I referred to the circumstances of the February 1974 General Election, brought about by the then Government's confrontation with the miners, and the speed with which, on our taking office, a settlement was reached.

After setting out all the Government had done for the industry, as printed in Appendix V, I made my appeal to the Conference:

Our record in fulfilling more speedily, more completely, than any other Government in history, the pledges we had made; our record in risking all on making a total reality of the Government's commitments on the social contract, all this has entitled us to ask for a corresponding commitment, for a response no less total.

I say this as one who has known the mining community intimately for *over* 30 years. I have been privileged to have been a friend of many of its national leaders and many of the MFGB[1] district leaders – from Ebby Edwards, Will Lawther, Jim Bowman through Ernest Jones to the present day.

I was concerned more than 30 years ago with the initiation of the most historic wages decision since 1926, when we re-instituted the *national minimum* wage, and signed the death-warrant of the hated wages-ascertainment system and district bargaining, which set district against district, and brother against brother.

Perhaps only a small minority of today's delegates, even of area leaders, ever worked under the wages-ascertainment system. But the miners of 1926, when they had lost all in the battle over wages and hours, fought on for another two desperate months in their resistance to district ascertainments.

In 'New Deal for Coal', 1945, I drafted, in consultation with miners' leaders, the detailed scheme for nationalisation of the industry, which, almost word for word, was the basis of the Labour Government's historic legislation which took the industry into public ownership.

Starting 30 years ago this month, I have had the privilege of representing many Lancashire mineworkers in the House of Commons.

Not as a stranger, therefore, do I again today address this Conference.

It was not as a stranger to the industry either, that, in January 1974, in that emergency debate for which we had demanded the recall of Parliament, I warned the then Conservative Government against the confrontation on which they were set.

I recalled the record of the mining community in peace and war; I reminded them of Winston Churchill's unstinted tribute to the miners of Betteshanger. I had told the heathen of Mr Heath's Goverment (I quote)

[1] Miners' Federation of Great Britain, their name when the sovereignty of the individual districts limited the national organization to a less than united status.

that the loyalty which they have shown to the nation, in peace and in war, is matched by the loyalty they cherished towards their industry, their pit, their comrades, their unshakeable beliefs, and their separate and individual, and often remote, mining communities.

But above all their loyalty to democracy.

I had, I said, concluded my Commons speech by telling Mr Heath:

Nobody has contributed more to democracy than have the mineworkers of Britain. They and their wives today constitute the solid rock of social democracy as much as they have ever done in the past 100 years. Government – any Government, whatever their political philosophy – should be proud to build upon that rock, instead of seeking to build upon the shifting sands of assumed political advantage.

I had ended by urging (I quoted)

The Prime Minister – that was the *then* Prime Minister – not to spurn, by any lack of understanding, all that that loyalty can mean *to* the nation.

It is now *Labour*'s Prime Minister, your Prime Minister, at a critical hour in the nation's history, enjoining this community, once again, to assert this loyalty *for* the nation.

It is not so much a question of whether that loyalty, that response, will be forthcoming in sufficient measure to save this Labour Government. The issue now is not whether this or any other democratic socialist Government can survive and lead the nation to full employment and a greater measure of social justice. It is whether any Government *so* constituted, *so* dedicated to the principles of consent and consensus within our democracy, can lead this nation.

What the Government is asking for the year ahead, what the Government has the *right* to ask, the *duty* to ask, is not a year for self, but *a Year for Britain*.

When I sat down Mick McGahey, Vice-President of the Union, who was sitting next to me, said, 'Well, you did what you came for.' I replied that I presumed that he did not agree with all I had said. He retorted that he did not agree with anything I had said, but predicted that Derbyshire and the West Midlands would be meeting late that afternoon. So it proved.

When the Executive met to consider the next day's proceedings the left-wingers knew they were beaten. A mandatory resolution in favour of the demand for an immediate £100 a week would not carry the Conference. Instead it was decided to keep the figure of £100 as a long-term, not an immediate, objective, as something they would 'seek'. Joe Gormley and his colleagues played the situation with consummate skill. Of course the £100 demand was on the table: the NUM would 'seek' £100, not demand it, still less make it a strike issue. The question was not even pressed to a vote in the Executive or Conference. Left-wingers, it is true, towards the end of the Conference, tried again to insist that the £100 wage was a 'demand'.

Len Clarke took the rostrum: 'You don't remove the word "demand" and put "seek" for the same meaning.' Joe Gormley firmly ruled: 'I don't think we are tied to the figure of £100. I have said that categorically.'

Following the Conference, the Executive on 11 July decided to hold a pit-head ballot, asking for support for the initiative then being discussed between the Government and the TUC to curb inflation. The result of the ballot was 60.5 per cent in favour, 39.5 per cent against, and the NUM Executive concluded an agreement with the Coal Board for a £6 per week increase, in accordance with the guidelines.

I flew back from Scarborough to London and chaired a ministerial meeting. Denis Healey's discussions with TUC leaders were making progress: the mineworkers' conference opened the way for a settlement. Denis Healey's timetable required a decision within the week. I was looking for a Government statement on the Thursday. By Wednesday, the day of the NEDC meeting, things were looking more hopeful. By this time I had had to fly to Edinburgh to be in attendance for the State visit of the King of Sweden, after which, following an audience of the Queen, I returned to London to see how far the Chancellor had progressed. Late night meetings of ministers to agree a draft statement culminated in Thursday's Cabinet, where our proposals for legislation to back up the agreement with the TUC were ratified. It had been clear to me from the Cabinet meeting the previous week that there would not have been a majority in favour of legislation to impose penal sanctions on unions or workers refusing to adhere to a pay formula. I had not let the Cabinet come to a clear decision, but a rough head-count based on what each minister had said made it clear that anything involving criminal sanctions was out.

Ten years of history under successive Governments have proved that in our democracy any formula for the statutory imposition of pay limits would prove to be the *ignis fatuus* of policy. A British Government, in peacetime, must proceed by leadership, agreement and consensus. The introduction of supporting legislation to an agreed settlement was another issue. This is what we sought. The White Paper we issued on Friday 11 July (Cmnd. 6151) was the result.

Parliament met at its usual time, 11.0 a.m. on the Friday. Most unusually for a Friday, Government and Opposition benches were packed. I rose to announce the Government's policy. The announcement and the subsequent questions, from both sides of the House, took an unusual seventy minutes, after which, with the ministers directly concerned, Denis Healey, Michael Foot and Shirley Williams, Minister for Prices and Consumer Protection, I took a press conference of nearly the same length, followed by television and radio interviews.

The full text is printed as Appendix VI. It was, necessarily, the toughest statement (Stafford Cripps not excluded) any Government had made in the House of Commons in peacetime on the need for pay restraint, the limits to be set, and the means to its realization.

The press, waiting hourly for news of splits and resignations, were ready to acknowledge, on such information as was available to them ahead of the statement, that agreement had been reached. On the morning before my statement the *Guardian* reported:

> The Prime Minister seemed last night to have pulled off yet another successful performance in his role as the Great Houdini of British politics by securing the agreement of his Cabinet to an anti-inflationary package which includes reserve powers without losing a single Cabinet Minister in the process.[1]

Without saying this, what was no less implied was that we had carried the TUC without an imposed diktat.

My statement to the press conference, and the answers to questions by the ministerial team, closely followed what I had said in the House. No one could gainsay the fact that the Government had secured a policy agreed by the two sides of industry, adequate to meeting the crisis, with legal backing to the consequential aspects of our decision, without invoking arid and legislative measures putting workers or their leaders in peril of criminal sanctions.

The *Guardian*,[2] reporting the day's proceedings, made this comment:

> The Prime Minister took Britain back to a full-scale, enforceable pay and prices policy for the third time yesterday, simultaneously succeeding in squaring the circle between statutory and voluntary controls to support the £6 a week pay limit. The limit is to apply virtually to the entire nation for the next 12 months.
>
> In a compromise formula worthy of a master of the art, Mr Wilson succeeded in reconciling Treasury demands for immediate reserve back-up powers with the well-known hostility to statutory pay curbs expressed repeatedly and in public by his Secretary for Employment, Mr Foot.
>
> The result is a deal which provides Mr Foot with a victory in his fight to prevent the inclusion of statutory penalties for breaches of the pay limit in the immediate legislation coming before Parliament in 10 days.
>
> But at the same time it provides the Chancellor with the assurance of the kind of back-up powers for dealing with an emergency which the Treasury regards as essential to reassure overseas creditors.

(We were in fact helped in reassuring the overseas creditors: the trade figures we were just publishing represented an annual deficit of £324 million, compared with an actual deficit in the year 1974 of £3,800 million.)

*The Times* commented in terms very similar to those of the *Guardian*:

> Mr Wilson yesterday seemed to have pulled off a feat of reconciliation that will go down in the annals of political wizardry as one of his greatest achievements; out of the Babel that preceded his publication of yesterday's White Paper from the political right, left and centre, he emerged with a Commons statement that produced not a single threat of resignation or instant revolution.
>
> At the end it was clear that, details apart, the measures were broadly acceptable, if not entirely welcomed, in all parts of the House ... apart from the occasional rumblings of discontent from expected quarters, it was clear that although many hurdles lay ahead of the Prime Minister and that next week's

[1] 11 July 1975.
[2] 12 July.

legislation will be looked at critically, there is unlikely to be a widespread revolt by the Labour left, while much of what the Government is proposing will be accepted by the Conservatives and other opposition parties.

The references to Houdini and wizardry were in this instance meant in a complimentary sense. The implication was that the unpleasant measures needed to deal with a national crisis were tailored in such a way as to be acceptable. The real point is that political acceptability is not the only test. They were endorsed by all the main economic interests, particularly management and unions, and at the same time were acceptable in the City and by overseas opinion as realistic.

In political comment there is a tendency – not evidenced in the texts cited above – to deplore a leadership approach which is accepted by ministers and MPs of widely different views. To bridge a deep political chasm without splitting a party or provoking dramatic ministerial resignations is sometimes regarded as something approaching political chicanery. This is to subordinate the realities of two hundred years of democratic politics to the demands of sensationalism. The highest aim of leadership is to secure policies adequate to deal with any situation, including the production of acceptable new solutions and policies, without major confrontations, splits and resignations. It may be bad for the headlines and news placards, but it has been sought and achieved by our greatest leaders, Conservative as well as Liberal or Labour. Baldwin, Macmillan and Churchill – both in wartime coalition days and in his peacetime premiership – always sought consensus. It is sometimes galling to be criticized for achieving it.

On 21 and 22 July the Government's policy, announced on 11 July, was debated in Parliament. It was carried by 327 votes to 269, a majority of 58 in a chamber where the Government no longer had an overall majority.

This was confidently cited by Denis Healey, when on the following day he moved the Second Reading of the Bill to give legislative effect to the policy announced on 11 July. A Conservative amendment to reject the Bill was thrown out by 320 to 260, and the Bill secured its Second Reading by 294 to 16, the Conservatives abstaining. The Committee stage began the next day. A Conservative amendment was rejected by only one vote, a number of Labour MPs abstaining. Others carried by 30 or 40 votes, but a left-wing Labour amendment moved by Eric Heffer was defeated by 229 to 39, the minority being made up mainly of Labour MPs, supported by Enoch Powell and a few Conservatives. The Committee stage went through the night and well into the following day. At 2.45 p.m. a Conservative amendment to the clause extending housing subsidies was defeated by 79, and at 4.36 p.m. the Bill was through its Committee stage. The Report Stage, which also went into the small hours, was less violently contested and the Third Reading was carried without a division at 5.0 a.m. It received the Royal Assent on 1 August.

# Chapter 7

## PARLIAMENT AND POLITICS

THE Parliamentary session from 29 October 1974 to the summer adjournment on 12 August 1975, and from 13 October to prorogation on 12 November, probably demanded more of its members, ministerial and back-bench, than any session in recent history. For sheer legislative output, together with the burden laid on Parliament by the outcome of the EEC renegotiations, it far transcends the busiest session of the reforming 1945–50 Parliament led by Clement Attlee.[1] The burden on individual members was the greater because, whereas Clement Attlee had a majority of nearly 200, we accounted after April 1975 for barely half of the MPs.

Mr Speaker Selwyn Lloyd was re-elected to the chair, and the new Parliament was opened by the Queen on 29 October. There was little surprise that the second 1974 Speech from the Throne foreshadowed one of the most formidable legislative programmes for many years. The Bills announced included some which had been prepared during the Short Parliament, and others were to give legislative form to the flood of White Papers issued in the weeks immediately before the Election.

Thus measures were promised to introduce a tax on capital transfers, to establish the Advisory Conciliation and Arbitration Service (ACAS) on a statutory basis, 'to tackle the abuses of "the lump" in the construction industry', and to ensure comprehensive safeguards for employment in the docks. Social legislation would increase existing social security benefits, including family allowances, make additional provision for the disabled, pay a Christmas pension bonus, and set up a new earnings-related pensions scheme. Bills were to be introduced to reform the law on rents and housing subsidies, and 'to enable land required for development to be taken into community ownership and to tax realizations of development value'.

On energy policy and the resources of the North Sea, the comprehensive programme announced by Eric Varley in the summer was to deal with coal, oil, natural gas and nuclear technology.

> Legislation will be introduced to regulate further the development of offshore petroleum, to establish a British National Oil Corporation with rights to participate in this development, to ensure that the community receives a fair share of the profits; and to provide for the acquisition of oil sites in Scotland.

[1] See p. 85n.

On industrial policy, measures would be introduced

to provide for the establishment of planning agreements and a National Enterprise Board; and to enable the shipbuilding and aircraft industries to be taken into public ownership.

Bills would be introduced to establish the Scottish and Welsh Development Agencies. Other legislation would be aimed at ending sex discrimination, to provide protection for policy holders of insurance companies 'and for people booking overseas holidays and travel who suffer loss as a result of the failure of travel agencies'. These two measures were a response to the V & G insurance scandal, and the collapse of tourist agencies in the previous year. A Bill was to be introduced to reform the law relating to adoption, guardianship and fostering of children.

It was one of the most formidable legislative programmes since the war, indeed in all our Parliamentary history. In many cases the Bill was as yet little more than a twinkle in a minister's eye, and even where White Papers had been issued before the General Election, the task of translating them into legislative form put a heavy burden on ministers and their advisers, the Law Officers and departmental legal staffs, Parliamentary draftsmen, on inter-departmental Committees and above all on the Lord President and Leader of the House who had to drive his colleagues to make sure that legislation was ready in time. And all this in a Parliament where the Government party had 317 members, after the election of Mr Speaker and his deputies, against 314 in all other parties.

Seventy-three Government Bills received the Royal Assent in the thirteen months of the 1974–75 Parliamentary session, that is excluding private Bills such as those promoted by public corporations and local authorities. Many of the Bills were of great length and complexity, such as the Social Security, New Towns, Iron and Steel, Offshore Petroleum Development, Petroleum and Submarine Pipelines, and Local Land Charges measures.

During the passage of this legislative programme the Government's minuscule majority was constantly in danger, from death – or later by-elections caused by EEC appointments – to say nothing of defections. On 5 March Bill Hamling, my Parliamentary Private Secretary, was taken ill in my room at the House. In addition to his general Parliamentary duties on the floor, he had volunteered for membership of the Standing Committee on the committee stage of the Finance Bill. He had sat right through the previous night in the Committee upstairs and told me that he intended to speak in a three-hour debate on the Norton-Villiers-Triumph co-operative, due to begin at midnight. Just after the previous three-line Whip business ended, most members went home. When he was taken ill I found a Whip and asked her to send her colleagues to every Commons exit and intercept a doctor MP. Fortunately they caught Dr Vaughan, Conservative MP for Reading, who immediately had Bill taken by ambulance to hospital, and stayed with him in the intensive care unit for three hours before coming back to report to me. Our very few Dr MPs of both parties are heroes at such times. Bill appeared to make a good recovery, but on 19 March, after being discharged from hospital, he suddenly died while laughing out loud at a television programme about Liverpool – he was a 'scouser'. His seat was lost to the Conservative candidate, Mr Peter Bottomley, who when taking the oath over the Treasury Bench turned to me to make a kind reference to his sadness at Bill Hamling's death. Labour's narrow defeat in West Woolwich was itself a tribute to Bill, who was a legend among all parties for his constituency service. Our majority now fell to one, 316 against 315. There it would have remained for a further eighteen months but for the defection of two Scottish Labour MPs to the 'Scottish Labour Party' which they formed in December 1975. In 1976 we lost Walsall North and Workington, on John Stonehouse's resignation and Fred Peart's translation to the Lords in Jim Callaghan's first Cabinet changes. (It is almost a by-election law that a seat vacated by a change of vocation is much more vulnerable than one vacated by death. Constituencies understand that all must die some time, but seem to resent an MP they have elected for a whole Parliament applying for the Chiltern Hundreds during the lifetime of that Parliament, as with Workington, and also Stechford and Ashfield when Roy Jenkins and David Marquand went to the EEC.)

An exiguous majority, or a titular overall minority, is not of itself a guarantee of repeated Parliamentary defeats. Attendance in the House becomes virtually compulsory, and abstentions on grounds of conscientious objection to Government measures become more rare – at least for a time.

The October General Election had meant the postponement of the annual conference. A special three-and-a-half-day conference was held in London from 27–30 November. All the resolutions submitted the previous summer for the October conference were scrapped by the Conference Arrangements Committee – many of them had been concerned with proposals of varying value for incorporation in the election manifesto. Such hardy annuals as the Chairman's Address and that of the Party Leader were maintained, but it was arranged – in addition to a business session concerned with changes in the Party constitution – to have a series of short debates, and even, in the interests of Party democracy, brief sessions to allow questions to be put to the Prime Minister and other ministers. (This was not a great success. The questions related to devolution, Northern Ireland, cuts in teacher training, the nationalization of the commanding heights of the economy, Arab terrorism, the wage-stop principle in social security, rents and rates, attacks on immigration controls, and aid to industry. The experiment has not been repeated.)

In my speech, as usual introducing the Parliamentary Report, I made two principal points. One was that Labour was now the 'natural party of Government', and should accept that responsibility and not continue in a posture of frustrated opposition. If the newly-elected Parliament went its statutory full period, until October 1979, we should have been in office nearly eleven and a half out of fifteen years from 1964. Having reported on the legislative and other changes we had made in the shortest Parliament since 1886, I quoted a tape-machine forecasting the Conference attacks we must expect to face, notably that 'the Manifesto on which this Election was won has not yet been implemented'. I claimed the right to plead for a little more time than the six weeks implied.

The other point was my attempt to up-date Keynes:

While we have moved on from Keynes, vintage 1936, our opponents argue as though he never even existed. He said when private investment plans are inadequate there must be public investment to secure full employment. What he had in mind was public works, roads, sewage and drainage.

That is why I claim the National Enterprise Board is the biggest leap forward in economic thinking as well as in economic policy since the war. For where private investment falls away, or even if it is not falling is on a scale far too small to ensure a high level of employment and modernization, when that is the position public investment is enlisted.

Investment, not to produce goods which our customers do not want or cannot afford, but to make the goods with which we can pay our way in the world and modernize Britain.

This is where we move the nation forward by a whole generation in our thinking and in our policy. And public investment, in deference to the late John Maynard Keynes, is to be mobilized, not to turn engineers into road workers, or for constructing drainage and sewage, but specifically directed in terms of the machinery, the plant, the research and development we so urgently need for the regeneration of British industry . . .

The one notable achievement of the Conference was the speech on the last morning by Helmut Schmidt, to which reference has been made. He carefully made no reference to a negative resolution toughening Britain's membership terms, carried on a card vote by 3,007,000 against 2,849,000, nor to a helpful resolution on the EEC referendum carried by acclamation.

Though we had not, despite the pre-Conference criticism, carried out the manifesto in six weeks, we were moving quickly on its implementation.

Barbara Castle's Social Security Act ended six years of legislative uncertainty. Dick Crossman had introduced a major measure in the 1969–70 session. The incoming Conservative Government in 1970 set it aside, and introduced a new measure. This, in its turn, though it reached the Statute Book, had not been put into effect when Labour returned to office in March 1974. There was a danger that social security legislation was becoming a game of pat-ball. Barbara and her Minister of State, Brian O'Malley,[1] set out with infinite dedication to produce legislation acceptable to both parties which

---

[1] Brian O'Malley died suddenly in April 1976, just as the measure was completing its passage through Parliament.

would endure for a political generation. In this aim they were supported, to his credit, by the Conservative shadow minister, Sir Geoffrey Howe. I remember hearing his welcoming statement on the car radio one Friday evening, on the way to Chequers. Barbara had followed my old chief, Beveridge, more than thirty years later, in carrying forward the nation's social security legislation for a generation. This had, in fact, been her aim. Following her publication of an outline, *Better Pensions*, and her study of reactions and comments, she had the Bill ready for the new session.

The first and fundamental change from the Beveridge reforms was based on the recognition that the ending of poverty and deprivation in old age and social distress could not be achieved by flat-rate contributions and flat-rate benefits. Two million out of seven million retirement pensioners, and half of the nation's elderly widows, were dependent on supplementary benefit, a right, but a right which had to be made good by verification of each applicant's individual circumstances. The Beveridge Report had highlighted the fact of 'two nations in old age', though his solution in terms of earnings-related pensions through funded schemes, firm by firm and industry by industry, in fact created a new two-nations situation. The new proposals were designed to integrate occupational pensions into a wider scheme of earnings-related schemes. They were aimed at a new partnership between the state and private schemes, not on the basis of strictly poverty-line benefits for the State pension, supplemented by private schemes where they existed, but by fixing the standards

> at the level necessary to remove poverty in old age, widowhood and disability, and then providing forms of State help to private schemes to enable them to meet the targets that we have laid down.[1]

So the principles underlying the legislation were:

1. that the pension must be adequate for everyone, in that there must be a redistributive formula to help the lower-paid;
2. that the scheme must have a much shorter maturity period than in the discarded Conservative Act, so that older workers could benefit;
3. that the proposals should recognize the changed status of women in society, getting away from the Beveridge doctrine of 'dependency' and providing that women at work should share equal responsibilities and enjoy equal rights;
4. that there should be an end to the discrimination against manual workers and that they should be assured equivalent benefits to those enjoyed by white-collar workers under salary-rated schemes;
5. the pension was to be inflation-proofed, and the Bill provided help to private schemes for this purpose.

[1] *Hansard*, 18 March, vol. 888, col. 1489.

The Bill provided, therefore, that the pension would have two components, a basic element which would reflect the amount of the flat-rate pension at the outset of the scheme, and an additional component giving, after twenty years,

> one quarter of a person's average earnings between the level of the basic component and a ceiling of seven times that level.

For those already in 'mid-career', with twenty or more years to go before retirement, there would be provision to 'load' their pension rights for this purpose.

Pensions would be reviewed every year to keep the basic element in line with earnings and the 'additional component' in line with wages. The basis for the final pension would be, not average earnings throughout a working career, but the best twenty years of earnings (after revaluation for price changes), irrespective of whether they occurred early or late.

Existing provisions discriminating against women were to go, and special provision was made for widows. Widowed mothers and other widows entitled to full pension were to inherit the whole of their husband's earnings-related pension entitlement – both the basic and additional components, plus any entitlement from their own earnings.

Disabled workers were to have their invalidity pensions made earnings-related.

The financing of pensions was based on a partnership between the State scheme and occupational pension schemes, organized and controlled by employers and representatives of employees. Contracting-out was to be allowed only on the basis that the rules, conditions and ultimate benefits in respect of independent schemes were to be not less favourable than those which would have been provided by the State. Funding would be on the basis of $5\frac{1}{2}$ per cent of earnings from the employee, $8\frac{1}{2}$ per cent from the employer. Under the State scheme pure and simple the rates would be $6\frac{1}{2}$ per cent and 10 per cent respectively.

Barbara ended her speech by saying,

> The message we are getting loud and clear from the people of this country is 'For heaven's sake let us settle once and for all the great pension debate that has been taking place for so long.'

With the ready response from the Conservative front bench, that was precisely what Barbara Castle achieved. It was one of the four great advances in social reform in this century: Lloyd George's social revolution in the Asquith Government, the implementation of the Beveridge scheme by the wartime coalition in the early forties, the Attlee-Griffiths social revolution of the late forties, and the Labour Government's achievement in the seventies.

The Committee stage, with full and constructive help from the Opposition,

5*

made amendments designed only to realize still more fully the aims set out on the Bill's introduction. It was due to come into effect in March 1978. Barbara had been dropped by Jim Callaghan when he formed his Government, and Stan Orme took over the administration of her Act. In March 1977 he published a simple guide 'New pensions: what you pay and how you benefit', explaining in detail the arrangement for 'contracted-in' and 'contracted-out' pensions. In June 1978 he announced new scales in the Social Security Benefits Up-rating Order, due to come into force on 13 November. The standard rate of the retirement pension was raised from £17.50 to £19.50 for a single pensioner, and from £28 to £31.20 for a married couple, an increase of 11.4 per cent in cash terms, and a substantial increase in real purchasing power.

In social terms the new legislation was the most important step forward since the reforms introduced by the Government of Clement Attlee (who moved the Second Reading of the Bill) more than thirty years before. But in economic terms, no one realized that with one measure we had created the greatest change in our financial system since the war. Ministers did not realize it, nor did back-benchers. Indeed hardly any observer in the City realized that we had carried through an economic and financial revolution perhaps greater than all the post-war nationalization measures put together.[1]

Meanwhile Northern Ireland affairs were constantly taking the time of Government and Parliament. For a brief time there were welcome signs of easement. Early on New Year's Day I flew back from a brief post-Christmas holiday in the Isles of Scilly. A meeting had been arranged with four Northern Ireland religious leaders, namely the Catholic Archbishop of Armagh, Primate of All Ireland; the Church of Ireland Archbishop, Primate of All Ireland; the Moderator of the General Assembly of the Presbyterian Church in Ireland; and the former President of the Methodist Church in Ireland. I had met all of them during my 1972 visit, and few men in the history of Northern Ireland had shown such leadership and courage as these four. The message they brought was one of hope. Although there had been no overt decision by the terrorists on either side to observe a Christmas truce, there had in fact been no violence over the Christmas period, and the de facto cease-fire had persisted into the New Year.

One illustration they used brought it home to us more than anything else could have done. Encouraged by the quiet conditions, youngsters, they said, actually went out to dances, for the first time since the troubles had begun. Girls of fourteen and fifteen went to their first Christmas party or dance. The party dresses they had bought two or three years before they now felt free to wear for the first time. If only it would last! Tragically the truce ended early in the New Year.

But mysterious things were happening. For whatever reason the IRA

[1] See Postscript 1 to this Chapter, pp. 146–8 below: *The Pension Funds Revolution.*

seemed to be moving towards an acknowledged cease-fire. Merlyn Rees kept me in touch. Early in February there seemed to be a chance.

On 9 February I was due to address the Labour Friends of Israel in the City of Leeds, part of which was represented in Parliament by the Northern Ireland Secretary. Throughout the afternoon and evening we were in touch through Downing Street, by means of the technologically advanced – and totally secure – system of communications. The signal I was awaiting had not reached me when I went on the platform. Halfway through my speech the message came, and shortly after 9 p.m. I interrupted my theme to announce a definitive cease-fire. Recognizing how hard Merlyn had worked for this, it was deeply moving for me to be able to announce it in Leeds.

The cease-fire, announced by the IRA provisionals, took effect from 18.00 hours on Monday, 10 February. The following day the Secretary of State made a statement to Parliament.

He indicated that if a genuine and sustained cessation of violence took place a new situation would be created in which there would be a progressive reduction in the commitment of the Army, both in numbers and in scale of activity, leading to a reduction to peacetime levels and withdrawal to barracks.

He also said that officials had put to Provisional Sinn Fein a scheme designed to make effective arrangements for ensuring that any future cease-fire did not break down. This had five main elements. First, a number of incident centres, manned by civil servants, would be established throughout Northern Ireland. These centres would be linked with his office in Belfast. Second, if developments occurred which seemed to threaten the cease-fire, these incident centres would act as a point of contact in either direction. Third, issues could be referred to his office in Belfast and clarified there. Fourth, cases referred up to the Northern Ireland Office would be considered, and a reply passed back to the incident centre for onward transmission. Fifth, if out of these exchanges general difficulties about the cease-fire arrangements emerged, then discussions would be arranged between officials and representatives of legal organizations to clarify them. There would be full consultation by officials with the security forces on these arrangements, which would cover only incidents arising directly out of the cease-fire.

Without ever renouncing the cease-fire, the first fatal assault by members of the Provisional IRA on a member of the security forces took place just three months later, on 10 May. For some months thereafter the frequency and intensity of attacks on the security forces remained at a lower level than in the preceding years, but sectarian assassinations continued at a higher rate.

Shooting incidents involving the security forces numbered 198 in the six months from 1 February 1975, against 1,021 in the same period of 1974: 11 were killed and 135 wounded, against 25 and 320 respectively in February–July 1974. But there were 640 shooting incidents against civilians, practically the same figure as in the same period of 1974, involving 104 deaths (82 in February–July 1974), and 974 woundings (against 1,007). Figures for the same period of 1976 showed higher figures for deaths, both of members of the security forces and civilians, despite fewer shooting incidents in respect of both categories.

Needless to say, ministers kept in close touch with the Irish Government. The Taoiseach, Liam Cosgrave, came over for meetings, we had discussions 'on the fringe' of the EEC summits in September and December 1974 and in Dublin in March 1975. Apart from these, I paid one special visit to Dublin.

Early in the morning of 17 November 1974 the news came that Erskine Childers, President of the Irish Republic, had died. When I came downstairs I went straight to Private Office and said that I felt I should go to the funeral service. My secretaries expressed their doubts: the Irish Government would not want me to go – the security problem would be a headache for them. The Foreign and Commonwealth Office were quite definite that I should not go. I told the office to get on to the Taoiseach and let him decide. He was clearly pleased with the proposal and said he would put it to the Cabinet, who were just convening. A few minutes later came their warm acceptance. In fact, I found when I arrived that many European Heads of State or Government were there, including monarchs and presidents. The Queen was represented by Lord Mountbatten, and Mr Heath was the third member of our party.

Security was impressive. After the service in Dublin's Protestant Church of Ireland Cathedral, we drove in the cortège of fifty or sixty cars which followed the hearse through the City. Innumerable green-clad soldiers walked along beside each car – until in the last stages, the cavalcade speeded up, and they were panting to keep up with us. The British party was cheered and cheered by the massive pavement crowds. They seemed to be telling us that a long and bloody chapter in Anglo-Irish relations was over, and this was echoed in the speeches of the Irish leaders at the lunch of heads of delegations in Iveagh House.

In February 1975, action had to be taken on the Civil List, Parliament's appropriation for the expenses of the Royal Household. In a statement after Questions on 12 February, I reminded the House that in 1971 a Select Committee had been set up to recommend permanent statutory provision, it was hoped for many years ahead. As Leader of the Opposition I had been a member. The idea was that a fixed sum should be voted which would permit of savings in the early years; this (augmented by accrued interest) could be drawn down in the later years of the reign as rising costs demanded. Section 5 of the Civil List Act 1972 required the Royal Trustees (the Prime Minister, the Chancellor of the Exchequer and the Keeper of the Privy Purse) to keep the annual expenditure under review and to report to the Treasury – who in turn must report to Parliament – if the funds were running dry. Because of inflation this situation was reached in 1975. Civil List expenditure rose by 16 per cent to £1,180,000, from 1972 to 1974, and was expected to increase by a further 18½ per cent to £1,400,000 from 1974 to 1975. The increase was almost entirely caused by increased wages and salaries, linked grade by grade with corresponding Civil Service rates: three-quarters of the List expenditure went in wages and salaries. These figures were purely in relation to the expenses incurred by the Queen in pursuance of her official duties, and included no contribution to the Privy Purse. To limit the income the Queen intimated that she would herself contribute £1,500,000 out of her own resources towards the 1975 list. From now on, no provision was to be made by Parliament to any member of the Royal Family except those who were children of a reigning monarch. In the debate on our proposals, I congratulated Mrs Thatcher on speaking for the first time as Leader of the Opposition: she expressed her party's support for our proposals.[1]

Inevitably Mr William Hamilton, self-appointed scourge of the monarchy and everything appertaining thereto, attacked the provision, and contrived to be quite offensive. Some of the exchanges are reproduced as Appendix VII, partly because of the intrinsic importance of the subject, partly to convey some idea of the flavour of Parliamentary exchanges, when serious proposals can be carried through the House with a certain good-natured acerbity at the expense of those who oppose them.[2]

Other speakers stressed the modesty of the estimate, recognizing that the Queen was Britain's Ambassador-Extraordinary in her foreign travels.[3]

Legislation to give effect to the decision was debated the following December.[4] I had prepared my speech in the aircraft returning from the Rome EEC Summit. On a day of miscellaneous business, which ran ahead of schedule, I was called at 5.45 p.m. The Chief Secretary to the Treasury, who was supposed to be winding up, came too late to hear the opening frontbench speeches, so I decided to wind up. Mr Hamilton came in weighed under with volumes of facts, figures and notes – it looked like being a long debate. He spoke in fact for half an hour, with much virulence. My first thought, replying to the debate, was to deal with his arguments. Suddenly I thought of a means of saving time.

> He will forgive me, I hope, if I do not respond to the courtesies which he addressed in my direction in the spirit in which he addressed them . . . Nothing that I might say in reply would in the remotest degree alter his views or affect his vote in the matter.

[1] *Hansard*, vol. 886, cols 373–6.
[2] See particularly the exchange with Mr Hamilton and Mr Andrew Faulds – in the latter case the references to the acting profession refer to his national popularity on television, notably as Carver Doone in the *Lorna Doone* series.
[3] In the substantial debate on the legislation to give effect to the decision, I pointed out that she was monarch of twelve countries, visiting them regularly.
[4] *Hansard*, vol. 901, cols 1980–2018.

He rose to the bait: 'That is right.' Thus encouraged, I replied,

> My Hon. Friend agrees with me . . . Therefore I shall not occupy the time of
> the House trying to convert him because it might lead to a rather late sitting,
> and at the end of it I might not succeed.
>
> In view of the kind remarks my Hon. Friend made about me, as he always
> does in these matters, I shall make one further reference to him. He referred to
> 'hangers-on' of the Royal Family. I doubt whether there is anyone better
> rewarded or who is a greater beneficiary from the existence of the monarchy –
> I would not wish to be so offensive as to refer to a 'hanger-on' – through his
> writings than my Hon. Friend.

The Second Reading was challenged by Mr Hamilton and others, and was
carried by 247 to 16. The whole process had taken just two hours. The
Committee Stage, despite amendments moved by Mr Hamilton, took just
forty-four minutes.

At this time I had a memorable, if brief, diversion from more pressing
problems. On 4 March I called on a very old and frail Charles Chaplin at the
Savoy Hotel, on the night he had received the accolade of knighthood from
the Queen. In the sixties I had been very keen to make such a recommendation to the Palace, but had met strong opposition from the Foreign Office,
on the ground that it would annoy the Americans. Regretfully, (and regret-
ably), I listened to this advice. Returning for my third administration, I was
damned if I would listen again, and the necessary submission went in. With
it I included the name of P. G. Wodehouse, a much-favoured candidate with
the Establishment, despite his naive insistence on visiting Hitler's Berlin and
broadcasting unpatriotic claptrap on their radio during the war. When the
1975 New Year Honours List was published both names were warmly welcomed by the commentators, and to meet that unforgettable Cockney was a
privilege never to be forgotten.

Meanwhile the legislation foreshadowed in the Queen's Speech ground its
way through Parliament. That was how it must have seemed to the Opposition, and to the Labour back-benchers operating on an almost constant-
attendance basis because of the knife-edge Parliamentary balance. The
Community Land Bill was a complicated piece of legislation designed to give
effect to the White Paper, Cmnd. 5730, of September 1974.[1] Only a Silkin
could do justice to its provisions, and indeed John Silkin, moving the Second
Reading,[2] paid filial tribute to the author of such legislation a Parliamentary generation before, with appropriate references to Lloyd George's
initiative in 1909, and those of the minority Labour Government in 1930.
He described the main objectives of the Bill, quoting the White Paper, as
being

[1] See pp. 45–6 above.
[2] *Hansard*, vol. 891, cols 236–45.

to enable the community to control the development of land in accordance with its needs and priorities and to restore to the community the increase in the value of land arising from its efforts ...

What the Bill does is to take the ownership of development land and give it to the community as a tool to achieve positive planning. Ownership enables the community to take the initiative in planning and to decide as a matter of positive policy where our development is to take place.

The Bill received its Second Reading by 263 to 240, the Liberal descendants of the aforementioned Lloyd George voting against it. It was carried on Third Reading on 14 October 1975 and received the Royal Assent on 12 November.

Meanwhile Ted Short, as Leader of the House, was consulting the parties about a remarkable, indeed quixotic, contribution to our democratic processes. Following an inquiry headed by Lord Houghton, he announced the Government's decision to propose to Parliament that financial assistance be provided for the Opposition parties in Parliament. The Liberals certainly needed it. The Conservatives have shown that when £2 million or so are required, there is an ample number of suppliers available for a touch, including enough to finance the staffing of their leader's office. The Government party would receive nothing.

Lord Houghton had suggested the provision of funds for all parties including the Government party, for all their work, outside as well as inside Parliament. The Government rejected subsidies for the parties' activities in the country, and excluded the Government party from access to the funds provided for work in Parliament.

When Ted Short tried to raise the issue in January he encountered some Parliamentary resistance on procedural grounds, but on 20 March he moved a resolution providing assistance, for Opposition parties only, based on a formula providing that £500 would be voted for each seat won by the party concerned, plus £1 for every 200 votes cast for it, at the preceding General Election, up to a limit of £150,000, provided that the party in question had two MPs elected, or, if only one, had received a total of 150,000 votes. The resolution was carried by 142 votes to 47.

But Parliament's main pre-occupation was with the major legislation announced in the Queen's Speech.

Two urgent and controversial Bills dealt with North Sea oil operations.

The Oil Taxation Bill closely followed the recommendations of the Public Accounts Committee, chaired by Edmund Dell in our opposition days.[1] Now, appropriately, it was he, as Paymaster-General and a Treasury Minister, who moved the Second Reading. Referring to the great and once-for-all benefit the country could receive from the treasures below the sea, he said,

[1] See pp. 38–40 above.

The first point is that not all of it will benefit this country unless the measures in the present Bill are enacted. Many of the original licensees are subsidiaries of foreign-owned companies, and there could be a large balance-of-payments loss through remittance overseas of their share of excess profits unless corrective action was taken. So one of the Government's first priorities is to ensure that new tax arrangements will protect the balance of payments by ensuring that the Government retain a significant part of the earnings of North Sea oil operations in this country. In fact the only way of doing this is by increasing the Government's share of our profits.

This Bill achieves that through the introduction of a new tax, the petroleum revenue tax, and the tightening up of the corporation tax régime which accompanies it . . .

The second priority, of course, is to increase the nation's revenues and to secure for the community a reasonable share of the profits of North Sea oil. We would patently not so do under the arrangements hitherto in force. We have a clear duty to provide for the public as a whole to receive a fair share of the benefit from the arrival of North Sea oil, and this is reinforced by the balance-of-payments considerations to which I have referred.[1]

He made it clear that though the Bill was designed to claw back revenues from foreign concerns, the tax provisions would not discriminate between British and foreign licensees.

Although the Bill represented a total reversal of the policies of the previous Government, by measures which had aroused great political controversy when we had attacked those policies, it received an unopposed Second Reading, and received the Royal Assent on 8 May 1975.[2]

A further complicated Bill relating to the North Sea was the Petroleum and Submarine Pipelines Bill, introduced later in the session. On 30 April the Second Reading was moved by Eric Varley, Secretary of State for Energy. He was in an exuberant mood.

This is a historic week for Britain and the British people. This is the week which will see the start of the passage through Parliament of measures which will place in the hands of the British people control of the last two basic resources the use and deployment of which are not answerable to the British people and their Parliament . . .[3]

(The other was the Community Land Bill, which had received its Second Reading the previous day.)

Eric Varley went on to quote from a speech I had made in Oxford just before polling day the previous October:

[1] *Hansard*, vol. 882, cols 459–60.

[2] While the Bill was still in Committee, Edmund Dell made a statement to the House on the Government's proposals for levying tax, including easier terms for smaller companies and less remunerative oil fields, and a lower incidence during the early periods of tapping the oil. The Petroleum Revenue Tax was set at 45 per cent (*Hansard*, vol. 887, cols 290–92). In 1978 the Government announced a further increase in the 'take' from the oil companies in respect of new fields under exploration.

[3] *Hansard*, vol. 891, col. 482.

'God gave the land to the people, He gave the seas to the people and the treasures beneath the seas. There is no record that when He made the firmament and the seas He ordained that the profits from the wealth beneath the seas should accrue in full to private investors or rich multi-national oil companies.'[1]

The purpose of the Bill was to supplement the Oil Taxation Bill in ensuring to the British people full participation in the benefits of North Sea oil.

Except for the United States, every major oil-producing and gas-producing nation in the world has taken participation in the producing industry. I am not referring only to the OPEC countries, but also to Norway, Canada, Australia, New Zealand, and all the EEC members with substantial oil and gas production or prospects – France, Italy, Holland, Ireland and Denmark.[2]

Although the Conservative Opposition were opposing the Bill, he quoted Mr Heath as having said – as Leader of the Opposition a year before – that he regarded 'carried interest' for existing licences as a major option and added that a Government could do what they liked with future licences. He further quoted the Opposition spokesman who a year before to the day had said in Oslo that 'the last Conservative Government had by no means ruled out' participation.

This was now to be assured by the establishment of the British National Oil Corporation (BNOC), which could hold licences as sole licensee, which would ensure to the community all the net revenues of successful exploitation of oil finds. It would hold the Government's participatory interest in production licences, in partnership with private companies, and could become sole licensee and operator in future licences.[3]

Though the Bill was opposed by the Conservatives and Liberals, the Second Reading was passed by 282 to 258. It received its Third Reading on 29 July, and became law on 12 November.

But the major legislation of the session covered the establishment of the National Enterprise Board. This had been party policy in two General Elections,[4] but even while the necessary legislation was being prepared[4] the need for it was sharpened by a totally unexpected crisis in private industry.

In September we had had to meet an overnight crisis in Ferrantis, a spearhead of British industrial innovation. It was caught by a severe liquidity crisis, exhausting its overdraft limits with the National Westminster Bank.

[1] *Hansard,* vol. 891, col. 482.
[2] *Ibid.*, cols 485–6.
[3] In the autumn of 1978 it was reported that a consortium headed by BNOC had discovered a rich find in a new area of exploitation.
[4] See pp. 29–31 and 33–6 above.

It did not stand high in the City: the brilliant Ferranti brothers were regarded as too theoretical and not profit-minded enough. In 1974 it was earning about £500,000 on a turnover of over £86 million. Just as a receiver was due to go in, the Department of Industry injected £8.7 million of Government equity finance, plus £6.3 million of loans. Management changes were made, and the somewhat sprawling company divided into five operating divisions. In 1977 it showed operating profits of over £6 million on a £125 million turnover. By 1978 NEB effectively held 62 per cent of capital, including non-voting shares about to be enfranchised, and Ferranti was ready for its first Stock Exchange listing.[1]

Sir Don Ryder (now Lord Ryder) had joined the Government service as an industrial adviser. We had announced that he was to become Chairman of the NEB when it was set up. In the meantime, following many post-war precedents, he was to head a shadow board in advance of its statutory establishment. Tony Benn wanted him attached to the Department of Industry, but I decided that he should be formally appointed, ad interim, as Industrial Adviser to the whole Government, and be attached to the Cabinet Office, reporting in fact direct to me.

The problem was that the NEB did not exist, and could not exist until the Industry Bill became law. But industrial crises have a habit of not waiting on legislation.

Before the NEB could become law, I was shocked to hear that British Leyland, formed in 1967–68[2] by the merger of the successful Leyland truck and bus manufacturing concern with the ailing British Motor Holdings (Austin-Morris *et al.*), was facing a liquidity crisis. Were it to go under Britain would be without any major nationally controlled motor firm, with devastating consequences for our balance of payments. Any necessary action would clearly fall within the remit of the NEB. Leyland, the Government was clear, had to be saved. I therefore asked Don Ryder, on 4 December 1974, to head an inquiry into the position, with a fairly clear remit to report on what was necessary to save the maximum possible out of the wreck.

Two days later the Secretary of State for Industry told the House of the serious situation the Leyland company was facing, and announced the inquiry Sir Don Ryder was to conduct. On 18 December Tony Benn announced the other members of the inquiry team. Two would be drawn from the members of the Industrial Development Advisory Board, set up under Mr Heath's Industry Act, 1972. From that time IDAB had earned a reputation for toughness in its inquiries: the two members of the Leyland inquiry were Mr R. A. Clark, Chief Executive and Deputy Chairman of Hill Samuel, the merchant bankers, and Mr Harry Urwin, a high official of the Transport and General Workers' Union with a lifetime's experience of the industry. The other members were a chartered accountant, a partner in Peat,

---

[1] See p. 149 below.
[2] See *The Labour Government 1964–1970*, pp. 439 and 482.

Marwick, Mitchell, and the former Chairman and Chief Executive of Ford of Europe, completing a formidable and experienced team.

The inquiry took the best part of three months. Though this meant a serious delay in getting the NEB established, it became clear that it would in fact have to be the instrument to provide help for Leyland, should that prove necessary.

Meanwhile emergency assistance was needed. In his 18 December statement the Secretary of State, invoking Section 8 of Mr Heath's 1972 Act, moved a Parliamentary resolution authorizing financial guarantees to Leyland's bankers, to a figure not exceeding £50 million. Despite strong Conservative criticism, the financial facility was endorsed by 149 to 13, the opposition being mainly Liberals and a handful of Conservatives.

The Committee reported on 26 March 1975. They revealed a situation even more serious than anyone could have realized in December. An abridged version of the Report, to avoid giving sensitive information useful to competitors at home and abroad, was published. After full Cabinet consideration of the issue, I decided myself to make the statement – necessarily a very long one – to Parliament about the inquiry and our decision.

The report, I told the House, recommended that the vehicle production industry ought to remain an essential part of the United Kingdom economic base, and that British Leyland should therefore remain a major vehicle producer. But urgent action was needed to remedy Leyland's weaknesses revealed in world markets. A capital investment programme was needed to enable new models to be introduced, and also an immediate and massive programme to modernize plant and equipment. The report was highly critical of Leyland's organizational structure as being harmful to its efficiency and future development.

Leyland should be organized in four separate businesses, dealing with cars, trucks and buses, special products and international activities. To this end there should be the maximum delegation of authority from the chief executive of the corporation to the four managing directors of these new units. More productive use must be made of existing and new capital investment; there must be more realistic manning levels and better mobility and interchangeability of labour.

The report estimated that the investment programme would cost about £1,500 million at constant prices over seven years, equivalent to £2,800 million on the assumptions made by the team about the future course of inflation. Half the estimated sum should be generated from within the company, but some £1,400 million (on the inflation basis) would have to come from outside sources. £900 million of this would be required up to 1978: £200 million of it should come from the continuation of existing temporary borrowing facilities, £200 million by a new equity subscription and £500 million by long-term loans. A further £500 million, it was estimated, would have to be found by means of long-term loans between 1978 and 1982. The proposed new equity contribution, it was recommended, should be by way of a rights issue underwritten by the Government. At the same time the Government should offer to buy out existing shareholders at 10p per share. In addition, as part of the financial reconstruction, the Government should be prepared to provide the whole of the further £500 million to British Leyland between 1976 and 1978, should no part of this be available from other sources.

> The Government accept the Ryder Report as a basis of future policy towards British Leyland and have already started upon discussions with the board of British Leyland with the aim of putting these proposals into effect. The Government agree with the proposal that they should offer to buy out existing shareholders and underwrite a new rights issue. In this way the shareholders will be given a fair choice between selling their shares at 10p each or retaining them and, if they wish, taking an additional stake in the company at the same price. The Government also accept that they may be required to provide £500 million of extra capital to British Leyland between 1976 and 1978 if none is available from other sources: the question of funds beyond that date will be a matter for later consideration. In return for this massive investment of public money the Government intend that they should have a majority shareholding in the reconstructed company.[1]

Meanwhile, to help with working capital, the Secretary of State, I said, would shortly be laying before the House a draft order seeking authority for an increase of up to £50 million in the guarantees already approved by the House of Commons. On that occasion the Secretary of State would inform the House of the Government's proposals for providing the longer-term financial support, a substantial part of which would come from the Conservatives' 1972 Industry Act, and introduce any necessary legislation.

Following the initial injection of equity capital in 1975, the Government would determine its releases of the further stages of Government funding in the light of the contribution being made to the improvements in the performance of British Leyland by better industrial relations and higher productivity: 'This is a condition to which the Government attach great importance.' For this reason the company would be required to put forward 'annual business plans' before further funds were provided, covering improvement in industrial relations and productivity and putting forward precise investment and operating programmes for specific Government approval within the system of planning agreements.

> The Government-owned majority shareholding in British Leyland will come under the National Enterprise Board once this new body has been set up, and arrangements for scrutiny will be worked out with the board. The aim will be to satisfy the criteria for the provision of public funds on such a vast scale while at the same time allowing the company to operate on an effective basis without day-to-day Government intervention.

[1] *Hansard*, vol. 890, cols 1742–8.

The commitments we were entering into were prodigious, and there could be no certainty that the cost of saving Leyland might not be even more than the working party had estimated.[1] But we could ignore neither the cost to the balance of payments nor the effect on employment if Leyland were suffered to go under. Leyland's direct exports from Britain in 1974 had reached almost £500 million. Moreover,

> The company employs over 170,000 people directly in this country, and the livelihood of several hundred thousand more is dependent upon it. I must tell the House that in this decision a million jobs are at stake.

There was no doubt about the gravity with which this announcement was received by all parties in the House. The Conservative Front Bench fairly asked for time to reflect on it. When however I emphasized the measure of the crisis, by saying that while the company was not bankrupt, failure of the Government to act on the lines I announced would have meant Leyland going into liquidation or a receivership, some Conservatives shouted 'No' to my suggestion that such action would have been the last thing MPs would wish.

As more Conservative back-benchers criticized the decision, I warned again about the loss of a million jobs, if the action on which we had decided were not taken. The announcement was warmly received on the Labour side, but it became clear that the debate to give Parliamentary approval to the expenditure could be very controversial.

When the British Leyland Bill came before the House for Second Reading it was strongly attacked by both Conservatives and Liberals. The vote was 282 in favour, 261 against. The vote on the Money Resolution authorizing the necessary expenditure was carried by a majority of 19. A further Financial Resolution to increase the December vote for interim aid was carried at midnight by 226 to 58.

Because of the unprecedented nature of the action taken by the Government, the Bill was not sent to a Committee of the House, meeting upstairs, but taken on the floor of the House. It went through speedily, and the one contested clause and the Third Reading went through with majorities of over 40.

Although the Chairman-designate of the NEB was in charge of the Leyland inquiry, and the NEB was to be the channel through which the massive contribution was paid, this body still had no formal existence. That depended on the enactment of the Industry Bill, which had been foreshadowed in the Queen's Speech. The Bill received its Second Reading on 17 February 1975, and was then referred to a Committee upstairs. Progress was slow. The Conservatives were fighting the Bill line by line, as of course they were entitled to do. On 12 May the Government came back to the floor of the House to seek a 'timetable motion', or 'guillotine' as the procedure was first

---

[1] It was.

known after Gladstone's Government lost their patience with obstruction from Irish MPs on his legislation. By that time the Industry Bill had had twenty-nine days in Committee, and the timetable motion restricted the remaining days there to eleven together with three days on Report (to the House in full session) and Third Reading. Even with the guillotine the Bill did not pass its Third Reading until 3 July, and – even though the Lords nobly agreed to sit in September on outstanding legislation – it was not until 22 November that the Lords' Amendments were disposed of, either by agreement or contested divisions, on one of which the majority sank to a mere seven. Moreover, in the summer the left themselves were becoming disenchanted with the measure. A group of them had fought the Remuneration, Charges and Grants Bill, which had put legislative teeth into the anti-inflation statement of 11 July, even to the point of voting against the Government. By November their disenchantment with the Government's policies was even more vocal, and though the Industry Bill went through, left-wing members tried to stiffen its terms, and made it clear that they regarded it as only a pale shadow of the proposals they had fought for in Opposition days.

They joined with the Conservatives, though from different ends of the Parliamentary spectrum, in criticizing the Bill's final form – even to the point of moving and voting on amendments – and when, almost at the end of the already unnaturally protracted session, on 22 October, the Lords' Amendments came up for acceptance or rejection, the House went right through the night to 5.46 a.m. It received the Royal Assent on 12 November, only seconds before the House was prorogued by Royal order to mark the end of the 1974–75 Session.

The Act not only made a legislative honest woman of the NEB;[1] it contained the framework for the 'Planning Agreements' which had so excited the National Executive's interest in the halcyon Opposition days of 1973. The relevant sections were warmly commended to the House, on Second Reading, by the Secretary of State, though, in accordance with the Cabinet's decision, they were commended to the House as 'voluntary in character'.

> The Planning Agreements will, we believe, allow us to move towards a more successful and constructive tripartite dialogue between Government, management and workers in the firms concerned, and managements will also get the benefit of greater disclosure of Government forecasts to help them in their own planning. These Government forecasts will be more likely to be accurate because they will be based upon a greater disclosure from the firms.

[1] The Secretary of State announced that the NEB would have an initial statutory tranche of £700 million with power to increase this amount, given Parliamentary approval, to £1,000 million. This sum, he explained, was in addition to the £550 million provided for under Section 8 of (Mr Heath's) 1972 Industry Act, subject to approval for further successive sums, and an unlimited sum under Section 7 of that Act. He went on to say that the Conservative Government of 1970–74 had provided public subsidies, by grants, incentives and other inducements, of £2 million a day.

Despite the Minister's assurance, the CBI became increasingly worried about the dangers, as they saw them, of Planning Agreements, and sent a very high-powered delegation to see me while the Bill was in Committee. Following my own reassurances, I took the opportunity, when addressing the CBI's annual dinner on 20 May, to stress the voluntary nature of the proposed Agreements, but they were hardly reassured.

In any event the TUC were in difficulties about them. Who should be the 'representatives of the workers' in the tripartite procedures? More than one leading trade unionist made it clear that his union's representative should be one of his own officers, either a regional representative or a 'national officer' specializing in the problems of the particular industry. Others, including the Secretary of State, Tony Benn, clearly wanted shop-floor representatives, presumably chosen by, and probably from, the shop stewards.

The more I thought about it, the more another anxiety plagued me. The Planning Agreements would be a charade unless the firm was going to reveal its plans, not only for this year's production, but for future developments, including, for example, in a scientific or technological undertaking, some new great advance, the success of which depended on total secrecy, especially so far as rival firms – foreign-based as well as British – were concerned. All advanced countries live in an age of industrial espionage. There are fortunes to be made in the sale or theft of industrial secrets. If the trade union representative, who under the Planning Agreements system was to have access to his firm's innermost secrets, were an employee, e.g. a shop steward, he would have to be tied to the firm for life, by some new statutory form of serfdom, to provide a guarantee against leakage or other abuse.

In the event, up to the time of writing, more than three years after the Second Reading of the Bill, not a single Planning Agreement has been negotiated in respect of a privately-owned venture; the only Agreement in force is with a publicly-owned industry – the National Coal Board.[1]

The NEB on the other hand has been a major force in industrial reorganization and modernization. By early 1979 the Government decided to make a massive increase in its resources. The statutory limit of £700 million (which could be increased by a Parliamentary vote to £1,000 million) was increased to £3,000 million, with provision for further increases by an Affirmative Resolution of the House of Commons to £4,500 million.[2]

Contrary to the revolutionary hopes which surrounded the NEB when it

---

[1] A Planning Agreement was negotiated with Chrysler UK in 1978, but the negotiations for the Peugeot take-over supervened: at the time of writing work on a new Agreement is just beginning. An Agreement was in course of negotiation with British Steel, but the crisis in the industry led to a new approach to the question of Government relations with steel.

[2] At this time the NEB's investment in industry had reached a little over £1,250 million. Investments taken over from the Government, including Rolls-Royce, amounted to £497 million; other investments up to the end of 1972 were £272 million, and investments in 1978 about £490 million.

was conceived in Opposition days, Eric Varley's department – following the spirit of the *Regeneration of Industry* White Paper – ensured that it would not operate like an industrial rogue elephant. It had to operate within the existing rules governing the provision of industrial finance. The Secretary of State promised Parliament that the guide-lines under which it would operate, in accordance with the Industry Act 1975, would be promulgated by him, and all the rules published. For example, while it could make loans, provide guarantees, engage in joint ventures or make any other form of financial commitment within a limit of £25 million for each project, above that sum it could act only with the approval of the Secretary of State. In all cases where a proposed commitment exceeded £10 million, or raised new or significant policy issues, the NEB should give the Secretary of State reasonable notice of its intentions, so that he could as necessary prevent or qualify such exercise of its powers.

The '*NEB guidelines: final version*' were published in the *Trade and Industry Journal* (24 December 1976), in the form of a statutory Direction to the NEB under Section 7(1) of the Industry Act. This statement covered more than three and a half closely-printed pages of the *Journal*.

The key passages are reproduced as Appendix VIII. The most important, set out in thick black print in the *Journal*, are designed to avow that the NEB, in acquiring shares or stock in any privately-owned listed company, must act in conformity with the requirements of the law and of existing Stock Exchange practice in respect of private take-over bidders. Where the NEB acquires shares enabling it to exercise control over 10 per cent or more of the effective voting stock it has to give notice to the Secretary of State, and also in cases raising new or significant policy issues. It has also to get his consent – as provided by Section 10 of the Industry Act – where the cost of acquiring share capital exceeds £10 million or where the acquisition would give the NEB 30 per cent or more of the voting rights of any company.

But NEB was not the only instrument with strong powers of intervention in industry. The 1975–76 Parliamentary session saw the establishment of the Scottish and Welsh Development Agencies, created and funded for the purpose of assisting new industrial ventures in the two countries. The Scottish Agency received £200 million (with powers to increase it to £300 million) and the Welsh Agency £100 million (with powers to increase it to £150 million for this purpose).

Both Agencies got off to a quick start. In evidence before the Committee of Inquiry into Financial Institutions, the Scottish Agency reported that in its first eighteen months it had investigated 152 cases for assistance, twenty-eight being accepted with a further twenty-five under assessment or negotiation. Of the original statutory provision of £200 million (rising to £300 million with Treasury and Parliamentary approval), some £100 million, it was estimated, could go quite speedily to investment in existing industry, and to industrial expansion. In this task it emphasized the importance of its authority to build factories and to buy land, claiming that it had already become one of the major industrial landlords in the country.[1]

In parallel evidence to the Committee, the Welsh Development Agency, working with direct Government assistance deriving from earlier powers, including the authority to reclaim land from nineteenth-century desolation, had already been responsible for £45 million manufacturing industry.[2]

In the Industry Bill 1978,[3] the Scottish limits of £200 million and £300 million could be increased, given Treasury and Parliamentary approval, to £500 million and £800 million respectively. The same legislation provided that the WDA's statutory limits of £100 and £150 million could be increased by order, given the relevant approval, to £250 million and £400 million respectively.

For some time I had had in mind a change of ministerial responsibilities in the industry area. This would have been very difficult, provocative indeed, during the period of the referendum, and public comment would have linked such a change with arguments over the EEC. But I felt that my intention should be known. During the Jamaica Conference, therefore, I planted a story – the only time I have taken such action in my whole period of office, 1974–76. The High Commissioner gave a reception for the British press corps in the garden of his residence. At an appropriate point I asked Harry Boyne, political correspondent of the *Daily Telegraph*, a paragon of discretion, to disengage himself in a little while, and go to a room the High Commissioner had reserved. I was waiting there and I stressed that while he could use the story – that Tony Benn was going to be moved, sideways, to another department – it should not be date-lined 'Jamaica'. As it happened, he was not returning direct to London, but having a month's holiday touring Florida. The *Telegraph* accordingly ran a story 'from our Parliamentary staff' that Tony was to be moved to pastures new. Strangely, though Fleet Street clearly took the story as authentic, the Lobby journalists, usually most active in political forecasting, failed to forecast the new Industry Secretary.

On the Monday evening after the referendum result I began my reshuffle, telling Tony I was moving him to Energy. He took it extremely hard, and it looked virtually certain that he would choose to retire to the back-benches,

[1] *Committee of Inquiry into Financial Institutions*, Evidence, vol. 6: Written and oral evidence of the Scottish Development Agency, pp. 149–87, and 189–209. See Annex I to the evidence, pp. 173–80, for some of the principal undertakings supported by the Agency, much of them through equity and convertible loan stock.

[2] *Committee of Inquiry*, Evidence, vol. 8: at the time of reporting the Agency had £25 million worth of factory building under construction, and a further £15 million on the drawing-board. On land reclamation, old colliery sites, etc., the Agency was planning to deal with 12,500 acres in the three years 1978–80. This compares with a figure for the whole of Wales of Government assistance for just eight acres in 1964, before the incoming Labour Government of that year smartly stepped up the programme.

[3] This Bill was due to secure its Third Reading in the Lords, before submission to the Queen for Royal Assent on the day the manuscript of this book in final form was returned to the publishers.

the last place where I wanted to see him. Late that evening Michael Foot
came to intercede on his behalf, but I made it clear that my mind was made
up, and told Michael – as I had emphasized to Tony – that Energy would be a
wonderful field in which to deploy *his* energy. Eric Varley, to whom I had
offered the job of Industry Secretary – saying that I was prepared to move
Gerald Kaufman over to help him – was very chary, and when he heard
through the grapevine of Tony's reaction came to tell me that he would not
accept if Tony resigned, as appeared highly probable. However, the next day
Tony came to see me again, and when I asked him straight out whether he
was refusing it, he said – not with his usual charm – of course he'd have to
accept it. Eric then came into line.

Within hours Tony had settled into his new role, which in fact has given
him more 'job-satisfaction' than his previous appointment. Not least, and I
suspect that he came to realize this, it gave him a closer contact with the
miners (a potential power-base for any future ambitions he might naturally
have been harbouring?). All this and North Sea too.

The July crisis and the overloading of the legislative programme created a
torrid Parliamentary situation. Not only were many left-wing Labour MPs
disenchanted by the pay legislation, to the point of actively opposing it, but
there was trouble from the Lords who, just as both Houses were due to
rise for the summer recess, found themselves faced with major legislation,
the Remuneration, Charges and Grants Bill being of top urgency, and the
Industry Bill waiting in the wings. At the same time the Government were
ploughing on with the Aircraft and Shipbuilding Bill, the one major nationalization measure of the 1974 Parliamentary programme. This was too much.
In fact, as already recorded, their Lordships nobly offered to meet during
the Commons recess, in October, to deal with the Industry Bill, a gesture
which must be unprecedented in modern times. In fact they met throughout
the week of the Conservative Party Conference. But, not unnaturally, they
made it clear that to ask them to occupy further time on the Aircraft and
Shipbuilding Bill, a major nationalization measure which had not even
gone through the Commons, was unreasonable.

James Callaghan and I returned from the Helsinki Conference just as this
constitutional crisis was coming to a head, and I was immediately involved
in meetings with the Leader of the House and the sponsoring ministers. We
accepted the deferment of the Aircraft and Shipbuilding Bill. But more than
that, as a result of representations from the House of Lords we entered into a
concordat, still effective and now virtually an unwritten rule of the constitution, laying down that the Lords should not be asked in any session to
receive a major Bill after Easter, except in a case of emergency.

The castaway Aircraft and Shipbuilding Bill was to face further storms on
its way to the statute-book. Introduced in the next session, 1975–76, it spent
fifty-eight sitting days in Standing Committee. Its legal standing was
challenged in the House by a Conservative back-bencher, Mr Maxwell-

Hyslop, as having an element of 'hybridity'. (A Public Bill is in order if it encompasses an entire defined group of persons, properties or assets, defined in general terms, but not if it takes in an individual concern outside such a group.) The Bill, it was ultimately held by a Speaker's ruling, included a different type of concern, the Marathon (Clydeside) shipyard, building vessels for the North Sea Oil operations. The Speaker's certification was unfortunately challenged by Michael Foot, now Leader of the House in James Callaghan's Government, by means of a procedural motion rejecting hybridity. In the vote on this motion, the House divided 303–303, the Speaker, following precedent, throwing his casting-vote in favour of the Government motion. Later activities of Mr Maxwell-Hyslop led to his hybridity argument securing the Speaker's approval. Weeks of examination followed by the Examiners of private bills, and when the Bill finally emerged, and was passed by the Commons, the Lords rejected the inclusion in it of ship-repairing yards. At the end of further protracted proceedings, when the Government asked the House to 'disagree with the Lords in the said Amendment' two right-wing back-bench Labour MPs refused to follow the Government's whip; the Lords' Amendment was carried and ship-repairing was excluded. The Bill itself, as so amended, finally obtained the Royal Assent on 17 March 1977, sixteen months after its first introduction in November 1975.[1]

---

[1] See Postscript 2 to this Chapter for later developments, and additional financial provision in respect of the NEB.

POSTSCRIPT 1: *The Pension Funds Revolution*

The growth of pension funds during and since the middle 1970s has created the biggest revolution in the British financial scene in this century. Surprisingly it was almost totally unperceived by political or even financial commentators until very recently. The *Hansard* parliamentary index records only four Parliamentary questions during my final two-year period at No. 10, 1974–76: three of these are about benefits.

Throughout the nineteenth century and the first three quarters of the twentieth, the main source of investment funds was the private sector. Inflation and the taxation policies of successive governments diminished the net contribution from private savings. For a brief period the investments of insurance companies in respect of life assurance took the lead, but since 1975 the pension funds have surged ahead, as the following table shows:

Net acquisition of assets by Life Assurance and Pension Funds

|  | £ million | |
| --- | --- | --- |
|  | Life Assurance | Pension Funds |
| 1974 | 1,466 | 1,445 |
| 1975 | 1,784 | 2,215 |
| 1976 | 2,101 | 2,970 |
| 1977 | 2,863 | 3,185 |
| 1978 (first 3 quarters) | 2,819 | 2,720 |

At the time of writing (early 1979) the current assets of pension funds total nearly £26 thousand million if we include those pension commitments funded through life assurance companies, amounting to £8 thousand million. In terms of new investment in a single year, the amount in 1978–79, as just defined, is about £6.3 thousand million, and is expected to reach £20 thousand million in 1985, of which £13 thousand million will be pension funds, and the rest funded pensions undertaken by life assurance companies.[1]

Much of the evidence submitted to the Committee to Review the Functioning of Financial Institutions stresses the extent of the financial revolution represented by the pension funds.

About 40 per cent are currently in Government securities, in land and property (including agricultural land) and most of the remainder in industry, principally equities, though much public comment has centred on investments by certain publicly-owned industrial funds in works of art, mediaeval

[1] Recent estimates suggest that the pension funds, including funds managed by life assurance companies, may hold an accumulation of £100 thousand million in industry by 1985.

chalices or urban development in the Rue Royale and other central areas of Paris. Economic commentators have pointed out that in the six years up to and including 1977, undistributed industrial profits have accounted for 76 per cent of gross domestic capital formation: *net* new investment by the pension funds and life assurance are 75 per cent of the balance.

Evidence submitted to the Wilson Committee and comment in the financial columns of the press have highlighted a number of consequences.

Pension funds' investment in industry is largely concentrated on a relatively small number of industrial concerns: around 200 public companies is the figure usually quoted. A considerable proportion of those are now, for practical purposes, controlled by pension funds, though their practice is not to intervene unless their investments are felt to be at risk. When anything untoward occurs, or is feared, institutional investors usually get together in Investment Protection Committees, in consultation with the Bank of England and other city institutions. In general, the funds invest little directly in smaller businesses,[1] though together they have committed investments in centrally controlled City investment institutions such as Equity Capital for Industry.

Investment in industry raises the question of the degree of intervention which is desirable to protect their interests, apart from crisis situations. In a BBC Money Programme broadcast I was asked about this, and commented that if they did intervene they were open to criticism, equally they were criticized if they did not: they just couldn't win. But information put before the Wilson Committee suggests that some at least, as well as insurance company investors, tend to keep in touch through regular visits by fund managements, or merchant banks and other advisers, with large companies, and that this is welcomed by the industrial firms concerned. But a familiar criticism of their investment policies is that by their heavy concentration on equity investment in a couple of hundred firms they are mainly investing in 'past performance', and that they contribute little to new industrial investment except when they take up their rights in 'rights' issues.

Another criticism is that within a very few years their domination of the City will be such that the Stock Exchange as it has operated in the past will virtually no longer exist – to use a phrase of my own, instead of creating a market it will be reduced to the status of an electronic score-board on a county cricket ground, simply recording what is happening on the pitch.

There is also the question of motivation. Their choice of investments as well as the issue of intervention is and must be dictated by one single duty – ensuring and maximizing the inflation-proofed pension which that young sixteen-year-old, who left school this summer, will receive on retiring from work in the middle twenties of the next century. Any other consideration would be a breach of a very solemn legal trust and a betrayal of the duties of

[1] Some do. The National Coal Board fund is one which does, also trying to concentrate in town centre improvement in formerly blighted coalfield areas.

the trustees, usually representing employers and workers in the firm or industry concerned. To divert for one moment from this motivation, e.g. to help the Chancellor of the Exchequer launch a new gilt-edged issue or to embody some concept of the public interest in an industrial investment, would be a denial of the purpose for which their binding trust was created.

A high proportion of pension fund investment is represented by the funds set up for nationalized industries and services. If one takes the Coal Industry Pension Fund, controlled by trustees appointed by the National Coal Board and the National Union of Mineworkers respectively, it will be recalled that the nationalization Act in 1947 took over 747 colliery companies at a cost, in terms of compensating shareholders, of £393 million, after many months of bitter Parliamentary debate. In so far as the fund is investing in industry, one might be justified in using the phrase 'indirect nationalization', which would be equally true in respect of the railways, steel, shipbuilding and the Post Office. The coal industry's 'indirect' nationalization would probably reach £393 million in a year or two, depending on current decisions about industrial investment, though of course this does not allow for inflation since 1947. Since evidence recently submitted to the Inquiry into Financial Institutions suggests that the main investment institutions now own something like 60 per cent of the equity of British industry, it could well be said that private industry is increasingly becoming 'nationalized' in this sense without a single debate, or even mention in Parliament, without Parliament even noting what is happening.

POSTSCRIPT 2: *The NEB and Industrial Assistance*

Because of the Leyland crisis a substantial proportion of NEB's original capital had to go into that particular rescue operation, the success of which is still in doubt at the time of writing – to a major extent, one would conclude, because of the appalling disputes record associated with the assertion of shop-floor power and the persistence of over-manning. £450 million has been invested by the NEB in British Leyland against an original NEB capital limit of £700 million. A further £657 million of private capital has gone into BL.

In December 1978 the Government introduced a further Industry Bill, raising the original £700 million[1] to £3,000 million, with provision for a further £1,500 million by an affirmative order of the House. The size of the increase is in part due to a desire to involve the NEB in such new and/or developing industries as computers and micro-processing and also to use the Board as a major instrument in regional development. But the Bill is designed also to ensure that all borrowing by subsidiaries, not just that under-taken by wholly-owned NEB subsidiaries, will be included in the new limit. Further needs of BL and the highly successful NEB-assisted Rolls-Royce Engines will have to come out of the new limit. Rolls-Royce has been granted £250 million to develop its new aero-engine, the RB-211, 535.

Against the success of the Rolls-Royce investment, the NEB, in addition to its BL difficulties, has fared badly with Herbert Limited (formerly Alfred Herbert), who were in difficulty in the 1960s in the days of the Industrial Reorganization Corporation.

But the NEB has done well with another highly criticized investment, that in Ferranti in 1974–75. At that time neither the City nor any private investor could have been easily persuaded to see Ferranti through its formidable problems, and the NEB's intervention was greeted with criticism and gloomy prognoses – here was the NEB taking over another lame duck: it was widely said that it would never see its £15 million back. Ferranti, characterized by superb technical leadership, was in financial and management difficulties in 1975. The Government, ultimately through the NEB, took over five-eighths of the equity and half the voting rights, on putting in £8 million, plus a loan of £6 million. By 1977–78 its deficit had given way to a profit of £9.1 million, and Ferranti has proved robust enough to seek a fresh listing in the market – netting the NEB £10 million on this once hazardous venture. It is interesting to compare the comments of the financial press at the time the NEB moved in, with the *Economist*'s headline on the latest developments, 'London spawns a supershare',[2] concluding with 'All told, Ferrantis is quite a sexy package', and forecasting a queue of pension fund managers for any shares that may come

[1] Increased, by an order earlier in 1978, to the limit of £1,000 million originally laid down.
[2] 9 September 1978.

149

on offer. It was because of the investment institutions moving out that the NEB had had to make their risky entrance three years ago.

The NEB, it will be recalled, refused to go into Chrysler when the crisis of November–December 1975 occurred. The Chrysler 1978 postscript was the sudden announcement that the British French interests were being sold out to Peugeot. Despite the heavy financial investment the Department of Industry had had to make in Chrysler[1] the Secretary of State saw no alternative to accepting the Peugeot deal.

An interesting comment on the growing acceptability of the NEB to the City – anxious as each institution is to justify itself to the Committee of Inquiry into the City – was printed in the *Financial Times* survey on 15 January 1979:

THE CITY is currently more remarkable for its new openness – to discussion, criticism and even change – than for the funds its component institutions are providing to British industry.

Companies have not placed it under great pressure for money over the past 12 months . . . if the City's institutions did not have to provide industry with much finance last year, they talked about providing it more than ever before. The clearing banks produced a thick volume describing and justifying their activities. The Bank of England published a guide to small company finance and urged the banks to underwrite loans to small businesses. Every section of the City had to justify itself before the Wilson Committee which in turn published volume upon volume of evidence. The Stock Exchange geared itself up to convince the Restrictive Practices Court that it should be allowed to continue in its current form. By the standards of the very recent past, very little in the City remained sacred.

At the same time, the City moved visibly in the direction prescribed by the 'mixed economy'. The Bank of England's growing involvement with industry became conspicuous when it organised the rescue of Spillers, the troubled milling, baking and petfoods group. Its governor, Mr Gordon Richardson, spoke out forcefully on the changes necessary in the management and ownership of British joint stock companies.

Banks, merchant banks, and other institutions in the business of providing companies with capital, became reconciled to the existence of the National Enterprise Board, the Government-owned agency which owns BL and Rolls-Royce and which seeks by interventionist investment to force the pace of Britain's industrial development. Two years ago the NEB was the City's enemy: today Barclays, Midland Bank, Rothschilds, United Dominions Trust, and Finance For Industry are only some of the private sector institutions which are working in partnership with it.

The NEB has made the running in this reconciliation. In the multiplicity of its activities it undoubtedly has had a gingering effect on the financial establishment. It has won respect with its entrepreneurial approach. Its required objective of a 15–20 per cent return on invested capital (apart from BL and Rolls-Royce) gives it respectability. Currently it is tossing balls into the air faster than they are landing. It is not until a day of reckoning comes in 1981 that the City finally will establish whether the NEB is playing the private sector's game.

[1] See pp. 195–9 below.

The three Party leaders, Edward Heath, Jeremy Thorpe, and the Prime Minister, Harold Wilson, share a joke on the occasion of Lady Churchill's eighty-ninth birthday and the launching of the Churchill Centenary Appeal, 1 April 1974.

Signing NATO's new Declaration of Atlantic Principles in Brussels, 28 June 1974.

During a visit to the bomb-blitzed city of Belfast, Mr Wilson pledges the Government's determination that 'violence will not succeed', 18 April 1974. With the Prime Minister are Northern Ireland Secretary Merlyn Rees (right) and Under-Secretary Stanley Orme.

*Below left* With Dr Henry Kissinger, US Secretary of State, 8 July 1974.

*Below right* Harold Wilson greets President Makarios shortly after he had been deposed as President of Cyprus, 17 July 1974.

The Labour Cabinet at No. 10 Downing Street.

The leaders of the Common Market countries on the steps of the Elysée Palace during the renegotiation of Britain's contribution to the Community budget, 12 October 1974. From left to right: Leo Tindemans (Belgium), Helmut Schmidt (West Germany), Poul Hartling (Denmark), Harold Wilson (United Kingdom), French Premier Jacques Chirac, Aldo Moro (Italy), Valery Giscard d'Estaing (France), Liam Cosgrave (Ireland) and (behind) Gaston Thorn (Luxembourg).

Chancellor of the German Federal Republic Helmut Schmidt, chats to the Prime Minister on his arrival at Central Hall, Westminster, to address the Labour Party Conference, 30 November 1974.

The Prime Minister during his address to the Conference.

*Above* President Ford and Harold Wilson at the Brussels NATO Summit Conference, May 1975.

*Left* In conversation with the Soviet Party leader, Leonid Brezhnev, at the European Security Summit Conference in Helsinki, 2 August 1975.

*Below* The Prime Minister makes his speech at the opening of the 62nd Inter-Parliamentary Conference in Westminster Hall, 4 September 1975.

The Commonwealth leaders on board the Royal Yacht *Britannia* at the Commonwealth Conference in Jamaica, 1975.

At the Press conference called after the Prime Minister's shock announcement of his resignation, 16 March 1976.

' HEATH GONE ... THORPE GOING ... WHAT D'YOU THINK, HAROLD? ... HAROLD? ... "

A cartoon by Franklin that appeared in the *Sun*, 17 March 1976.

A cartoon drawn specially for the Prime Minister by Franklin which has never been published before.

Harold Wilson greets the Queen on the steps of No. 10 Downing Street on the occasion of his farewell dinner.

The other element in industrial strategy in 1974 to 1976 was the programme of industrial assistance under Section 8 of the 1972 Act. Whereas assistance under Section 7 is confined to 'assisted areas', there is no geographical bar on Section 8 schemes, which are of two main types:

a) Schemes of aid to encourage the modernization and development of specific sectors of industry. Each scheme is 'tailor-made' to meet the needs of the particular sector, after assessment of its problems. Schemes have been introduced in fourteen sectors since 1974.

b) General schemes not directed at particular sectors. Within this category there have been two schemes to encourage major investment in manufacturing industry: the Accelerated Projects Scheme, introduced in April 1975 to stimulate the bringing forward of projects during the recession, and the more general Selective Investment Scheme which followed it in December 1976. (The Energy Conservation Scheme is a third Section 8 general scheme of a different character, designed to encourage energy saving projects in industry and commerce. Another general scheme, the Product and Process Development Scheme, was introduced in July 1977 under the Science and Technology Act 1965; this makes selective financial assistance available for the development of new products and processes by manufacturing industry.)

Under these schemes assistance of £250 million was made available up to June 1978, for nearly 1,500 projects, with total project costs of £1,560 million; at that time there were further applicants under consideration which could lead to a further investment of over £2,300 million.

The National Economic Development Council (Neddy) has received progress reports on these schemes as part of its sector-by-sector reviews of British industry, and the reports have also featured in evidence before the Committee to Review the Functioning of Financial Institutions. It would be quite wrong to regard the great majority of them as public works schemes to cushion the suffering caused by unemployment. They have of course created new employment, but still more important has been the modernization of a number of industries, many old and traditional, which are now able to compete more effectively at home and abroad – at the same time giving a boost to new ventures. Amongst those substantially modernized or developed are ferrous foundries, machine tools, clothing, paper and board, slaughter houses and poultry meat processing (partly to meet EEC requirements), printing machinery, textile machinery, wool textiles, non-ferrous foundries, electronic components, drop forging and footwear, as well as general cross-industry investment to increase instrumentation and automation, or energy conservation.[1]

---

[1] For a study of the working of the programme in the wool textile industry – combing, worsted spinning, woollen spinning, worsted weaving and woollen weaving, see Maurice Corina in *The Times*, 12 September 1978.

6

# Chapter 8

## EAST–WEST: NORTH–SOUTH

THE period from October 1974 to the Parliamentary recess beginning in August 1975 was one of intense international activity. In addition to the renegotiations of the terms of our entry into the EEC, described in Chapter 5, the major events were the visits paid by the Foreign Secretary and myself to the United States and the Soviet Union in January and February 1975, the Commonwealth Conference in Jamaica in May, and the Helsinki Conference on Security and Co-operation in Europe (CSCE) from 30 July to 1 August 1975.

Since my return to Downing Street in March 1974 I had met President Nixon on two occasions, notably the celebrations in Brussels of NATO's twenty-fifth anniversary on 26 June, and President Pompidou's funeral service in Paris on 6 April. Mr Nixon was on his way to Moscow and discussed his plans there. In passing he referred dismissively to the Watergate accusations. By August 1974 he had resigned, and was succeeded by Gerald Ford. It was not until January 1975 that I made my first official visit to Washington to meet the new President.

On 29 January I spent the day in Ottawa for talks with Prime Minister Trudeau and his colleagues. A good deal of the discussion was about the forthcoming Commonwealth Conference in Jamaica, and the economic consequences of the oil-generated world inflation. That evening we flew to Washington – and almost failed to arrive in one piece. Just as we were landing and close to stalling speed an aircraft just taking off hurtled towards us – the ground staff had talked us in in the wrong direction. Thanks to the presence of mind of the RAF pilots we zoomed up, it seemed almost vertically, with what must have been a great strain on the aircraft's structure. We landed safely, and went to Blair House, the President's guest-house across Pennsylvania Avenue from the White House. At 10.30 next morning we arrived for the formal welcoming ceremony the White House lays on in the grounds. Bands played, troops marched – on this occasion the White House had decided to honour us by dressing them in the British uniforms of the period of the War of Independence! After the national anthems and an inspection of the guard of honour, brief speeches followed and we then went indoors for the first formal meeting. The President was attended by Henry Kissinger; we fielded the Foreign Secretary and Sir John Hunt, Secretary of the Cabinet.

Until lunch we discussed economic affairs, with particular reference to the world energy problem, the crisis facing developing countries as a result of oil shortage and the escalation of oil prices, and of food and raw materials. We were both concerned that the establishment of the oil price control through OPEC should not be followed by the creation of Phosphate-Pec, Bauxite-Pec, or Banana-Pec, all of which were being discussed by the producing countries concerned. We discussed with them proposals we were preparing to lay before the Commonwealth Conference, to which the Americans were quick to give general support, subject to examining the specific methods we were proposing.[1] We also discussed the line we should be taking in Moscow the following month, with particular reference to the negotiations designed to prevent the proliferation of nuclear weapons and the Strategic Arms Limitation Talks (SALT). Our discussions then and on the next day revealed close agreement on Dr Kissinger's step-by-step approach to a limited agreement between Egypt and Israel.

The afternoon was taken up with meetings with the Foreign Relations Committee of the Senate and the Foreign Affairs Committee of the House of Representatives. In the evening there was the traditional White House dinner with full protocol, and speeches by the President and myself.

After the necessary press conferences, TV and radio interviews, my speech and answers to questions at a Washington Press Club lunch, and the Foreign Secretary's briefing of the EEC Ambassadors to Washington, we were ready to fly to New York, where the next morning we met with Dr Waldheim and his colleagues. Most of the discussion was about the Middle East, particularly the Kissinger approaches, and about the breakdown of talks over Cyprus as a result of the intransigence of the Turks.

Dr Waldheim was concerned to outline his worries about the General Assembly, whose recent meetings had been even more marked than ever before by a ganging up of the majority of the Afro-Asian delegations. I agreed that it was certainly true that the Assembly had given the world the impression of a shambles and had given great encouragement to and all the ammunition desired by critics of the United Nations and of the Third World. I told him we had discussed this very pressing problem in Washington, and also with Pierre Trudeau, who had suggested that we should try to influence the forthcoming Commonwealth Conference. While Commonwealth Prime Ministers' meetings do not take binding decisions, they present an opportunity for thirty-four countries to discuss all aspects of world affairs. One of the most recent problems, it seemed to us, was that the Governments of Arab oil-producing states had been able to buy their way into the hearts of the Third World, which we said was particularly sad after all the aid and development training which the Israelis had given them. At the Jamaica Conference we would hope to try to persuade them that while, through their massive membership, the UN, and certainly the General Assembly, had become their fief, their sheer weight of numbers and oratory were not

[1] See pp. 161–4 below

enough to warrant their taking action effectively to destroy the United Nations.

We concluded our discussions by indicating the main features of the commodity initiative we should be putting forward at the Jamaica Conference in May.

The account of the Moscow visits, less than a fortnight after the Washington meetings, will necessarily be considerably longer. The White House talks were mainly an up-dating of the meetings I had had with the President in Brussels and Paris, which were to be followed by two more in the summer. The Kremlin talks were the most comprehensive a British Prime Minister had had for many years. I had myself paid three visits in 1964–70 (one for the British trade fair)[1] and Harold Macmillan's visit in 1959 had covered a great deal of ground. But the importance the Soviet Government clearly accorded to the February 1975 talks – the time allocated at all levels, and the thoroughness with which they had applied themselves to the agreements and protocols we were intended to sign – went beyond the Macmillan visit. The 1975 talks covered more ground than any since Winston Churchill's historic visits in the Second World War.[2]

We touched down at Vnukovo airport, Moscow, at 4.0 p.m. local time on 13 February, and were met by Prime Minister Kosygin. After the national anthems and a march-past by a formidable body of troops, we walked to the airport building. The walls were plastered with large posters of welcome in Russian and English, and outside was a larger gathering than I had seen before of Muscovites, waving their own and British flags. This Russian rent-a-crowd, deployed whenever Soviet hosts want to highlight a visit, was explained by Mr Kosygin as Moscow citizens who had given up their work to give us a welcome. The road from the airport carried a similar message. Alternate lamp standards were decorated with crossed flags, not only on our side of the road (the usual form for a Grade A welcome) but on the other side of the two-way system. (I commented to one of our staff, who had not been there before, that the test would be the array of flags, if any, on our return to the airport at the end of the visit.)

The Prime Minister took us to our dachas on the Lenin Hills, and after a brief stay we were taken to the Kremlin to meet General Secretary Brezhnev and the Prime Minister. There was unusual press interest, as Mr Brezhnev was known to have been ill, seriously it was thought, and had been away in the South for some weeks. This was his first public appearance. The photographers and TV men covered him from every angle; following their withdrawal we took our places on opposite sides of the huge table.

After a few opening words of welcome, Mr Brezhnev said he had noted that the Conservative Parliamentary Party in Britain had just elected a lady as

---

[1] See *The Labour Government 1964–1970*, pp. 213–15, 253–6, and 489–93.
[2] See Winston Churchill, *War Memoirs*, vols IV, pp. 425–49, and V, pp. 197–209.

their leader. This would give me someone to woo. I said that indeed our so brief relationship had started with a honeymoon period: on her first day as Leader of the Opposition I had paid her a visit in her room at the House of Commons as a gesture of courtesy. No doubt the gloves would be coming off soon.

In the first instance, Mr Brezhnev went on, we should discuss the question of strengthening and developing the relationship between Great Britain and the Soviet Union. No doubt our meetings would touch on economic matters, but the most important issues to discuss were political matters. The Soviet Government had no strict protocol or agenda to suggest, but he hoped we would feel that the discussions should be entirely free. (In the car from the airport Mr Kosygin had said that the Soviet leadership would leave with me the 'guest's privilege' of proposing the order of the agenda, but it might be sensible to have a wide-ranging discussion of a general nature to begin with. I had agreed.)

Mr Brezhnev who, in Russian fashion, desperately mixed serious discussion with badinage, referred to the several hundreds of troops at the airport that afternoon: they were, of course, the Soviet spearhead for attacking Europe.

I suggested that the talks should, of course, deal with the possibilities open to us for strengthening and developing the bilateral relationship over a wide range of subjects, and with contacts between the two Governments on world affairs during the forthcoming important phase of international conferences and assessments. In the field of bilateral matters, there should be a discussion of what could be done to increase trade and industrial co-operation, and participation in joint ventures, including the development of the Soviet Union's vast raw material resources, as well as of its technological and scientific manufacturing interests. There would also be possibilities of co-operation in cultural and scientific matters to discuss, including co-operation in medical research.

On international affairs, I said that as co-depository with the Soviet Union of the Non-Proliferation Treaty, Her Majesty's Government would like to discuss measures to reduce the risk of the spread of nuclear weapons and of competition between countries in nuclear weapons. The two sides should therefore consider what they could do together at the Review Conference due to be held the following May on these matters and also on chemical weapons, biological weapons and others.

Ministers, together with our accompanying experts, should review progress in other international conferences, including the Law of the Sea, the talks in Vienna on 'Mutual and Balanced Force Reductions' (MBFR), and those in the Geneva preparatory meeting aimed at getting the Conference on Security and Co-operation in Europe (CSCE) into being that summer. Progress, I said, had been slow in these Geneva talks. There had been some improvement in recent weeks but things had not yet gone anything like far enough. The Foreign Secretary and I were anxious to see sufficient progress made there for us to be able to hold the Summit later that year – we hoped, indeed, in the summer.

Mr Brezhnev asked what other matters we should like to discuss during our stay. James Callaghan raised the problem of the primary producers, facing increased costs of fertilizers and other essentials. Stressing the need for a fair return to primary producers in developing countries he referred to the work we were doing on world commodity policy.

We then returned to a more detailed discussion on the CSCE. Mr Brezhnev pointed out that not only had I emphasized the need to get the Conference in session: the United States, Helmut Schmidt of Germany and Aldo Moro of Italy had urged a speedy clearing up of problems so that the CSCE could meet. Predictably he was, in the talks, repeatedly to divert discussion into another dimension by criticizing America – the United States, he said, had sent to West Germany two brigades armed with nuclear weapons. They were not ICBMs, so they were not covered by the Strategic Arms Limitation negotiations, but if you were killed it did not make any odds which weapon had done it. (This is, of course, a familiar ploy: from my meetings with Molotov and Vyshinsky nearly thirty years before, I remember that all threats to peace derived from American actions.)

We should not waste our time, he said, on the fine points of 'Third Baskets' – the provisions for the CSCE dealing with human rights, reunification of families, nor even the integrity of states, the inviolability of frontiers and so on. There was a debate going on at that very time on the size and location of the zones in which all military manoeuvres had to be notified. These were not serious matters compared with hundreds of nuclear installations in West Germany. If the United States were prepared to take away those installations, the USSR would be prepared to proclaim the movement of even a single regiment right as far as the Urals. What people were worried about was the possibility of a terrible catastrophe, as a result of which the entire *white* race (*sic*) could perish. He knew what was meant, that was why he was dedicated to strengthening peace. That was the policy handed down by Lenin and that was what mattered, not baskets and cages. This was again familiar material: the Soviet Union wanted peace; any differences in approach or self-protective measures by other countries of their own interests, or any statement of their own approach to peace, was flirting with war.

I decided to get down to cases, and the need for an early summit on security and co-operation in Europe. Geneva had already established a number of useful confidence-building measures on which we should be able to agree. Mr Brezhnev had spoken of Third Baskets: 'the question involved might seem small in relation to the major issues of world peace, but they were part of the staff of life for ordinary people.' Mr Brezhnev had also spoken of the proposed agreement on the inviolability of frontiers. This was an issue of vital importance to Germany. My understanding of the Geneva discussions so far was that it was possible to reach agreement about the words to be used, but not on the question where – in any Conference document or communiqué – those words should come. This was surely a question which could be settled by mutual agreement, even if it meant putting the words in more than one place – putting them where the Soviet Government wanted them and elsewhere where the West wanted them. If we could not agree at Geneva, it was time to settle these matters in Helsinki, or wherever else we could agree to meet.

Mr Brezhnev picked up the reference to the peaceful change of frontiers. I replied that Britain would not support forced changes in frontiers. We *would* support the inviolability of frontiers. There must be some way of agreeing where to put the relevant words. As we reached the end of the meeting I suggested that the Foreign Secretary and the Soviet Foreign Minister should together get down to these questions on the Third Basket and on the inviolability of frontiers. Using a Russian word, I suggested the two of them should give a '*pinyok*' to the work of the officials at Geneva. The official record shows that this attracted 'Laughter' on the Soviet side: it also translates the word as 'push'. The Russians knew that a more correct translation would have been 'kick in the rear'.[1]

The following morning we met again from 11.0 to 1.20. Mr Brezhnev said he had intended that we should discuss bilateral questions. (In the end these were left to Mr Kosygin.) But, he said, he had had talks with his colleagues on the CSCE and they were ready to discuss the subject, so that a decision could be reached for inclusion in 'the documents'. The Middle East and Cyprus too. He suggested – and we agreed – that the two Foreign Ministers should work it out together. In the event, the Middle East was to come up again when I met him on the following Monday. On Cyprus, Jim Callaghan deplored recent Turkish moves on the island. When asked about the Common Market situation, I explained the principles on which the renegotiations were taking place. For his part Jim took up with Kosygin the problem of Portugal and the need to safeguard the independence of Mario Soares. I was to revert to this subject with the Soviet leaders during the Helsinki Conference.[2]

We were then entertained to lunch in the Kremlin by our hosts – the full treatment. Late in the afternoon we reached the time for speeches: both rather long and each requiring subsequent translation. (It always intrigues me to notice that each minute of the English text of a speech requires something like two or three minutes to render in Russian.) My own speech, partly going back to the changes in Moscow and the world since the trade agreement I negotiated with Mr Mikoyan in 1947, was mainly directed to explaining our position on the key issues for Helsinki.

[1] I knew the word because in the 1947 trade negotiations Anastas Ivanovich Mikoyan, then trade minister and deputy premier, had made a pun on the name of the Ministry of Food member of my delegation, Frank Pinnock.
[2] See pp. 172–3 below.

There had been trouble in the Foreign Office before we left for Moscow over one phrase I intended to use, of all things 'peaceful coexistence'. It seemed to be a dirty collection of words. While it was all right given the western interpretation, the Soviets had construed it differently. For me to use it would be to accept their interpretation. This I could not understand. If I used it, it would bear my interpretation. In any case Clement Attlee had not only used it, he had embellished it. To refuse to use it would be accepting the Russian right to interpret its meaning. The argument went on, though I was going to use it; when James Callaghan joined us in Moscow – he had visited Poland on the way there – he fully agreed with my intention. In my lunch speech I put it this way:

> ...what we have learned as we have lived together in this ever-shrinking world . . . is that, whatever our differences, we are in a very real sense members of one human family. Clement Attlee, a great leader of our country, who was Prime Minister when I first came here as a young trade minister, himself said in the context of the threat to world peace created by the menace of thermo-nuclear warfare, 'The only alternative to co-existence is co-death.'
>
> The challenge to world statesmanship is to find the basis on which we can co-exist.

Mr Brezhnev later picked up the Attlee quotation with great relish, and returned to it more than once.

In his own speech[1] he recalled

> The great Victory of the Powers of the anti-Hitler Coalition and the freedom-loving peoples over the Nazi aggressors and enslavers: there are grounds to recall that the Soviet Union and Great Britain have behind them the experience of a combat alliance in the fight for a just cause. You and I, Gospodin Wilson, like others of our generation, remember well enough that this was an alliance not only of Governments; it was also a fighting alliance of our armies and our peoples and a historic example of successful co-operation regardless of differences in social systems.

There was no reference to the leaders of that alliance. Stalin was already a non-person. Winston Churchill had presumably forfeited his right to a place in the pantheon of peace with his 1946 speech at Fulton, Missouri, and his call for an alliance against Soviet aggrandizement.

He spoke hopefully about the CSCE:

> ... a good start has been made. The All-European Conference on Security and Co-operation is working, though not at a very fast pace. This forum of 33 European States with the additional participation of the United States and Canada – a forum unprecedented in the continent's history – is called upon to lay a durable foundation of peace and good-neighbourly co-operation on the soil of Europe for a long historical period. No small amount of work has already been done, but in our conviction far from all that is necessary is being done . . .

[1] Printed as Appendix X.

He took a somewhat tough pro-Arab line on the Middle East:

> There are some who seem to want to offer the Arab peoples something like a
> soporific in the hope that they will calm down and forget about their demands
> for the restoration of justice, and the complete elimination of the consequence
> of aggression. But a soporific knocks you out only for a short time, and then
> you wake only to be faced with the same real life with all its problems.

He did not however take the Palestinian line that Israel had no right to exist:

> All this indicates that there is no substitute for a genuine and enduring peaceful
> settlement. And its postponement is inadmissible unless complete neglect is
> displayed for the destinies of the countries and peoples of the Middle East
> (*naturally, including Israel, whose people can hardly be interested in living end-
> lessly in a country converted into a military camp*)[1] and for the destinies of
> universal peace.

He knew perfectly well where I stood on these questions, and that I had
insisted in the then Shadow Cabinet that the Parliamentary Labour Party
should vote on a three-line Whip against the Heath Government's decision to
withhold spares and ammunition for British equipment supplied to Israel by
previous Conservative and Labour Governments during the Yom Kippur
War in 1973. Indeed, Said Hammami, London representative of the PLO
whom I knew well, and who was murdered by Palestinian extremists in
London in 1977, had told me that when Yasser Arafat had visited Moscow
in 1973, Mr Brezhnev had said, 'Why don't you talk to Harold Wilson? He
has more influence with the Israelis.' He was to return to the subject at our
final meeting the following Monday.

On the Saturday and Sunday we were in Leningrad, accompanied by
Deputy Prime Minister Kirillin, a Leningradian, and saw once again some of
the wonderful sights of that beautiful city, particularly of course the Hermit-
age, the relics of the Czar's palace then in course of restoration, the
fortress-prison of St Peter and St Paul, as well as the cruiser *Aurora*, said
to be the oldest ship afloat anywhere in the world, and the vessel from which
the shell was fired at Kerensky's Social Democratic forces in 1917, and which
ensured Lenin's victory.

We went to a gala ballet performance, the ballet at the Kirov theatre,
formerly the Czar's Mariinsky theatre – re-named by the Soviets after a
Communist who was murdered in the twenties. As we sat in the state box,
unchanged from Czarist times, James Callaghan leaned over and asked me
what it felt like to sit in the Czar's seat. 'Fine,' I replied. 'How do you feel,
sitting in Rasputin's?' Tragically, the leading ballerina slipped and fell in one
of her most difficult sequences. There was a shudder of horror from the
audience: I immediately asked for a special bouquet to be obtained and sent
to her dressing-room in the interval. At the end of the performance she
received an uproarious ovation from the entire audience.

[1] Author's italics.

6*

The two sides had a final meeting on the Monday morning, after which Mr Brezhnev asked for a brief restricted session, himself, myself, Sir John Hunt and the Soviet interpreter, immediately before the signing of the 'Agreed Statement' and other documents.

He simply asked me how I saw the Middle East situation. I expressed support for Kissinger's step-by-step approach, spoke of the hopes of a Sinai settlement which would involve Israel's relinquishing Abu Rudeis, but said they would not surrender any strategic area such as the mountain pass adjoining the oil wells. They would, in my view, have to come to terms with the Palestinian problem, but would be unlikely to yield territory in the Gaza strip, Sinai or – most of all – in the narrow belt of Israeli land between the Jordan and the coast. The Soviet leader made no comment.

We then went to the spectacularly-staged signing ceremony. The Joint Statement covering our talks is printed below as Appendix IX. The other five statements, declarations and 'programmes' covered Medicine and Public Health, the 'Long-Term Programme for the Development of Economic and Industrial Co-operation between the United Kingdom and the Union of Soviet Socialist Republics', the Programme for Scientific and Technological Co-operation between the two countries, the United Kingdom–Soviet Protocol on Consultation, and the Joint Anglo-Soviet Declaration on the Non-Proliferation of Nuclear Weapons.[1]

After the signing Prime Minister Kosygin came to a farewell lunch at the British Embassy. The speeches were brief, but Mr Kosygin, speaking without notes, used one phrase to which my attention was later drawn by the Soviet interpreter, doyen of them all, Viktor Sukhodrev:

> The talks between the British Prime Minister and Foreign Secretary and L. I. Brezhnev and all of us were truly historic and this visit will be a major factor in the history of Anglo-Soviet relations.

Mr Sukhodrev told me in the car that the particular word used by his Prime Minister, translated as 'historic', had a very special significance. It was usually used only to describe the historic defence of Leningrad against the Nazis – and Mr Kosygin had been, of course, the Mayor of Leningrad and architect of its defence at that time.

On the return to the airport the flags were still on both sides of the road, and the number of Moscow citizens who had 'given up work' to cheer us on our way had risen.

EEC meetings apart, the other major international conference of 1975 was the Commonwealth Heads of Government Meeting in Kingston, Jamaica, in late April and early May. It was the sixth I had attended. The first had been chaired by Clement Attlee in 1949, when nine Heads of Government

[1] The texts are printed in full in the White Paper presented by the Foreign and Commonwealth Secretary to Parliament on our return to London, Cmnd. 5924.

(including Rhodesia) and their advisers had been easily accommodated round the Cabinet table in Downing Street. Three I had chaired in London, in 1965, 1966 and 1969, and in addition had attended the Conference in Nigeria in January 1966 immediately following the Rhodesian 'unilateral declaration of independence' – a conference to be tragically followed by the murder of our host Abubakar Tafewa Balewa three days after the conference ended.

The arrangements were prepared by the Commonwealth Secretariat established by the 1969 Conference and given permanent accommodation in Marlborough House. But there was a not insignificant essay in pre-planning on which I insisted, to the dismay of the Foreign and Commonwealth Office. I said our delegation would sit there as 'Britain', not as 'United Kingdom'. The protocol experts had powerful arguments against this apostasy. My argument was more simple. Each country was due to be represented by its Head of Government. I was not going to sit next to Uganda if, as was always possible, Amin was going to be there. There are occasions when good taste must override protocol. This was one. Just before the conference I met Duncan Sandys by accident in the House of Commons lobby. He had great experience of Commonwealth affairs. He entirely agreed with me, and indeed said that even in pre-Amin days he had always insisted on the title 'Britain', despite protocolaire objections.

The Foreign and Commonwealth Office withdrew their objections, and I sat comfortably between President Seretse Khama of Botswana and Prime Minister Trudeau of Canada. In the event Amin did not turn up, but the point had been made.[1]

For several months we had been preparing an initiative for the Conference, namely on a world commodity policy, the need for which had been underlined by the oil and commodity price boom which followed the Middle East fighting in October 1973. It was a subject on which I had been keen from my days as a young minister, in 1946, when Clem Attlee had sent me to head the British delegation to the UN sixteen-nation conference on food, agriculture and commodity policy in Washington from September 1946 to January 1947.[2] In Opposition I had written and lectured on these matters, and in Government had spoken at successive Commonwealth conferences from 1949 onwards.

The departments were set to work on the theme in the autumn of 1974' under the general direction of Sir Donald Maitland, head of the Foreign Office's economic department.[3] In February I had given to President Ford an

---

[1] Perhaps Amin recalled the Singapore Conference of January 1971 when President Obote was unseated in an armed revolution staged by Amin during his absence there. I had repeatedly warned Milton Obote against him.

[2] See the debate on 6 February 1947, *Hansard*, vol. 432, cols 1986–2002, in which on Attlee's proposal I put the conference achievements and our contribution on record. Also *War on Want* (Association for World Peace, 1952), and my *The War on World Poverty* (London, 1953).

[3] Later HM Ambassador to the European Economic Community, Brussels.

outline of our proposals, which had a warm response, and also informed our partners in the EEC. The result was our initiative taken at the meeting of the Jamaica Conference, on 1 May 1975. At the same time we published a major study of the raw material situation, commodity by commodity, to indicate how our proposals would work.[1] As the conference drew near we were aware that we were in an intellectually competitive situation. Mr Forbes Burnham, Prime Minister of Guyana, had taken the lead among developing countries in working out plans for strengthening their economic power vis-à-vis advanced countries. There was even competition between us on who should open the economic debate, but he generously waved me on. For my part I was ready to join him in calling for acceptance of the fact, as I put it,

> that the relationship, the balance, between the rich and poor countries of the world is wrong and must be remedied. That is the principle on which my proposals rest: that the wealth of the world must be redistributed in favour of the poverty-stricken and the starving. This means a new deal in world economics, in trade between nations and the terms of that trade.

I called for a General Agreement on Commodities, to set alongside the General Agreement on Tariffs and Trade, signed at Geneva in 1947, when I had been ministerial head of the British negotiating team:

> First, we should recognize the interdependence of producers and consumers and the desirability of conducting trade in commodities in accordance with equitable arrangements worked out in agreement between producers and consumers.
> Second, producer countries should undertake to maintain adequate and secure supplies to consumer countries.
> Third, consumer countries for their part should undertake to improve access to markets for those items of primary production of interest to developing producers.
> Fourth, the principle should be established that commodity prices should be equitable to consumers and remunerative to efficient producers and at a level which would encourage longer-term equilibrium between production and consumption.
> Fifth, we should recognize in particular the need to expand the total production of essential foodstuffs.
> Sixth, we should aim to encourage the efficient development, production and marketing of commodities (both mineral and agricultural) and I should like to emphasize forest products – and the diversification and efficient processing of commodities in developing countries. We should not deduce from two centuries of history that there was any divine ordinance at the creation of the world under which providence deposited the means to primary production in certain countries, it was ordained that those minerals, or other products, should be exclusively or mainly processed in other countries.
> In saying this I repeat that in any general agreement, or other means to

---

[1] My speech setting out the principles and the 110-page supplementary document *World Economic Interdependence and Trade in Commodities* were laid before Parliament and published as Cmnd. 6061.

advance, we must lay heavy emphasis on the special needs of the poorest countries.

Now in practical terms, if we are to give specific content to these general commitments, specific action is called for. This action should, in my view must, include measures directed to the following ends:

1. To establish better exchanges of information on forward supply and demand.

2. To elaborate more specific rules to define the circumstances under which import and export restrictions may be applied to commodities.

3. To encourage the development of producer/consumer associations for individual commodities.

4. To give fresh impetus to the joint efforts of producers and consumers to conclude commodity agreements designed to facilitate the orderly conduct and development of trade. This could be done

   First, by identifying commodities appropriate to the conclusion of such agreements;

   Second, by analysing commodity by commodity the appropriate mechanisms for the regulation of trade within the framework of such agreements (including international buffer stocks, co-ordination of nationally held stocks, production controls and export quotas);

   Third, by examining ways in which any financial burden arising from these mechanisms may be appropriately financed.

5. To agree that the regulatory mechanisms incorporated in any international commodity agreement would be directed towards the maintenance of market prices within a range negotiated in accordance with the principles enshrined in the fourth general commitment.

6. To establish the framework of a scheme for the stabilization of export earnings from commodities.

These proposals will obviously need detailed study. There are already in prospect negotiations on a number of individual commodities including coffee, cocoa, tin and wheat. The United Kingdom has always belonged to previous commodity agreements and we shall play our part in the negotiations for these new agreements. Commodities will also be an important subject in the multilateral trade negotiations which are now getting under way and the European Community has stressed in its mandate for these negotiations its intention to take account of the interests and the problems of the developing countries and in particular of the least developed in all sectors of the negotiations.

Some commodities are of special, if not exclusive, importance to Commonwealth producers, tea and jute, for example, which have not shared in the recent commodity boom. Can we agree to tackle the problem of these commodities as a matter of urgency?

As my colleagues will see, in my specific proposals I have suggested that we look afresh at the possibilities for reducing price fluctuations. This could be done either through internationally held buffer stocks or through co-ordination of national buffer stocks and you won't find that the answer that is right for one is right for another commodity. At the same time my proposals recognize that commodities produced by the poorest countries are not on the whole susceptible to price stabilization agreements.

That is why I have suggested, as a complement to price stabilization, that we should examine schemes to stabilize export earnings. I propose this for a number of reasons. Such schemes are particularly helpful, one might almost say essential to countries where production is hit by drought or other natural disasters.

The proposals were well received by the Conference, though Forbes Burnham's more radical proposals, involving a degree of dispossession of assets of advanced countries, inevitably had a special appeal for Afro-Asian and Latin American Heads of Government. So far no progress has been made, and the gap between rich and poor has remained – in some respects it has grown wider. President Giscard's totally abortive North–South Conference, from which Britain was virtually excluded,[1] did not direct itself to the aims we had set forth.

The final communiqué – with its reference to Lomé, so important to the referendum campaign[2] – was agreed in our final session, and laid before Parliament on our return.[3] It recorded also our appointment of Sonny Ramphal of Guyana as the new Secretary-General of the Commonwealth Secretariat, in succession to Mr Arnold Smith of Canada; proposals for a Commonwealth Investment Bank; a report on the working of the Commonwealth Youth Programme; proposals for the future of the Commonwealth Foundation; and special studies on multinational corporations, a possible Commonwealth Centre for specialized medical services, the position of women in Commonwealth countries, and the 'brain drain' from less developed countries to more advanced countries in the Commonwealth and elsewhere.

Inevitably the Conference provided facilities for bilateral meetings outside the Conference Hall. I had two, for example, with Sheikh Mujib of Bangladesh – tragically he was murdered in a palace revolution on 15 August 1975 – and separate meetings with almost all Heads of Government. A number of the fringe meetings were directed specifically to action in Rhodesia, where the situation had been dramatically transformed by the Portuguese revolution and the new status of Mozambique. The Foreign Secretary and I had two meetings with African leaders.

On 2 May we met President Kaunda of Zambia and President Nyerere of Tanzania: a second meeting took place on 5 May with them, together with President Seretse Khama of Botswana, and Joshua Nkomo of Rhodesia. They knew they had no hope of persuading us to use military force through the newly-opened Mozambique to bring down Ian Smith's Rhodesian régime. But they pressed us to supply arms and money for the guerillas based in Mozambique and elsewhere, and operating or seeking to operate across the Rhodesian borders. This we flatly – and I am sure courteously – refused to do, and all their arguments and blandishments failed to change our minds. We did however agree, if the matter was pressed, to convene an early con-

[1] See pp. 201–3 below
[2] See p. 107 above.
[3] Cmnd. 6066.

stitutional Conference, whenever the auspices looked right for political change in Rhodesia.

On another occasion we met Bishop Muzorewa, a visitor to the Conference, who was pursuing a very different policy for changing the internal situation in Rhodesia.

The labyrinthine Geneva preparations for the Conference on Security and Co-operation in Europe (CSCE) went on so long throughout the spring and summer of 1975 that it became very doubtful whether we should be able to convene in Helsinki before the autumn. The Soviets gradually gave way on their procedural objections to certain agenda items, particularly those relating to human rights. Even so there was a last minute hiccup owing to a procedural disagreement between Greece and Turkey over Cyprus.

This problem was resolved and the Conference duly opened in Helsinki on 30 July. The 'Final Act'[1] was duly signed by all participants on 1 August. The meeting was as significant for the many bilateral meetings 'on the fringe' of Conference as for the official proceedings in Finlandia Hall. In straight bilaterals I met separately with President Ford, President Kekkonen our host, and the Heads of Government of Italy, Greece, Czechoslovakia, Turkey, Yugoslavia, Ireland, Poland and the Soviet Union. In addition the Foreign Secretary and I had a working breakfast with President Ford and Henry Kissinger; we gave a lunch at HM Embassy with the Americans, Germans and French at Head of Government and Foreign Minister level; and there were two simultaneous lunches respectively for the Heads of Government and Foreign Ministers of the EEC countries. The dinner given by President Kekkonen at the President's Palace gave further opportunities for bilateral talks before and after the dinner.

The main subject we discussed with the Americans was the increasingly serious situation in the Middle East. From the time of my Washington visit on the way back from Jamaica in May, I had been clear that President Ford was going through an 'agonizing reappraisal' over relations with Israel. He warned me that unless there were substantial moves to peace, involving a real change in Israel's attitude to their Arab nations, particularly in Sinai, the traditional American support of Israel would give way to a much tougher attitude. On a visit to London Dr Kissinger warned me that the President was working up to a definitive statement in June which would come as a great shock to the Israelis. In the event the statement left things open, but Kissinger in his shuttle movements between Jerusalem and Cairo was putting increasingly tough pressure on Israel. It was well known that I was very close to the Israeli leaders and was felt to be broadly pro-Israel on the basic questions – despite perfectly friendly relations with President Sadat and Prince Fahd of Saudi Arabia, both of whom paid official visits to London during this time.

[1] Laid before Parliament and published as Cmnd. 6198.

Equally the Americans knew that I was in touch with the Israelis in London, and had arranged to keep in touch with Israel's London Ambassador while in Helsinki. Moreover, on arrival in Helsinki on Tuesday 29 July I was contacted by Eppi Evron, a former minister in London and a personal friend. He explained that, having been working hard, he had decided to have a holiday, and had been able to borrow the Helsinki flat of the Israeli Ambassador to Sweden, who was accredited to Helsinki as well as Stockholm! He visited me after midnight, and the Americans were, of course, informed of our exchanges.

The following morning James Callaghan and I breakfasted with Ford and Kissinger; the Secretary of the Cabinet was with us and Ford had General Scowcroft there. The President expressed his gratification at the success of our referendum, and also his congratulations on our White Paper, earlier in the month, on inflation. He was optimistic about expansion in the US economy, as he was later at the Rambouillet Summit in November – only to be proved totally wrong in the event. American harvest prospects were good: this was welcomed by Jim Callaghan, who said that they were uniformly bad in the East European countries he had visited on the way to Helsinki, as they were in Russia. I perceived no sign of sorrow on the President's part at this news: the Americans were clearly hoping to secure some political dividend, however limited, from any export of grain. Jim reported briefly on his tour. He had been impressed by Gierek in Poland, but had found Hungary depressing. The lesson he had brought back from his visit was that it was important to put pressure on the Soviet Union on détente, particularly in relation to a forward movement on MBFR.

On the prospects for Helsinki, the President said that his administration was under some criticism about the CSCE, fears being expressed, notably on Wall Street, that he would give away too much. He asked about public reaction in Britain: we had to report very little press or public interest in the subject.

He asked us our impressions of the situation in Portugal. I summed it up as very gloomy. It was reported that Antunes was out of the Government. We had, I said, discussed the position at the Brussels EEC Summit when at an after-dinner meeting Giscard and I had been asked to raise the question with the Portuguese delegation to Helsinki, though it was doubtful whether we should be able to achieve anything useful. The Americans thought that though there could well be Soviet help getting into the country, there was no reason to think that the Soviets had engineered the position. I commented that there was no need to assume that they had. From all accounts Portuguese leftism, Communist or whatever it was, was really a strange hybrid creed deriving from Marxism, and embodying Leninism, Maoism and Trotskyism as well as other expressions of 'liberation' doctrines.

We all expressed anxiety about Italy, where it seemed that a Communist Government, or one incorporating a Communist element, seemed a real possibility. The Labour Party for many years had tried to help bring the Italian Socialists together, but all to no avail. They were the soft under-belly of the European Democratic Socialist movement and some of them were said to be refusing to form a government without Communist support. Our influence on them had ebbed, and the two Socialist parties were hardly on speaking terms. One had to consider the consequences for NATO. However, the Swedish Prime Minister had convened a Socialist Leaders' conference in Stockholm, where we all planned to break our journeys on the way home, and where we would be joined by Mitterand of France and Soares of Portugal, as well as the leaders of the two Italian Socialist parties.

Other matters we discussed were Turkey and the US Congress's refusal to supply arms, Cyprus – and whether Italy could help to mediate there. We also had some discussion on the Middle East, including the moves by the Afro-Asian block to expel Israel from the United Nations at the forthcoming Assembly.

The Americans had clearly expected me to pass on their warnings to Israel via Eppi Evron. I saw him later in the day, and made it clear that Israel was in danger of over-pressing. Not only did the Israelis want a more advantageous territorial settlement than the US thought possible: Kissinger was trying to negotiate while the Israelis were shouting the odds in public – in Attlee's phrase, nailing their trousers to the mast. Kissinger regarded his task as difficult enough: the Israelis were making it harder by 'shouting' all the time. These public utterances were likely to make Sadat feel that he was presented with an ultimatum. Kissinger could not go on carrying the can to Egypt in such circumstances. In any case, he had ended his shuttle missions. He would be prepared to return to the Middle East only to tie up the terms of an agreement between the two parties. On the UN threat I told Evron that Britain and the United States were in touch, and that we should be stiffening our Socialist colleagues at Stockholm at the end of the week to combine in resisting the Third World countries' attempt at the forthcoming General Assembly to expel Israel. I pressed him to ensure that Rabin, the Israeli Prime Minister and Socialist Party leader, was present at the Stockholm meeting.

The following day we hosted a lunch at the British Embassy for France and Germany as well as the US (again with Foreign Ministers present). We had talks in the garden over sherry, and afterwards over coffee, as well as a full discussion at lunch. Ford again explained his position on Israel, again clearly angry at Israel's habit of going public on matters under close negotiation. He was, he said, by no means fully committed to the Israeli case: they were taking a risk by the way they were acting. He made clear that he was not willing to put American troops into any peace-keeping role, for example, in the Sinai passes between Israel and Egypt. The Israelis, he said, going back to his pre-June position, should understand that if the agreement they were working for did not materialize in August, he would make his long-projected statement of reappraisal in September. Hopes we and the US had entertained that we might persuade Giscard to back our joint position were met by Giscard's refusal to commit himself to support it.

After we had discussed Portugal, Giscard raised the question of the world economy. We accepted his idea of holding an early meeting together with Japan, and, it was later agreed, Italy. This was how the Rambouillet Summit came about.[1]

Secrets are hard to keep on such plans, particularly where European statesmen are involved. The following day the EEC delegates had lunch together. In the evening all delegations were invited to President Kekkonen's dinner in the Palace. I arrived to find Giscard under furious attack from the other Europeans, who had been tipped off about the Rambouillet meeting. Giscard defended himself, with my support, but it was clear that the other West European leaders felt that the cohesion of the EEC was at stake, bitter particularly at any suggestion that within the EEC there were first- and second-class citizens. That Rambouillet was unlikely to be a once-for-all operation increased their bitterness, and it has, of course, been the fact that similar conferences have taken place at frequent intervals right up to the present time.

Considerations of space forbid a record of all the other Helsinki bilaterals in which we were involved, but the one with Portugal is worth describing at some length. In common with our EEC partners and social democratic colleagues we were dedicated to doing all we could to help our democratic socialist colleagues in Portugal. In the spring James Callaghan had visited Portugal to address a socialist meeting with Mario Soares. The Stockholm meeting of labour leaders was being called specifically to consider the Portuguese situation, and in September European socialist leaders with Mario Soares were to come to Downing Street to set up a 'Committee of Solidarity' to support Portuguese democracy. Soares was to visit and address the Labour Party Conference at Blackpool. But in Helsinki it was Portugal's military President, Costa Gomez, whom we had to meet. Not only Britain, but all our EEC colleagues, were committed to support a democratic solution there, a decision underlined by our offer of substantial economic help, conditional on Portugal's becoming a 'pluralist democracy' based on free elections.

Costa Gomez met us supported by his military colleagues from the Armed Forces Movement, as choice a bunch of thugs as I have ever met.

I began by saying that we had met his Prime Minister at the NATO Council meetings in Brussels, and his colleague Antunes had called on me in London. Her Majesty's Government were gravely disturbed by recent events in Portugal and the continuing march of events from day to day. We had been

[1] See pp. 184–8 below.

heartened by the revolution sixteen months earlier. Above all we trusted that the commitment given by Portugal's leaders to the establishment of 'pluralistic democracy' still held firm. We wanted to make clear our desire to give all possible support and assistance: he would have seen the statement of the EEC Heads of Government Conference a fortnight before. All EEC leaders were unanimous in linking closer economic and financial co-operation between the EEC and Portugal to the development of a pluralist democracy.

The President would realize that the EEC Ministers and indeed the Commission would not be willing to finance a dictatorship of any kind. But we looked forward to a closer and warmer co-operative relationship with a Portugal clearly moving on the path of democracy, based on the people's choice in a free election. The Council of Foreign Ministers had looked forward to meeting Major Antunes on 22 July, though this had not occurred.

I reminded him that Britain was Portugal's oldest ally, over a period now reaching six hundred years. But when Caetano, the right-wing leader, had been invited by our Conservative predecessors to visit London, I had protested strongly in the House of Commons, and after news reached us of the Wiriamu massacres in Mozambique, I had called on the then Government in the House of Commons to cancel the visit. For this I had been strongly attacked in wide sections of the British press. Not only was there our longstanding alliance. We were both members of NATO. Article 2 of the North Atlantic Treaty committed all members of the Alliance to democracy. We had been greatly encouraged by the first news of the revolution and decolonization in Mozambique and Angola – events which the President had described in his own speech in Helsinki.

But now we were gravely disturbed at the news reaching us. We were not concerned who were the leaders of Portugal – that should be for the people to decide – but there were increasing signs that the freely-expressed will of the Portuguese people was being rejected. I hoped he would be able to reassure me.

Costa Gomez thanked me for the frankness with which 1 had spoken. He had to say with equal frankness that the United Kingdom and her allies in NATO and elsewhere in Europe were looking at the matter from a distorted point of view. He wanted to make clear that Portugal intended to establish a 'pluralist socialist system' where all individual liberties would be fully assured and protected. He was familiar with the criticism that the Portuguese mass media were dominated by a certain Party. But this was unfair, because he could say that the freedom of the press was so open and full that in fact everyone could speak and criticize as they wanted. Indeed, freedom of the press had caused difficulties, for example, in Angola.

Portugal was not a dictatorship as he felt I was suggesting. If he and his colleagues had wanted a military dictatorship they would have created one on 25 April 1974, when they were backed by 90 per cent of the country.

It was a difficult moment for Portugal, facing as they were an economic recession. But he foresaw that if they could master the economic crisis they would be able to lead the Portuguese people to their final aim of a pluralist socialism and thereby attain a political form where they would be able to emain both in NATO and in other organizations of which they were members.

I took up his reference to the economy and referred to my talks with Antunes in Brussels, and challenged what Costa Gomez had just said about democracy.

First, about the freedom of the press which the President had mentioned, what about the newspaper *Republica*, which was not being printed?

Second, if what I myself had said to the President at this meeting had been said by me publicly, would the Portuguese press have printed it? The British press often said critical things about the British Prime Minister because as a free press they were entitled, indeed in duty bound, to do so.

Third, when the President talked about social democracy did he mean that the Government would be chosen by the vote of the people? I had been beaten in 1970 by the Conservatives, and immediately accepted the decision, as the Conservative Prime Minister did in 1974. Britain had two elections in 1974. Did President Costa Gomez's definition mean a democracy where a party which gained a majority in the election could govern without the approval of the present rulers?

The President took up my reference to the *Republica* newspaper, and sought to explain it away as a conflict between the workers and the management which had turned into a conflict between the Portuguese Socialist Party and the workers. (Translation: the Government had imposed censorship through the printing unions they controlled.) It could not be denied, he went on, that newspapers had their own political orientation and often had to give in to pressure from the workers. But there was no doubt that it was not the Government or any official body which had limited the freedom of the press. He thought it would be necessary to pass legislation to make the newspapers and broadcasting 'more responsible'. He had had contacts with all parties represented in the former Government, which had represented 80 per cent of the people, and they had agreed that responsible people from the political parties and officials from the Ministry of Social Communications should study the problem thoroughly and put forward proposals for a solution.

As for his ideas of democratic socialism, he thought that as soon as legislative elections had taken place the winning party should be invited to form a Government by itself or in coalition. 'Invited', I asked, 'by whom? By the President?' He replied, 'Invited by the President'. In practice this would mean by 'certain Ministers led by military men'. That is, by the Ministers of Defence, Intelligence and Information: this should be for three years.

James Callaghan asked whether the Assembly would, as had been envisaged, meet in September and draw up a Constitution? Would it prepare elections? When would these take place?

Costa Gomez said that when the Assembly was at work, then there would be legislative elections followed by the election of a President of the Republic.

I asked him to elucidate his phrase 'social democracy'. Did he mean socialism in the sense of a socialist like Dr Soares – who had secured the biggest vote – or 'socialist' in the Communist sense? Costa Gomez replied that *in theory* he meant democracy as seen by Soares, but he had to say frankly that sometimes the Portuguese Socialist Party had confused the people in the country a little with its speeches and statements and had got away from its very principles.

I asked whether the Armed Forces Movement had the popular support of the country, and if he thought they had, how he and his associates knew this was so. How had it been tested? President Costa Gomez said that on 25 April 1974 90 per cent of the country had supported them. Today that support had obviously decreased, but he could tell me that a majority of the country were still with the revolution. He knew this because of all the contacts between the military and people in the country. This proved that the people still welcomed the military. He went on to refer to the social progress sponsored by the AFM, especially in rural areas, such as electrification, schools, and in the health field.

James Callaghan said that nothing I had said called in question our basic position that the people of Portugal should be free to choose their own government. But we felt that the right of choice was not being demonstrated.

Costa Gomez replied that the Portuguese revolution had two parallel lines. There was the 'elected line', which they used to get information in order to know exactly what the political tendencies were in the country. Then there was the 'revolutionary line' by which they intended to establish a direct link between the Armed Forces Movement and the people, aimed at discovering deficiencies and identifying the aims and aspirations of the people! They would use that link to understand better what the country really wanted. They all thought that the two lines would ultimately converge and were not incompatible. One line had a political finality, the other a social finality.

James Callaghan then raised questions of labour unrest, lock-outs and interference with trade unions. The Portuguese President seemed to be mystified by such inferences, so I asked him to drop me a letter when he had examined the points Jim had raised. It never arrived.

Finally, reverting to the 'two lines' of the Portuguese constitutional system as he had described it, I said that when the President had been explaining them to us, he had demonstrated his thesis with his hands – on the one hand this; on the other hand that. The question which occurred to me was, which hand would ultimately be round the people's throats?

On that note we withdrew, singularly unimpressed and deeply worried about the future of Portugal. Fortunately for Portugal and democracy, Costa Gomez ceased to have any control over his country when he gave way to President Eanes on 27 June 1976.

Bilateral talks with other Heads of Government can be dismissed more briefly. The conversation with President Kekkonen, as on previous occasions, was friendly. The Foreign Secretary and I congratulated him on his organization of the Conference, and thanked him for all he had done for his many guests. We then turned to mainly bilateral matters, particularly trade and industry, including British Leyland's plans for developing trade there. James Callaghan reported on his pre-conference visits to East European countries. Again our meeting with Gierek of Poland related mainly to trade, and to points raised in the Foreign Secretary's visit the previous week.[1] Following up the Anglo-Polish agreement in 1974, we were negotiating about further contracts: in particular opening up the question of exporting ships to Poland from British yards.

The talks with President Tito were again in very general terms, but our talks with the Turkish Prime Minister – with whom I had a longer talk at dinner – were mainly on Cyprus, and proved quite unrewarding. Mr Demirel was still smarting over the US Congress decision not to supply arms, and James Callaghan told him that the discussions we had had were of the chicken and egg variety – Congress would not agree to the provision of arms until Demirel delivered in Cyprus; Demirel would make no move over Cyprus until he got the arms.

But the talks with Brezhnev were more to the point. They began, as usual, with a not very intellectual joke, this time perpetrated by us. At the Moscow talks he had once pretended to walk away with my Cabinet red box, saying he would now be able to learn all our secrets. Some wag in the Foreign Office suggested prior to Helsinki that we should present him with a red box, inscribed in Russian characters with his official title, just as in Westminster boxes bear the title of the minister concerned. I approached him with it – again he sought to impound it, and was quite surprised to see the inscription. Needless to say, it had its own individual lock and key, as is the practice in London.

We were meeting at the very end of the Conference just as copies of the Final Act were being assembled on the platform for signature. But I was anxious to press him on Portugal.

He began by referring to our Moscow meetings. While it was true, as many speakers at the Conference had pointed out, that not every problem had been solved, and there were still questions which should be elaborated and discussed further, a very good beginning had been made. The final declaration was a strong political and moral document. He was sure that both the

[1] See p. 166 above.

Soviet and the British peoples had been pleased with it when they saw it. It was now up to the two countries' leaders to implement it. My own visit to Moscow had been an important landmark on the road. The document we were both about to sign instilled the conviction that grounds existed for better developments in European relationships than ever before.

Time was passing. I told him there was one problem which I wanted to mention specially and about which I felt great anxiety. On the agenda for détente was the position of Portugal. Britain was greatly disturbed about it and I hoped that he would use all his influence to ensure that the situation was resolved in a way which accorded with the wishes of the Portuguese people. I had seen President Costa Gomez earlier in the day. But since time for discussion was so short, I would like to send him a memorandum about the question.

He replied that he would just like to say 'two words'. Portugal was an independent state. The Soviet Union was in no way involved in the situation. They were not sending arms to Portugal. But the situation was complicated. Gromyko intervened to say that this was an internal affair of the Portuguese people. Brezhnev went on to comment that many people had approached him in Helsinki during the Conference. He and his colleagues would think the matter over when they returned to Moscow to see what could be done. The Soviet Union had not started the Portuguese revolution.

Emissaries were coming in to say that all the other signatories were on the platform and awaiting us. I concluded by saying that I should make it clear that the British Government had welcomed the revolution and the dismissal of Caetano. But we were very worried at what was happening. We agreed to keep in touch.

So far my Helsinki memoirs have dealt exclusively with bilateral and wider meetings outside the Conference itself. The Conference was opened by a speech of welcome by the President of Finland, followed by an exordium by the emissary of the Secretary-General of the United Nations. It was then open to national delegates.

The order of speaking had been decided by ballot, an Italian girl on the Secretariat having drawn names out of a box. The first name drawn out was the United Kingdom. A further ballot installed me as Chairman of the Conference for the final session on 1 August.

My opening speech – of about fifteen minutes – covered a wide canvas on détente[1] and on the high hopes raised by our agreed text on human freedoms. One paragraph, better than the others, was written, let it be said, by the Foreign Office, and it was much quoted:

[1] In view of the revived interest – and, now, disappointment – in the Helsinki Conference created by the dissidents' trials in Moscow in 1978, I reproduce the text as Appendix X. For a systematic analysis of the Moscow trials and other developments set against the Helsinki Final Act see the Parliamentary written reply by the Foreign Secretary to a written Parliamentary Question I had tabled (*Hansard*, 13 July, 1978 Written Answer 215W).

Détente means little if it is not reflected in the daily lives of our peoples. And there is no reason why, in 1975, Europeans should not be allowed to marry whom they want, hear and read what they want, travel abroad when and where they want, meet whom they want. And to deny that proposition is a sign not of strength but of weakness.

This phrase was picked up by a number who were present. Referring to the speech when we met at the President's dinner that evening, Secretary of State Kissinger told me that when I had sat down President Ford had told him to re-write his speech in a grander style to compete with it.

President Giscard had a neat response to one of my more pompous opening notes:

In territorial coverage, in representation at top level of almost every State, large and small, it so far transcends any previous European meeting, that it makes the legendary Congress of Vienna of 1814 and the Congress of Berlin of 1878 seem like well-dressed tea parties,

making the rejoinder that Vienna had much more to be said for it. Heads of State danced the night away, leaving Prime Ministers to do the work. Helsinki would not go down to history for its 'Congress Dances'; Heads of State had to work just as much as Prime Ministers.

The final Act of the Conference, signed by all the Heads of Government, was a comprehensive document. It was not in any way amended in Helsinki, having been finalized and agreed in Geneva.

The document ran to fifty-two octavo pages when printed as a Commons White Paper. Its preamble ended with these words:

Motivated by the political will, in the interest of peoples, to improve and intensify their relations and to contribute in Europe to peace, security, justice and cooperation as well as to rapprochement among themselves and with the other states of the world.
Determined, in consequence, to give full effect to the results of the Conference and to assure, among their States and throughout Europe, the benefits deriving from those results and thus to broaden, deepen and make continuing and lasting the process of détente.
The High Representatives of the participating States have solemnly adopted the following . . .

It went straight on to the section 1(a) 'Questions relating to Security in Europe'. After pledging themselves to détente, the Act embodied a 'Declaration on Principles Guiding Relations between Participating States', with particular reference to 'Sovereign equality, respect for the rights inherent in sovereignty . . . Refraining from the threat or use of force . . . Inviolability of frontiers . . . Territorial integrity of States . . . Peaceful settlement of disputes . . . Non-intervention in internal affairs . . . Respect for human rights and fundamental freedoms, including the freedom of thought, conscience, religion or belief . . . Equal rights and self-determination of peoples . . .

Cooperation among States . . . Fulfilment in good faith of obligations under international law . . .'.

Section 1(b) listed 'Matters related to giving effect to certain of the above Principles'.

Document 2 was headed 'Document on confidence-building measures and certain aspects of security and disarmament'. The Conference adopted 'Prior notification of major military movements' – exceeding 25,000 troops . . . 'Prior notification of other military manoeuvres . . . Exchange of observers . . . Other confidence-building measures'. This part of the report also covers 'Questions relating to disarmament'.

The third main section is headed 'Co-operation in the Field of Economics, of Science and Technology and of the Environment', and covers eighteen pages. The fourth section, 'Questions relating to security and co-operation in the Mediterranean', is a bare page and a half. The final section, also covering eighteen pages, deals with 'Co-operation in humanitarian and other fields', dealing in particular with 'Contacts and regular meetings on the basis of family ties . . . Re-unification of families . . . Marriage between citizens of different states . . . Travel for personal or professional reasons . . . Improvement of conditions for tourism . . . Meetings among young people . . . sport . . . Expansion of contacts . . . Improved circulation of, access to and exchange of information – print, films, broadcasts – co-operation in the field of information and the improvement of conditions of journalists.' There are long sections on cultural exchanges, and co-operation and exchanges in the educational field, and in science and the study of foreign languages and civilizations.

The final two pages deal with follow-up action. To secure the acceptance of these fifty pages of principle and action was a great achievement. In the three years since their adoption it is disappointingly true that they have been more a statement of principle than anything approaching a reality.

In the conference itself most of the speeches were off rather than on the precise words which had been agreed. Each speaker took one or more passages as a text for a wider speech, or spoke of the magnitude of the achievement of getting a document on which we could agree – and on the size and splendour of the occasion.

The Foreign Secretary and I returned to London via Stockholm. Olof Palme, the Swedish Prime Minister, had invited all of us Labour Premiers at the Helsinki Conference to break our journeys there for a brief morning conference followed by lunch. Socialist leaders who were not Prime Ministers, such as Mitterand and Soares, came over specially, and, as we had suggested, Prime Minister Rabin came from Israel.

The question of the UN Assembly resolution over Israel was quickly dealt with. All the Heads of Government at Stockholm promised full support for Israel, and we undertook to use our individual influence with as many UN delegations as possible. In the event, the move was not pressed by the Afro-Asian bloc.

The greater part of the meeting was devoted to Soares and the problem of strengthening democracy in Portugal. Again, all possible help was pledged, and EEC Labour Heads of Government undertook to seek the support of our other Community colleagues. It was decided to create a 'Committee of Friendship and Solidarity with Democracy and Socialism in Portugal', consisting of Willy Brandt (no longer German Chancellor but still chairman of his party), Bruno Kreisky, François Mitterand, Olof Palme, Joop den Uyl, and myself, to meet in Downing Street in September.

I was able to summarize the Government's record on overseas affairs at the Party Conference in October:

> We all remember, and anyone studying the records of the NEC, and of Conference since the war, might estimate that the NEC has probably spent 60 per cent of the time it devotes to policy discussions, and Conference 40 per cent, on overseas affairs.
>
> In some years these discussions were directed towards a very friendly and always constructive criticism of the Labour Government of the day. In other years, long years of opposition, we were trying to shape Party attitudes about what we thought the then ruling Conservative Government should be doing in foreign affairs.
>
> The fact that there have been less deep and fundamental arguments about overseas affairs in the last 18 months of Labour Government is not a reason for ignoring foreign affairs this week.
>
> On the contrary, what I can point to is a record of achievement and influence in significant areas of world affairs which I believe to have been unparalleled by any Government, Labour or Conservative, at any time since the war – and indeed long before that.
>
> Let us take, first, relations with the United States. I know that not everyone here is equally enthusiastic on this subject, though during the Referendum campaign I thought I detected a new-found insistence in certain quarters – unexpected quarters[1] – that we must do nothing to endanger our transatlantic relations. I am sure this enthusiasm was not a passing phenomenon. (*Laughter*)
>
> What I was able to tell the Executive three weeks ago was that relations between Britain and the United States are now closer, are now more constructive, both in political and economic issues, than at any time in the political life of most of us and that judgment is not mine – it comes from American leaders.
>
> Over the years we have had many debates about relations with the Soviet Union and other East European countries. The situation in 1975 has been described as 'historic'. Not my phrase – it is that of one of the top Soviet leaders during my visit last February.
>
> The Commonwealth. Anyone who was present at the meeting of thirty-five Commonwealth Heads of Government in Jamaica last May would have concluded – as my Commonwealth colleagues did – that Britain's relations with the Commonwealth, again both political and economic, had never been better in our history.

[1] Left-wing.

This is partly because Rhodesia no longer divides the Commonwealth. Tragically it divides only the African parties within Rhodesia, to the immense satisfaction of the white régime.

It is also because South Africa does not divide us. The Commonwealth was torn apart a few months after Labour lost office in 1970 by the Conservatives' insistence on supplying arms to South Africa.

On taking office in 1974, as in 1964, I gave immediate instructions that arms to South Africa should be stopped forthwith. (*Applause*) The arrangements to end the Simonstown Agreement followed soon after. And your Government it was that declared the South African presence in Namibia to be unlawful and called upon them to withdraw.

Again with Europe. Following renegotiation, the Government gave the people the final right to decide, as we had promised in our Manifesto.

The people decided.

And the way we conducted the campaign – particularly the then much-criticized 'agreement to differ', within the Cabinet, within the Executive – fulfilled my very confident prediction at the time, which many doubted, that the Party would come out of that campaign not weaker but stronger, not divided but more united.

That is what happened. The issue was settled by the people themselves and it has now been virtually accepted.

The argument is over.

We are using our influence, Jim Callaghan at the Council of Ministers, both of us at the regular Summits, not only to assert British economic interests and those of a wider Europe but on political matters too. Remember it was the Commonwealth Prime Ministers who recorded – on their own initiative, not mine – that 'British membership of the Community was of value in encouraging the Community to be more outward looking to the rest of the world.'

I ended by referring to a challenge I had made to the National Executive:

Relations with America; with the Soviet Union; relations with the Commonwealth; relations with Europe, particularly directed towards democracy in Europe.

That was my report to the National Executive three weeks ago.

Following that report I felt justified in asking my colleagues, some with 30 years in Parliament, some with a record of political activity going back well before the War, if they could recall a time, and if they could to name the year, when relations with the United States were better.

If they could recall a time, and name the year, when relations with the Soviet Union were better.

If they could recall a time when relations with the Commonwealth were better.

If they could recall a time when relations with Europe were better.

Still more, could anyone name some halcyon period when relations with America, with the Soviet Union, with the Commonwealth and with Europe were better than now – and all at the same time?

Not one such era was recalled by my very experienced colleagues on behalf of Her Majesty's Government; not one year was nominated.

In twenty-two years on the Executive this was the first time that we could record a measurable period of absolute silence on the Executive. (*Laughter and applause.*)

Today, to this Conference, I put the same thought – is there anyone here, however long their apprenticeship and work in the Labour Movement, who can answer those questions, who can name a comparable period? You do not need to answer now. Take your time, I will give you notice of the question and you can let me know.

No one did.

# PART III

*August 1975–April 1976*

# Chapter 9

## SUMMITS AND CRISES

T HE remaining two chapters of this book cover the period from August 1975 to my leaving Downing Street on 5 April 1976. Until the new Parliamentary session was opened by the Queen's Speech on 19 November, life was relatively quiet. From then until the end of the year it was the most hectic I have ever known either as Prime Minister or as a member of Clement Attlee's post-war Cabinet. From the New Year, with the exception of Northern Ireland, things moved at a more measured rate until Easter. Major international conferences were confined to the Rambouillet gathering of the Heads of Government of the six major industrial powers and two hardly notable EEC summits at Rome in December and Luxembourg in April.

The flow of distinguished visitors to No. 10 showed no sign of abating, nor has it done so since James Callaghan became Prime Minister. Among the Heads of Government were President Sadat of Egypt and President Nyerere of Tanzania, the Prime Ministers of Greece, Papua New Guinea, Jamaica, Mauritius, Portugal, Iceland (for bitter discussions on the cod-fishing crisis), Federal Germany, the Netherlands, Luxembourg and the Irish Republic. Vice-President Rockefeller, the Governor General of Australia and the Deputy Prime Minister of New Zealand, Prince Fahd, the Foreign Minister of Saudi Arabia, the Foreign Ministers of Poland, Brazil, Sweden, Israel (twice), Zaire, Spain, France, and Mr Gromyko of the Soviet Union were visitors, as were the New Zealand Minister of Foreign Trade, the Lord Mayor of Berlin, Mr Schlesinger, the US Defence Minister, the Soviet Minister of Foreign Trade, the Iranian Minister of Commerce, the Secretary-General of CENTO, Señora Allende of Chile, Governor Wallace and Senator Church, the Speaker of the Egyptian Parliament, in addition to a high-level US industrialists' mission we had invited to report to their people on Britain's industrial efforts and modernization, not to mention deputations from individual Parliaments and a group of young Israeli socialists. Most of the Heads of Government and Foreign Ministers such as Mr Gromyko came on official visits, with reciprocal dinners and lunches to fit in, as well as many hours of conference time in the Cabinet room.

The new term began with the world Inter-Parliamentary Union Conference in Westminster Hall, opened on 4 September 1975 by the Queen, with speeches by the Lord Chancellor, Mr Speaker and myself, followed by dinner and other gatherings.

The following day I chaired the meeting in Downing Street of European Socialist leaders which we had arranged in Stockholm to discuss the Portuguese question, at that time rent with division and hostilities between Communist and non-Communist members of the armed forces, with followers of the right-wing liberator, General Spinola, with Dr Mario Soares, the Socialist leader and Foreign Secretary, attempting to create a viable democratic government after nearly forty years of Fascist rule. How difficult, not to say dangerous, life was for him we did not fully appreciate until he told us that he had to sleep with a fire-arm under his pillow, and on several nights each week had to flee from the house in which he was sleeping to another, to save his life. European Governments, through the EEC, had pledged massive financial subsidies to Portugal on condition of her adopting democratic government, and the Downing Street meeting was directed to ensuring that this help was effective, and that as Governments and social democratic parties we were doing all we could to protect and establish democracy. We set up the International Committee of Solidarity and Friendship with Portugal's democracy under Willy Brandt, with each of our countries represented.

Later in the month I paid an official visit to Romania on the invitation of President Ceaucescu, whom I had met on a previous visit when we had been in Opposition during Mr Heath's administration. He is a leader of immense fascination, a great student of history and statecraft, who has survived, one surmises, by being able to play off the Russians against the Chinese, who in part sponsor him. He has been described as a liberal abroad and a hard-line disciplinarian Communist at home. He rejoices in analysing Soviet philosophy and politics from a historical background, and would certainly endorse the view expressed nearly thirty years earlier by George Kennan (Mr X) when he said that Russia has changed Communism less than Communism has changed Russia.

On this visit I was accompanied for the first time by a small group of junior ministers – from Energy (a former Scottish miner), and Trade and Agriculture, and one result, following an all-night sitting, was a substantial trade agreement significantly increasing our exports to further Romania's industrial and agricultural development. Building on an earlier agreement, negotiations began, leading now, as these words are being written, to a major repeat order for British civil aircraft.

The following week we began to assemble in Blackpool for the Party Conference, the first 'normal' one for two years – the two intervening gatherings being the three-day assembly in London after the second 1974 General Election,[1] and the charade in Islington just before the EEC referendum.[2]

It was my fourteenth year as Party Leader. I knew, though very few others did, that it would be my last. I had no anxieties about this particular Conference. Labour Party Conferences are not usually difficult, though once

[1] See pp. 124–5 above.
[2] See pp. 106–7 above.

in a while, as later in 1976 and 1978, they are impossible. I arrived there from the North-East, where, as a life-long railway enthusiast and retired railway historian, I had been visiting the 150th anniversary celebrations of the Stockton and Darlington Railway. A speech had to be prepared and this was virtually completed on the Thursday night. Friday, as usual, was taken up with the National Executive meeting, which went on until the late afternoon.

One of the chores of Party Conference is the long period an NEC member has to be in attendance – Thursday night to Monday morning – before the Conference actually begins. NEC members worried about their seats, or concerned with the 'compositing' of resolutions on the Saturday afternoon, find some useful employment in this period, or in appropriate caballistic activities. But all this takes place in a very markedly hot-house atmosphere, with NEC members, delegates, lobbyists (including the growing number of professional lobbyists by whom conferences are becoming increasingly infested), failed barkers, and pressmen discussing the form and calculating the odds. I opted for Chequers; as it happened the US Secretary for Defence was visiting London and there was much to discuss. Also Danny Kaye, whom I had known for nearly thirty years, was conducting an orchestral concert in the Festival Hall, giving me time to catch the night sleeper to Liverpool in time to read the lesson at the Conference service in Blackpool Parish Church. The NEC Sunday afternoon meeting presented few problems, and Conference duly began with an excellent Mayoral welcome the following morning.

Traditionally the Party Leader, whether in government or opposition, moves the adoption of the Parliamentary Report. I was concerned, in what I knew would be my last speech to Conference, to do four things.

The first was to put on the record what the Government had done, and was proposing to do, in implementing the two manifestos on which the elections of February and October had been fought. The second was to report on Britain's relations with major world powers and groupings of states, whether in Europe or the Developing World. The third was to take a knock at subversives and trouble-makers, whether on the extreme left or the extreme right. The fourth was to speed the process of securing acceptance, as we celebrated seventy-five years as a Party, by the delegates of Labour as the 'natural party of government', no longer just a party of protest – while in fact embodying in government our ancient role as the party of protest against social evils and economic inequities.

Extracts on these four themes from the speech are set out at some length in Appendix XI, to give some idea of the relations between a Labour Prime Minister and Conference nineteen months after our return to office, and also to summarize some of our legislative and other achievements not recorded or discussed above. The passage on overseas affairs has been set out above in Chapter 8, pp. 176–8.

Conference went away in a better mood than at any time for many years.

7

The following week was the Conservative Conference, which my colleagues and I did not in any way seek to upstage. I spent part of the time quietly visiting service establishments in the south-west.

On 3 November in Aberdeen the Queen took part in a ceremony to start the flow of oil from the BP operations in the Forties Field to the mainland and on to the Grangemouth refinery in the Firth of Forth. BP, their contractors and their suppliers had overcome massive, indeed unprecedented, problems in their task. The oil had to flow in water more than 300 feet deep for 95 miles out of a total length of 110 miles, through the deepest large-diameter pipelines ever laid on the sea bed. The sea platform had to be able to withstand a 'one-in-a-century' wave rising to 94 feet, and a maximum wind velocity of 130 miles an hour. Platforms twice the height of Big Ben had to be placed in these hostile waters.

My only contribution to the proceedings, in a very short speech, was to lose two noughts in my estimate of the value of oil discovered *up to that time* in British waters. At current prices the correct figure was in fact £200 thousand million (200 American billions), more than had been found, on the international oil industry's 'proved and probable' formula, in all the seas surrounding the coasts of the United States, including Alaska. 'It is not entirely misplaced humour when I have told our friends abroad that a British Minister of Energy will be Chairman of OPEC in the early 1980s.' Britain was expected to be self-sufficient in oil by 1980, and in balance-of-payments surplus as a result of our reduced dependence on oil imports by 1977. The 1977 target was in fact realized, but with a lower margin of surplus than had been expected, involving the estimators in doubts for the future.[1]

On 5 November the National Economic Development Council met at Chequers for a full review of all the work that had been done over a year and more on industrial strategy, with particular reference to the modernization and investment capabilities of nearly forty industries, each subsequently surveyed in depth by 'sector' working parties.[2]

During the week-end between the end of the 1974–75 Parliamentary session and the Queen's Speech, the Rambouillet Conference took place. This conference of the free world's six leading industrial powers was a characteristically imaginative proposal of Giscard d'Estaing, even though it had inevitably upset EEC leaders at Helsinki. It took place, after very careful

[1] The balance-of-payments out-turn in these years was:

£ million
1973  —  999
1974  −3,551
1975  −1,855
1976  −1,137
1977  +  406
1978  +  109 (provisional at the time of writing).

[2] See *The Governance of Britain*, pp. 117–18, and the text of my statement after the meeting; Appendix VI, pp. 205–7.

preparation, at Francis I's magnificent palace at Rambouillet from 15 to 17 November. A great deal of care had been taken with its preparation, each Head of Government nominating a very senior official to join in meetings to work on the agenda and administrative arrangements.

Rambouillet was an ideal setting for those who would be accommodated there, just Heads of Government, Foreign and Finance Ministers and Principal Private Secretaries. All other officials, ambassadors and advisers had to stay in Paris, being flown in and out on each of the two days by helicopter. Giscard's austere ideas about note-taking, which meant, as at his EEC summit, that Foreign Ministers were reduced to the role of minute-writers and messenger boys, were ruled out by a revolt on the part of Giscard's guests.

Helmut Schmidt opened a discussion on the world economy, setting out four objectives.

On trade, we should agree to ward off the world-wide trend to protection, maintain and support the OECD[1] initiative to expand trade, and call for the speeding up of the negotiations to reduce tariffs, under the aegis of GATT.[2]

On financial and economic policy, there should be closer co-operation between Central Banks, aimed at promoting an agreement at the International Monetary Fund two months later, in January 1976. (This mountain in labour was to produce its usual mouse.)

On developing countries, action to promote their recovery by financing their balance-of-payments gap.

On commodities, the projected consumer–producer dialogue was relevant, but would probably take a long time to produce significant results.[3]

President Ford was optimistic. The US package of half a dozen economic indicators was moving in the right direction. He confirmed my reference to a sudden and unexpected boom in automobile production in the US – an industry which was usually regarded as a pace-maker for the American economy.

I expressed agreement with Schmidt's analysis, and encouragement at Ford's bullishness. In Britain our balance-of-payments position was improving. Two years earlier the fourth quarter of 1973 had recorded a deficit at an annual rate of £4,000 a year, almost before the rise in oil prices had begun to hit us. But already our non-oil deficit had been converted into a surplus, and before long our own production would be covering about a third of our national consumption. I referred to the acceptance by the unions and employers of the Government's inflation policy and forecast that increases

[1] Organization for Economic Co-operation and Development, formerly known as OEEC.

[2] General Agreement on Tariffs and Trade, established in 1947 as a temporary measure to discourage economic nationalism, pending the coming into force of the Havana Charter on its ratification by the US Congress. In the event Congress did not ratify, and GATT has lasted, so far, for over thirty years, confirming the French proverb that it is only the provisional which endures.

[1] See p. 185 above.

in the price level would be at an annual rate of about 10 per cent – not on a year-on-year basis, which I have always regarded as statistically illiterate, but on a seasonally-corrected basis. (In the event both Ford and I proved too optimistic. The US economy lurched into a further depression: our inflation rate in the second half of 1975 was still running at an annual rate of over 13 per cent.)

Miki of Japan and Aldo Moro of Italy both warned against moves into protectionism. Giscard was surprised at American bullishness. In Europe Governments had large budgetary deficits, yet falling production was general. He saw two threats ahead. First, any hopes of an export-led recovery would fail because of the low purchasing power of the intended customers. Second, budgetary deficits would have to be cut back sooner or later, and this would put a brake on industrial expansion. Events have confirmed his forecasts.

The following day, Monday, began with an informal discussion between Heads of Government on international affairs. It was agreed that what was said there should not be revealed outside. After this long interval there is no harm in recalling that a good part of the talk related to Spain and the prospects for building democracy there. Giscard was at that time in closer touch with the Spanish situation than the rest of us.

When the Conference resumed in plenum I was asked to open. Country by country, I said, there seemed no early hope of escaping from recession. In a very real sense we were facing the greatest challenge since 1947. A major new initiative was called for, as imaginative as the Marshall Plan of that year had been. For the reasons given by Giscard, such a plan should be directed to a significant extent to the problems of the Third World. Even so, we should be unwise to expect speedy results.

Ford called for tariff cuts, accompanied by non-tariff measures based on international negotiations aimed at stimulating trade – in particular working for the elimination of tariff and non-tariff barriers to trade, our goal being to secure this objective in 1976. (It seemed to me that he was ignoring a generation – two generations in fact – of Congressional obstruction to reducing trade barriers.) He concluded by pressing for meaningful and preferential treatment for LDCs (less developed countries), *and* for an improvement in the 'trading régime' for exchanges of agricultural products – an obvious hit at EEC agricultural protection.

Schmidt called for a declaration which would reject protectionism,[1] renew the OECD initiative, step up GATT provisions for opening up trade, and settle international issues about credit for exports. This last item seemed to be aimed at preventing a *sauve qui peut* competition in undercutting export credits, which led me to some pointed remarks directed at France. In our

[1] Three years later he has still not succeeded in rallying his coalition partners, particularly Herr Ertl, the Agriculture Minister, on this proposition so far as farm products are concerned.

trade agreement with the Soviet Union earlier in the year we had been repeatedly pressed to ease our credit terms to the levels which France was offering on major contracts. The Russians had carefully avoided telling us what the French terms were, and the French authorities had been equally obscurantist. Western countries should compare notes about iron-curtain trade and pursue a common policy on credit terms. This visionary approach of mine has still to become a reality.

I raised the problem of competition on textiles, especially subsidized exports from countries in the East European bloc and the Far East. We all faced problems of survival in our respective textile industries, but a distinction must be made between a planned and controlled run-down and a laissez-faire policy leaving our industries open to measures which would destroy them during the recession and leave them no chance of recovery when world trade conditions improved.

The finger had been pointed at Britain, as our colleagues believed that we were planning to introduce a régime of quotas and other protective measures against them and the world in general. This I disavowed – though there was very strong pressure from industry, and indeed some ministers, in favour of sweeping protectionist policies – while reserving our proper right to protect our industries against blatant subsidized competition from certain East European countries (and Spain), particularly in men's suits and suitings, and in footwear. Our colleagues' fears had apparently been aroused by statements emanating from members of the National Executive Committee of the Labour Party. These were repudiated.

Giscard was, even for him, unusually reserved on many aspects of trade. He did not disguise the fact that he was holding a great deal back for the North–South economic conference about to open in Paris.

At the beginning of the session during the late afternoon of the Sunday, Giscard accepted our proposal that we should discuss energy, raw materials and world development together, and he asked Ford and me to open the discussion with a double presentation.

Ford told us of his impressive plans to reduce American dependence on oil. His Alaskan pipeline would soon be in operation. (In fact it was very slow coming on stream. The oil refused to move. In the event, Rolls-Royce Engines, never slow to see an opportunity, came to the rescue. Jet engines were inserted into the pipe at suitable intervals to blow the oil through.) There was, further, to be an Outer Continental Independence Agency set up to minimize fuel imports.

More than two and a half years and three summits[1] later, President Carter at Bonn outlined new plans to reduce US dependence on imported oil. Old hands seemed to recall having heard the speech before. US imports in the energy area had risen from an annual rate of $7.6 billion in 1973 to over $40 billion in 1978. The first half of the year which saw the Paris summit showed

[1] The intervening summits were in Puerto Rico and London.

an import of $11 billion, the first half of the year leading up to Bonn, one of $19 billion.

My own contribution was a restatement of the commodity proposals Britain had put forward in Jamaica. But I took the opportunity to stress, in addition, the question of credit terms for East European trade. On this I circulated a document to my colleagues about the inordinate number of international agencies concerned with world development, 'Point Four', now the 'North–South' problem: Giscard through his North–South conference was adding yet a further dimension. I told them I had been introduced to this subject in 1946 when Attlee had sent me to head the UK delegation to a sixteen-nation conference on world development. Though playing my part in adding to the proliferation in our work preparing FAO – and proposing more when I wrote *War on Want* six years later – I was alerted by the wise words of one of Britain's most experienced and trenchant administrators, P. J. Grigg, former Permanent Secretary to the War Office, and later Secretary of State for War in Churchill's wartime Government. In 1946, in Washington, where he had become Britain's Executive Director to the International Bank for Reconstruction and Development (IBRD), he warned me of the large population of 'beach-combers' in Washington getting in on the world development racket.

The Parliamentary session had ended on 12 November, and the 1975–76 session was opened with the Queen's Speech on 19 November. It was considerably less ambitious than its predecessor of a year earlier. Indeed, it was a mark of the troubles we had had in the heat of the summer that we had to reintroduce the Shipbuilding and Aircraft Bill. This fared little better in the new session and did not reach the Statute Book until 17 March 1977. Its Parliamentary Odyssey from its first introduction in April 1975 had taken almost two years.

A disappointment to the supporters of devolution for Scotland and Wales was the clear indication, confirmed in the debate which followed, that we were not planning to get the measures through Parliament in the new session:

> My Government will bring forward legislative proposals for the establishment of Scottish and Welsh Assemblies to exercise wide governmental responsibilities within the framework of the United Kingdom.

The key phrase was 'legislative proposals'. The Government had decided to publish a White Paper setting out the policies recommended, but not in statutory form. On so important – and controversial – a constitutional issue, it was felt that Parliament should have a searching debate on the Government's first thoughts informed by public debate, particularly in Scotland and Wales, the areas most directly affected. In the debate I announced that the White Paper would be laid before the House on 27 November, and would be followed by an extended debate. Meanwhile the Government would be preparing legislation on the lines of the proposals, subject to any changes considered necessary in the light of the Parliamentary and public debates. 'For these reasons', I explained that afternoon,

> the Government are not insisting, even if it were possible and proper to insist, that the House should complete the whole legislative process in this present session.
>
> Whatever view any Hon. Member takes, I think he will agree, whether he supports the principles of the White Paper or bitterly opposes them, that we must ensure that the final form of the legislation is responsive to the national debate and to the parliamentary debate, not only on the White Paper but on the text of the Bill.[1]

A Bill introduced in November 1976 failed to make progress, and when a timetable (guillotine) motion was defeated the following February with the help of Labour votes, it was dropped. In the 1977–78 session two Bills, the Scotland Bill and the Wales Bill, were introduced, and on this occasion, virtually making the carrying of a guillotine motion a matter of confidence, the Government was able to persuade Parliament to lay down a strict time-table. Both Bills were introduced on 4 November 1977, and received their respective Second Readings on 14 and 15 November, their timetable motions on 16 November. Again the Conservatives, with considerable Labour support, moved 'wrecking' or near-wrecking amendments, for example, on the timing of the respective referenda, and, more serious, a provision that no 'Yes' vote on a referendum would be accepted as effective unless supported by 40 per cent, not of those voting, but of the electorate entitled to vote, including many who would abstain. With these provisions the Bills received their respective Third Readings on 27 February and 5 May 1978. The Lords, in their turn, introduced further amendments, including an insistence that voting should be by proportional representation. (This was reversed by the Commons.)

Other Bills foreshadowed in the Speech from the Throne included one 'to ensure comprehensive employment safeguards for dockworkers';[2] to meet the United Kingdom's obligations under the International Energy Agreement, to control energy supplies in conditions of shortage, and to implement policies of energy conservation;[3] to phase out private practice from NHS hospitals;[4] to abolish selection in secondary education;[5] to extend Post Office banking services and to reform and extend the activities of trustee savings banks;[6] and to strengthen the law on racial discrimination.[7] Two measures which had great appeal, not only for our supporters, were the transfer of housing from new town development co-operations and the New Towns

---

[1] *Hansard*, vol. 901, col. 30.
[2] Second Reading 10 February 1976; Royal Assent 22 November.
[3] Second Reading 22 March 1976; Royal Assent 18 November.
[4] Second Reading 25 April 1976; Royal Assent 22 November.
[5] Second Reading 4 February 1976; Royal Assent 22 November.
[6] Second Reading 16 May 1976; Royal Assent 29 July.
[7] Second Reading 4 March 1976; Royal Assent 29 July.

Commission to elected local authorities,[1] and the legislation announced to abolish the agricultural tied-cottage system in England and Wales.[2]

Devolution apart, it was not an ambitious programme, reflecting as it did the Government's appreciation of the difficulties we were facing with our minority position in Parliament. Similar legislative programmes in earlier years would have been greeted as a thin Speech, Oppositions always having to be careful about using the phrase 'a thin Queen's Speech'. The Conservative Opposition on this occasion faced no such temptations: their aim was to present it as Socialism red in tooth and claw, compounded with malignancy and a malicious seeking to settle old political scores.

Whether or not the Speech was 'thin', the majority at the end of the five-day debate was decidedly so. With the Liberals, Scottish and Welsh Nationalists and Ulster Unionists voting against the Government, the Opposition amendment was defeated by only six votes by 294 to 288.

The Health Bill was related to Barbara Castle's programme of fulfilling the manifesto proposal to phase out pay-beds. This was a highly controversial proposal both within the profession and on the Westminster political scene. The February and October 1974 manifestos had committed us respectively to 'phase out private practice from the hospital service', and to 'continue the progressive elimination of prescription charges and phase out private pay-beds from National Health Service hospitals'.

As Labour saw it, and particularly Barbara, there were two problems. One was the long waiting period for operations and other hospital treatment in cases which were perhaps quite serious though not of course involving a threat to life, as compared with fee-paying patients who could usually get speedy admission to a private hospital and its operating theatre. The other was the suggestion of discrimination within a National Health Service hospital. Barbara wanted to end the dual system within the NHS premises, and severely cut down the facilities at private hospitals. In particular, at a time when public expenditure limitations precluded the building of urgently needed NHS hospitals, she was concerned with schemes for building more exclusively private hospitals.

The General Medical Council was dedicated in its unanimous opposition to her policies, and highly articulate in the presentation of their case. In all my ministerial experience in handling deputations from industry, transport, local government, trade unions, educationists or back-benchers, to say nothing of Soviet, American or EEC ministers, I must yield the palm to the doctors for their sheer vigour of presentation. Dockers may employ more colourful oratory; doctors direct their scalpels to the specific portions of the anatomy which their long training suggests as being most vulnerable, much of their argument being prima facie highly convincing, totally so if one accepts their basic principles. The medical profession throughout the country

---

[1] Second Reading 23 March 1976; Royal Assent 15 November.
[2] Second Reading 4 May 1976; Royal Assent 22 November 1976.

should never complain about the advocacy at the call of their elected leaders.

It was not only argument. Barbara had to face also industrial action, particularly by junior doctors. The Conservatives not unnaturally seized on the crisis by selecting the health service for a whole day's debate, as is the Opposition's right, on the Queen's Speech. Opening the debate she referred to the action of the junior doctors in defiance of their leaders' proposal for a ballot, in introducing a forty-hour week, and dealing with emergencies only. Even if the money had been there she could not have met the demand presented to her. Junior doctors the previous April had received pay increases of from £13 to £30 a week, and the pay policy then – as in the years immediately preceding and immediately following – precluded a further increase in less than twelve months, as well as limiting increases to £12. She had offered to spread the £12 million available for redistribution and removal of anomalies, but the juniors demanded figures of £17 million, £25 million and still higher ranges. In the ballot of the 14,000 who voted out of 20,000 junior doctors, 12,000 accepted the general principles of the *form* of the Health Department's new contract, but of these 12,000, 7,000 voted for industrial action on the *quantum* and 5,000 against. She proposed that the new supplementary payments should begin at forty-four hours; they demanded that these should begin at forty hours.

The dispute was aggravated by medical opposition to the Government's policy to phase out pay-beds from NHS hospitals. As Barbara put it,

> To Labour Members the right to free and equal medical care for everyone through the NHS is a cardinal principle ... The issue of pay-beds, with the opportunity it gives to patients with money to jump the queue, is seen as a bitter affront to those thousands of staff who are dedicated to the principle of a free Health Service ... We are not proposing to abolish private practice outside the NHS. On the contrary, we propose to reaffirm in the legislation the rights of consultants and doctors generally to practise privately.[1]

She offered to continue negotiations on the phasing-out process, while accepting the pay principle in private hospitals.

These proposals were rejected.

There is a time in the affairs of governments, Conservative and Labour, when deadlock becomes total, and ordinary human agencies are impotent to deal with the situation: the superhuman is then invoked and a telephone call is put through to Lord Goodman. In this case we learnt that he was already hovering, having been approached by certain hospital authorities and doctors. I had already had meetings with the BMA. Lord Goodman, commuting between Downing Street and the doctors, had a series of meetings with Barbara and myself. By mid-December we were able to put a proposition to Cabinet. It was an incredibly difficult week in Cabinet terms – the Chrysler settlement and the final determination of the public expenditure

---

[1] *Hansard*, vol. 901, cols. 353–5.

7*

allocations for the coming financial year, with projections for the succeeding four years, had to be agreed.

On 18 December Barbara announced the settlement on the lines Lord Goodman had proposed. The profession put on record their continuing opposition to the phasing out of private practice and reserved their right to influence Parliament on the issue. The legislation to be introduced by the Government would embody two principles: first, that private beds and facilities would be separated from the NHS, and second, that the Government would recommit itself to the provision of the National Health Service (Amendment) Act 1949, asserting the right to private practice by entitling doctors to work both privately and in NHS establishments.

An independent Board was to be set up by the Government, consisting of an independent chairman, two members of the medical profession acceptable to the profession, and two members appointed after consultation with NHS staff and other interested parties.

> The criteria under which pay-beds and facilities would be phased out in the legislation will be the reasonable availability of alternative facilities for private practice. It is accepted that there are some pay-beds and facilities which on this basis and on the basis of their under-use could be phased out without delay.

The Bill was therefore to contain a schedule giving details of 1,000 pay-beds which were to be phased out of the NHS within six months of Royal Assent – the schedule to reflect the criteria mentioned and to be subject to consultations with those concerned.

> ... The phasing out of the remaining pay-beds would be determined by the independent Board which should be guided by the following criteria: that there should be a reasonable demand for private medicine in the area of the country served by a particular hospital; that sufficient accommodation or facilities existed in the area for the reasonable operation of private medicine, and that all reasonable steps had been, or were being, taken to provide those alternative beds and facilities. This would be kept under continuous review. Where all reasonable steps were not being taken, that would, after due warning, be in itself grounds for withdrawing pay-beds and facilities in the hospitals concerned ...[1]

During the protracted negotiations on the pay-bed issue it became widely agreed that it was time for a general look at the working of the Health Service, now more than a quarter of a century old. Accordingly the Queen's agreement to the appointment of a Royal Commission was announced on 17 October, and reported to the House of Commons on 20 October.[2] Its terms of reference were wide:

---

[1] *Hansard*, vol. 902, cols 971–2. The Bill received the Royal Assent on 22 November 1976.
[2] This procedure was not unnaturally criticized by the Leader of the Opposition, and I had to explain that as the announcement was urgently awaited, it had been done in this way owing to my absence from London on the 17th, visiting Liverpool for a meeting with the shipping industry, followed by a tour of industrial areas in North West Lancashire (*Hansard*, vol. 898, cols 35–7).

To consider in the interests both of the patients and those who work in the National Health Service the best use and management of the financial and manpower resources of the National Health Service.

A later written answer announced that Sir Alex Merrison, Vice-Chancellor of Bristol University, had been appointed Chairman. At the time of writing the Commission is still at work, and evidently concentrating on the wider questions of the NHS, rather than on the specific issue of pay-beds.

One of the problems inflating Health Service costs was the fussy and bureaucratic structure created in our Opposition days by the National Health Service Act, which became law in July 1973, following the Conservative 'reform' of local government the preceding year. It reversed the principle which Richard Crossman had put forward in 1970, shortly before Labour went out of office. He had proposed more effective democratic control of the Area Health Authorities. Attacking the Conservative Health Service changes, in February 1973, I referred to the 'fetishism' of the Treasury and the Civil Service generally about appointing the members of the governing authorities. The Crossman proposal had rejected the previously accepted doctrine that Whitehall nomination was necessary to secure financial responsibility.

Unless the appointed members were to be drawn exclusively from Whitehall or consist entirely of district auditors there is no such guarantee. What tends to happen is that the appointed members can become a self-perpetuating oligarchy frequently influencing Whitehall's choice of nominees to fill casual vacancies.

But this was not all. The Conservatives were insistent on a two-tier system with expensive and duplicatory Regional Executives. In government before 1970 and in opposition, therefore, we made clear that we opposed a system of control by nominees. Dick Crossman's White Paper had provided that doctors *plus* local authority representatives would form a majority over the Ministry custodians.

The Conservative Government's White Paper and Bill reverses this. Denied membership of the Executive bodies at the Area and Regional level, the consumer of the services – and this means give or take a few who opt out, every man, woman and child in Britain – is allowed access to meaningful control only through a body which Shirley Williams describes in the debate on the Consultative Document as 'The strangest bunch of administrative eunuchs any department had yet foisted on the House, a seraglio of useless and emasculated bodies'.

This had been our warning before taking office. But the decision had been taken and legislation enacted before Labour took office in March 1974. Coupled with the NHS in our criticisms in Opposition and Government was our attack on the wasteful reorganization of local government by the establishment of the two-tier system.

The results of the 1970–74 'reforms' of the National Health Service and local government were that NHS administrative and clerical staff increased by 23 per cent between 1970 and 1974, and local government staff by 13 per cent.

I referred at some length to NHS reorganization, and the wider problems of the use of manpower, in a speech at the annual joint conference of the Association of Municipal Authorities and the County Councils Association at Eastbourne on 19 November 1975.[1]

In local government, as recorded earlier, there were over 2½ million people employed against 1½ million fifteen years earlier, an increase of 67 per cent, very much higher than the increase in central government manpower. In particular – fearing for my safety on leaving the hall – I emphasized the proportion of local authority employees actually providing the services as against those constituting the supporting staff. Sections of the audience were clearly angered by my reference to 'Chiefs and Indians', 'teeth and tail', and the 'administrative overload' which meant economy at the sharp end, the people doing the job, dealing with those who need help.

On health service manning I pointed out that whereas in 1964 doctors, including GPs, were just over 52,000 and the administrative and clerical staff just over 48,000 – the doctors in a majority – by 1974 the figures were 63,000 doctors and 79,000 in the administrative and clerical grades.

Clearly these trends reflected pressures put on the services concerned by central government under successive Governments. But in both the NHS and in local government generally the problem was aggravated by legislative 'reforms'.

My Party when in Opposition strenuously opposed the reorganization imposed on England and Wales. We had accepted the principles of the report of the Redcliffe-Maud Royal Commission on Local Government in England with its stress on unitary authorities, and we feared – and we were right in the event – that the two-tier system would be expensive in terms of manpower and money. But the change having been made, we recognized that to thrust yet another reorganization upon the long-suffering Councillors and ratepayers would be a

---

[1] This was one of two major speeches to organizations covering great areas of our national life, the other being to the National Council of Social Service in London on 10 December. The four weeks from 19 November to 17 December 1975 were a period of peak load for public speeches, many of them requiring several hours of preparation. On 19 November was the principal speech of the Parliamentary year on the Queen's Speech, on the 20th the Local Government Conference at Eastbourne, on the 28th two speeches at hospital openings on Merseyside, on the 29th two Labour rallies at Carlisle and Newcastle, on 3 December the first annual Patrick Blackett Memorial Lecture at Imperial College, on 6 December the Degree Ceremony at Bradford University and the London Labour Mayors' Association dinner in Bloomsbury, on the 10th the National Council of Social Service, on the 12th my speech in Guildhall on receiving the freedom of the City of London, and on 17 December the Association of American Correspondents. The same four weeks included visits by the President of Tanzania, the Prime Minister of Mauritius, and the Soviet Trade Minister, the Rome EEC Heads of Government Conference on 1 and 2 December, a working dinner with the Terry Working Party on the film industry, two receptions for International Women's Year, the Queen's annual Diplomatic Reception, and a Parliamentary speech on the Queen's Civil List Bill. All this and Chrysler too.

burden not to be tolerated. I made clear in a speech at Newcastle in February 1973 that despite our views on the changes, the incoming Labour Government would not throw the whole of local government into the melting pot, with all the disruption and unsettlement that would create. The Secretary of State for the Environment said earlier in the year, when addressing the Association of District Councils, 'Reorganization is a fact and I do not have any proposals to undo it; after one major operation I doubt if the patient is yet strong enough to undergo another.' Local government must now be given time to settle down and solve the problems created by reorganization. It would be wrong to face it with a period of further uncertainty, which could only be damaging for services and for staff; though we reserved the right to amend the Act, both in general, and on individual boundaries, where that might be needed.

So it has been to the time of writing – and likely to remain so. The Environment Secretary[1] has meanwhile concentrated by administrative means on strengthening the position of the big cities within the county areas, for example, in civic functions extending beyond their own municipal boundaries, though this hardly diminishes the cost and confusion caused by the dual bureaucracy.

At the end of October I had received reports of a statement made in Detroit by the chairman of the Chrysler Corporation indicating a cut-back in production, and the probable closure of their British subsidiary, Chrysler (UK). Eric Varley, Secretary of State for Industry, immediately sent him a message demanding clarification.

The previous January I had met with the American Chrysler President, Lynn Townsend, and their Chairman, John Riccardo, at a small dinner organized by Sir Eric Roll (now Lord Roll), whose merchant bank, Warburgs, acted as Chrysler's UK adviser. Sir Don Ryder had been with me, and the visitors presented a gloomy prognosis of their company's prospects, with particular reference to their British subsidiary. In early 1974, they had said, the slump in the American car industry had meant a cut-back from an annual rate of $10\frac{1}{2}$ million to $8\frac{1}{2}$ million. In November the production rate had fallen to $5\frac{1}{2}$ million. Many plants had been laid off in the US, and he warned me about prospects in Britain. The fall in UK sales was 28 per cent; there was a serious liquidity problem in the British company, and he was considering applying to Finance for Industry (FFI) for a £25 million loan. Chrysler very much wanted to stay in Britain, but they were now taking over direct control of the British management. It was agreed that they should get together with Don Ryder. The crisis occurred nine months later.

When the Government received news of the sudden announcement in Detroit, we immediately requested Mr Riccardo's presence in Britain. On Sunday 3 November he arrived with his team at Chequers. A quick dinner was followed by a formal meeting in the Great Parlour. We had hardly begun when, symbolically, the lights blacked out through a local power failure: someone said the lights were going out all over Europe. Certainly for

[1] Peter Shore is the Minister referred to: these words were written before the change of Government.

Chrysler, as Mr Riccardo quickly made clear. I told them I had asked them to come over because of his announcement in America, made with no prior consultations. We were faced with a fait accompli. Chrysler should explain what options were open.

He explained that Chrysler (world-wide) had lost $255 million in the first nine months of 1975. He had had to make the reference to Britain, he said, because if he had not done so the facts would have been deduced by the press. The position of the British company had deteriorated seriously during 1975. The parent company had invested about £65 million in Chrysler (UK) and given them loans of £19 million. Since Chrysler had taken over the former Rootes group in 1967 losses had reached £70 million, £18 million in 1974. The final out-turn for 1975 was likely to amount to £40 million, and the forward estimates for 1976 were of still heavier losses.

The Chrysler Board had given him full authority to come to Britain and take any decisions he regarded as necessary to deal with the situation. But in return he had undertaken that any solution proposed would not involve any further cash investment in the British company, and that indeed it had to show an immediate operating profit.

He could see just two options.

The first was to transfer the complete ownership of Chrysler (UK) to the British Government on a 'going concern' basis. The second was to transfer the majority interest to the Government with Chryslers holding a minority interest.

If either option were agreed Chryslers would be willing to provide advice and help to the new company on technical, marketing and managerial questions. He and his colleagues saw no other solutions to the problem but were willing to discuss any proposals that the British Government might put forward. If no mutually acceptable proposal were forthcoming, the Corporation would have to take steps to liquidate, and this process would have to start at the end of November 1975 – that was in less than four weeks. 'Liquidation', he went on to explain, did not mean the formal appointment of a liquidator or receiver, but it did imply that production would be stopped immediately, and action would begin to sell off the company's assets. The time needed to complete the operation could not be estimated; it would be possible to sell off some inventory items fairly quickly but negotiations for the sale of major plant would take some time.

Chrysler realized, he went on, that this kind of action could involve serious disputes with the labour force, and he envisaged sit-ins in the main factories. The company would, of course, be liable for considerable sums in respect of redundancy payments, but when these were set against the tax reliefs available to them in the United States he estimated that over a period of years there would be no net expense to the corporation in this respect. He also recognized, he said, the effect on the corporation's international reputation – but this had to be weighed against the potentially disastrous cash-flow Chryslers were facing.

Naturally an old Parliamentarian had a few choice words with which to greet this cool abdication of responsibility, above all in human terms. When I used the word 'blackmail', and the accusation that he had held a pistol at the heads of the Government, under-statements though they were, they were thoroughly justified; the already unpopular tribe of multi-nationals had done anything but improve its image. Mr Riccardo had blithely talked of Her Majesty's Government taking over Chrysler UK as a 'going concern', a misuse of our common language even on the figures he had cited. It had an ageing model range, a seriously deteriorating penetration of the market – down to around 5 per cent – and on what he had just said the prospect of continuing losses into the indefinite future. He himself, responsible for the direction of the company, had shown that there was little or no prospect that whoever took over the company could make it viable even in the long run.

The Chrysler representatives commented that on certain assumptions the British company could be made viable even on a relatively low market penetration. If productivity were raised to levels comparable with that of other concerns, products updated and market penetration raised to 10 to 12 per cent, then there could be an operating profit in 1977. True, an essential part of this process would be the development of a new model at a cost of about $150 million of new money, and that model at best would not be on the market before June or July 1977; he conceded that there would be severe difficulties in maintaining production until that time.

Were all this true, it seemed odd that he should now be throwing in the towel. Where was the new model, and who was responsible for its absence from the scene?

The Iran Government's assembly contract for completely knocked down (CKD) kits of British manufactured parts could be profitable; 1976 should show a profit in this contract of £2 million, which would maintain employment for around 2,500 workers, mainly in the Coventry area. But he conceded that it was unlikely, if the rest of UK operations were closed down, that the Iran operation could be kept going. When we asked him if the more profitable production of commercial vehicles could be maintained, he confessed that it was not possible to keep the commercial side going as a separate entity, though it might be sold to another manufacturer. In January 1975, he went on, Chryslers had estimated that a package of £100 million would be needed to rescue the British company. Since then the situation had greatly deteriorated. He could not immediately estimate the cost of restoring viability, but would arrange for figures to be supplied to the Department of Industry.

When pressed about greater integration of Chrysler's British and French subsidiaries, again he was negative. Until 1973, he said, Detroit had had in mind a much greater degree of integration between the two countries and had begun to design their model range accordingly. But when the British company's profit situation deteriorated so seriously in 1974 this idea was rescinded. He went so far as to suggest that the decision to produce the Simca

1300 (C6) – the Avenger – in France, meant that the decision not to integrate had been taken, leading to the further deterioration of the British company. Labour relations in Britain, measured by disputes disrupting productivity, compared unfavourably with what was achieved in France. Chrysler's programme for joint consultation in Britain, going far beyond anything previously tried here, had had no effect.

He was sharply told that although he had explained the difficulties they faced, it seemed nothing less than extraordinary that given the amount of consultation which had existed between the company and the Government, they should now decide to move so precipitately, and without any notice whatsoever had made their announcement in the US, and then descended on Britain to tell the Government that they were declaring 27,000 people redundant in four weeks. Summing up, I said that although I understood the difficulties of the Chrysler Corporation in relation to their British company, it seemed to me that the British Government was being asked at unreasonably short notice to assume responsibility for a company whose future performance and viability were a wholly unknown quantity. Nevertheless, without any prejudice to the Government's decision, I was prepared for further talks between Chrysler and the Department of Industry, to consider the options he had aired – and any others that might be put forward. Meanwhile I was sure that Chrysler would agree that no further hint should be given of what had been said. Officials representing both sides of the table should prepare a short agreed press statement to be issued that night.

In the next few weeks the Cabinet and its committees were deeply involved in the Chrysler crisis – I chaired four Cabinet committee meetings, and five times it came before Cabinet itself. In view of the leaks about ministerial consultations – practically the only ones in the twenty-five months from March 1974 to April 1976[1] – I have no hesitation in saying that Eric Varley and his department were wholly resistant to the Chrysler proposals or any variation of them. Press stories[2] suggested that Harold Lever's intervention changed the Cabinet line. Certainly he was seeking an alternative solution, but my own reaction was influenced far more by the arguments of Willie Ross and his Minister of State, Bruce Millan, about the effects on Chrysler's establishment at Linwood near Glasgow. The Linwood factory had been built on virgin land and was regarded as a symbol of Cabinet responsibility for a new deal for industry in Scotland. Harold Lever was concerned about the Iranian assembly contract, and was sent out there for talks with the Shah

[1] I quickly knew who had leaked. He got his head thoroughly washed, and was warned that a repetition would mean resignation.

[2] Media reconstructions of the Government's internal discussions reached an all-time high in a Granada TV representation of a Cabinet meeting on the issue. All the Cabinet members were represented by Parliamentary lobby correspondents; I was represented by David Watt, then of the *Financial Times*. It was an unrecognizable caricature of that or any other Cabinet meeting. Even the Cabinet table was the wrong way round, and a turning-point attributed to 'Harold' (Lever) was directed to the wrong Harold, though his Iranian visit was a major contribution to the final decision.

and his officials. The idea that we should maintain the Iranian connection by arranging for them to assemble Leyland Marinas was rejected by Iran. In the confrontation between Eric Varley and Willie Ross I came out firmly for the Linwood proposition.

By this time Chrysler had been driven into a negotiating posture. Their first assessment was that a transfer of the British facilities servicing the Iranian project to Linwood would cost £19 million, and there would be over 10,000 redundancies in the Midlands. There would be a loss of £61 million over four years.

A not entirely united Cabinet reached its decision in mid-December, in the week which saw our final settlement of the 1976–77 public expenditure programme, and the settlement of the long dispute with the doctors. The proposal to which we were working provided that Chrysler UK would receive a Government subsidy, plus a continuing Chrysler contribution and Chrysler management. The Iran operation would continue. The Government would not, repeat not, take over Chrysler's liabilities, but would bear the first £40 million of the 1976 loss, and half any additional losses in 1976–79 up to £20 million in 1976 and again in 1977, £15 million in 1978 and £10 million in 1979, a total commitment of £72.5 million. We would also guarantee the £35 million loan from the Consortium of English and Scottish clearing banks provided it was counter-guaranteed by Chrysler Corporation.

Chrysler then accepted this in principle but would not accept any part of the £55 million required for capital investment and the development of the new model. They would move the 'Avenger' from Ryton to Linwood giving Ryton the C6 'Alpine' produced in France as the Simca 1307/1308. The entire cost of bringing the 'Alpine' to Ryton was forecast to be around £10–12 million, all of which would be funded by Chrysler Corporation. The balance of capital expenditure to develop the 'Sunbeam' 424, and to modernize and rationalize production facilities, would be borne by HMG by means of two loans, a 'guaranteed' loan of £28 million (guaranteed by Chrysler Corporation) and a 'secured' loan of £27 million (secured on the assets of Chrysler UK by means of a debenture).

On 16 December Eric Varley announced the package to Parliament, making clear that the Government had not been prepared to accept any scheme until only a week before, when Chrysler had stated that it was prepared to stay in Britain and that Chrysler UK would have the parent company's full support. Summing up the prospective cost, he set the total potential commitment at £162.5 million but this included the guarantee obligations and assumed that the maximum contribution to net losses would be paid. An agreement was signed on 5 January 1976. In the debate which followed the statement the Conservative Front Bench condemned the proposed agreement root and branch, and warned of the total cost falling on the taxpayer.

The following day the House, after an acrimonious further debate, passed, by 287 to 266, the Secretary of State's motion to authorize under Section 8 of the (Conservative) Industry Act 1972 the financial commitment of 'sums exceeding £5 million but not exceeding £162·5 million'.[1]

December 1975 was by far the most hectic and harrowing month I experienced in nearly eight years as Prime Minister, indeed in the eleven years and over of my Cabinet experience. The one escape was for two days for the European summit in Rome at the beginning of December. It meant, of course, a great amount of documentation and briefing meetings, though it proved almost a non-event.

President Giscard reported on the Rambouillet Summit, the very occurrence of which still rankled with some of the Prime Ministers who had not been invited – evidence that the Community was drawing apart instead of coming closer together. The Commission's President not unnaturally supported this criticism. Helmut Schmidt pointed out that none of the mostly declaratory seventeen points in the communiqué infringed the EEC's field of responsibility. I pointed out that the essence of Rambouillet was not decision-making, but analysis. No institutions had been or would be set up: everything discussed was to be pursued through existing bodies.

The one new proposal Rome discussed was our plan for tighter control of expenditure within the Community. Drawing on my experience as chairman of the House of Commons Public Accounts Committee (1959–63) I called for effective Parliamentary control through the European assembly, including power to summon and examine the heads or 'accounting officers' of the Commission's principal spending departments. There was general agreement among our colleagues, though it still cannot be said nearly three years later that effective and democratically audited control exists even today. This will now have to await the election of the European Parliament in the summer of 1979. Just as the Westminster Parliament did not begin to become effective until it challenged the royal spending power, so, in a different way, Parliamentary control is required to get a grip on the vast sums spent by Brussels. The big spenders in Brussels are not the members of the Commission, if one excludes some of their bureaucratic proposals for standardization.[2] The huge bills imposed on EEC countries come from

[1] In July 1978 Eric Varley, an opponent of the Chrysler rescue in 1975, announced that only £7.5 million of the £162.5 million remained. Chrysler was doing badly in Britain, and, as in 1975, was incurring losses in America. Varley was making his announcement against the background of weekly losses of £1.2 million at Linwood through a strike. It will be recalled that saving the Linwood plant had been a decisive factor in the Chrysler rescue. But in the following month, Peugeot made a take-over bid for Chrysler, to which the Government agreed. As a result the guarantee obligations were taken over by PSA Peugeot Citroen and the 'loss subvention' thus became less than the potential liability at the time of the 1975 rescue.

[2] In recent years there have been proposals, in the blessed name of harmonization, for laying down standards for nearly everything from Euro-bread and beer to the Euro-sausage, and one extraordinarily lunatic proposal to require the Kentish hop-growers to build mesh fences to separate the Kentish male hops from their female counterparts, in order to impose on them equality of misery with the regimented French male hops – in

national ministers, particularly the agricultural ministers. Helmut Schmidt has repeatedly complained that the farm ministers, not least his own, get completely out of control – including their own Governments' control – when they sit down together. In so far as restraint has been imposed in the last two or three years, this has derived from decisions taken at summit level – and also from the constructively obstructive performances of the British Agriculture Minister, John Silkin, in refusing to be budged in his campaign for economy and against the excesses of standardization.

It was not inappropriate that in Rome the meeting moved on from economy to Parliamentary accountability. Most of the continental Heads of Government wanted to lay down a firm date for community-wide elections: June 1978. We had to report that Britain could not be ready, though we accepted the principle of direct elections in place of the present system of selection by nomination from existing national Parliaments.

We needed more time for consultation in Parliament and with the respective political parties (the main hostility came from within the Labour Party). Denmark was not even able to commit themselves to elections in principle. It was not until the summer of 1976 that the European Council was able to agree on the principle, the allocation of seats and the timing – the spring of 1979.

The reason why the Rome Summit was so negative and disappointing arose from Giscard's proposal for an international summit conference on world economics – due to convene in the week before Christmas. It was to be genuinely 'North–South', with the participation of Governments from the advanced and the developing worlds. But it was not to be comprehensive. The French President decided who would be invited to participate, on the basis that it would be sufficiently representative in the countries chosen to be capable of discussing the world's problems. No EEC country would attend except France – as host. The President of the Commission, M. Ortoli, would be there virtually as an observer.

This imposed exclusivity had been strongly opposed by James Callaghan at the meetings of EEC Foreign Ministers. He felt that Britain should be at the Paris Conference, for we were as much involved through the Commonwealth in the problems of the developing world as was Paris through France Outre-Mer.

The Foreign Secretary was on a fair point though not in any sense a major point of principle. I backed him mainly out of loyalty, for it soon proved he was out on an uncomfortable limb. In truth, I considered that the Conference

---

what is normally regarded as the more sexually permissive society. This proposal, like most of the others, foundered through national objections, though as recently as the summer of 1978 the bureaucrats have attempted to lay down standards for the vinegar which customers of fish and chip shops in Yorkshire, Lancashire and other leading culinary centres slosh on their purchases. The proposal here was to ban the use of the dilute acetic acid favoured by British epicures, in favour of wine vinegar, the consumption of which would help to reduce the level of the EEC 'wine lake'.

would prove such a dreary failure that it hardly mattered one way or another whether Britain was represented. But Jim made the sound point that since oil supplies and prices would be an important issue, we should be there as the Community's only oil producer – an observation which could be guaranteed to raise Giscard's hackles, and those of others.

I said that we were prepared to be represented by the Commission when there was agreement amongst us on the line to be taken. There was no such agreement – certainly none on so central an issue as oil pricing. If Britain could not be there we would certainly refuse to be bound by any decisions of the Conference.

But what rapidly appalled me was the vehemence of our colleagues in denouncing this proposal as anti-'*communautaire*'. This was not for individual countries. We were a Community. The President of France would be there.

Helmut Schmidt, Thorn and Giscard himself said this was a test of the credibility of the Community. Referring to oil, Schmidt said that if Britain were there he would oppose Canada as joint chairman, and Norway as a participant. (How he would do this as a non-participant was not clear.) The Community was showing an unaccustomed degree of unity – against Britain.

I proposed a compromise. First, could we agree together on the target oil price? If so, then let France be there as our (self-appointed) representative. She could carry the EEC ticket into the conference room. But for a few minutes she would pass the card to Britain, who would speak briefly and then hand the ticket back.

We had taken up most of the morning. We adjourned for lunch – and agreed to meet at 4.30. Clearly the Community was facing a crisis caused by *Perfide Albion*. When we resumed Giscard said that he found the British insistence on this question 'somewhat irritating'. By this time I was just finding it somewhat boring. Denmark supported my compromise, and suggested that a British representative, sitting there, should be 'invited' by the President to speak. Ortoli agreed with the proposal provided we did not go beyond the mandate, whatever that was.

The deliberations dragged on into the evening – about ten hours in all, including lunch. The Foreign Secretary and I were due back for an important division. Messages were sent to the Opposition in Westminster asking to grant us valid pairs, which they agreed to do. The argument grew more vehement and increasingly boring. From time to time we adjourned, walked round the room, meeting in clumps, Helmut or Giscard breaking away to sound us out. Tempers were becoming frayed: trains and planes were being missed. Jim and I were very much in Coventry.

In the end, and with a very bad grace – matched, I am sure they felt, by equally bad grace on our part – they accepted my proposal. It was agreed that the Minimum Selling Price (MSP) for oil should be $7.50, Helmut Schmidt reserving his position at seven dollars. Jim was to receive the EEC ticket, but to speak for no more than five minutes. The EEC later ordered this to be reduced to two minutes!

In the remaining half-hour we cleared the rest of the business. Our colleagues raised the issue of protection – knowing we had our horns locked with Chrysler they feared that any deal would include protection against imports from Europe. The long-discussed Passport Union was agreed, as was my own proposal of earlier in the year, that our Ministers of Justice, the Interior, Home Secretaries, should meet to co-ordinate action against international terrorism. The first meeting took place the following February and proved useful.

Otherwise the Conference had been an acrimonious waste of time. We had seen the EEC at its worst: no doubt our colleagues thought they had seen wayward and selfish Britain at ours. I had felt it right to back the Foreign Secretary on a point of minimal importance, particularly in view of the reaction he met. In the event, when he spoke on the opening day, 16 December, his watch stopped while recording his two-minute speech. He was variously reported in the British press as speaking from 10 to 12 minutes, but reporting of his speech was minimal, most reports commenting on the anger of his EEC colleagues. As for Giscard's North–South Conference, it dragged on through the whole of 1976, finally expiring on 2 June 1977, with a 133-page report, signifying nothing, one of the longest non-events in post-war international history.

I left Rome feeling that if anything were ever to destroy in men's minds the great concept of European unity, it would not be a wrong decision or some cataclysmic upheaval. It would simply be that the EEC had become a bore. Three years after Rome that anxiety has not disappeared.

But the following day I had to report to the House – the worst reception I had, not least from our own people, in the two years. Jim Wellbeloved, now Defence Under-Secretary for the Army, denounced me in unprecedentedly violent terms for insisting on the Foreign Secretary's rights to speak in Paris, and was cheered by the Conservatives and by Labour pro-marketeers. When, after dragging on for nineteen months, the Paris Conference ended, none mourned its passing and few reported its discussions.

I felt it was right to back Jim, more out of loyalty than any enthusiasm for the Paris Conference. It was a very minor issue; even so it was the only time I had even the slightest disagreement of approach on any of the countless issues we had had to discuss together in those two years.

For other reasons, the Luxembourg Conference the following April was just as unproductive. The fires that were lit by Giscard's welcome creation of the European Council seemed to be damped down, and hardly a meeting in the following two years has seemed – at least to most of us on the outside – to be any more productive of achievement, with the exception of the Bonn Summit in July 1978, which led to the Schmidt–Giscard proposal on the European Monetary System, EMS.

The crowded week of Chrysler and the doctors' negotiations was also the week when we agreed the expenditure estimates for the coming financial year from 1 April 1976. It was more than usually difficult. Inflation had aggravated the already considerable problem of accommodating all the different claimants: defence, social services, housing, aids to industry, regional programmes, Wales and Scotland. Unless the Chancellor was going to be faced with the need to force up taxation – already endangering incentives at indeed all levels in industry – to intolerable levels, the departmental demands had to be reined in even more severely than in previous years.

On the Friday morning, 12 December, which mercifully ended that crowded week, Cabinet, adjourned owing to the weight of business from its normal Thursday morning meeting, was still finalizing the expenditure estimates, the Chrysler settlement and the doctors' question. I saw the estimates safely through and it was left to the Treasury to prepare the weighty tome setting out all the departmental programmes, spelt out in the minutest detail.[1] Not only are the figures set out for Parliamentary approval for the coming fiscal year, but forward estimates for the following four years are appended, item by item and sub-head by sub-head, following a decision of the then Labour Government in 1969. For the second year the proposed expenditure limits are pretty firmly decided, though subject to final decisions over the following year. For the third, fourth and fifth years the figures are increasingly less firm and subject to unpredictable expenditure items such as provision for unemployment benefit and other social payments, to say nothing of defence and other estimates contingent on world developments. The published *Supply Estimates* in recent years have tended to approach 900 pages, and close on 3 lb weight.

The 1976–77 Estimates and those for 1977–78 were particularly difficult to agree. After countless meetings between Joel Barnett, Chief Secretary to the Treasury, and the major spending ministers, the gaps were narrowed in meetings with the Chancellor. The Cabinet had agreed for the latter year that the provisional figures agreed the year before should be cut by £3,750 million. When Cabinet met on 5 December to take the final decisions, the Chief Secretary had reached bilateral agreements covering £2,600 million. £1,150 million were still to be found. Joel Barnett listed possible options adding up to £2,300 million – double that figure. In the event agreement, with great difficulty, was reached on £1,035 million.

Cabinet still had to approve the Chrysler statement when I had to leave for Guildhall for the Freedom ceremony. My wife and I were driven to the Law Courts, where a state coach was waiting – one of those ordered for Queen Victoria's Coronation in 1838. It was a bitterly cold morning for the ride through the City. Not only that, the gentle swaying of the coach could well

---

[1] For a description of the detail and the coverage of the annual volume of *Supply Estimates* see *The Governance of Britain*, pp. 68–9, and a photostat of two typical double pages of the 1975–76 Estimates, Appendix IV, pp. 198–201.

have led to a variant of sea-sickness had it gone on very much longer. I began to understand why one high Palace official had told me that he regularly took a couple of Kwells for the annual journey by coach for the State Opening of Parliament. So cold were my hands even after the procession through Guildhall to the dais, that I could hardly grip the quill-pen to sign my name in the book of Freemen: it must be the most illegible in the register.

Nevertheless it was a beautiful if somewhat terrifying ceremony. In my short speech I naturally referred to the role of the City in our fight to bridge our overseas payments gap, the theme of my speech a month earlier at the Lord Mayor's Banquet.[1] But also I referred to the role of the City in the fight for democracy – its role when Charles I sought to arrest the five members; the City's trained bands barring the King's troops at Turnham Green. And when the Protectorate itself turned away from democracy it was the City who welcomed back a monarch, while joining with Parliament in ensuring that neither he nor any successor should ever be allowed to hold our country in thrall again.

On Wednesday 17 December I was the guest of the Association of American Correspondents for their pre-Christmas dinner. Normally this would have been a light-hearted occasion, but I had decided some weeks before that I would use the occasion to appeal to the United States about the amount of money and arms flooding across the Atlantic in support of terrorists in Northern Ireland. I was, in fact, due to go to Northern Ireland the next morning, but for obvious reasons I could not inform them of this. My words, sent straight to the US, and widely published there, concluded with the following:

The financing of IRA terror, brutality and murder by misguided Irish-American sympathisers is a threat to those Irish-American links, because it is a threat to the people, majority *and* minority, Protestant *and* Catholic in Northern Ireland, and to the people in the South.

The British Government's responsibility is for the maintenance of law and order in Northern Ireland. Since the outbreak of violence began there in the summer of 1969, almost 1,400 people have been killed. The defence forces, the British Army – who, it should be remembered, went in in August 1969 to

[1] 'This year net invisible earnings have been running at £115 million a month, in the figures as published. But here I might draw the veil aside to indicate a small, intellectual dialogue the First Lord of the Treasury has been having with the other Commissioners of that august body. The monthly figures of invisible receipts, as published, are struck after including not only private sector invisible debits, but also net Government expenditure abroad, including for example the troops in Germany, Foreign Office overseas expenditure and part of our overseas aid. If that were not included, the achievement on invisibles would be seen to be considerably higher than I have said' (10 November 1975). The Committee on Invisible Exports has produced a number of reports segregating the private sector surplus. On this basis, their *Annual Report for 1977–78*, p. 5, estimates an increase in the net surplus from £1,087 million in 1968 to £4,354 million in 1977. They foreshadowed a fall for 1978, mainly because of increased overseas spending on developing North Sea Oil supplies.

protect the Catholic population – the Army, the Ulster Defence Regiment, and the police have lost nearly 370 of their men killed.

Killed, let it be clearly understood, not by a gallant band of men courageously fighting for their country's freedom against an army of oppression – which is the kind of myth they would like to foster in the United States – but killed from behind, or in the dark, indiscriminately by gun, bomb, and knife in pursuit of an ideology overwhelmingly rejected through the ballot box; killed not by men protecting the minority population, but men who are terrorising them.

Grievous though the number of deaths are among the defence forces, the number of civilian deaths is far worse. Over 1,000 men, women and children, including babes in arms, have been murdered: blown up in ships or in cars; shot in lonely farmhouses, mown down in the bars and clubs of Belfast, Londonderry and elsewhere.

In addition about 16,000 soldiers and civilians have been injured or maimed in this campaign; most of them in the bombing, but some of them – 200 this year – by the barbaric practice of shooting away the kneecaps of the victim, perhaps leaving him crippled for life.

Because it must be clearly understood in the United States that American money, the million and more dollars that have flowed from there to Ireland since 1971, has directly financed these murders, this maiming, this indiscriminate bombing, as have munitions smuggled illegally from the United States to Ulster and to the Irish Republic.

For example, those who subscribe to the Irish Northern Aid Committee, the principal IRA fund-raising organisation in the USA, are not financing the welfare of the Irish people, as they might delude themselves.

They are financing murder.

When they contribute their dollars for the Old Country, they are not helping their much-loved shamrock to flower. They are splashing blood on it.

Nor are they helping the minority Catholic population.

The vast majority of the Catholics in Northern Ireland, courageously represented by Gerry Fitt and his Social Democratic and Labour Party, abominate those killers who excuse their assassinations by saying they are acting on behalf of the minority population. The Catholics abominate, too, those of their former kinsmen, now separated by two, three or four generations, who from the safety of their own homes in the United States are playing the role of vicarious merchants of death.

The fact is that most of the modern weapons now reaching the terrorists in Northern Ireland are of American origin – possibly as much as 85 per cent of them. They are bought in the United States and they are bought with American-donated money . . .

I cited the leaders of Catholic opinion in Ireland, North and South, and in Britain, who had wholeheartedly condemned this bloody traffic: John Hume, deputy leader of the SDLP, himself many times threatened both by the IRA and by so-called Loyalist para-military groups; Jack Lynch, former Prime Minister of the Republic: Liam Cosgrave, the then Taoiseach.

So has Cardinal Conway, the Primate of All Ireland, North and South. Let no one on either side of the Atlantic impugn the right of the Cardinal Archbishop to speak on behalf of the Catholic communities of Northern and Southern Ireland. So has the Roman Catholic Bishop of Birmingham, where twenty-one people, mostly youngsters, were murdered in the bomb outrages in those pubs in November last year. The Catholic Bishop of Derry has specifically condemned the flow of money and arms. Are there those who claim to speak with more authority for the Irish Catholic community, than the Bishop of Derry?

They know that every dollar subscribed to the IRA is a dollar to undermine democracy in Ireland, to substitute gun law for Parliamentary government . . .

You, better than anyone else, can strip away the romantic legends, the myths of 1916 and all that, to which the IRA still so calculatedly cling.

You can tell the people back home that the killers of today have nothing remotely in common with the patriots of sixty years ago. That the men of the IRA are to the men of the Easter Rising what Al Capone was to Garibaldi. That they are prolonging the agony of Ireland, and so are all those who support them from afar.

My final quotation was from Conor Cruise O'Brien, who had said that the last thing Ireland wanted from the American people was ' "help" which promoted violence on this island. Quite a lot of that sort of help has come here in the form of dollars. Those dollars mean death.'

Embassy and consulate staffs in the United States reported very wide coverage of these warnings. The Central Office of Information asked me to record a radio programme for an American network, which in the end was transmitted by over 900 local stations.

My last duty before Christmas was, in fact, to visit Northern Ireland, which I did on Thursday 18 December. We were flown by helicopter from Aldergrove airport to Ebrington Barracks, Londonderry. From there we went on to visit 42 Heavy Regiment, Royal Artillery, the Strand Road police headquarters of the Royal Ulster Constabulary. There we found the Chief Constable in a state of high excitement. He had just – for the first time – received a Christmas greetings card from his opposite number in the Garda, the uniformed force across the border. From there we went to Fort George to visit the Third Battalion, Light Infantry.

I spent some time talking to eighteen or twenty fully accoutred infantrymen just about to go out on a routine patrol. I chatted to each – most of them were from Merseyside, some from my constituency. The last two I met were from Aberdeen and Oadby, Leicestershire. They then went out on the streets.

When we reached Belfast an hour later we were told that these last two had both been killed when a booby-trap bomb went off in a car about which they were suspicious. It was my fourth visit to Northern Ireland since the eruption of violence in the sixties, but this was by far the most tragic incident, underlining the degree of mindless violence and the vulnerability of our troops.

From Derry we flew to Stormont, landing on the castle lawn, and had lunch with the Secretary of State, his ministerial colleagues and officials, who were specially joined by the chief officers of the Security Forces, police and military. In the afternoon I flew on to Ballykinler in County Down and spent some time, first with men of the Queen's Lancashire Regiment, and also with some of their wives in their social clubs. Next I met members of the Third

Battalion of the volunteer, part-time Ulster Defence Regiment, another group whose members have faced murderous attack in their homes and elsewhere.

It had been a grim day – the worst of all my Ulster visits.

But before the New Year was more than a few days old there was worse news to come from Northern Ireland.

# Chapter 10

## FINALE

THE New Year began with a series of the worst atrocities Northern Ireland had seen. Fifteen people were murdered in the first week of January. The fragile Christmas 'cease-fire' was over. The murder campaign had become increasingly centred on County Armagh. In 1975, of the fourteen Regular soldiers who had been killed in the Province, nine had been done to death in Armagh, as well as one Regular policeman, one reserve policeman and five members of the Ulster Defence Regiment. In the same period thirty-nine civilians had been murdered. County Armagh had a 280-mile long frontier with the Irish Republic, and the pattern was for terrorists to cross the border, do their victims to death, and slip across one of the innumerable border crossings before the security forces could move in on them.

In the first week of the New Year, on 4 January, five Catholics were killed in their homes by Protestant extremists. The following day eleven Protestants were returning home from work at the textile factory in the village of Glennane in a mini-van. A man carrying a red torch waved the bus down, and a dozen or more armed men appeared. The Catholic driver was moved aside. The eleven were forced to get out, stand on the road, and were brutally shot down, the murderers again escaping across the frontier. Ten were dead, the eleventh was taken to hospital for an emergency operation.

The following morning I met senior officials, later to be joined by the Secretary of State, and the following day chaired the Northern Ireland Committee of the Cabinet. In the afternoon I called in Conservative leaders for discussion. Meanwhile, plans were prepared for a meeting on the Sunday at Chequers, attended by the Secretaries of State for Defence and for Northern Ireland, the GOC commanding the forces in Northern Ireland, and the Chief of the General Staff. I told them we must put the Special Air Service Regiment (the formidable SAS) into the province, concentrated on Armagh. It was agreed to move up the Spearhead Battalion and station them in Armagh.

When Parliament met the following day, 12 January, I announced these moves.[1] The SAS, I said, would be used for patrolling and surveillance – the House knew they would not always be in uniform. Extra police had been moved into the area, including the Special Police Group and the RUC's Anti-Assassination Squad. In addition, two battalions of the Ulster Defence

[1] *Hansard*, vol. 903, cols 27–30.

Regiment were mobilized and put into action, under the direct control of the GOC and the Chief Constable. The security forces had stepped up their activity throughout the area: the House would not expect me to specify all the measures in detail, but examples were:

1. More check-points for vehicles and people.
2. A much more extensive use of personal identity checks.
3. Increased surveillance operations, particularly along the border.
4. More extensive use of existing powers under the Prevention of Terrorism (Temporary Provision) Act 1974 to question people within a mile of the border.
5. More house searches in the area because of intimidation of householders.
6. Full use – but no extension – of existing powers to arrest and question suspects.
7. '. . . as the House knows, this border presents a special problem, but not all of the gunmen operating in Armagh escape to the other side of the border after their cowardly attacks. A number of practical steps are in hand. A new information system, based on automatic data processing, is to be introduced by the Army to handle existing records so that information can be processed and acted upon more quickly. More border roads can be closed if this is necessary for security reasons. We are studying urgently a number of other measures for the greater control of vehicle movement, including a possible system of passes for vehicles using those unapproved border roads which are being permitted to remain open. But we must be sure that any measures we take will be effective and not merely consume manpower without hindering the gunman.'

I went on to refer to closer co-operation with the Republic including a meeting between the Secretary of State and the Minister for Justice in the South, the previous Thursday. There was increasingly close and valuable co-operation between the RUC and the Irish police (the Garda), and the police forces on both sides of the border had been strengthened and the programme of 'joint activity' strengthened.

Mrs Thatcher and other Opposition spokesmen gave us their full support.

We felt that the situation had now become so serious that all parties at Westminster should not only be working together, but be seen to be doing so. Accordingly, I invited the Conservative leadership, and representatives of the Liberals, Scottish and Welsh National parties, the Ulster Unionists and the SDLP to meet at Downing Street for a completely free disclosure of the facts known to us and an equally free discussion – while, of course, leaving any of the invited parties uninhibited in any criticisms of proposals they might wish to make in the House. In addition to discussion meetings we also provided graphical 'presentations' of film and statistical material on the main

Northern Ireland issues, followed by questions and discussion. This went on for three or four weeks until the situation again – by Northern Ireland standards – became relatively quiescent.

The day after the Northern Ireland statement I opened a five-day debate on devolution, based on our now definitive proposals set out in a White Paper.[1]

The first aim was as far as possible to put the Scottish National Party in baulk by giving the Scots a clear choice between a greater control over their own affairs, nearer their home, through the Scottish Assembly, and ministers responsible to it, as against SNP separatism. Quoting Winston Churchill's writings on the First World War,

> The Allies floated to victory on a sea of oil.

I said that was precisely what the Scot Nats were trying to do. The parallel between them and the Douglas Social Credit Party in Alberta, I told the house, seemed a clear one. When Social Credit took control there, the utter economic impracticability of its proposals was disguised for a time by the discovery of oil in that province – even then it helped them to survive only for a short time. Now the cry was 'Scottish oil' – never 'North Sea oil', as their shouts always made clear. We in the south never talked of English gas: it was North Sea gas.

I challenged them on the vast help a United Kingdom Government and Parliament had made available to Scotland. Less than a month earlier we had signed the agreement with Chrysler. The maintenance of the Linwood plant had been crucial in our decision. Would a Westminster Government or Parliament have fought to save Linwood in a separatist Scotland? Would a separatist Government have had the resources, or the Britain-wide power, to have negotiated with Chrysler on all their British properties? Or the complex at Bathgate? I could have referred to Ferranti. What would be the prospects for workers on the Clyde in a separatist Scotland when the world faced a recession in shipbuilding?

After arguing against the ingenious, but in our view unworkable, Liberal proposals for a federalist situation, I explained our White Paper proposals.

There would be directly elected assemblies in Wales and Scotland, with real powers. In Wales the powers would be exercised in respect of executive powers, and in Scotland they would be legislative as well as executive. An idea of the powers devolved could be derived from current financial provisions.

In the case of Wales, about £850 million would have been involved in UK expenditure for the services to be transferred to the new Assembly.

In Scotland, public expenditure in the financial year 1974–75 had been, on

[1] Cmnd. 6348. The speech is set out in *Hansard*, vol. 903, cols 207–29.

services now proposed for devolution to the Edinburgh Assembly, about three-fifths of the total identifiable public expenditure in Scotland. Had the devolution proposals been operating in 1974–75, some £2,000 million would have been on devolved services – including a block grant of about £1,300 million, with contributions towards loan charges; about £300 million would have been met from local authority revenue raising and about £500 million from capital borrowing.[1]

The Lord President, Edward Short, who had masterminded all the Government's work on devolution since 1974, spoke on the second day to give a very full explanation of the legal powers transferred, and the precise working of relations between the Assemblies and Parliament.

Despite the disagreements between – and within – the main parties the level of debate over the five days was high. Mrs Thatcher, in a highly critical speech, quoted Burns so effectively as to win the praise of the Secretary of State for Scotland, Willie Ross, himself a regular first choice among Burns Night orators. He in turn quoted the poet,

> But Maggie stood right astonish'd,
> Till, by the heel and hand admonished,
> She ventur'd forward on the light,
> And, vow! Tam saw an unco' sight.

At the end of the full five-days' debate, the House voted. Two amendments had been moved. The first, in the name of the Conservatives, was defeated by 315 to 244, the Scottish Nationalists and Liberals voting with the Government. The second, moved by the SNP, was lost by 304 to 27, the Conservatives abstaining and the Liberals voting for the amendment.

The main question, asking the House to take note of the White Paper, was carried by 295 votes to 37, those in the 'No' Lobby including a very mixed group of Conservatives, Ulster Unionists, and one Labour member.

The Government had made clear that we were not hoping to carry the devolution legislation in the 1975–76 session, but were counting on seeing it on the statute-book in 1976–77. This hope failed.[2] The Bill covered both Scottish and Welsh devolution, and had an exceedingly rough reception, not least from an active group of Labour back-benchers from Wales and Scotland, and some from England, who made common cause with the Conservatives on 22 February 1977, in refusing the Government timetable motion (guillotine) by a vote of 312 to 283. The debate languish d and the legislation died.

In the 1977–78 session two Bills for Scotland and Wales got their Third Readings on 29 June and 31 July respectively.

For Parliament devolution has been a bore. But it has helped to weaken

---

[1] The problem of reconciling the figure of £2,000 million with the addition of the three figures (£2,100 million) is explained in *Hansard*, vol. 903, col. 224.
[2] See p. 189 above.

the forces of separatism. Perhaps the very fact that it has been so boring will be a factor persuading many people, not least many members, that now the legislation is through, the important thing is to make it effective, in due time amending it – perhaps strengthening it – but not making it a shuttle-cock between the main parties, confusing elections and wrecking the legislative programmes of future Governments.[1]

At the week-end James Callaghan and I flew to Elsinore on the invitation of the Danish Prime Minister for inter-party talks. The Hamlet environment was itself exciting, though the conference environment, in one of the Danish Labour movements' residential week-end study course establishments, less so. Instead of being round a table, as at Chequers in 1974, and Stockholm in 1975, it was held in an auditorium, with a large concourse of spectators and hangers-on of various kinds. The agenda was well-planned, involving four or five of us in opening up a subject, followed by general discussion. Inevitably

---

[1] After the text of this book was sent to the publishers, the referenda have taken place in Wales and Scotland.

In Wales the result was utterly decisive 58.8 per cent of those entitled to use their suffrage actually voted. Of those, 46.9 per cent voted against the package of limited devolution put before them; 11.9 per cent voted for, a majority of nearly four to one.

In Scotland the situation was more complicated. A number of Labour MPs, south and north of the border, had carried an amendment which would have the effect of nullifying any vote which failed to produce a pro-devolution majority vote of less than 40 per cent of the number of votes recorded.

The figures announced by the national Returning Officer on 2 March 1979, were: pro-devolution 32.85 per cent, anti-devolution 30.78 per cent and non-votes 36.37 per cent. Thus the required statutory 40 per cent criterion was very far from being met. Even the narrow majority of those who had voted was open to question, in that pro-devolution advocates, including two Scottish ministers, had advised opponents of devolution that their opposition could be just as well recorded by abstention as by voting against, since an abstention would operate against the achievement of a 40 per cent majority. Public opinion polls subsequently suggested that abstentionists acting on this advice totalled over 2 per cent of the total vote, which if polled could have led to a small majority against devolution.

The results presented the Cabinet with a grave problem. The law required the Government, should the 40 per cent 'Yes' vote not be reached, to lay an Order before Parliament which, if carried, would lead to the repeal of the Devolution Acts. The Government took three weeks after the declaration of the referendum poll to reach a view. There had been some hopes in the Cabinet that having laid the repeal Order, their own supporters would vote the other way and keep devolution alive. But strenuous inquiries by the Government Whips revealed that some forty or so Government back-benchers would join the Conservatives in killing devolution. After a long period of reflection, the Prime Minister called for inter-party talks, which were rejected by the Conservatives. The Scottish National Party, while still hoping for effective measures of devolution, tabled a motion of 'No Confidence in Her Majesty's Government'. This was taken over by the Conservatives who tabled a No Confidence motion of their own.

Although the Scottish Nationalists and the Conservatives were on opposite sides of the devolution fence, they combined forces in the vote on 28 March 1979, and with the help of the Liberals and most of the Ulster Unionists, defeated the Government in the No Confidence division, by a single vote, 311 to 310. The Government immediately decided that there was no alternative to a General Election, and the following day advised the Queen to dissolve Parliament. The date of the General Election was fixed for 3 May – its immediate cause therefore not being industrial disputes, pay policy, or the piling up of garbage in the streets during the strikes of public service unions – it was the impasse caused by the response of Scots and Welsh in the devolution vote.

I was given world economic planning with particular reference to the Third World.

François Mitterand was billed to speak on the problems of the Mediterranean countries, which he extended round Gibraltar to Portugal. I had to go out of the room: when I went back to the Conference Jim Callaghan alerted me to what he regarded as a rather worrying speech. I listened for a few minutes to him in French and then put on the headphones. This was worse. He was making a really passionate appeal for a socialist/communist electoral alliance in such countries as – he listed them – Turkey, Greece, Yugoslavia after Tito, Italy, France, Spain and Portugal; a socialist/communist electoral alliance which, if backed by the voters, would be followed by a coalition Government. I immediately moved the adjournment of the Conference to attend upon the Mayor. When a few of us got together over the Mayor's whisky, we decided on the order of speaking, Palme, Brandt, Joop den Uyl of the Netherlands – and I was given the task of the hatchet job. We were all of us totally opposed to what was suggested. Omitting the speech I made, I quoted for the benefit of the Europeans one of the most moving and poetic creations of our mutual classical English literature:

> There was a young lady of Riga,
> Who went for a ride on a tiger,
> They ended the ride
> With the lady inside,
> And a smile on the face of the tiger.

This led me to invent a new concept, 'Mitterandisme'. Euro-communism is a development involving the creation of Communist parties in individual West European countries, acknowledging little or no rapport with Moscow, but aiming each to establish 'Communism in one country'. Each – Italy, Portugal, Spain, France—has its own distinctive national version. There is little that established traditional parties can do about its arrival in each country, except either ignore it or fight it. 'Mitterandisme' on the other hand involves a conscious and deliberate system of alliance, coalition or working arrangement country by country between the democratic socialist party and the Euro-communists.[1]

The electoral alliance between François Mitterand and M. Marchais, the French Communist leader, in preparation of the French Assembly elections in March 1978, was the first formal alliance of the kind he had advocated. In the event it virtually broke as the Communists repudiated the originally agreed policy and stiffened their policy demands over a wide area of industrial policy, particularly nationalization.

---

[1] For a fuller treatment of Euro-communism, see my article in the *Guardian*, 5 November 1977 and an article in the *Spectator* by Hugh Thomas on 10 December 1977. The *Guardian* article led to a formal protest by the French Socialist Party to the National Executive Committee of the Labour Party, who issued me with a formal rebuke. This I noted but have not troubled to acknowledge.

While we were at Elsinore, I became involved in what proved to be a highly significant event in the European context.

The leading EEC countries had raised with me at the two previous meetings of the European Council the question of the succession to M. Ortoli as President of the Commission. There was a general view that one of the three new countries who had acceded to the Community in 1972 should hold the Presidency, and Britain was first choice. From March 1974 it had been assumed by them and by us that Christopher Soames would be our nominee. I was certainly prepared to nominate him, though there were some muted grumblings because of his tendency to be outspoken – not a bad qualification in Europe. About his total European commitment there could be no doubt. But in the autumn of 1975 he became seriously ill, and there were not unreasonable doubts on whether he could face up to all the rigours of the job.

James Callaghan discussed this with me in one of the more boring passages of the Elsinore conference – I think the Italian Socialists were speaking.

He said that EEC Heads of Government during the week-end had approached him about the situation arising from Soames's illness. He naturally wanted to put forward the name of George Thomson, a former Labour minister who was the other British Commissioner, and who had for years been his close friend. I knew that some of the European leaders considered him something of a lightweight, and that there was a real danger that if we sought to insist upon him they would turn to another country. 'What about Roy?' I said. The Foreign Secretary took this up with enthusiasm – but would Roy take it? I had no idea, but thought it worth while to take soundings. Helmut Schmidt – making it clear that he was speaking for others – said this was what they were waiting to hear. I had no idea whether Roy would be remotely interested, but I felt I should sound him out on our return to London.

It was a most difficult subject to broach. Our relations were by this time extremely good, though they had not always been so. I had asked him in 1974 to take over his 1964–67 Home Office appointment, because his resignation from the Shadow Cabinet over the referendum had taken him out of the mainstream, and his re-emergence as one of the twelve elected Shadow Cabinet members in 1973, which I had welcomed, did not enable me to appoint him either as Foreign Office spokesman or Treasury spokesman, even had I wished to do so, because James Callaghan and Denis Healey were firmly ensconced in the Shadow FO and Treasury posts.

Soon after our return from Elsinore Gaston Thorn came over to London to see me, and in turn asked about the chance of our nominating Roy. He made it clear that he had been talking to other Benelux leaders. I replied that it was much in my mind, but would Roy take it?

Roy came to see me. My task was difficult. I began by referring to a similar

8

interview with R. A. Butler just after the 1964 election.[1] Rab had been blamed for the narrow Labour victory because of an interview in a train with a journalist, when he had been somewhat defeatist about the election results. The Mastership of Trinity had become vacant, and knowing his Cambridge loyalties, and the fact that his uncle had been Master, I said that in approaching him about it I was not seeking to remove a redoubtable opponent. I should just hate to hear afterwards that he would have liked the post – a Royal appointment. He immediately said I should not assume that he would turn it down: could he sleep on it, and also consult his wife? The next day he accepted it. So, I told Roy, I was not playing tricks; he would be most difficult to replace, but knowing his deep European commitment I would hate to feel he had not had the chance. Moreover, European leaders wanted him. He fully accepted the sincerity of the offer, but he had to say he did not want the job. However, he had to go to Paris ten days later for the EEC Justice Ministers' conference I had proposed, and was due to meet Giscard – so could it be held over? The very next day he wrote to me and said he was very interested – would I please keep the appointment open.

This was a problem which concerned the timing of my impending resignation less than a month hence. I did not want him to lose the opportunity of running for Leader, and this was one of the factors weighing with me against any postponement beyond mid-March. Even before he went to Paris, he had decided. James Callaghan was kept in the picture: it was to his credit and those around him that Roy's acceptance was not peddled to the PLP electorate during the contest for the leadership in March and early April.

On the morning of Saturday 24 January I addressed the annual conference of the Welsh Labour Party, and then rushed off to Chequers for negotiations with Mr Geir Hallgrimsson, the Icelandic Prime Minister, who had come to England to discuss the armed deadlock which had arisen over British trawlers fishing in Icelandic waters. This had been a traditional fishing ground for trawlers from Hull, Fleetwood and elsewhere and there had been rough harassment by Icelandic armed coastguard vessels. Royal Navy frigates had gone to the area to protect them. This had involved a number of clashes, the daring seamanship of the frigates meaning that the Icelandic marauders frequently had to pull away to avoid collision. The Icelandic Government was a somewhat rough-neck coalition, with the second party extremely hawkish about our trawlers.[2] Threats were made that Iceland would leave NATO, where she had and has a key role to play in Atlantic defence. Negotiations

---

[1] See *The Labour Government 1964–1970*, pp. 75–6.

[2] James Johnson, an MP for Hull, was right when, following my Parliamentary statement on the talks, he said, 'I accept' Mr Hallgrimsson has internal difficulties with a hostile Cabinet, perhaps a hostile Parliament, and perhaps a hostile population on the pavements' (*Hansard*, vol. 904, cols 426–7).

were refused until Dr Luns, the NATO Secretary-General, persuaded the Icelandic Government to send a high-level mission to London.

During lunch and for the rest of the day we discussed quantities of fish, and Icelandic harassment of our trawlers.

On Sunday 25 January I had a rest from cod. There was a problem to settle about North Sea oil. British Petroleum had been given a special position in tapping and marketing, in effect as a chosen instrument on behalf of the British Government. But they were a world-wide organization – as witness the oil pipeline from Alaska. On the face of it there was an important conflict of interests. In its North Sea capacity BP had a special responsibility, but it was also a world oil power, and it would be difficult for them to become a divided personality. Tony Benn suggested that he and I should meet their chairman and deputy. He reminded me of an occasion when the question of merging the British Motor Corporation and Leyland was in issue. I had asked Donald Stokes of Leyland and Sir George Harriman of BMC for dinner at Chequers, and there the marriage had been duly arranged. Would I, he suggested, arrange a similar evening with himself, the Chairman of the new British National Oil Corporation, Lord Kearton, and the Chairman of BP and his colleagues.[1] We discussed the problem for several hours: I then proposed a solution. BP should remain a world-wide corporation, but they should create a North Sea subsidiary to be called, e.g., BP (Dogger Bank) Limited. Operationally it would be detached from the main company. Staff would be specially seconded from the parent company, and be reinforced by new recruits. But while so seconded they should have no contact with the parent organization. This was quickly agreed, and however illogical a compromise – as so many typically British solutions are – it has worked.

It was back to Icelandic cod in the morning. Mr Hallgrimsson began the discussions by declaring that both our countries had supported a 200-mile limit at the United Nations Law of the Sea Conference (UNLOSC), and that UNLOSC was about to announce that the relevant 'Coastal State' would decide the total size of the catch in her waters. His UNLOSC claims were far from the truth. At the time of writing, two and a half years after our Chequers meeting, UNLOSC is as far from an agreement as ever; on present form it looks like discharging its mandate in God's good time, perhaps not in the lifetime of those of us who met in January 1976. Iceland, he went on, had no surplus catch to allocate to other countries; already a third of their fishing fleet was laid up. While recognizing the problems for Grimsby, Hull and other British ports, he proposed an agreement which would (1) take account of the fact that Iceland alone should decide the size of the 'Total Allowable Catch' (TAC); (2) agree on measures to conserve fish stocks; (3) within those parameters consider what could be done for the fishermen of Britain.

The discussions were long and tedious. There was, inevitably a clash of

[1] See p. 136 above.

interests. My colleagues and I were concerned for our trawler-men from the north-east and the north-west, an important minority community with a romantic calling, to say nothing of the preferences of our consumers. But what we had to realize also was the fact that the fishing industry was vital for our guests. While Iceland is not a single-industry nation, fishing is vital to her economy and a way of life for so many of her people. Even British Members of Parliament for fishing ports were ready to concede the strength of Iceland's case.

Moreover, we were conscious of the vital role Iceland plays in our North Atlantic defences. We were anxious to get as fair a deal as possible for our own industry, recognizing that Iceland herself had cut her own industry back, and had come to an agreement of only limited generosity with West Germany.

The talks dragged on. We deputed our respective scientists to seek to agree on the facts and figures. For two days we argued about the TAC and our share of it. James Callaghan tried vainly to split the difference between our minimum demand and their maximum offer, only to find their maximum repudiated. In any case it was not just cod, but included other varieties of various degrees of edibility and consumer preference.

By the Tuesday both sides were spawning statistical solutions. They pressed us to adopt the solutions the Canadians had accepted – which would have given us 50,000 tons annual catch. I tried a few essays. If TAC were fixed at 265,000 tons for cod, and allowing 15,000 for the Germans, Scandinavians and others, Iceland might take 170,000 and Britain 80,000. This was rejected. I tried a more sophisticated formula. Iceland's unequivocal right to fix the TAC would be acknowledged, we should have $x$ per cent of it, provided our share did not fall below a floor figure of $y$, or rise above a ceiling figure of $z$. This went better, provided we could agree on translating algebra into arithmetic. I suggested 28 per cent for $x$, with a minimum of 65,000 and a maximum of 75,000 *plus* 10,000 tons of other varieties. He suggested 60,000 and 75,000 *including* other varieties.

Meeting again on the Tuesday, in my room at the House of Commons, he said he would go home 'and fight' for 65,000 (*including* 10,000 other varieties) but could not say there was any certainty that his proposals would be accepted. But he would try – Britain to have 25 per cent of TAC (cod) with a minimum of 55,000 and a maximum of 60,000 tons. We, of course, reserved our position on the catch, but asked how long the agreement would last. He offered two years back-dated to November 1975. We said the agreement should begin with the signature, and last as long as their undertaking to Germany, i.e. into 1978.

The Foreign Secretary dangled a long-term economic agreement before him, with help, e.g. a tied loan on soft terms as long as Iceland faced balance-of-payments difficulties. Hallgrimsson undertook to examine these possibilities and give us his final answer on the Thursday. It became clear that he could get no response from his coalition partners and he flew back without an agreement, leaving us without any cod except what could be caught under Royal Navy protection. Very soon the fish and chip shops of the north and elsewhere were using their ingenuity with substitutes, the most striking – and popular it appeared – being those produced by Chinese caterers, and the more ingenious members of Britain's immigrant population.

It was a sad story, disastrous indeed for some of our fishing ports – the facts were as Jim Johnson stated them in the House, justifying the ancient truth that one cannot very far negotiating with a Prime Minister facing the kind of problems for his major industry that our guest was.

At the beginning of February 1976 the House had to elect a new Speaker. Selwyn Lloyd had occupied the Chair since 1971 on the resignation of Horace King (later Lord Maybray-King).

The Conservatives and Liberals let us know that they would support our choice of George Thomas, since March 1974 Chairman of Ways and Means and Deputy Speaker. His election was a matter of great delight to me. In the late forties I had seen him successfully presiding over the House, sitting as a Committee of Ways and Means on the annual Finance Bill. Those were the days when all stages of the Bill were taken on the floor of the House.[1] He was appointed as a member of the panel of Deputy Chairmen of Ways and Means, recruited for its successive stages, and this was where he first proved his ability in the Parliamentary chair. As a very young minister I decided that if I were ever in a position to influence the choice of Speaker in a later generation I should support him. Not many would have regarded him as Speaker material in those days. In his own Church and in Wales he was well known as a somewhat outlandish left-winger, often away from Westminster, once turning up somewhere on the wrong side of the Communist lines in Greece. But as a minister from October 1964 to June 1970 he had impressed the House as equally successful in the Home Office as an Under-Secretary of State, at the Commonwealth Office as Minister of State, and at the Welsh Office as Secretary of State. In that capacity he had to play a leading part at the Investiture of the Prince of Wales in Caernarvon Castle on 1 July 1969. He was not Welsh-speaking, in common with many sons of the South Wales valleys, but he was well tutored.

In my speech of congratulation on his election as Speaker I referred to another occasion, when he sought to address the Lord Mayor of Caernarvon in the language. The Welsh translation of Lord Mayor is, I understand, *Arglwydd Faer*. In his enthusiasm George proceeded to address him as Arglwydd Mawr (or as one record has it 'Fawr' – the female version), the translation of which is 'Almighty God'.

He has proved a good and sociable Speaker, popular in all sections of the

[1] See p. 27 above.

House, and has built on the practice of his two immediate predecessors in his exchange visits with other presiding officers, particularly in the developing world.

Between 22 January and 11 February I had a number of speeches, mainly economic and industrial: the French Chamber of Commerce, the Overseas Bankers' Club, the Birmingham Chamber of Commerce and Industry, and the Parliamentary and Scientific Committee. On 4 February I held a party at No. 10 for the excellent and courageous non-doctrinaire Northern Irish trade union leaders, and at the week-end a series of constituency engagements, when I went down with a severe feverish cold. Fortunately on arrival in the small hours at Chequers my condition was correctly diagnosed by the Scottish Chief Wren, who prescribed a nationalist hot toddy of such potency that the flu germs conceded, and I was just fit enough to receive the Federal German Chancellor the next morning for a discussion on the next round of European economic talks. To preserve him from infection we drove to Northolt Airport in separate cars, before taking part in a brief press conference and series of TV interviews. We had a formula – now canonized by three years of Anglo-German repetition. We were at one in what needed to be done: each country must pursue separate and national, but co-ordinated, paths to economic salvation.

Then a new and potentially dangerous event took place. Angola was torn apart by internal warfare supported on one side by external aggression. The ruling régime sought help from outside. Certain British recruiting agents, including some with a record in Northern Ireland, began to recruit mercenaries from Britain for service in Angola. Very soon alarming stories began to hit our headlines. In the fighting some of the mercenaries proved ineffective against their determined, Cuban-led adversaries, and a number were lined up and summarily executed by some of the thugs leading them. Pictures appeared in the British press and on television. Evacuated from Angola, forty-four of the surviving mercenaries flew into London airport and were questioned by the police. Three had been seriously wounded.

Our laws, despite the Foreign Enlistment Act, were powerless to deal with the situation, and I announced in the House the appointment of a Committee of Privy Counsellors, led by Lord Diplock, together with Sir Geoffrey de Freitas and Sir Derek Walker-Smith, to inquire into the whole issue, including the adequacy or otherwise of the Foreign Enlistment Act, relating to the recruitment of mercenaries. Reggie Maudling for the Opposition had the previous day spoken strongly about this 'bloody business', though Mrs Thatcher, whom I had consulted before making my announcement, was doubtful whether any checks could or should be placed on foreign enlistment.

As British citizens have within present recollection fought for many different causes overseas – (Hon. Members: 'Not for money') – any Act of this kind can be operated not according to whether the Government approve of the cause but only according to objective tests laid down by law about British interests. Will the Right Hon. Gentleman confirm that the Foreign Enlistment Act makes no distinction between whether those who fight overseas are paid or are volunteers.

In reply I confirmed that the question of the Foreign Enlistment Act had been relevant in a number of past cases, particularly the Jameson Raid in South Africa. Certainly more recently many British Jews and others had gone to Israel to fight in the Yom Kippur War. This case seemed to be different:

> If murder has been committed or is alleged to have been committed abroad, even in Africa, by any British citizen against another, those who committed the offences are liable to be charged in this country in respect of such action if the facts support such a charge.[1]

The Diplock Committee reported the following August. In general it recommended no change in the existing law to prevent a UK citizen from accepting service as a mercenary abroad. But it proposed that any new legislation

> should be directed to empowering Her Majesty's Government to prohibit recruitment in the United Kingdom of mercenaries for service in specific armed services abroad. The activities prohibited under this head should be widely defined so as to include publishing information as to how or where to apply for employment as a mercenary or how to get to the place where such employment is available, and making any payment or taking part in any arrangement to facilitate or promote such employment.

Such an Act should be brought into effect in any particular case by Order in Council, or other appropriate statutory instrument requiring affirmative resolutions by both Houses of Parliament specifying the forces to which it is to apply.

During this period the Queen gave three successive receptions at Buckingham Palace for firms and individuals who over the past few years had received the Queen's Award for Industry. Few of them would have known that the original idea had been put forward by Tony Benn. He had come to me soon after the formation of the 1964 Government with the idea that Parliament should initiate an award to industrialists for export achievement or advances in technology. I pointed out that the Queen, not Parliament, was the fount of honour. However, it seemed an excellent idea, and I asked the then Federation of British Industries to prepare a plan, under the leadership of the Duke of Edinburgh. Any firm, large or small, could apply – and a considerable number of the awards have gone to very small firms. Those so honoured were entitled to fly a large banner over their factory or company headquarters, and to use the Award symbol on their company letterhead. A

[1] *Hansard*, vol. 905, cols 236–47.

committee of industrialists chaired by the Duke of Edinburgh adjudicated on each year's applications, and usually rather less than a hundred awards have been made in each annual list, announced on the Queen's birthday – her real birthday, not the official birthday in June which is the occasion for the Birthday Honours List. In addition to recognizing achievement, the use of the symbol on a firm's letterhead has played no small part in further advancing exports.

During these weeks I was receiving reports of unhappiness in the Civil Service about constant press and Parliamentary attacks on 'the bureaucracy'. To reply to these I decided to take advantage of the fact that Cyril Plant, head of one of the Civil Service unions, had been elected Chairman of the TUC General Council. As Minister for the Civil Service, therefore, I arranged a party at the Civil Service Department in his honour.

In my speech I appealed to Disraeli's classic reply to Gladstone on public expenditure.

> 'Mere abstract and declaratory opinions in favour of reduction and retrench-ment are of no use whatever. I have so often maintained it in this House that I am almost ashamed to repeat it, but unfortunately it is not a principle which has yet sufficiently entered public opinion – expenditure depends on policies . . .'

But, I went on,

> If expenditure depends on policy, so do the numbers of those who, by no decision of their own incidentally, are required to make that policy effective. And of course some of the policies introduced over the last ten years are inevitably staff-intensive. I have referred to the Health Service, and the parallel development of personal social services within local government. The same applies to the revenue services, the Inland Revenue and Customs and Excise. Successive Chancellors of all Parties have sought to introduce refinements into existing taxes in addition to inventing new ones. The motive – apart from revenue – has frequently been the desire to counter avoidance and thus make the system more fair, or to introduce systems of different treatment between individuals, based on 'cancellarian' canons of equity and social justice. Some new taxes, such as VAT, introduced in 1973, have inevitably proved staff-intensive, as everyone I think knew they would.
>
> And the demand is not just for more work to be done, but for more compli-cated and sophisticated work. I have referred to the increasing complications of tax work in the cause of fairness. The same goes for social security. The developing relationship between government and industry imposes new, sophisticated demands on both partners. And of course the traditional public service functions of safeguarding citizens' personal safety are becoming more difficult, as recent events are unfortunately demonstrating more and more often.

Replying to criticism of civil servants' pensions – they had certainly been treated quite generously – I commented that the relevant decisions had been taken by the Conservative Government in 1971, the then minister describing the Bill as a 'far-reaching and overdue reform'. There had been no criticism at that time by the Labour Opposition or anyone else.

This speech was widely reported in the serious press, and welcomed by the Civil Service.

Meanwhile an interesting constitutional issue was arising over the question of evidence before Select Committees. Dick Crossman, at my request, had extended the range of Select Committees in the late sixties. By this time they had proliferated quite extensively, to the point where attendance there was detracting from attendance in Parliamentary debates. A number were generating sub-committees armed with all the powers of requiring the attendance of witnesses enjoyed by the main Committees. One of these set out to examine the history of the Chrysler affair.[1] The December leaks had featured, indeed greatly exaggerated, the role played by Harold Lever, the Chancellor of the Duchy of Lancaster. The sub-committee in question summoned his appearance before them. This I vetoed, and was questioned in the House on the matter. Precedents, so far as they existed, were murky. There had been a case centuries before where a member had been summoned to appear, had refused, and was committed into custody – at which point he decided to respond to the summons.

The Chairmen of the principal Select Committees met, and deputed Mr du Cann, Chairman of the senior Committee, Public Accounts, to see me. I explained the decision I had reached. There would be no Downing Street interference with the attendance of any minister summoned to answer questions arising out of his departmental duties. Indeed, I went further. If a Select Committee felt that the subject raised matters within the purview of another minister's duties, he also could be asked to attend. I took the case of a ministerial action taken in connection with the EEC, e.g. at some EEC ministerial meeting – for example, in the agricultural field. If the Committee felt that the question under examination directly affected the work of another minister, for example, the duties then carried out by Shirley Williams (later Roy Hattersley) on prices and consumer protection, then it was appropriate that such a minister should attend as well as the Agricultural Minister. What I could not accept was the suggestion that any minister referred to in press stories as having taken a particular line in the Cabinet on the question, having no relevant departmental duties, should automatically be subject to a Committee summons. Apart from the fact that such summonses could be based only on leaks, there would be a crossing of lines of departmental responsibility. Such invitations might be based on pure press speculation.

There was a particular problem here in respect of ministers holding no departmental portfolio, such as the Lord President, Lord Privy Seal and the Chancellor of the Duchy of Lancaster, who from time immemorial have chaired Cabinet committees, or have been sent on missions by Prime Ministers. To call them would blur existing ministerial responsibilities, and impair collective Cabinet responsibility.

Edward du Cann went back to report to his fellow-chairmen. I heard

[1] See above pp. 195–200.

8*

nothing more of the problem, nor so far as I am aware has it been pursued.

The rest of February was quiet – a speech to the Parliamentary and Scientific Committee, a visit from the Prime Minister of Luxembourg to discuss the forthcoming EEC summit in his capital, a call by the Speaker of the Egyptian Parliament and a meeting with Northern Ireland church leaders.

In that month my appointments' secretary, Mr Colin Peterson, concerned among other issues with Prime Ministerial recommendations to the Queen for appointments to Bishoprics, had completed discussions with the Church authorities for a new procedure. This was made possible by the creation of a new Church authority between ecclesiastics and laity, the Synod. Our agreement, to be ratified by the Synod in July, involved a closer relationship between the appointments' secretary and the Archbishop's secretary and others concerned with senior church appointments.

Following diocesan consultations, the church authorities would submit two names to the Prime Minister, indicating their preference as between the two. The Prime Minister would then make his recommendation to the Queen, not necessarily choosing the name of the one preferred by the ecclesiastics. He would further have the right, though this would be regarded as an exceptional procedure, to ask for a third name to be submitted, should he have difficulties about the first two.

Even this agreement did not end controversy since some ecclesiastics feel that No. 10 should have no place in the nominating procedure. But both my successor and I had to point out that a nomination to the episcopal bench is directly or indirectly a nomination to the High Court of Parliament, for not only do the two Archbishops but also the Bishops of London, Durham and Winchester automatically become members of the House of Lords, but others, up to a total of twenty-one, take their place there on the basis of the seniority of their sees.

During the first week of March I went to Liverpool, where I held a press conference to launch a statement on my proposals for reform of the law on contempt and defamation in return for press understanding on privacy. My proposals were first put forward to press proprietors on 9 December[1] and were later worked out in detail in the 4 March statement:

In the Government's view changes in the laws on Contempt and Defamation which would, in the interests of the press and the public, increase the right of the press and the broadcasting authorities to comment on issues of public concern, must be balanced by voluntary measures, agreed with the Press, to guarantee the individual citizen and his family an effective right of Privacy. For what is or should be meant by the right of Privacy is extremely difficult to define, and particularly to define it in legal terms.

No less than five Bills or draft Bills attempted to do this in the years between 1961 and 1970. Nevertheless, other countries have embodied such a right in

[1] See pp. 228–9 below.

their statute law. For example, the German Federal Republic, France, the USA, and, in Canada, British Columbia.

I went on to deal with the problems of defining privacy in these terms:

A friend of mine with great knowledge of the Press, but not a lawyer, thought that the shortest and most satisfactory definition would be a clause which said 'Newspapers will accord to the general public the same rights of Privacy they accord to their own proprietors, or even the proprietors of other newspapers.' This, however, might be thought to be an unwarrantable intrusion into the freedom of the Press. But clearly we would need an effective means of ending those practices, easy to recognise, difficult to define, which are offensive to a citizen's privacy and not an issue of public concern.

While no decisions have been taken, the Government would like to draft, in consultation with the Press and broadcasting authorities, following the public debate which the Green Paper should stimulate, a Code of Practice or Statement of Policy to govern the treatment of the Privacy question by all concerned. That is the way we should proceed. But I repeat a voluntary code must be effective. For what it comes down to is the question of enforcement of the Code of Conduct or whatever Instrument we are able to agree on. The present constitution and practices of the Press Council do not, in the view of the Government, seem adequate to meet the need. While a voluntary embargo by the Press on intrusions into privacy may cover 90 per cent of the cases which at present give offence, there must be an effective sanction imposed by the Press which would make any would-be Code-breaker think seriously before doing so. If only one or two newspapers break the Code they put heavy pressure upon the others to do so.

We are left with the problem of defining invasions of Privacy. Matters like intrusion in the private grief, for example, of a bereaved family, may perhaps be relatively easy to define and I believe there will be a general willingness to comply with the definition. . . .

Again, there is also much public criticism of some of the so-called revelations in the gossip columns of certain, though by no means all, newspapers. It might be impossible to stamp out entirely the payment of money to get spicy information from waiters, cloakroom attendants, taxi drivers and others, and self-control must therefore be in the hands of those who produce the papers or broadcasts, with the ultimate power of machinery to which I have referred on an all-industry basis. But let me add that in my view protection should not be forthcoming for public persons in cases where their public actions could endanger security in any way, or any protection which might be instrumental in hushing up bribery or corruption at local or national level, whether involving officials or elected persons.

In this connection my speech and published statement referred to the European Convention on Human Rights, Articles 8 and 13, beginning with the quotation:

Everyone has the right of respect for his private and family life, his home and correspondence.

Article 13 states that

> Everyone whose rights and freedoms set forth in this Convention are violated shall have an effective remedy before a national authority notwithstanding that the violation has been committed by persons acting in an official capacity.

This was an important offer to the press, because of their understandable concern about restrictions on their freedom under the Official Secrets Act, and also the sub judice rule. For example, the *Sunday Times* had been fighting the thalidomide case for more than a decade, and were inhibited from publishing what they had discovered because the matter was before the courts under a libel action against the *Sunday Times.*

Attempts to raise the matter in the House had foundered because of the sub judice rule, but in our Opposition years I had persuaded Mr Speaker Selwyn Lloyd to accept the proposition that whatever the laws in respect of the press, Parliament could not be muzzled and that we should be free to debate the thalidomide issue. For what might otherwise occur was that a matter of great public importance could be precluded from debate in the press and in Parliament by the issue of a writ which was not proceeded with for many years. Mr Speaker accepted my submission, which meant that Parliament was once again in control.

Writing rather less than three years after my speech of 4 March, I have to report that no progress has been made on my proposal. There is still no statutory provision of privacy, despite the European Statutes quoted above. Nor have the press problems in relation to defamation and contempt been eased.

From my own experience since leaving No. 10, I would suspect that certain organs of the press have shown that they cherish the right to invade privacy more than they would welcome any easements of the law in respect of defamation and contempt.

In that week I had chaired – as was my practice once a quarter – the meeting of Neddy in the Millbank Tower. The following day, 4 March, the Taoiseach, Mr Cosgrave, came over for talks on Ireland, with particular reference to security. The talks were in no way difficult. Our shared interest in security across the border had been underlined by the recent events in Armagh.

But just as we were about to meet for lunch on Friday 5 March, an entirely unrelated event occurred, destined to lead to very serious economic developments.

I looked at the No. 10 ticker-tape just before going up to lunch. The pound had fallen fractionally, less than half a cent, below two dollars. The Maginot line had been breached.

During the crisis which had broken on 30 June 1975, the £ had fallen below $2.20. For months we had been told that two-twenty was the critical level.

Below that the oil sheikhs would take their money out of Britain. This was urged upon ministers by the Treasury, when they were reacting to the June crisis by their rapidly-prepared and statutorily-based incomes policy. The mineworkers' conference and the 11 July statement had held the situation, but the £ had steadily fallen from $2.1725 on 1 July to $2.1415 on 1 August, $2.1060 on 1 September and $2.0430 on 1 October. It was held about that level, sometimes with Bank of England help through buying sterling with the sale of dollars and other currencies, until in January and February it hovered between $2.02 and $2.03.

A few days before 5 March James Callaghan, about to go abroad for an extended tour, had voiced his anxieties to me. The Treasury weren't bent on forcing the £ down further, were they? Would I perhaps call a meeting on his return of the key ministers who dealt with these matters, to make quite sure there was no fatal slide? I told him that I, too, was carefully watching the decision. Certainly no decision had been taken, and the Treasury had given no hint of any move below the two-dollar market. We would be meeting on this and other questions, but not until he returned.

On seeing the tape I sent for the Chancellor, and somewhat heatedly asked him if he was aware of the fall below $2.00, and whether this had been foreseen, or even arranged. He was most reassuring. He had seen the figure. What had happened was that a sudden demand for sterling had unsettled the market, and the Bank of England, apprehensive that sterling would rise too high – and thus make our exports less competitive – had sold sterling to keep the rise within bounds. Unfortunately they seemed to have over-reacted and the £ had gone just over the two-dollar edge. But this was not an action based on policy. It would be held at two dollars.

But in the volatile foreign markets the reaction was far different. The Rubicon had been crossed. The Emperor had no clothes. There was no shortage of metaphors, only of buyers of sterling. It was only later that I learnt that the markets had for long heard rumours that the Treasury had been harbouring a fetish based on the belief that the real value of the £ should be $1.88.[1] Perhaps this was so. Perhaps they were right, but it was in flat contradiction to what the Chancellor believed and to his words of reassurance. When the foreign exchange market closed on Friday, sterling stood at $1.9820.

The fall continued. On Monday 8 March, sterling fell a further five cents, despite heavy Bank of England support, to $1.9425; the following day to $1.9145. On 11 March it rallied to $1.9355, falling to $1.9265 on Friday 12 March. Apart from national considerations, this was worrying news to me personally. I had set Tuesday, 16 March, for announcing my resignation from the premiership.

When Labour returned to office in March 1974 I then decided that I should

[1] For apparent confirmation of this see the *Sunday Times*, 14, 21 and 28 May 1978 (reprinted in octavo), *The Day the £ Nearly Died*.

not continue as Prime Minister for more than two years, even assuming that
we won the second election, which was inevitable and could not be long postponed. If possible I hoped for an earlier date, and for some time had the
Party Conference of October 1975 in mind. My first target was to get the
EEC negotiations through, followed by the referendum. This was achieved
by June 1975, but was followed by the payments crisis of July. The consequences for Britain, and for other nations, of the oil price inflation and
commodity boom, was greater and more enduring than either major party or
most commentators had recognized. Labour was attacked for pursuing
policies in 1974 based on the realization that there was little or no hope of
*increasing* living standards. By 1975 it was clear that our anti-inflation and
related policies had to be based on a severe *reduction* of real wages and
salaries. The acceptance by industry and the nation of these policies was not
achieved until the mineworkers' conference and the events which followed.
Not until the TUC Conference of September 1975 could there be real confidence that we were set on the right path, and even then the steady fall in the
value of sterling and the vulnerability of our overseas payments caused
repeated anxieties.

By that autumn I had set March 1976 as the time, on or around my sixtieth
birthday on 11 March. This would give adequate time for my successor to be
elected before Easter, and for him to be settled in well before the local
elections due in May.

In September, on the annual visit to Balmoral, I informed the Queen's
Private Secretary that I intended to submit my resignation six months later.
George Thomas spent the first week-end of October at Chequers, and I told
him, too, of my intention. On 9 December I formally told the Queen at my
weekly audience that 11 March or thereabouts would be the date. That was
not my only engagement on 9 December. Lord Goodman, at that time
Chairman of the Newspaper Publishers' Association, had suggested that I
should meet the principal proprietors and chairman to discuss the future of
the press. The disappearance of any newspaper diminishes democracy itself:
I had seen in recent years the death of *Reynolds News*, the *News Chronicle*
and the *Daily Herald*. The *Guardian* and *Observer* were in those days
believed to be perennially at death's door, *The Times* for a long time
vulnerable. There were doubts how long the *Daily Express* would survive its
creator's death. I had worked out, and circulated to relevant ministers,
proposals for an injection of capital on a non-discriminatory basis, conditional on both sides of the industry putting their house in order on questions
of pay and industrial relations including over-manning and lightning walk-
outs. In addition, as remarked above, I had formulated proposals for some
kind of understanding between Government and Fleet Street under which
legislation would be introduced to ease their burdens under the archaic laws
relating to defamation and contempt of court, in return for an active move
by the press designed to provide a real measure of privacy for the individual

citizen and his family. On the question of cash support, the Royal Commission on the Press set up in April 1974 had been asked to give this priority and produced an interim report specifically recommending substantial but conditional financial help.

The dinner with the press chiefs had been fixed for 9 December, the night I had formally informed the Queen of my resignation date. At the end of the evening I said to our host, 'Oh, Arnold, I mentioned that matter to the Queen.' He felt I had done it a little crudely, and that my meaning would be recognized – but it was not. My reason for doing this was that when I finally resigned I knew I could safely count on at least one or two papers knowingly saying that my real reason was not the one stated: in those last months paper after paper was telephoning anxious inquiries about stories that I had this or that serious syndrome, most of them terminal. In those few weeks stories they had received diagnosed heart disease, one or more strokes, cancer in almost every part of the body, and leukaemia. Putting them all together would have reduced me to the state of the hero of *Three Men in a Boat*, who on reading an A to Z medical directory discovered that he was suffering from every known affliction except housemaid's knee – the one thing I had.[1]

The 9 December exercise was designed to make such stories less likely, and also to discourage others attributing my 'sudden' resignation to an impending national crisis, or as one newspaper blatantly sought to suggest, some great revelation which would shortly break on the world – whether a bank robbery or genocide was not specified.

In that week after the 5 March sterling crisis, I woke each day wondering whether something would occur to force me to postpone my resignation. The strength of sterling was one continuing factor. Wednesday 10 March almost produced another.

Parliament was due to approve the Paper on the public expenditure programme for 1976-77[2] on which the Cabinet has experienced so great a trauma the previous December. Our Parliamentary managers did not even ask the House to approve the White Paper. The motion was in general terms, not even asking the House simply to take note of it.

In the evening I was at one of a succession of birthday parties, having arranged to return with Jim Callaghan for the 10 o'clock vote. As I went through the division lobby the Whips told me we were facing a heavy defeat. Thirty or more of our back-benchers were abstaining to show their dis-

[1] One Sunday popular paper had telephoned the Lord President about my 'stroke', revealed by a slight limp for a day or two. Edward Short was able to reassure them that I had twisted my knee playing golf.
[2] The motion moved by Denis Healey and designed to be acceptable to Labour backbenchers was in these terms: 'That this House, in rejecting the demand for massive and immediate cuts in public expenditure which would increase both unemployment and the cost of living, recognizes the need to ensure that manufacturing industry can take full advantage of the upturn in world trade by levelling off total public expenditure from April 1977 while keeping under continuous review the priority between programmes.'

agreement about the spending cuts we had made – and, many of them would say, our excessive defence expenditure. A Conservative amendment was defeated by 304 to 274. But when the 'Main Question' was put, the vote was reversed: Ayes 256, Noes 284. Thirty-seven Labour members had abstained.

I had already left the House to return to my party, and so missed the noisy inquest which always crowns a Government defeat. There were comments on my absence, though the Lord President adequately coped. But the Cabinet, meeting the following morning, clearly had to take action.

I proposed that we simply asked for a vote of confidence. If we won, that would expunge the previous night's defeat. If we lost, it would mean a General Election. This was, so far as my researches and memory confirm, the first formal vote of confidence in nearly eight years as Prime Minister. It seemed to me, considering it, a rum way to spend my sixtieth birthday, just five days before the day I was due to announce my resignation.

The Lord President informed the parties of a change of business. For technical reasons the vote would be on a motion to adjourn the House, but no one was in any doubt that it was a motion of confidence. I decided to keep my speech brief and pointed.

But as it was Thursday I had to take questions first. In a supplementary to a question referring to departmental ministers, a Conservative raised the question of the previous night's defeat. Wishing me a happy birthday, he asked,

> Why . . . did he shuffle off the responsibility last night for answering on the future of his Government to the unfortunate Lord President while he stayed skulking in his room with the door locked and the lights out, hiding?

I replied,

> If the door was locked I am not responsible for that. If the lights were out it was because I had gone to my birthday party.

Just before the debate was due to begin, I was on my last question. Left-wing members who had abstained the previous night seemed keen to reassure me that it was really the Conservatives of whom they disapproved. Since, as I saw it, their mass abstention had given aid and comfort to the Conservatives, I commented that I was glad that Dennis Canavan, after a good night's sleep, was less kindly disposed to the Conservative Party than he had appeared the previous night. After other supplementaries, Eric Heffer thought it necessary to throw the mantle of his protection around Dennis Canavan:

> Is my Right Hon. Friend aware that my Hon. Friend the Member for West Stirlingshire (Mr Canavan) was not well disposed to the Conservative Party, and that Hon. Members who abstained on last night's vote did so precisely because the Government had pursued Conservative policies in relation to public expenditure?

Concerned that whatever the rationalization of their decision, thirty-seven had given aid and comfort to the Conservatives, I replied – it was a completely unprepared answer to an unforeseen question –

It is always an arguable question about promiscuity whether one is more open to criticism for going into the bedroom or being the lapdog outside the door.[1]

Eric Heffer retired hurt, and there was a sudden *frisson* among my frontbench colleagues, one of whom said 'That's one down: if that's what he says to a question what will his prepared speech be like?'

The answer was, very much the same. I had prepared a speech of no more than ten minutes, but the barrage of supplementary questions and my never-conquered bad habit of rising to supplementaries and interruptions, extended it to double that length. I include one extract only:

The fact that this decision of confidence has to be put today at all arises out of one of the most unholy Parliamentary alliances in the history of Parliament. Nothing like it has been seen since the Shinwell-Winterton alliance, described in its day as 'arsenic and old lace'. This time, it is 'arsenic and red chiffon'.

What happened last night was an alliance of Hon. Members who would not normally be seen dead with one another. The distinction on this occasion was that the Conservative Opposition, who voted last night, had begun the debate by tabling a serpentine amendment, which was voted down, and which was designed, in its snake-like way . . . to get unaccustomed allies from this side of the House. But my Hon. Friends must recognise that they were giving their sedentary support to an Opposition who throughout the debate, which centred on public expenditure, had the following record: first, the Opposition would not tell us what they would cut; secondly, they did not tell us what they would increase.[2]

I quoted the Shadow Chancellor's admission that the expenditure cuts they were proposing would increase unemployment. What had happened was a curious reprise of the votes the previous August on incomes policy. Then, the Conservatives had abstained while the Left voted against the Government; now the Left abstained while the Conservatives voted. After all the Conservative propaganda about left-wing Marxists, now they embraced the Marxists as allies.

The vote of confidence was carried by 297 to 280, with 16 March just five days away.

Even so, I had one fear – a further crisis in sterling. All was calm up to the end of the week, and on Monday the 15th I arranged with the No. 10 switchboard that I would be called at 6.0 a.m. the following day, so that I could hear the latest market report from Singapore. The plan for that morning also provided for No. 10 to inform the Treasury at official level of

[1] *Hansard*, vol. 907, col. 624.
[2] *Ibid.*, col. 634.

the announcement, so that the Bank could be put in the picture and made ready to intervene should there be any short-run disturbance in the foreign exchange market.

The occasion planned for my statement was a Cabinet meeting on Tuesday 16 March. Tuesday is not a normal day for the Cabinet to meet, but in any week where business is heavy it is quite usual to meet on Tuesday as well as Thursday. As it happened – and this was unusual – the agenda for Thursday, the 11th, was quite heavy – and added to by the Government's defeat on the Wednesday night. A meeting on the 16th would have been necessary in any event, and no suspicions were aroused.

By arrangement with the Queen an audience was arranged at 9.30 a.m. for me formally to tender my resignation, to take effect as soon as a successor was appointed. At 10.30 Cabinet met. I began by saying I had a statement to make.[1] I reported on my visit to the Queen and my formal announcement of my resignation.

My four administrations, I said, had been 'happy' Cabinets, despite the problems we faced. But I had by this time presided over 472 Cabinet meetings, and thousands of meetings of Cabinet Committees, and answered over 12,000 Parliamentary Questions. I then summarized our achievements, and outlined my plans for setting, through the Chairman of the Parliamentary Party, the electoral machinery for choosing a new leader, emphasizing the need for speeding up the usual procedures. I would remain in Parliament for as long as my constituency would put up with me: I should not go into industry or full-time academic work or take paid employment.

The Cabinet was clearly taken by surprise. The Lord Chancellor and one or two others asked if there was any question of my reconsidering the decision. There was not.

I left them there, as there was work to do. Apparently they agreed to make a statement, and despatched Shirley Williams and Tony Benn to a Committee room to prepare it, and this was duly issued:

> In the Prime Minister's temporary absence from the Cabinet meeting, this morning the Cabinet approved the following statement and directed that it should be issued to the Press:
>
> 'Cabinet this morning learned with deep regret of the wholly unexpected message which the Prime Minister had earlier conveyed to the Queen. They would have wished it otherwise. They must respect what he has described as a personal and irrevocable decision. The Prime Minister has carried the burdens of leadership with outstanding wisdom and dedication. The whole Cabinet wishes to place on record immediately its sense of loss and its profound gratitude to Harold Wilson for the unique service he has given to his country and his party over the past thirteen years.'

The press were clearly caught by surprise. The London evenings, and such

[1] The text of the statement made to Cabinet and subsequently issued to the press is reproduced as Appendix XIII.

provincial evenings as I saw, printed their stories, including qualified eulogies and lengthy – long prepared – obituaries. So did the mornings. Even I was amazed at their recall of long-forgotten incidents. I asked one of them whether the suddenness and surprise had not meant that, in the main, they had raided their mortuaries/morgues for copy. These are the press mausolea where one's obituary notices are kept, fresh and ready for an unforeseen heart attack or assassin's bullet. They confirmed that indeed was the quarry to which they rushed.

Some were surprisingly friendly and fair. Peter Jenkins, who had been one of my more austere and mordant critics, despite or perhaps because of a long and friendly relationship, had made one comment a few days before my announcement, in a piece for my sixtieth birthday:

> Mrs Margaret Thatcher is having to come to terms with a powerful Government led by a powerful Prime Minister which has stolen some of her more fashionable creations and even borrowed Sir Keith Joseph's coat-of-many-colours.
>
> With only 39 per cent of the vote at the election of October 1974 Mr Wilson has put together what is really a powerful ruling coalition. Temporarily at least he has answered the question, 'Who rules the country?', and exploded the notion, so fashionable only a year ago, of ungovernability. The country does have now a kind of National Government appropriate to a deep economic crisis.
>
> . . . On his 60th birthday next month Mr Wilson will be able to drink a cheerful toast to the vanquished who have fallen below the gangway. His Government does not dare, and perhaps never will, to speak openly the language of German Social Democracy, but that is the direction in which their policies are now pointing. Like it or loathe it, the face of British politics has been virtually transformed, all in the space of less than nine months.[1]

This statement in its way meant more to me than many others, equally friendly, a week later. But others, too, who had wielded the club or rapier for thirteen years – some for a generation – decided that an era had ended. I was no longer a threat, I was not coming back and they could afford to be generous. But, as I had forecast, the headlines the next day were looking to the future, for British political journalists prefer to compete, with varying degrees of foresight and accuracy, to predict the future rather than simply record what has occurred. I had told my PPS and others that the next day's headlines would be 'IT LOOKS LIKE . . .'. So it proved. The press, each having taken quick soundings from their contacts in the Parliamentary Labour Party, were unusually unanimous in saying, 'It looks like Jim.' And they were right.

On the whole I think most of the political correspondents welcomed my resignation, on professional grounds quite apart from other reasons. They had the resignation story to write up, their assessments both of my reasons for going, and of nearly eight years at Downing Street, and thirteen as Party

[1] It was just eight months since the Mineworkers' Conference.

Leader. There was all the excitement of the election of a new Leader, and the prospects of a change of style, not to mention Cabinet changes.

But there was perhaps, at least for many of them, a further reason. The press – and this is no criticism of them – in the main prefer a situation of confrontation. A few, perhaps, are of this mind for political reasons. A Labour Prime Minister faced with a choice of alternatives must needs, though deciding the issue on its merits, either please his party, or taking a 'right-wing' decision infuriate some of his supporters in the House, and almost certainly the latter-day National Executive Committee. If the choice goes the first way, he is open to attack for putting party before country if the alternative is chosen, then the headlines refer to 'splits' or 'anger' – always an enjoyable theme.

I was regarded as one who tried always to work for a formula which would unite the party (for example, the July 1975 pay policy)[1] – and if it was one which had not been aired in the press there was disappointment and a feeling of deprivation. Many of the comments on my resignation referred to my constant desire, others even said ability, to unite the party – a latter-day Baldwin in fact. I do not regard this as a condemnation – indeed many reviews of my *A Prime Minister on Prime Ministers* have referred to my 're-habilitation' of Baldwin, that is in the period before Chamberlain's ascendancy and the appeasement of Hitler.[2] But a good old-fashioned confrontation generates more news and livelier comment. To the extent that, again as many of my 'obituaries' conceded, I had kept the party united through such crises as the Common Market, the adoption of the anti-inflation policy in July 1975 – not to mention speedily ending the nuclear row after becoming leader of the party in 1963 – I was something of a disappointment.

To produce a policy on which the party could remain united, despite unhappiness on one or other wing – or both – inevitably evoked the phrase 'devious'. But in my view a constant effort to keep his party together, without sacrificing either principle or the essentials of basic strategy, is the very stuff of political leadership. Macmillan was canonized for it. No Labour leader can expect such an outcome: indeed in an articulate party such as Labour, formed out of so many diverse views and pressures, it would be folly to expect it. More Conservative back-benchers are born with a stiff upper lip (though this phenomenon is becoming more rare), some with a primeval obligation to support their leader, right or wrong. I prefer the Labour Party – and so, I suspect, do the press.

[1] See pp. 120–1 above.

[2] For instance, Mr Patrick Cosgrave, well known as a speech writer for both Mr Heath and Mrs Thatcher, in an article in the *Spectator*, 20 March 1976, reprinted in *Harold's Years*, edited by Kingsley Amis (London, 1977) entitled 'The Nicest Prime Minister': 'There are of course Trollopian times when the only business of government *is* to exist. It seems unlikely, however, that the historian will judge that the Wilson era was one of them; and his final epitaph is therefore likely to suggest that he was a palliator of crisis, not a man who could solve great problems. He is Labour's Baldwin; and he will like Baldwin be remembered as a simple man who became an enigma.'

That afternoon, being a Tuesday, was a day for Prime Minister's questions. Clearly to the very few in the know it would be no ordinary Tuesday.

On being called I was greeted with generous cheers. My first question was from Peter Blaker, one of my most avid hunters, who has since survived, in a mysterious kind of half-life, as a member of the Gang of Four dedicated to the pursuit of James Callaghan. His question was to ask me – though he already knew – whether I had received the Interim Report of the Royal Commission on the Press. His prepared supplementary would have been exactly the same as if he had asked a stock form of question, for example, whether I had plans to visit Timbuctoo. As it was a somewhat special occasion, Mrs Thatcher rose to wish me well, personally she said, in my retirement, and went on predictably to propose that my successor should call an immediate General Election. I thanked her, dealt with her main proposal – and she surprisingly came back by suggesting a date for the poll. Jeremy Thorpe put his question in friendly terms – leading to murmurings, which Mr Speaker answered by saying, 'This is a special occasion.' So it proved: all the other questions were directed to the occasion – except for one Labour back-bencher, who was avid to castigate the *Daily Telegraph* for offering the Tribune Group space to put their case following the inclusion of their highly respected Lobby Correspondent, Harry Boyne, in the New Year Honours List. The other leaders, SNP, Enoch Powell speaking for the Ulster Unionists, and Edward Heath, spoke to the 'special occasion' theme. Edward Heath was particularly – and characteristically – generous,

As the Prime Minister and I faced each other across the Table for ten years of our leadership of our respective parties, may I say that any man who has been able to lead his party as skilfully as he has for thirteen years and been Prime Minister for eight years, having won four General Elections, deserves the fullest tributes for his achievements during that time? May I thank the Right Hon. Gentleman for the courtesies that he always extended to me when I was Leader of the Opposition and for the way that he responded to my invitations during the time that I was Prime Minister? May I congratulate him, after his retirement from office, on joining the party which is the only one to have doubled its numbers in the course of a year?

– a reference to the 'party' of ex-Prime Ministers still in the House. As I pointed out, there would now be five ex-premiers, including three not in the House, Lord Eden, Mr Macmillan and Lord Home of the Hirsel.

Bill Molloy put a kind supplementary – was I aware that in deciding to relinquish my post as Prime Minister and the leadership of our party I would most justifiably and honourably have the good wishes not only of the Parliamentary Labour Party but of all the ordinary folk in the great Labour movement outside the House?

One feature which distinguishes it is that it was his decision to relinquish his office and the leadership of the party. He goes without any knives in his back. (*Interruption.*)

I took the opportunity, besides thanking him and commenting in my most friendly way on the lethal customs of the Conservative Party, to make it clear that my decision was not a sudden one:

> I communicated it to you, Mr Speaker, many months ago.
> *Mr Speaker*: That is correct.[1]

Meanwhile the election process by eliminating ballot for choosing my successor was put in hand. I had seen Cledwyn Hughes, the Chairman of the Parliamentary Labour Party, immediately after my statement to Cabinet, while the meeting was in fact still continuing, together with the Secretary of the Parliamentary Labour Party. They agreed to my suggestion of speeding up the processes required by an eliminating ballot.

The first vote, declared on 25 March, showed Michael Foot just ahead with 90, against Jim Callaghan's 84, Roy Jenkins with 56, Tony Benn with 37, Denis Healey with 30, and Tony Crosland with 17. Tony Crosland was automatically eliminated, and Roy Jenkins, very much disappointed by his vote, was persuaded by his supporters to withdraw. Tony Benn also withdrew, and threw his support behind Michael Foot. The second ballot, on 30 March, led to the elimination of Denis Healey with 38 votes, Jim Callaghan leading Michael Foot by 141 to 133. The final run-off on 5 April gave Jim Callaghan the verdict by 176 to 137.

On Tuesday 23 March the Queen and Prince Philip honoured her retiring Prime Minister by dining at Downing Street, with members of the Cabinet, my own family and friends, including the Vice-Chancellor of Bradford University. It was a happy and informal occasion. (Although the Queen's car had been called for 10.30 she in fact stayed until a quarter to twelve.)

As this was a private occasion it would not be appropriate to quote the Queen's gracious speech. In my reply of thanks for her many kindnesses and generous understanding, I pointed out that in her twenty-four years on the throne, she had seen off six Prime Ministers, more than Queen Victoria had at a similar period in her own reign. She had, in fact, received resignations from six, but 'three came back to haunt her', Derby, Palmerston and Russell.

Meanwhile, in these last days, the work of government went on. Denis Healey continued to consult me on his developing budget. I stuck to engagements already made, opening a new factory extension in Prescot, attending the schools national swimming championship, a lunch for Foreign Minister Gromyko, a film industry seminar, opening the new *Daily Express* building.[2]

---

[1] *Hansard*, vol. 907, col. 1128.

[2] Sir Max Aitken and I had had worries over this engagement, set for 31 March. A large plaque had to be erected in the entrance, but if the leadership election was completed on the second ballot, the words 'Prime Minister' would be inappropriate. I suggested that a blank space should be left immediately above that line, so that the word 'Former' could be inserted. In the event the voting did not end until 5 April.

The principal engagement was the European Council, to be held on 1 April in Luxembourg, which held the Presidency for the current six months. By this time it was virtually certain that James Callaghan would be elected early the following week, and naturally most leaders were anxious to have talks with him. They were extremely kind to me. Giscard gave me a present of a beautiful carriage clock, a Breguet. This gesture nearly ended in disaster. When the brown paper parcel was carried into the Embassy and placed on a table, a security guard saw it, and suspecting a bomb, rushed out to put it in a bucket of water. Fortunately he was intercepted in time. Helmut Schmidt gave me a striking picture of Hamburg, which I had twice visited as his guest: 'From his Hamburg friend'. Another beautiful picture, of Luxembourg, hangs also in my study.

The conference itself was as much a non-event as its predecessor in Rome, if anything more so. The only significant items in the communiqué took little discussion, the formal announcement that the Lomé Convention was to come into force and an anodyne statement on Rhodesia.

On the first day we were due to have a discussion on economic and monetary policy. Giscard said it would amaze public opinion if Heads of Government were not to exchange views on the situation, though he suspected that the practical consequences of our discussions would be small.

Helmut Schmidt said he would speak as an economist, not as Federal German Chancellor. One has often been tempted to think this was the role he preferred, but on closer study there was no difference. The Keynesian heresy had to be extirpated, and Milton Friedman at his best could not have excelled him, despite deploying the arguments at much greater length. He was, as usual, speaking from strength, and did not waste words denying it. Pay increases in Germany were 'minimal', though there was no interference in pay settlements by government.

I reported on the British situation, picking up his emphasis on the 'three disciplines', money policy, budget policy, incomes policy. Britain's printing of new money in 1973 had been the highest in the Community: in 1974 we had been about the middle of the range, by late 1975 we were well among the lowest in the table, apart from Germany which had a nil net rate. It was in fact to Germany we were all looking for a measure of reflation which could help to lead the trading world to higher levels of employment. At the time of writing, nearly three years later, it would appear that little has changed.

I opposed the Commission's proposals for new Committees or institutions. We should work through what existed, the Monetary Committee, the Finance Ministers' meetings, and, not least, the monthly meetings of central bank Governors in Basle, which included the head of the Federal Reserve.

At the end of the discussion we had to decide what should be said to the press. The highest common denominator was a feeling that nothing should be said to the press, but since Gaston Thorn, as chairman, would have to meet journalists, it was decisively agreed that he should say just what he thought, provided that he made it clear that he was speaking only for himself.

The second day provided a miserable experience. We had to take firm decisions on EEC-wide elections, due for the spring of 1978. At least we agreed that whenever they took place they should be in the same week – we wanted them at the time of our borough elections. If they could not be on the same day, the ballot-boxes should be sealed until all countries had voted. There were fears of early declarations affecting the voting elsewhere. Britain was unwilling to commit herself until we knew how many seats we should have in the European Parliament. On the proposals before us Scotland with 5.2 million population, and Wales with her 2.7 million, would both have fewer seats than Luxembourg with its 350,000. Denmark could not commit herself.[1]

Any progress at all on this question was ruled out by the problems Italy was facing. Aldo Moro was receiving grimmer and grimmer news from his own legislature, who were riven by the debate and the voting prospects on the most divisive question Rome could face – abortion. With his Parliament at crisis point, it was impossible for his Christian Democrats to discuss problems about the European Parliament with the other parties.

The meeting ended with no agreement. For once we had concluded the agenda ahead of time for adjournment. We discussed the Tindemanns Report on the development of greater cohesion in the Community. This led nowhere. Helmut Schmidt raised the question of the kind of environment in which we met. We always had palaces or grandiose conference rooms, too big for so small a gathering. We were dominated by the huge boxes built high in the wall for interpreters to give us simultaneous translations in four languages. Why should we not meet in a cosier atmosphere, a small room, each of us with an interpreter sitting behind us whispering into our ear? This I resisted, without stating my reason. With an enthusiastic interpreter one would get no peace. It is necessary sometimes to sit back and take stock, as well as to prepare interventions. Discussing these acute problems before lunch, and with the freedom of one self-discharged from future conference service, I suggested the translation apparatus should have a music channel.

The real value of Luxembourg lay, clearly, not in the conference sessions, but in the discussions Heads of Government were able to have with James Callaghan. Half-way between the penultimate and the final ballot it was clear that he was set for victory.

The week-end was peaceful – a visit to Chequers' nearest pub for the final pints, for the benefit also of the photographers. There was no point in trying to catch up with the foreign telegrams or the papers for discussion at Cabinet committees.

[1] This problem was solved, with apparent ease, at a succeeding meeting of the Council, and the British Parliament has legislated to provide for the election. Just before the proofs of this book were received the country voted, almost exactly confirming my gloomy, but witnessed, prophecy that the turn-out would be 32 per cent, and the number of Labour seats won would be 17.

My last official engagement was the Monday Cabinet – a Budget Cabinet. Denis Healey outlined his proposals in some detail. He was going to increase the tax on cigarettes, but not pipe-tobacco, which he explained was much consumed by retired persons. I asked him if he was intending to include this in his Commons speech. He was – and the following day he repeated it with a nod towards the Front Bench below the gangway, the traditional seat for former Prime Ministers on the Government side. It went well.

At 3.15 Cledwyn Hughes came to my room at the House to give me the result of the final ballot. I telephoned the figures to the Queen's Private Secretary. At Party meeting, Jim made his speech of acceptance and thanks. I followed with my congratulations and pledge of full support. Michael Foot and Roy Jenkins spoke in similar terms, Roy making a particularly kind reference to me. I asked him for a copy of his speech, which he duly sent me, with a charming letter saying how much he had misunderstood what I was doing – a reference to my handling of the Common Market issue which had ended with the Party, with whatever individual misgivings, accepting the decision to remain in Europe.

From Party meeting I went straight to the Palace to tender my formal resignation. Contrary to the views of some text-book writers, a retiring Prime Minister does not advise the Queen who should be sent for, still less is there any truth in one proclaimed view that if the Queen asks for his advice she must accept it.[1] This was never so. All I did, following the modern practice appropriate to elective party leaders, was to say that she was already aware of the voting figures I had sent her, which meant that Mr Callaghan was elected leader of the Parliamentary Labour Party.

We then exchanged official farewells and I sped on my way to Chequers. The No. 10 diary which records every movement and meeting in a Prime Minister's day summed it up superbly:

3.15  The Prime Minister saw Mr Cledwyn Hughes in his room at the House.

5.15  Drove to Buckingham Palace for his final Audience of the Queen, to tender his formal resignation to the Queen.

Afterwards Mr Wilson drove to Chequers for the night.

[1] Compare R. C. K. Ensor, *England 1870–1914* (Oxford 1936), p. 215.

# Epilogue

This epilogue is being written after the General Election of 3 May 1979, when the Conservatives were returned with a majority of 44 overall, and 71 over Labour.

It has been said that Labour had exhausted its mandate, carried through its legislative programme and run out of steam as a result of nearly eleven years in office in less than fifteen years. In so far as it ran out of steam, this was in a sense true from the time when it could no longer command a majority in the House, dating from the loss of the West Woolwich by-election in 1975 and the subsequent defection of two MPs to the short-lived Scottish Labour Party. The intervention of the International Monetary Fund Cheka in the autumn of 1976 put a stranglehold on the Government's economic policies. The Lib-Lab pact under-wrote the Parliamentary majority, but even so the Government was living on borrowed time.

Yet most of the measures foreshadowed in 1974 became a reality through legislative and administrative action, and the final Queen's Speech drafted by the Labour Government proposed new and constructive action for the last session of the Parliament.

It was the pay issue and the turbulence of the winter of 1978/79 which, it can now be seen in retrospect, caused the downfall of the Government, Ministers bravely, but somewhat unrealistically, nailed the figure of 5 per cent pay settlement to the masthead. Whether a higher, but still austere. figure such as 8 or 8½ per cent might have been accepted, at least as a guide-line, has been the subject of much argument. But the unions, torn internally by years of imposed or induced wage restraint, with differentials dangerously narrowed, and the lowest-paid in industry after industry moving into mili-tancy, took to the streets. Garbage piled up and rotted in the streets. Physical violence in the lorry-drivers' strike, picketing and closure of schools, and – worst of all – action preventing the burial of the dead, affronted the nation. Three Members of Parliament (two ex-ministers and a former Party chairman), whom I asked to forecast the result of an election held at that time, separately estimated 'one hundred Tory majority'.

James Callaghan strove to avoid an election held in the shadow of the garbage heaps, and looked forward to the summer or even the autumn.

The Duke of Wellington, commenting on the fall of Sir Robert Peel, said in reference to starvation in Ireland, 'It was rotten potatoes did it all. It was that which put Peel in his damned fright.'

If, for a time, it was rotten garbage that threatened the Labour Government, it was devolution which forced it to the country. The Scottish and Welsh referenda led to a motion of no confidence tabled by the Scottish Nationalists, which was promptly taken over by the official Conservative Opposition. By one vote the motion carried, recalling yet again Winston Churchill's 'One is enough'. So it proved. The Prime Minister announced that the Government would put its case to the country. It did, and the country gave its answer on the third of May.

# APPENDICES

Appendix I Statement by the Minister for the Disabled on action taken since his appointment, as updated to December 1978

The following checklist sets out the decisions and the action taken by this Government since March 1974 to provide new help for disabled people and their families.

*Social Security*

Non-Contributory Invalidity Pension (NCIP) for men and single women: now 130,000 beneficiaries.

Mobility Allowance for an estimated 120,000 new beneficiaries, including severely disabled children.

Introduction of Non-Contributory Invalidity Pension in lieu of 'pocket money' allowance for long-stay patients in mental hospitals: 56,000 beneficiaries.

Extension of Non-Contributory Invalidity Pension to married women incapable of normal household work: 43,000 beneficiaries to date.

Invalid Care Allowance for men and single women who look after severely disabled relatives: approaching 6,000 beneficiaries.

Social Security benefits, including benefits for disabled people, up-rated five times since March 1974. Further up-rating in November 1978.

Raising of therapeutic earnings limit for recipients of Invalidity Pension, Non-Contributory Invalidity Pension and Unemployability Supplement.

Legislation enacted for earnings-related Invalidity Pension, an easing of the age conditions for Invalidity Allowance and 'home responsibility protection' for a person who has to stay at home to look after a relative needing care.

Increase in Private Car Maintenance Allowance for War Pensioners.

Attendance Allowance payable to foster parents of handicapped children as from 29 August 1977.

Increase in Car Maintenance Allowance for War Pensioners and others.

Industrial Disablement Benefit for victims of byssinosis (not extended to new categories).

Industrial Injury provisions for occupational deafness introduced and currently under review.

Industrial Injuries Advisory Council asked to consider whether asthma caused by exposure to substances encountered at work should be prescribed as an industrial disease.

Viral hepatitis prescribed as an industrial disease.

Vinyl Chloride Monomer induced diseases prescribed as industrial diseases.

Easing of conditions for entitlement to industrial death benefit in certain cases of death from pulmonary disease.

Study of the problems faced by disabled people in relation to membership of occupational pension schemes.

Attendance allowance extended to kidney patients dialysing at home.

*Other Financial Help*

£12.1 million paid to Rowntree Trust Family Fund for disabled children.

Extension of terms of reference of Rowntree Trust Family Fund to include *all* severely disabled children.

Government help for Thalidomide children.

Vaccine damage payments scheme.

Coal Industry Pneumoconiosis Compensation Scheme. Limited right of appeal on diagnosis of pneumoconiosis introduced and proposals announced for extending right of appeal.

## Financial Support of Voluntary Organisations

Much increased financial support for voluntary bodies.

Government financial support for Crossroads Care Attendants Schemes.

First-ever grants to three major voluntary organisations for the hearing-impaired.

Grants for three voluntary organisations helping to find adoptive parents for handicapped children.

Grant to assist Royal Association for Disability and Rehabilitation, formed by merger of the Central Council for the Disabled and the British Council for Rehabilitation of the Disabled.

Grant to the Scottish Council on Disability, including assistance towards Mobile Aid Centre.

Grants for Scottish Workshop for the Deaf conference.

Grant to the Scottish Council for Spastics for the provision of Sheltered Housing for disabled people.

## Co-operation and Consultation

Better co-ordination between Government Departments.

UK co-sponsors UN Declaration of 1981 as an International Year for Disabled Persons.

Closer liaison with voluntary bodies.

Wide-ranging Seminar on Disablement held at Sunningdale.

UK co-sponsors UN Declaration on the Rights of Handicapped People.

Approaches to non-government organizations.

DHSS/Post Office Liaison Committee on aids for the physically and sensory handicapped.

Personal Social Security Council's new group on 'People with Handicaps'.

## Hearing Impairment

Phasing-in of new behind-the-ear hearing aid for up to one million hearing-impaired people: over half a million already supplied.

Special hearing aids for children and young people.

Advisory Committees on Hearing Impairment.

Institute of Hearing Research and first English out-station established.

Audiological Medicine – a new specialty.

Development of audiology services.

Co-ordination with DES on audiological equipment in schools.

Guidance for Hearing Aid Users.

Up-dating of NHS hearing aids.

Hospital Ear Nose and Throat Services – Design Guide.

Introduction of Hearing Therapists.

Staff Training on Deafness.

Government help for the Private Member's Bill to enable the Hearing Aid Council to draw up a code of practice to govern advertising of privately dispensed hearing aids.

## Visual Impairment

Increase in Blind Person's tax allowance.

Capital grants proposed for pilot residential units for deaf-blind adolescents and young people.

New NHS Optical arrangements of special help to people with severe loss of vision.

Appointment of additional Blind Persons' Training Officers.

New Government circular to local authorities about admission of guide dogs to certain premises.

British Rail agree to admit guide dogs to sleeping-cars.

*Mental Handicap*

National Development Group for the Mentally Handicapped set up.

Development Team for improving services available to mentally handicapped people.

Programme Planning Group on Mental Disorder.

Jay Committee on Nursing and Care of the Mentally Handicapped.

*Aids*

Funding of Special Units at selected hospitals to work specifically on aids and equipment.

Assessment of aids and equipment for physically handicapped people at Rehabilitation Centres.

DHSS assumes financial responsibility for 'Equipment for the Disabled' from the National Fund for Research into Crippling Diseases.

More environmental control aids made available for disabled people.

Advisory Group on Medical and Scientific Equipment and Aids and Equipment for the Physically Disabled.

Development and general introduction of cosmetic calipers for NHS patients.

Improvements to wheel-chair service.

Review of wheel-chair service.

Development of a swivel-walking device for spina bifida patients.

Catalogue of and guide to environmental control equipment for the severely disabled.

Working Group on patient support systems.

Study of personal hygiene and eating aids at Loughborough.

Development of a chemical closet for home use (production started in February 1977).

Study of stairlifts and personal passenger vertical lifts for disabled people.

*Mobility and Transport*

Further parking concessions for all 'Orange Badge' holders.

Extension of 'Orange Badge' scheme to include the blind.

Petrol allowance restored (and doubled) for drivers of government-supplied invalid vehicles.

Financial and administrative support for major new voluntary organization: Motability.

Extension of exemption from Road Tax (vehicle excise duty) to Mobility Allowance beneficiaries or their nominees.

Exemption for certain disabled people from the statutory restrictions on car hire-purchase and rental or leasing terms.

Disabled people now automatically entitled to priority in taking driving tests.

Provision of facilities for disabled people at motorway service areas (including signing them on motorways).

Concessions to 'Orange Badge' holders at most tolled crossings.

Disabled drivers now able to supervise 'L' drivers.

Two distinctive traffic signs prescribed and supplementary signs, exempting disabled people from vehicle traffic prohibitions, may now be used.

Public Transport: special arrangements for disabled travellers by British Rail, and easier access into new rolling stock.

Concessionary fares for disabled people.

In consultation with the Government, London Transport review travelling problems faced by disabled people.

New bus design now being tested in London.

Government help for Private Member's Bill to exempt mini buses used by certain voluntary organizations from Public Service Vehicle Licensing Scheme.

Research study of the needs of disabled drivers and passengers.

*Education*

Introduction of discretionary allowance of up to £160 to disabled students whose disability leads to additional expenses in connection with their studies (to be increased to £180 on 1 September 1978).

Integrated education of handicapped pupils given new impetus by the passing of Section 10 of Education Act 1976.

Report of the Warnock Committee on education of handicapped children and young people published 24 May 1978.

Improved provision for the needs of disabled people in educational establishments.

Survey of Further Education provision for young adults with handicaps.

Guidance on the discovery of children requiring special education and the assessment of their needs.

*Employment: Rehabilitation, Training and Job Opportunities*

Publication by Manpower Services Commission (MSC) of 'Positive Policies' – an employers' guide to employing disabled people.

Decisions on the future of the employment quota scheme, sheltered employment for disabled people and related matters.

Scheme of grants to employers towards the cost of adaptations to premises or equipment made to enable disabled individuals to obtain, or retain, employment.

The inception, on 4 July 1977, of an experimental Job Introduction Scheme, to provide financial assistance enabling certain disabled people to undertake a trial period of employment with an employer, where there is reasonable doubt as to the person's ability to perform a particular job.

A revised and simplified scheme designed to help severely disabled people with their travel-to-work costs introduced on 5 July 1978.

Increases in allowances paid to people going on employment rehabilitation courses.

Increase in the number of Senior Disablement Resettlement Officers in the Employment Service Division of the MSC.

Under the MSC Special Programme for young people additional opportunities have been provided at Employment Rehabilitation Centres for disabled young people.

Increased budget in the Employment Service Division for work in hospitals.

Arrangements made by Manpower Services Commission in co-operation with DHSS for hospital patients to spend part of each week at an ERC. Plans made to run young persons' work preparation courses at all ERCs.

Establishment of an employment rehabilitation research centre and the commencement of its research programme.

Planning in progress for rebuilding of the pioneer ERC at Egham. A new double-stream ERC has been built at Preston, opening Autumn 1978.

A systematic evaluation of Young Persons Work Preparation Courses has been carried out by the Hester Adrian Research Centre. Research commissioned by ESD in May 1976.

Residential Training Colleges Working Group set up to examine the services they provide, their relationships with the employment and training services of the MSC and their role for the future.

Pilot study carried out of employment opportunities for disabled people in an Area Health Authority, to find out where within the Health Authority disabled people are already employed, and to discover what further employment opportunities might be afforded them.

Introduction of literacy/numeracy training at one RTC and decision to continue in view of results achieved.

Introduction of special courses for the less able at one RTC (ITWE).

Introduction of a Pre-Vocational Assessment Course at one RTC.

Introduction of the Release for Training (RFT) scheme for disabled people who are already in employment but experiencing problems which can only be resolved by a period of intensive training.

Increase in provision of individual training – with employer arrangements.

Major expansion in the range of publicity material available to assist disabled people to obtain and keep employment, particularly the launch of the Employment Service Division's new rehabilitation and resettlement magazine 'Outlook'.

Publication in the DE Gazette of figures showing quota performance of public sector employers – nationalized industries, local authorities, area health authorities and Government departments.

Issue by the Civil Service Department of a Code of Practice on employment of disabled people in Government departments.

Research programme started on the training needs of disabled people.

On 1 April 1978 the MSC introduced its Youth Opportunities Programme which comprises a number of different schemes, including remedial courses, work preparation and work experience. Young disabled people are eligible for all elements of YOP and parts of the programme are specifically designed to help them.

*Housing*

Strong new guidance on housing needs.

Marked increase in special housing provision for disabled people.

Consultation paper on adaptations to housing.

Awards for good housing for disabled people.

Government help for the Rating (Disabled Persons) Act 1978.

DOE Circulars to New Town Development Corporations requesting greater provision within their tenancy allocation policies for housing elderly and disadvantaged families, including the physically and mentally handicapped.

Promotion of EEC-Funded Study of Housing and Care for disabled people.

*Access and Designing for Disabled People*

Appointment of Silver Jubilee Committee on Improving Access for Disabled People.

Awards for best public buildings for disabled people.

Government help for Private Member's Bill extending the access provisions of the Chronically Sick and Disabled Persons Act 1970 to places of employment.

Publication in June 1978 of technical guidance on designing and adapting government buildings to meet the needs of disabled employees and members of the public.

Pressure on public and other bodies to improve access and services for disabled people, e.g. special low counters for wheel-chair users.

Improvement of facilities for disabled people in the National Theatre.

Home Office Circular on Access to Polling Stations.

Advice on the adaptation of premises to meet the needs of disabled employees has also been given to Employment Service Division for use by Disablement Resettlement Officers in discussion with private sector employers.

Access for Disabled People – Design Guide and Wall Chart.
Incorporation into building regulations of standards for ramps for wheel-chair users and others.

*Research*
DHSS Research Liaison Group set up to look at research needs in the disablement field.
DHSS assumes financial responsibility for research team supporting work of Rowntree Trust Family Fund.
Research into work, personal and social difficulties of handicapped people seeking employment – conducted by Neil Fraser, University of Edinburgh. (Due to finish December 1978.)
Research on the relevance of services to disabled adolescents – conducted by Dr Dingwall and Professor Raymond Illsley, University of Aberdeen.

*Miscellaneous*
District Handicap Teams set up.
Extension of War Pensioners' visiting scheme.
Zero rating of VAT on aids and appliances for disabled people and also on medical equipment for donation to a hospital for the purpose of treatment or research.
Remedial professions – improved status.
New arrangements for dental treatment of handicapped patients.
The provision of special rehabilitation facilities at the Birmingham Head Injuries Centre for people who have suffered severe head injuries (in co-operation with Area Health Authorities).
Meeting on classification and assessment of impairment and handicap held in London in October 1976.
Extension of special concessionary TV licence arrangements for people in old people's homes.
Increasing the number of disabled people, or people representing their interests, appointed to the Nationalised Industries' Consumers' Councils.
Government's White Paper on Sport and Recreation of 1975; its emphasis on the needs of the disabled.
Issue of new edition of 'Help for Handicapped People' and 'Help for Handicapped People in Scotland'. Further revisions to be published in November 1978.

10 December 1978                                          Alfred Morris

Appendix II *Guardian* report of New York speech on incomes policy, and leading article, May 1971

Mr Wilson has done more in America than assure President Johnson that Yorkshire is the Texas of England. His paper in New York last night on 'collective bargaining in a free society' is the result of his six years' experience of our central economic problem, inflation. His eyes are wider open than when he entered Downing Street, yet his views have a remarkable consistency with those he argued in the mid fifties as Shadow Chancellor. They have become the accepted wisdom about voluntary incomes policy, and they remain the holy grail to which most sensible thinking in the Labour movement, and indeed in Britain, is directed.

The Labour movement badly needs leadership on incomes policy at present. Two of the more obnoxious aspects of current union behaviour are the phlegm with which the TUC seems to accept that unemployment of more than 800,000 is something upon which Mr Heath should act swiftly and dynamically, but is something that has nothing much to do with the rest of us; and the blatant hypocrisy which sheds crocodile tears for pensioners while contributing to a tearaway inflation. It is no answer for the unions to point to the Government's parallel entrenched position. Neither can act without the other.

As for a statutory incomes policy, it is comforting to its opponents to see what a man who has had the levers of power in his hands for six years thinks about its weaknesses. Mr Wilson's Government was forced into such a policy by crisis. He knows that other Governments can be forced in that direction also – and doubtless, as a politician, would enjoy watching Mr Heath eat so many words. But Mr Wilson shares none of the current illusions among his political friends and others who have joined the fashionable outcry for statutory control. The conditions he lays down for it amount to the imposition of a siege economy. It must be applied only in times of national emergency, and for a short period (otherwise anomalies will 'discredit not only the policy, but even the system of society in which it operates'). It would have to be accompanied by improved social services – difficult as this is during such a crisis – and by politicians on such provocations as regressive tax changes, speculative gains, and luxury spending. Short of a ban on the spending of money except between consulting adults in private, Mr Wilson could not have gone much further. Yet this is the lesson of the former Prime Minister's experience in office, and it deserves attention.

His faith resides still in a voluntary compact between the Government and the two sides of industry. Mr Wilson sees this coming, most probably, out of some kind of national crisis. In this he is in line with a growing school of thought, though whether the trauma will be unemployment, unacceptable inflation, and/or a payments crisis remains to be seen. The policy would provide voluntary restraint in wages and prices, expansion, full employment, fair tax policies, and a social wage. There is much detail, but wide gaps. This is not Mr Wilson's blueprint, for in this field he cannot be an architect, only a bargainer. This is his negotiating position. There would be a lot of horse-trading before the TUC vetting committee, which he rightly regards as vital, got down to work.

Yet whether in opposition or in government there are a number of questions Mr Wilson will have to answer in talks with the TUC. He speaks of a 'guarantee of full employment' in return for wage restraint. Would this be at a specific level? And would there, in return, be a norm for wages? He envisages a restored Prices and Incomes Board, variously described as authoritative, imperative, 'capable of

251

commanding acceptability', yet 'endowed with powers'. Which powers? Mr Wilson rules out a total system of price control, which would become 'increasingly bureaucratic and irrelevant', but he wants 'parallel action' (with that on wages) to control prices that centrally affect family spending – such things as rent, bread, milk, school meals, fares, and clothing. Again, what action?

For all the unanswered questions, it is good to see Mr Wilson searching again for solutions to our most intractable economic problem. And before the year is out the Prime Minister and his colleagues would be wise to begin stealing the Leader of the Opposition's clothes.

A voluntary prices and incomes policy is 'the pattern of the future for democratic societies' Mr Harold Wilson claimed in New York last night.

The Opposition Leader told an International Symposium on Public Employment Labour Relations that the 'compact' he envisaged would include: a guarantee of full employment by the Government; restraint of 'key prices' by manufacturers; and restraint of wages by unions. This would lead to higher growth and higher wages for the future. He attacked attempts to control wage levels by deliberately raising unemployment.

Mr Wilson said:

Not long ago the pundits thought that if unemployment rose in Britain to 700,000 – at one stage they even said 500,000 – no trade union would dare to ask for increased wages, and no employer would be financially able to grant increased wages. Now that Britain has topped the 800,000 figure and has a higher rate of male unemployment even than the United States, this theory has been discredited, since wage claims and wage settlements have in no sense abated.

And it is a fact that wage settlements in the private sector, at any rate, have not de-escalated with rising unemployment – nor is it easy to see how they can with prices rising more rapidly than ever. I have always been doubtful, and recent events have strengthened my doubts, whether there is any acceptable figure of unemployment which of itself can reduce or eliminate wage claims.

Even if there were such a figure, and it would have to represent an inordinate increase even above present levels, it would mean such a cutback in employment and in profits, that investment would be reduced, productivity would fall as a result, unions would intensify restrictive practices to ensure – so far as they could – that their workers did not work themselves out of a job, unit costs would increase, but prices, if they fell at all, would be unlikely to fall to the point where smaller wage increases became acceptable.

Equally, the theory that employers would resist wage claims in such a situation is being proved to be a fantasy. The firm with a tight cash flow, perhaps even on the margin of bankruptcy, will not necessarily, as the theorists argue, resist wage demands; it is at least as likely to give in to a wage demand – it cannot face a prolonged strike – because it cannot afford to be out of production, with no income from the sale of its products. While standing charges are continuing, the cash freeze is becoming critical, even lethal.

We have to think therefore in very different terms. We have to think in terms of industrial democracy, without which nineteenth-century concepts of political democracy have no meaning.

And I set out not as an assumption, but as a fact, that – to the extent that a voluntary policy of restraint can be accepted – economic society as a whole can permit a degree of higher production, leading to higher productivity, with all that means for fuller employment and for higher wages in the future; first, because this encourages investment, second because this creates conditions in which work-sharing and restrictive practices are no longer seen as a necessary safeguard of living standards.

. . . The lesson of our experience is that a statutory freeze can only be of short duration, in a national emergency, before anomalies make it totally unworkable and, as they do so, discredit not only the policy, but even the system of society in which it operates.

Most of the lessons to be drawn from statutory control of incomes apply, if only to a slightly lesser degree, to the voluntary incomes policy – its greater acceptability if it is associated with national crisis; its totality and fairness; the absence of provocative incomes or gains elsewhere, the social service supplement – the social wage helping the industrial wage – and the absence of discrimination between the public and private sector.

But it is particularly true of a voluntary agreement, which must depend on cooperation and acceptability, that restraint in wages and salaries will not last long if prices – and especially key prices – are rising. By key prices I mean in the expenditure of an average household – rents, bread, milk, school meals, commuter fares, whether by rail or bus, shoes and clothing, particularly children's shoes and clothing.

. . . I believe that a unique opportunity was created in Britain by our economic success, and, at some moment of time, this will be true of other countries, including the United States, when the achievement of a balance-of-payments surplus, or even equilibrium, will make possible a voluntary compact between Governments and industry – both sides of industry – in which the Government can go forward boldly with economic policies necessary to increase production, knowing that this need not lead to inflation so long as it could count on industrial cooperation and restraint.

I conclude with the conditions of such a compact. The first is parallel action on prices. Not, of course, all prices. Modern industrial society, modern consumer requirements, modern design and selling, would make it impossible for a total system of price control, which could only become increasingly bureaucratic and irrelevant. I am referring to the main elements in family expenditure.

The second condition is that machinery (like the Prices and Incomes Board) . . . imperative, authoritative, capable of commanding acceptability, is needed.

Thirdly, parties to the compact must have the feeling that they are part, and an essential part, of an all-out national effort. It may be a national effort to rescue the nation from economic crisis. In a more general sense it must be part of a national effort to raise living standards to an extent that they have not been raised before.

But, in a modern democracy, the parties to the compact cannot play their part unless they feel and know that they are part of a united nation, a united society, a national family protected against the divisive factors of those who seek division for their own political or industrial power.

They must be able to feel that the sacrifices, the restraint, the efforts they are called upon to put forth must be related to a guarantee of full employment. They must be satisfied that there will be adequate provision for the less privileged within the community.

The compact means that there must be adequate provision for those who cannot work, for the sick, the disabled, the old, but also for those who, at work, are among the low paid, and for those with the largest family commitments.

There cannot be an industrial wage policy without a policy for the social wage. And, equally, they have the right to demand a fair tax system, a system of taxation which is indeed an extension of a social security system based on the principle, 'from each according to his means, to each according to his needs'.

For, if we are to ask workers by hand and brain to renounce economic rewards which some, at least, could demand and win through the free play of market forces, if we are to ask them to renounce part of their freedom, then it can only be because society creates the conditions in which they are prepared to make this sacrifice for a wider and greater social purpose. A sectional sacrifice, perhaps, a short-term price, for a long-term gain for themselves and for the community.

## Appendix III Extract from Statement on EEC renegotiations to London Labour Mayors' Association on the eve of the Paris EEC Summit, December 1974

On Monday and Tuesday the Foreign and Commonwealth Secretary and I will be in Paris for a meeting of the Heads of Government of the European Community countries, a group which will, I think, come to be known as the European Council. This is a follow-up to the successful informal exchange of views between Heads of Government on economic and other questions in Paris early in September.

A great deal of work has been put into preparing for these high-level talks. Certainly to judge from the meetings I had with the German Federal Chancellor at Chequers last week-end, and with the French President in Paris on Tuesday, we shall be discussing together world economic problems, particularly inflation and unemployment, energy, international trade, and the challenge to the world's financial system caused by the growing surpluses held by oil exporting countries. To get a clearer idea of where we all stand, and the greatest possible identity of view on these matters, will be of the highest importance.

We are not meeting exclusively or even mainly to talk about Britain's renegotiations of the 1971 terms of entry into the European Community, though that will not be far from the minds of any of us.

But it is imperative that our partners in Europe should know exactly where the British Labour Government stands – where indeed we have always stood.

The position I have put forward on behalf of the Party since the terms of entry into the Community became known in 1971 has been totally consistent, and indeed it is the line we have taken ever since the time when, during the previous Labour Government, we made our first approaches to Europe in 1966.

We said then, we say now, that entry on the right terms would be good for Britain and good for Europe. But at no point over these years have I disguised my conviction that we should reject terms which would cripple Britain's ability to solve her own problems, and prevent Britain from making the contribution to Europe of which she is capable. The kind of terms we proposed in 1967 are precisely the kind of terms for which we are negotiating now.

When I read the assessment of commentators who have shown their blind and fanatical commitment to entry regardless of the terms, the people who now commend us for seeking the right terms in place of those they so eagerly supported in 1971–72, it is plain that it is they who have changed, not the Labour Party or its leader.

We are negotiating with a real intent to succeed, and what we are negotiating to achieve precisely follows the resolution which I put before the National Executive Committee in July 1971, and commended to Conference the following October.

The specific issues with which we are concerned were set out in the Manifesto which we put before the country in February, and restated in the Manifesto for the October election. In both these elections the British people have endorsed our policy on the Community, and accepted our pledge that 'within twelve months of the election we will give the British people the final say which will be binding on the Government – through the ballot box – on whether we accept the terms and stay in or reject the terms and come out'.

The position of the Government is clear.

'If renegotiations are successful, it is the policy of the Labour Party that, in view

255

of the unique importance of the decision, the people should have the right to decide. If these two tests are passed, a successful renegotiation and the expressed approval of the majority of the British people, then we shall be ready to play our full part in developing a new and wider Europe.

'If renegotiations do not succeed, we shall not regard the Treaty obligations as binding upon us. We shall then put to the British people the reasons why we find the new terms unacceptable, and consult them on the advisability of negotiating our withdrawal from the Communities.'

That was what we said in the February Manifesto. That has been the policy of the Labour Party, endorsed by Conference; it is the policy of the Government, endorsed by the people.

Our negotiations stand or fall on the issues set out in our policy. And they were set out clearly by the Foreign and Commonwealth Secretary in his first statement on these matters to the Council of Ministers of the Community at the beginning of April.

I am not sure even now how fully they are understood or appreciated by all those with whom we are negotiating; so I will summarize them again tonight.

(1) Major changes in the Common Agricultural Policy, so that it ceases to be a threat to world trade in food products, and so that low-cost producers outside Europe can continue to have access to the British food market.

(2) New and fairer methods of financing the Community budget, so that our contribution to Community finances is fair in relation to what is paid and what is received by other member countries.

(3) Rejection of any kind of international agreement which compelled us to accept increased unemployment for the sake of maintaining a fixed parity, as was required by the proposals then current for a European economic and monetary union.

(4) The retention by Parliament of those powers over the British economy needed to pursue effective regional industrial and fiscal policies.

(5) An agreement on capital movements which protects our balance of payments and full employment policies.

(6) The economic interests of the Commonwealth and the developing countries must be better safeguarded. This involves securing continued access to the British market, and, more generally, the adoption by the enlarged Community of trade and aid policies designed to benefit not just 'associated overseas territories'.

(7) No harmonization of value added tax which would require us to tax necessities.

Those are the terms we seek, and it is on our success in achieving them that the issue will be decided. They are the terms on which every Labour Member of Parliament, every Labour candidate, all of us, fought two General Elections.

For me, for the Government, the guidelines for the negotiations are set out in the Manifesto. Whatever the outcome, we shall abide by them.

It stands to reason that provided we get the right terms – but only if we get the right terms – I shall commend them to the British people, and recommend that we should stay in and play our full part in the development of the Community.

I have made this clear again this week, and I shall repeat it at the meeting of the European Council next week.

Having put the issue twice to the people within this year, I owe it not only to the Party, not only to the British people who endorsed our Manifesto, but also to those with whom we are negotiating, to make it clear that those are the terms and we do not seek to add to them.

I have been concerned to read a number of press reports, which might mislead our partners in Europe, to the effect that there is only one issue that really matters – the size of Britain's budgetary contribution. This question is important, but satisfaction on this is manifestly not enough.

That is why I have throughout been emphasizing the importance of the other issues.

We have already made substantial progress on some of them. As a result of a decision by the whole Community, the Common Agricultural Policy is to be subject to a thorough review and stocktaking.

But already the Minister of Agriculture has in urgent and critical negotiations succeeded in securing the necessary freedom in Britain to act, for example, on beef.

And on sugar, where the terms we so strongly criticised in 1971 have now been proved to be – as we said they were – insubstantial and inadequate, we have at last secured what our predecessors failed to obtain: guaranteed access for 1.4 million tons of sugar from the developing countries of the Commonwealth. While perhaps the Conservatives cannot be blamed for failing to see that 1974 would end in conditions of a world shortage of sugar, it is ironic that this shortage coincides with the very moment they set for ending our right to import from Australia, and the guarantees for Commonwealth developing countries whose firm continuance we demanded.

On the Manifesto requirement about arrangements for developing Commonwealth countries, good progress has been made. The negotiations this summer in Jamaica covering African, Caribbean and Pacific countries were marked by considerable success by Judith Hart in extending the arrangements under Protocol 22. We believe that similar concern should be shown for the Indian sub-continent, but I for one would like to pay tribute not only to our negotiators, but to the response which they were accorded by our partners.

There may be good reason for hope that our requirement on VAT may be not too difficult to meet, and clearly European Economic and Monetary Union is receding into a more distant perspective.

Problems of parliamentary authority are going to require a great deal of imagination, but the specific problem referred to in the Manifesto of the powers of Parliament in relation to fiscal, regional and industrial questions should be capable of a solution. There need be little difficulty over the fiscal issues. On industry we are concerned with one or two specific matters, notably steel. The regional question is not so much one of the Regional Development Fund, where progress is being made; it is much more a matter of each country – and we all have problems here – being able to take whatever action is needed on a basis which does not offend against the Community rules of fair competition nor create difficulties for our partners.

Different countries have evolved different techniques for dealing with their regional aids, because regional problems can vary considerably within an individual country. Particularly in the industrial situation which we and our partners face, it may sometimes be necessary to act speedily and with a certain degree of originality.

I made clear earlier in the week that what we are concerned to do is to redistribute employment opportunities and industrial expansion as between prosperous areas and those most in need of development – *within Britain*. I think it is right that each country should have a reasonable degree of freedom to act quickly in an emergency, subject only to an obligation to justify any action to their partners. But I would repeat an assurance I have already given that we do not want to get into competitive bidding against others in the Community. We should all be working within the same rules of fair trading competition.

I believe very strongly, and I want our colleagues in the Community to recognize this, that what we have said in the Manifesto about the ability to continue to import food from our traditional Commonwealth suppliers is something which is very important to our people. These have been traditional suppliers to Britain. But it is not just a matter of trade. There are deep personal and family relationships for many of our people with countries in the Commonwealth. I have forty-three close relatives in Australia, descendants of my four grandparents, more than four times as many as I have in Britain. I am not unique in this. And in addition to family ties there are very many who recall the response of the Commonwealth when Europe's freedom was in danger, many who developed close personal friendships within the Commonwealth. I trust that our friends in the Community will not underrate this very powerful feeling in Britain, or the importance of the Commonwealth relationship which we can bring into the Community with us. But in pressing for some understanding of these problems, we do not seek to change the basis on which the European Community is founded. Indeed we believe that the adjustments we are asking for are readily compatible with the principles of the Community.

It is in the best interests of Britain and of other members of the Community that we proceed with all reasonable urgency to settle the outstanding problems which face us in the renegotiation. We shall be meeting in Paris against the background of an increasingly grave world crisis. We should all be free as soon as possible, whatever the outcome of the negotiations, to give that crisis our full attention. I hope that Monday and Tuesday will provide the highest possible measure of agreement between us on how these problems should be approached.

I believe that the necessary speed and urgency, combined with the thoroughness that is needed, can best be achieved if Ministers, accountable to their own people, now take charge. At the Press Conference which Herr Schmidt and I held at the conclusion of our talks last Sunday, I said: 'I would like to see the negotiations coming under much clearer political direction by politicians who know what is important to their own country, their own electorate, as well as to the countries with whom they are negotiating and their electorates'. This was immediately endorsed by the Federal Chancellor, who said 'I very much agree with the British Prime Minister, that political questions in the first and in the last instance are to be solved and answered by political animals. They can be prepared, and must be prepared of course, by civil servants of various capacities, but we ought to be aware that what we are facing are political questions that are not very likely to be solved by legal procedures'.

For various reasons – changes of Government in other Community countries, our own second General Election – we have not before now been able to bring the vital remaining issues to the point of decision. Now, in simple sporting terms, the Foreign Secretary and I want to get the ball out of the scrum.

It is frequently said, not only in this country, that in Brussels there is a great concentration of bureaucrats, jurists and even theologians. You find them not only in the Commission, but to some extent even in national delegations visiting Brussels for particular Councils or Committees. However that may be, we have now reached the point where the result is more important than the game.

There is a famous story about a Welsh Fifteen at Cardiff Arms Park. For twenty minutes, ankle deep in mud, the forwards hardly released the ball from the scrum for a moment. At last it emerged to the scrum half, who passed to the fly half, who then kicked it high over the Grandstand. A search party set off to look for it, and after ten minutes had not returned. One of the Welsh pack – or it may have been the English – was heard to say: 'Never mind the ruddy ball, let's get on with the ruddy game'.

We must take great care that we do not become so obsessed with the game that we lose sight of the ball. So let's get it out of the scrum. It has been there so long that I would like to know if it is in fact oval or oblong or banana shaped or even flat. I want to get it into the hands of the three-quarters, the politicians, those with authority to move. Then let's see if we are able to score the try or not.

For many years I have been accused of putting Party interests or the requirement of Party unity before all else. I do not think Party unity is necessarily an unworthy aim, particularly for the Leader of the Party.

The fact is, as others have admitted so clearly, that the Labour Party is divided on this issue. So are the Conservative Party, even though they have more ruthless means of suppressing freedom of thought than a democratic party would consider to be right. So are the Liberals. I have no doubt that the other parties represented in the House of Commons reflect this same division, which runs right through opinion in this country.

But at a time when the pro-market commentators, whose regard for me two or three years ago fell a little short of enthusiasm, are now beginning to sing a different tune, let them realize this. While I do not apologize for doing all in my power to get this Party *united*, what I can claim to have done since 1966 is to keep this Party *consistent*. And this is what our Manifesto means. We will work wholeheartedly for the success of the European venture if we get the terms for which we have asked and the endorsement of the British people. But if we do not, we believe that our national interest would not be served by accepting a situation which would undermine our economic strength, and our capacity to protect our national as well as our wider international interests.

Mr Chairman, I thought it right in advance of this vitally important meeting next week to set out for our own people and for those to whom we shall be talking, the position which, as a Party, we have taken up, the position which the British people have endorsed, the position which is the policy of Her Majesty's Government.

Appendix IV Introductory Statement to Dublin meeting of the European Council on the renegotiation of Britain's terms of entry into the EEC, March 1975

Mr President, Colleagues:

Since it falls to me to be the first of your guests to speak I would like to extend to our Chairman the very warm appreciation of other Heads of Government for the splendid arrangements made to welcome us on this occasion. Also pleased – you told me this – to be first British Prime Minister in the Castle since Asquith in 1911. This is the first meeting of the European Council. It is an event of significance in the history of Europe; and it is fitting that it should occur in this magnificent historic setting. I hope that our discussions here will mark a positive step towards closer understanding. That is my purpose and I am sure that others will share it.

Since we last met in Paris and discussed what we have called renegotiation – which some prefer to call the British problem – we have seen substantial progress made in the Council to resolve points of difficulty which we had raised and to steer the Community in directions which we regard as right, not just for us, but for the Community as a whole and for the world outside. I should like to thank your Governments and the Commission for your readiness to consider in a helpful spirit the questions we have raised. The Community has demonstrated that it is ready to approach problems which member states raise in a flexible and pragmatic way.

Today there are just two points remaining, the budget and New Zealand, on which I must again ask my fellow Heads of Government to focus their attention. If we can resolve them in our talks, the way will be clear for the British Government to reach its verdict on renegotiation and to declare its position to Parliament and the people before Easter. That is the timetable I would like to follow. I ask you therefore to join me in making the final political effort to reach agreement on the outstanding points today.

Before I come to them in detail I would like to make a few brief remarks on renegotiation in order to remove misunderstandings which may have arisen. *First*, I would like to make it clear that I do not intend to raise any new subjects, nor will any new subjects be raised by us in the period between now and the Referendum. Let me also repeat that we have throughout conducted renegotiations with the intention of succeeding and obtaining terms which the Government could commend to the British people. I cannot prejudge what view the Cabinet will take; and, until the Cabinet has reviewed the results as a whole, I cannot declare a personal position. I believe indeed that it would be prejudicial to the Cabinet decision if I were to do so. But if the Cabinet accepts the outcome of renegotiation, then it is my firm intention to put the favourable results which we have achieved and the advantages of membership of the Community clearly before the British people. We shall not be neutral when the nation makes this historic decision. But only if the renegotiations meet the outstanding points: those on which we made progress in Paris, and those where we seek a solution here in Dublin, I am convinced that we shall be able to campaign actively for Britain to remain in the EEC.

*Second*, I know that some of you are concerned that even when renegotiation is over, Britain will still be a reluctant partner in the Community, that we shall go on seeking changes which will be damaging to the established pattern of Community life. Let me make it quite clear that this is not so. If the Referendum endorses

British membership, we shall have British national backing for that membership, which was not the case from January 1973. We shall bring our own constructive contribution to the pursuit of common goals. Of course we shall continue to seek improvements where we think improvements desirable. That is the right and duty of any Member. The CAP stocktaking, proposed by the German Government, is a good example. So is aid to countries other than the African, Caribbean and Pacific countries. But we will be playing our part in all the developments of the Community in a constructive spirit and as a Member with a vested interest in the cohesion and well-being of the Community as a whole.

I should perhaps just say a word about steel in view of some of the things I have read since the Foreign Secretary made his statement in Brussels. Let me repeat that this is not an issue which we are putting forward for settlement before the Referendum. Therefore I am not asking you to undertake any commitment about this in Dublin. If there is an opportunity later in our discussion I can explain briefly the points we would want to examine and perhaps discuss with the Community after the Referendum and as part of normal Community business.

Subject to the views of the Chairman I will now turn to the two items we have to settle in order to complete renegotiation. First the Budget. Second New Zealand.

## The Budget

The budget problem is perhaps the most difficult and intractable which we have raised in renegotiation. It is, I think, generally agreed that the existing arrangements are likely to have an unfair impact on the United Kingdom. This was the only conclusion which could be drawn from the Commission's Report last autumn, and Heads of Government duly drew it at their Paris meeting when they decided that a corrective mechanism should be set up as soon as possible.

At the end of January the Commission produced the very helpful report which is before the meeting and it was decided at the 10/11 February Council that we should take this as a basis for discussion. I very much hope that the meeting today will confirm that decision. We shall be in real difficulties if we further complicate a difficult situation by looking at new ideas. Naturally there will be points on the Commission Report which we or others will wish to raise. But as M. Thorn so rightly said in the Council, the Commission Report must be more nearly a point of arrival than a starting-point.

It seems to me that there are three main outstanding problems which this meeting ought to try to settle this afternoon. I will explain what they are in a moment. If we can reach a consensus on them our officials can prepare a draft declaration overnight for us to consider tomorrow. They can at the same time settle all the other points in the Commission's Report on which there are outstanding reserves. These points are in my view subsidiary.

The three main points are:

a. the balance of payments criterion;
b. the size of the refund; and
c. the VAT slice, where the Commission have made the suggestion that the total of this should be a ceiling on a Member State's refund and where the French Foreign Minister put forward a rather different version.

I should like to explain my Government's views on these three points.

As my colleagues, the Foreign Ministers, will know, the Commission's suggestion that a Member State with a balance of payments surplus should not qualify would cause an unsurmountable difficulty. The Community should not add to the already stringent criteria about relative GDP per head and relative growth rates an additional criterion relating to the balance of payments. It may not be necessary for me to repeat today why we think that this is irrelevant and would be harmful. I hope that we can agree to drop it.

Then there is the size of the refund. We think that the Commission, in their natural efforts to make their report acceptable all round have made these suggestions too restrictive. This fact, taken together with the two-thirds limit and the sliding scale system proposed, would mean that the United Kingdom would be unlikely ever to secure a refund of much over half the gap between our GDP share and our budget share. I think that there is general agreement now that this gap is likely to be about 7 per cent in 1980 and to decline thereafter in the natural course of events. I put it to you that it is not an 'equitable solution', in the words of the formula about unacceptable situations which gave rise to the title of the Commission paper, for a Member State with a GDP per head below 85 per cent of the Community average to pay 3 per cent or 3½ per cent more than its GDP share of the budget. This would be particularly difficult to defend when certain other Member States with GDP per head well above the Community average would be paying two or three percentage points below their GDP share of the budget. The Community will not function well, to use the wording that Heads of Government adopted in Paris in December, if one Member State is at a permanent disadvantage in this way. What would its attitude be to Community expenditure? What would be the effect on Convergence which, we are all agreed, is our aim?

I would be grateful therefore if the meeting could concentrate on this crucial question. We should like to remove the two-thirds limitation and improve the sliding scale arrangements so that the United Kingdom would get back a more substantial part of the gap than the Commission suggest.

If an improvement of this kind cannot be made the outcome will come under severe criticism in Britain. I know that each percentage point will cost all of the other Member States something, their budget share, whatever it may be, of the additional refund. If there is to be a corrective mechanism it ought surely to ensure an actual refund of at least three-quarters of the gap.

Finally, I come to the VAT point. I hope that the French Government will be prepared to work on the basis of the Commission version here. I am bound to say that even the Commission version causes us certain difficulties. In some circumstances it could have an effect on the size of the refund, particularly in the early years of the operation of the mechanism. We do not really accept the logic of what the Commission suggests.

To sum up, this whole question is complicated. In addition to the points I have raised, we could discuss at length whether 85 per cent of Community GDP per head or growth rate at 120 per cent of the Community average are the right percentages for a Member State to qualify. There are other points which Member States might wish to raise. But I should like to suggest that we avoid arguing about these and all make an effort to go along with the Commission's suggestions on these subsidiary points. I hope, Mr Chairman, that you can concentrate the discussion today on the three main points of substance I have mentioned and that we can reach a consensus on them this very afternoon, so that an agreed draft declaration can be prepared overnight. Even if we cannot reach full agreement this afternoon, a draft declaration should still be prepared by officials tonight, with as few square brackets as possible, so that Heads of Government need spend as little time as possible on this matter tomorrow.

## New Zealand

We fully understand why the question of access for New Zealand dairy products is not an easy one for the rest of the Community.

But the links between the British and New Zealand people are peculiarly close: New Zealand is not 'just another developed country'. The British people cannot understand why these links should be permanently damaged by our membership of the Community. They think that the Community's willingness to respond to these deep emotions is a test of the Community's ability to take account of the political interests of its members.

The New Zealand dairy industry has been traditionally dependent on the British market. They are now diversifying both their markets and their economy. We entirely favour what in any case would have been a natural development. But they need a long time to do this. We cannot accept that the Community should impose unnecessary burdens on them meanwhile.

This has always been a crucial issue both for this and the previous Labour Government. I made my concern quite clear when I toured Community capitals in 1967. I criticized the arrangements negotiated by the previous Government in 1971 as far from satisfactory. New Zealand has always figured high in the list of our renegotiation requirements.

Of course we do not wish to override the procedures laid down in Protocol 18. It is for the Commission to produce a proposal, and for the Council to agree on it. But the British people need the political assurance that the Council's eventual decision will be on the right lines. This is why we look to the Heads of Government to issue a political declaration, with which the President of the Commission would of course be associated, and which would indicate the broad lines along which the Community would be ready to proceed after 1977.

The Foreign and Commonwealth Secretary tabled a draft declaration in the Council on 3 March. This reflects our latest talks with the New Zealanders. It covers the three important problems of price, quantities and butter equivalent.

*Price* The New Zealanders are particularly concerned about the pricing provisions in the existing Protocol. It is now widely recognized in the Community that the price provisions in the existing Protocol are inadequate. They do not provide a basis upon which the initial prices could be updated from time to time. The need for a review of prices has been particularly apparent against the background of the rapid world inflation over the last two years. Last year the Community had to review New Zealand's prices under the Protocol on an *ad hoc* basis, and agreed to an 18 per cent increase. But looking to the period after 1977, it is, in our view, necessary to lay down a clear basis for fixing prices for New Zealand dairy products and adjusting these from one year to the next. This is something to which New Zealand as well as the United Kingdom attach particular importance.

*Quantity* The declaration proposes that the access quantity for the three years 1978–80 should be fixed at a level closely related to deliveries in 1974 and 1975. It does not specify figures, which would have to be settled in the review later this year. However, in 1974, New Zealand supplied some 124,000 tons of butter equivalent. Our estimate of supplies during 1975 is 134,000 tons. Taking the two years together, it seems likely that this formula might point to a figure between 125,000 and 130,000 tons of butter equivalent. This, of course, is below the access quantity for 1977 in the Protocol – around 143,000 tons of butter equivalent. The reference to butter equivalent would allow for some New Zealand cheese to be imported according to availability and the market situation.

Especially as we contemplate an access quantity below the figure for 1977 in the present Protocol, we consider that it would be reasonable in the course of the review to avoid further degressivity by fixing a firm figure for an initial three-year period after 1977. It would be necessary then to provide for the arrangements for subsequent periods after 1980 to be fixed by the Council. The quantity for 1981–83 would, for example, fall to be decided in 1978.

*Duration* The declaration recognizes that it is for the Commission to present detailed proposals for decision by the Council in the review of the Protocol. We should be grateful if the Commission could put forward these proposals before the end of April. This would allow adequate time to carry through the review before the summer holidays and to reach a conclusion before the New Zealanders hold their elections in the autumn, as they wish.

## Statement on Steel, 11 March 1975

I should like to say a further word about steel and the problems it presents to Britain as a member of the European Community. At the outset of the negotiations, the Foreign and Commonwealth Secretary mentioned steel as having problems for us. There can be no complaint that these were not reached earlier, because for months, by mutual consent, no progress was attempted on negotiation until the second British general election was over in October. We have also needed to have experience of the practical problems as regards steel arising from Community membership. But I mentioned steel in my public speech in December and I referred to it at Paris.

We have a steel industry of which the greater part is, and has been for many years, publicly owned. That fact creates problems neither for us nor for other members of the Community. And I know that you will confirm that neither membership of the Community nor the ECSC Treaty itself, nor any rules and practices developed under the Treaty, derogate in any way from the right of Britain or any other member country to extend the boundaries of public ownership or even to take the whole industry into public ownership. That is not and has not been in question.

But Britain is a mixed economy, and steel itself is part State-owned, part privately-owned. We are concerned to help ensure that the operations of the private sector also do not offend against the basic rules and principles, for example on competition, operated under the Treaty. There are problems about prices in the private sector, and also mergers in that area. We believe these can be overcome.

The principal problem relates to control of investment within the private sector.

When Britain joined the Community, the then British Government moved in Parliament to repeal statutory powers which gave the Government certain controls over *private* steel investments. But the Commission equally appears to have no power of control, while the advice we have had suggests that there could be difficulties if we ourselves moved to fill the vacuum by introducing new legislation.

In Britain today, a problem has arisen – in South Wales – where a private firm, not British, not controlled from any member country or countries of the Community, but controlled from outside the Community, seeks to build a new plant. This at a time when, in the interests of efficiency, the British Steel Board is closing down older plants in areas of high unemployment. Because of the repeal of all investment control powers, we have no power to act.

We could take powers to deal with this problem without conflicting with the Treaty. But, externally-owned steel undertakings apart, there are still other problems to be solved.

When, as part of our common effort to fight inflation, Her Majesty's Government holds back the level of new investment in the public steel sector, it is unacceptable that the private sector should be free to expand where it wants, and by as much as it wants, thus adding to the inflationary pressure on resources. There are location and regional problems, too, especially for areas where steel men have been made redundant by technological change involving the closure of elderly plants.

It may well be that other Member countries have already met with this and similar problems. I presume that such problems have been resolved, after consultation where necessary, in ways compatible with the Treaty – for no country has sought to amend the Treaty.

I should be very grateful to learn from your experience. That might save my Government a lot of trouble. We are not now proposing Treaty amendment. We would much prefer to avoid it. It is the last thing we seek in view of its implications. There may be administrative or other ways of dissuading potential investors – environmental controls, planning controls, industrial development certificate controls, or other means. There is always the possibility of extending public ownership; and we reserve the right to do this if necessary. If we could find one or other of these ways, or indeed some other way, of dealing with this problem in conformity with the Treaty, that would be the kind of solution we seek. But it is of vital importance to us that the problem be solved.

I end by reconfirming that we are not making this an issue to be settled in these negotiations or before the referendum. As I have made clear, provided that the problem is understood and acknowledged, we are now prepared to leave its solution, in a spirit of consultation and advice, to the future work of the Community, if after the Referendum we remain as a member.

Appendix V Extracts from speech to National Union of Mineworkers'
Conference, Scarborough, 7 July 1975

We had stated in our Manifesto our determination to work out a new strategy *for* the
coal industry, *with* the coal industry. We had pledged ourselves to re-examine,
jointly – Government, the NUM and Coal Board – the Industry's future, and to
produce a plan to ensure it within three months.

The Secretary of State for Energy, then Eric Varley, himself a former mineworker,
was given Cabinet authority to sit down with the industry and work out that plan.
It *was* produced within the three months we laid down. It was announced to
Parliament. It was discussed at the NUM Conference.

Let me remind you of the main conclusions of the plan, unanimously agreed
upon between the Coal Board, NUM and Government. They were these:

*First*, the coal industry has an assured long-term future.

*Second*, potential demand exists over the next ten years for up to 150 million tons of
    coal a year from the British coal industry, *provided it can be economically produced.*

*Third*, taking account of the inevitable exhaustion of existing mines, a massive
    investment programme will be needed to stabilize deep mined output at 120
    million tons.

*Fourth*, open-cast output can and should be expanded to 15 million tons a year.

*Fifth*, at long last a scheme of compensation for pneumoconiosis sufferers should
    be drawn up and put into operation.

*Sixth*, miners' pensions should be radically improved.

The Coal Board is pressing ahead with its investment programme as it promised.
So far 24 major colliery projects have been started which will provide 8 million
additional tons of coal each year. They are aiming at starting work, before the end
of this year, to develop the capacity necessary to produce nearly half the extra 42
million tons annually, which they are planning.

The new confidence in the industry's future is reflected in the recruitment figures.
1974, following the settlement of the dispute in the industry in March, was the first
year since 1957 when the number of miners increased. So far this year the NCB has
increased its workforce by more than 3,000 compared with an increase of 545 in the
same period last year and a reduction of more than 6,000 in the same months of
1973.

\*　　\*　　\*

Now the future of the coal industry is where it belongs – in the hands of those who
work in it and the hands of those who run it.

Their decisions and their actions, *your* decisions and *your* actions, will decide
whether coal is to retain the competitive price advantage which above all guarantees firm employment prospects and good wages.

That is the reality so far as the future of this industry, and above all the future of
jobs in this industry, are concerned. No resolution which may be passed this week
can affect that reality.

If ever coal becomes uncompetitive again – and this is true of any industry – then
it begins its decline. The greater the uncompetitiveness, the faster the decline.

It is natural that trade unionists should seek to negotiate as high an income as they can, for the comfort of themselves and their families. It is natural that others, on both sides of industry, should wish to do the same. It is certainly natural, when prices have been rising at the rate they have, that everyone should seek to protect their living standards against inflation.

But if, as a result, the rise in prices, the rise in the cost of living generally is not only perpetuated but aggravated, then that natural intention turns to dust and duff and spoil.

Hardly anyone gains, except at the expense of others. Sometimes those others are in the low-paid industries, who are entitled to look to their stronger brethren for support. Sometimes at the expense of the sick and disabled – of whom the miners have always borne a tragically disproportionate share – the old and the deprived.

Industrial actions have their social consequences, usually for those least able to bear them. The price of coal has too often, and literally, been a crippling one for the miner; bodies shattered, lungs destroyed, children orphaned. The strength of the mining community throughout its history has been that it is a community, in good times and, more frequently, in adversity.

But that strength would become a weakness if ever the mining community were to become isolated from the national community – if the mining industry ever said 'whatever the state of the economy, whatever the nation's crisis, we will protect ourselves from its effects'.

The Government have made it clear that every public industry must now pay its way within its income. You can't get a quart out of a pint pot. That includes the coal industry. Increases in wages and other costs mean, as they did last year, an automatic, almost simultaneous, announcement of higher coal prices.

We all know what happens when costs increase. Everyone pays. The consumer. The coal-using industries. The mineworker and his family pay too – for example, when electricity prices rise as an inevitable consequence.

If, for example, there were a settlement on £100/85/80, this would inexorably add £5.25 a ton to the present average of £16.40 a ton: £21.65, an increase of 32 per cent. Against oil, against nuclear power, coal would lose its competitive edge, become the poor relation once again.

There is no alternative to, no escape from, reality. If I ask 'How can this cruel chain of circumstances be avoided?', some will say, of course, that it can be avoided by subsidies.

But subsidies have to be paid for. Paid for out of taxation.

The inevitable result, therefore, is that almost before you have started to enjoy the proceeds of a settlement beyond what the nation can afford, the Chancellor has got to put up taxes – the only way left to pay for it.

\*     \*     \*

The roots of this movement are buried deep in the history and suffering of the unemployed. It was to end economic and social injustice that we were born.

The action the Government has decided to take is not in pursuit of some economic textbook or theory. It is not a question today, in the crisis that Britain faces, of choosing between inflation and unemployment. Inflation is causing unemployment. We cannot have a little of one and less of the other. The more inflation we have the more unemployment we have. And if we were to tolerate the rates of inflation reached in recent months, then no industry would be secure, no job safe.

The battle against inflation is a battle for exports, for a greater measure of economic independence in an interdependent world. But, no less, the battle against inflation is a battle for full employment. Lose the battle against inflation and the battle for full employment is lost before you begin. Lose the battle against inflation, and there is no hope of stopping unemployment rising much higher.

This is true of coal.

In present circumstances, there can be no question of Government subsidies to pay for the cost of any increases over the odds, or in some way to cushion the consumer against the effect of the increases.

There can be no more borrowing for this purpose. It is the Government's job to get borrowing down in the period ahead, not increase it.

Nor can there be any loading of excessive costs on the public by charging more. That would make inflation worse, not less.

To continue wage awards on the scale of recent months would be to eat the seed corn. In the coal industry, it could only come out of the programme to which the Government is pledged as a result of the tripartite – Coal Board, NUM and Government – examination of a year ago, and approved by your Conference last year. Such an act would be crazy, even suicidal with all that means for future employment in the industry. It's not on.

I am proud, quite apart from the long-term investment like the major schemes not far from here and in other parts of the country, that the ingenuity of the Board and the NUM with Government backing, has been directed on relatively short-term expenditure and investment to save pits in danger of closing, even to reviving mining activity on an economic basis in areas where past closures have practically meant the end of a coal field or a mining industry. I am thinking of projects to extend the lives of mines like those at Longannet in Scotland, Horden in the North East, Silverdale in the Western Region and Ollerton in Notts. My fellow Yorkshiremen here are pressing for the re-opening of Thorne colliery at a cost of between £40–£50 millions. I can't pronounce on that, it's a matter for the economics of the industry. What is clear is that *if vast amounts are taken out of the industry in pay settlements over the odds there'll be less available* for saving precariously situated pits, or re-opening closed ones.

For we must all face the fact that there is a limit to what this or any other industry can spend, and that what goes up in the flue is not available to provide warmth and comfort for those who need it.

Any democratic assembly can pass resolutions, and mean them. But no resolution can alter the immutable facts that resolutions and what they lead to have to be paid for, and in the end they are paid for the hard way.

The Labour Government returned to office sixteen months ago on a national mandate to unite a bitterly divided people, whose divisions culminated in the previous Government's pitched confrontation with the mining community: returned to office on the mandate we had sought to govern by consensus and consent.

Appendix VI 'An Attack on Inflation': Statement in the House of Commons on the Government's Pay Policy, 11 July 1975

With your permission, Mr Speaker, I should like to make a statement.

The House will recall that 10 days ago my Right Hon. Friend the Chancellor of the Exchequer made a statement on the attack on inflation, and announced the determination of the Government to bring down the rate of domestic inflation to 10 per cent by the end of the coming pay round next autumn, and to single figures by the end of the year. He referred to the consultations with the TUC and the CBI which had been taking place directed towards achieving an agreed voluntary policy with, in particular, effective arrangements about pay consonant with that cost-of-living target. He undertook that by the end of this week the Government would make a statement about those consultations, setting out the Government's judgment as to whether a voluntary policy, which was both viable and effective, had been reached.

The house will have seen the statement endorsed by the General Council of the TUC on Wednesday, and regardless of party the whole House will pay tribute to the extent of the TUC's achievement. Yesterday I described it as an achievement unexampled in peace or war by the free democratic trade union movement in this country.

The Government have decided to accept an overriding limit of £6 per week for pay settlements during the next pay round, a figure consistent with the aim of reducing the rate of inflation to 10 per cent by the late summer of next year. Our policy is based on consent and willing cooperation within our democracy. We reject, for the reasons I have so frequently stated, the idea of statutory policies based on criminal sanctions against workers.

My Right Hon. Friend and I have been in close consultation with the CBI and the TUC during these 10 days and we have set out our policies for the attack on inflation in a White Paper, copies of which will be available in the Vote Office when I have sat down. In the White Paper we have set out the Government's proposals, directed to strengthening the fight against inflation right along the line, covering both the public and the private sectors.

The Government have decided that the cut-off for the increase of up to £6 shall be £8,500. We are also proposing some transitional arrangements to deal with inequities which would otherwise arise for certain groups which are expecting shortly to implement their annual agreements under the present TUC guidelines. It is, however, a requirement of the new proposals that no settlement can be approved within 12 months of the previous settlement.

I must make clear that while the Government accept the proposal for a flat-rate limit of £6, this is not an entitlement – it is a maximum. It will have to be negotiated by established collective bargaining procedures, and it is not a requirement on employers who simply cannot afford to pay it.

The Government are concerned – as the TUC has shown that it is – that unions or groups of workers who make a settlement early in the pay round should legitimately be able to demand protection against the action of other groups which, on past experience, might prejudice their position by negotiating considerably bigger settlements later in the round.

We intend to ensure observance of the new pay policy by employing the full battery of weapons available to which my Right Hon. Friend referred 10 days ago.

269

As employer, the Government will ensure that all settlements in respect of its employees in the Civil Service, the National Health Service and the Armed Forces comply with the pay limit. They will call on all other public sector employers to do the same. As paymaster and treasurer, on behalf of the taxpayer, for publicly-owned industries and services, the Government will use all their powers to see that settlements are made within the pay limit. They will ensure that the money available is strictly controlled and that none is available for the payment of increases over the agreed limit.

This means that for the nationalized industries and services, no money will be made available for excess settlements, whether by subsidies, whether by permission to borrow or by loading excess cost on the public by increasing prices or charges. There will be a strict limit on expenditure. Those seeking to negotiate settlements above the agreed limits, by whatever means, must face the certain consequence that there will be an inescapable cut-back in the current expenditure of the board or corporation concerned, directly affecting employment in that industry.

There must be no less stringent control in respect of local authorities' spending. There will be urgent discussions with the new Joint Consultative Council and with the Convention of Scottish Local Authorities.

In this as in other areas, legislation will be necessary to supplement and strengthen the policy we have worked out with industry. The Bill will be introduced next week.

So far as local authorities are concerned, legislation will be brought before Parliament to enable the Government to restrict payment of rate support grant to individual local authorities so that no grant is forthcoming in respect of any part of a settlement made in breach of the pay limit – any part of the settlement, not just the excess. No rate support grant increase will be made in such cases. Moreover, unless there is a tighter restriction on the numbers of staff employed, the Government will further have to restrict the scale of provision of grants.

In addition, if this proves necessary, as a further sanction the Government will be prepared to use their powers to control local authority borrowing, including access to the capital market, to reduce the capital programmes to individual local authorities to offset any excess expenditure on pay settlements.

In the private sector the Government will use all their powers against any breach of the pay limit. The Bill will relieve employers of any contractual obligations which would otherwise compel them to increase pay by more than the limit.

In the field of price control the Bill will ensure that where an employer breaks the pay limit, not only the excess but the whole pay increase will be disallowed for the approval of price increases. This sanction will also be applied to nationalized industry prices.

From now on the Government will not give discretionary assistance under the Industry Act to companies which have broken the pay limit. Contracting Departments will also take account of a firm's record of observance of the pay limit in their general purchasing policy and in the awarding of contracts.

The Government believe that these measures are necessary to secure compliance by all employers with the policy I have stated, but if our faith in the agreed policy is disappointed, if there are any who seek to abuse a system based on consensus and consent, or to cheat by any means, the Government will not hesitate to apply legal powers of compulsion against the employers concerned, to ensure compliance. We must have these powers in reserve.

Legislation has therefore already been prepared, for introduction if need be, which, when applied to particular cases, would make it illegal for the employer to exceed the pay limit. If the pay limit is endangered, the Government will ask Parliament to approve this legislation forthwith.

The fact that pay increases are to be negotiated within a flat-rate limit will rightly give preference to the low-paid worker. But the House will see in the White Paper the extent to which the Government intend to act to restrain prices. In present circumstances a general price freeze is not realistic and would simply depress investment and aggravate the unemployment problem. But the Government's policy on prices, in addition to acting as a sanction against recalcitrant employers, is also designed to provide the necessary assurance to employees, required to justify the flat-rate pay limit.

The Government will therefore continue the present strict prices control enforced under the Price Code. We shall introduce legislation to extend the control powers beyond 31 March 1976, when they would expire. As the pay limit comes into full effect, the Government intend to ensure that the rate of price increase for a range of goods of special, strategic importance in the family expenditure will be held to about the 10 per cent target. The CBI and the Retail Consortium, which we have consulted, are prepared to enter into immediate discussions with the Government to achieve this price limitation programme.

The Government have decided also to finance many more consumer advice centres to assist consumers who have complaints or queries. We shall encourage more work on local price comparisons and will accelerate the programme of price display and unit pricing.

To assist with the cost of living during this period, and particularly to protect the living standards of lower-income families and pensioners, the Government have also decided to delay the phasing out of food subsidies which was announced in the last Budget. This will involve an expenditure of an additional £70 million in the period 1976 to 1977. Local authority rents were frozen by the Government between March 1974 and March 1975 but increases are now in the pipeline because of pay increases and other inflationary influences. For the period 1976 to 1977 the Government propose to limit rent increases so that rents do not rise faster than prices generally. This will mean that on average rent increases next spring will be of the order of 60p a week rather than £1 a week or more. For this purpose the Government will provide an extra £80 million.

The Government believe that this comprehensive programme – with any further action which we deem necessary – will bring about in a fair and equitable manner the desperately needed reduction in the rate of inflation.

We reject massive panic cuts in expenditure. Some which have been suggested would not only have acted directly to increase the cost of living and so aggravate the inflationary problem, but would have added to the numbers unemployed. The action we are proposing will improve employment by restoring confidence, promoting investment, and increasing the competitiveness of British industry, both in export markets and in the saving of imports.

Unemployment has already reached an unacceptably high level in this country, and it is small comfort to record that in the deepest world recession since the 1930s unemployment has so far risen less in this country than elsewhere or that we have been more successful in maintaining the level of industrial production.

My Right Hon. Friend the Chancellor has already announced the increased opportunities for training and retraining, as well as measures to help people to move to newer employment and a plan for a temporary employment subsidy to assist firms located in areas of high unemployment. The Government will introduce the temporary employment subsidy at the earliest possible moment. I must make it clear, however, that this subsidy will not be available to companies which exceed the pay limits. We shall also take, as the White Paper makes clear, special temporary measures to encourage the training and employment of school leavers and other young people in industry.

I said that we reject the panic measures in the field of essential expenditure, including the social services. The best guarantee against a reduction in social standards is to bring the rate of inflation down to the level we have indicated for next summer and beyond. But we certainly will continue our efforts to contain the demands on resources made by public expenditure programmes.

We have made clear our intention to apply cash limits, as opposed to limits based on resources measured at theoretical constant prices, as a means of ensuring financial discipline, in central Government, local government, and publicly-owned industries and services. Urgent work is in hand to ensure the extensive use of cash limits in the coming financial year.

Without trespassing unduly on the time of the House, it is not possible in this statement to set out the full range of Government controls and actions which we intend to use to fortify the agreed policy as set out in the White Paper.

But I must leave the House in no doubt about the Government's total will and determination to use to the full all the powers we hold, in both the public and the private sector. This is not all. The legislation which we shall bring before the House next week will significantly extend the powers at the disposal of the Government to strengthen controls, to close loop-holes, to frustrate cheating, and generally to secure compliance with the new pay limits.

When Hon. Members study the White Paper[1] I hope that they will be ready to endorse its concluding words:

> The Government seek the support of the nation in breaking the inflation which threatens our economy. The measures the Government, the TUC and the CBI are taking are designed to last right through the next pay-round until price inflation has been brought down to single figures and we have reached agreement on how to arrange our affairs so as to avoid a resurgence.
>
> This is a plan to save our country. If we do not, over the next 12 months, achieve a drastic reduction in the present disastrous rate of inflation by the measures outlined in this document, the British people will be engulfed in a general economic catastrophe of incalculable proportions. If we do succeed, as we are resolved to do, we can turn with fresh energy and hope to tackle the fundamental problems which will still face us on constructing an economy in which high pay is earned by high output.

[1] Cmnd. 6151.

# Appendix VII  Statement on the Royal Civil List, 13 February 1975

Mrs Thatcher:

Is the Prime Minister aware that the Opposition welcome his statement and agree that proper provision must continue to be made for the Royal Household and the performance of its official functions? This is our most precious asset.

In view of the inflationary conditions prevailing, which affect the Royal Household and its staff as much as anyone else, we believe that the time has come to look at the way in which we provide for the Civil List. We shall, of course, carefully examine any legislation which the Right Hon. Gentleman chooses to lay before the House.

The Prime Minister:

With your indulgence, Mr Speaker, may I say that I know that I speak on behalf of all my Right Hon. and Hon. Friends when I congratulate the Right Hon. Member for Finchley [Mrs Thatcher] on her outstanding success in being elected leader of her party. We wish her happiness in and enjoyment of a life which she knows she can expect to be exciting but sometimes arduous and difficult. From a study of the Right Hon. Lady's speeches, I have formed the impression that there may well be a deep gulf between her and me in our respective political philosophies, but, having worked closely with her three immediate predecessors, as I have, I know that political disagreement between us need not mar the work that we have to do together in Parliament, and I look forward, as I hope she will, to the meetings behind your Chair, Mr Speaker, and to the informality and, to judge from my experience with her predecessors, the intimacy, which such meetings afford.

Mrs Thatcher *rose* –

The Prime Minister:

I apologize to the Right Hon. Lady. I did not answer the very important question she put to me. That is an oversight. I thank her for what she said at the beginning. It is absolutely right that the House should have not only abundant time to debate these matters but abundant time to think about them. That is why I think that the legislation will be best introduced very much later on this year so that Hon. Members in all parts of the House, whatever their views, can give thought to them. As the Right Hon. Lady says, we must think about this whole question.

There was an all-party Select Committee three years ago of which I and others were members. We went into these things very fully indeed, as the Right Hon. Lady knows. Speaking for myself – other Hon. Members may form a different view – on the whole I think that the right decision was taken at that time.

Mrs Thatcher:

I know that it is important not to speak too often from this Dispatch Box, Mr Speaker, but may I respond to the Prime Minister's kindness? I know that we shall have hard things to say to one another across Dispatch Boxes, but I hope that we shall be able to keep the mutual respect of keen antagonists which I think is in the best interests of parliamentary democracy.

Mr Thorpe:

Is the Prime Minister aware that the Right Hon. Lady appears to have bowled him over at least through half of his questions? Whether that is a sign for the future I know not. Is the Prime Minister aware, further, that it is singularly appropriate today to congratulate the Right Hon. Lady on becoming the first lady of this House, which we hope is not a contested position, at least for the immediate future?

Does the Right Hon. Gentleman remember that some eight years ago he was kind enough to assure me that the relationship between party leaders was one of warmth, friendliness and total understanding? We hope that the Right Hon. Lady will live to enjoy that relationship.

Would the Right Hon. Gentleman agree that inflation inevitably hits any Head of State under whatever system it is operating, and the Head of State of this country is not immune from those processes? Would he also bear in mind that some of us who sat on the Select Committee on the Civil List believe that the present system is not only psychologically unfair but is totally misleading?

Will the Prime Minister again have a look at the Crown estates, which admittedly have the benefit of having been freed from death duties but which none the less are surrendered to the Exchequer at the beginning of each reign? In 1970 those revenues were as much as £3½ million. Would he consider the possibility of those revenues being paid into a joint Exchequer board for the actual expenses which the Chancellor of the Exchequer, and perhaps an official from the Royal Household, could agree, as the Inland Revenue does already in other matters, were wholly and properly incurred in the discharge of the Royal functions and see that this surplus was paid into the Exchequer each year? That would be much more accurate and much more fair.

Finally, so that we get these matters into perspective, will the Prime Minister confirm that the cost of discharging the functions of the Head of State of this country is slightly less than the cost of running the Embassy in Paris?

The Prime Minister:

I thank the Right Hon. Gentleman. He is, of course, right when he says that inflation hits Heads of State in common with everyone else. In fact I think the more accurate phrase to use is that it hits any large employer. The increase referred to in the statement which I made this afternoon, which is required because of the statutory requirement of the report by the trustees, is largely because of wages and salaries. I am sure no Hon. Member begrudges the fact that the Royal servants received roughly the same wages and salary increases as those in comparable work and in comparable – in many cases the same – trade unions. No one disputes that.

The Right Hon. Gentleman was right when he said that this cannot be regarded as an increase in pay, notwithstanding the rather tendentious headlines we have seen about 'Increase in Queen's Pay'. It is not an increase in pay. It is not an increase in salary. The Queen has received no salary since the 1972 Act. It is in fact a reduction, not an increase, in the real value of the finance made available. In part it reimburses her as a very large employer on behalf of the nation for what she in an inflationary situation over three years has had to pay in increased wages and salaries . . .

Mr Paul Dean:

Is the Right Hon. Gentleman aware that his statement today will go some way to deal with the grossly unfair and misleading remarks which have been made outside? Does he agree that since the Crown surrendered various rights in exchange for the Civil List, the State has made a handsome profit out of the Royal Family, quite apart from the enormous debt that we owe them as ambassadors for Britain and the Commonwealth throughout the world.

The Prime Minister:

Yes, Sir.

Mr William Hamilton:

Is the Prime Minister aware that the vast majority of Members on this side will be appalled at the statement that he has made this afternoon, and that I suspect that the vast majority of our supporters outside will share that view?

Does the Prime Minister know – I am sure that he does – that there is a tax-free income available to the Crown of not less than £300,000 a year from the Duchy of Lancaster which, if it were taxed, would be more than £14 million a year, and that that is likely to increase over the next few years? Does he not think that it would be desirable for us to return to the principle of having a Select Committee to go into all the details instead of this proposal being passed by an order of the House, which we shall not have the opportunity to amend?

Will not the Prime Minister accept – [Hon. Members: 'Too long.'] – that the whole of the Parliamentary Labour Party took the view, when the Civil List was debated, that we should establish a Department of the Crown – in other words, treat it as another Department of State, with an annual Vote? His proposals this afternoon fell very short of that. We knew that he was a member of the establishment, but he does not need to go on all fours to prove it.

Mr Rathbone:

On a point of order, Mr Speaker. Would you give me some guidance? Should not the Hon. Member for Fife, Central [Mr Hamilton] have declared an interest in the subject to which he was speaking, in that he has gone out of his way to seek publicity for a book which he has published about the Royal Family and he is now making use of the House of Commons in order to further the sales of his own creation?

Mr Speaker:

It is not a convention of the House that interests have to be declared during Questions.

The Prime Minister:

The views of my Hon. Friend the Member for Fife, Central [Mr Hamilton] on this matter are well known and have been well canvassed over many years. Indeed, he has every right in a free country, as I said of another politician yesterday, to speak for himself and some others. But he does not have the right to claim to speak for the majority of the British people. Naturally, I do not accept some of his remarks. I know how strongly he feels and it will perhaps be better for me to pass them by.

My Hon. Friend referred to the Select Committee of which he and I were both Members and in which we played a considerable part together.

Mr William Hamilton:

I was a full-timer.

The Prime Minister:

My Hon. Friend has always been a full-timer on this subject. Some of us have to spend time on other subjects.

My Hon. Friend did not point out that in the debates on the Bill that followed the Select Committee the procedure under which I have to take action today, as required by law, was not contested by a vote called by either of the Front Benches of the major parties or by him.

Mr Hamilton:

I was away.

The Prime Minister:

Perhaps my Hon. Friend was away. Some of us were full-timers at that time.

Mr Hamilton:

I was away sick.

The Prime Minister:

If my Hon. Friend was in his sick-bed, I understand and withdraw that remark.

Mr Hamilton:

My Right Hon. Friend should have known that.

The Prime Minister:

My Hon. Friend will be aware that, in his absence, even those whose support he claims did not move an amendment to the Bill relating to the procedure under which my Right Hon. Friend the Chancellor of the Exchequer and I are required to act.

I was interested in what my Hon. Friend said, because the point was pressed in our discussions. Incidentally, in most votes in the Select Committee he and I voted on the same side, but perhaps for slightly different reasons [Hon. Members: 'Oh.']. I am not accusing my Hon. Friend of guilt by association. I am just saying that we did.

My Hon. Friend suggests that the Royal Household should be treated as a Department of State. I think he will realize the implications. If it were a Department of State – in other words, an employing Department – with 75 per cent of its total expenditure being staff costs, it would be automatic for that Department to come to this House to ensure that there were votes of sufficient money to pay those wages and salaries . . .

Mr Faulds:

Does the Prime Minister agree that most people iu this country believe that the services of Royals, even at the expenditure of such moneys, are cheap at the price if they prevent the emergence of populists such as President Powell or President Wedgie Benn?

The Prime Minister:

My Hon. Friend is the second of those behind me to parade his favourite obsession this afternoon.

Mr Molloy:

My Hon. Friend is a fifth-rate actor.

Mr Skinner:

He wants a job.

The Prime Minister:

My Hon. Friend had a Shadow job once. I have the greatest regard for my Hon. Friend. Indeed, I remember when he acted as sponsor to the would-be President Taverne. Leaving aside the concluding words of my Hon. Friend's remarks, which he read beautifully – he needs a new script writer, if I may say so – I agree with his opening words.

Mr Faulds:

On a point of order, Mr Speaker. Even from my Right Hon. Friend, for whom I have such high regard, I cannot accept the accusation that I ever read my questions or that anybody writes my scripts.

The Prime Minister:

That was the point. I apologize to my Hon. Friend. I was not suggesting that he was reading his question. That would be out of order. I was saying that I thought that he was following his own script. When I suggested that he should change his script writer, I meant that he should have someone other than himself to write for him.

## Appendix VIII  Guidelines for NEB Investments, 24 December 1976

*Acquisitions and Disposals*

The Secretary of State intends that in making acquisitions the NEB should have the same opportunities (within an agreed strategy) and the same obligations, and be subject to the same body of good practice, as institutions and companies in private ownership. The NEB and their companies are subject to the fair trading legislation. The Secretary of State has directed the NEB to act in accordance with the City Code on Takeovers and Mergers and, where relevant, the Stock Exchange rules in 'Admission of Securities to Listing'. The NEB have no special powers of compulsory acquisition but they have the same rights to acquire shares as are provided to businesses established under the Companies Act 1948.

When the NEB take a holding in a company they will normally seek to do so with the agreement of the company's Board. The Government do not accept, however, that the NEB should be able to buy shares in a company only with the agreement of its directors. To do so would place the NEB at a major disadvantage compared with other businesses and would give directors power to override the right of shareholders to sell their shares on a voluntary basis. Before acquiring, without the agreement of the directors of the company in question, shares or stock in a listed company which give an unrestricted right to vote, and whose acquisition would entitle the NEB to exercise or control the exercise of more than 10 per cent of the votes at any general meeting of the company, the NEB shall give the Secretary of State reasonable notice of their intention to acquire these shares or stock and of the size of holding which they wish to acquire eventually in the company. In addition, in the case of any acquisition which raises new or significant policy issues (whether or not the acquisition is one of which notice must be given in accordance with the foregoing requirements of this paragraph) the NEB shall give the Secretary of State reasonable notice of their intentions. After giving notice in accordance with this paragraph the NEB shall wait for a reasonable time before acquiring the shares or stock. This will give the Secretary of State the opportunity to decide whether to exercise his power of specific direction in relation to that acquisition. For the purposes of this paragraph a 'listed company' is a company to which Section 33 of the Companies Act 1967 applies.

Section 10 of the Industry Act 1975 requires the NEB and their subsidiaries to obtain the consent of the Secretary of State when the cost of acquiring share capital exceeds £10 million or where the acquisition would give the NEB 30 per cent or more of the voting rights unless the acquisition is covered by a general authority which the Secretary of State has given. (In considering proposals by the NEB the Secretary of State will have regard to the fact that the Panel on Takeovers and Mergers would normally require that a person acquiring 30 per cent or more of the voting stock in a listed company should make an offer for the whole of the stock. It is therefore possible that if the NEB acquired 30 per cent or more of the voting stock they might be committed to further purchases.) The Secretary of State has given a statutory general authority under which subsidiaries of the NEB may acquire 30 per cent or more of the share capital in a company providing the acquisition is not opposed by the directors of the company and the cost of the total shareholding in the company does not exceed £0.5 million.

The NEB shall consult the Director General of Fair Trading (who has the duty of making recommendations to the Secretary of State for Prices and Consumer

Protection about possible mergers qualifying for investigation) before entering into arrangements or transactions which may constitute or result in the creation of mergers qualifying for investigation by the Monopolies and Mergers Commission under the Fair Trading Act 1973. The NEB shall also use any power they may possess to ensure that their subsidiaries consult the Director General of Fair Trading in the same way.

Under Section 2(4) of the Industry Act 1975 the NEB have the power to dispose of any securities including voting shares. Before exercising this power, the NEB shall obtain the approval of the Secretary of State to the disposal of any voting shares or stock held by the NEB. The NEB shall also use any power they may possess to ensure that the Secretary of State's approval is obtained by their subsidiaries before those subsidiaries dispose of any such shares or stock which they hold. But the approval of the Secretary of State will not be required for the disposal of voting shares or stock held in a company by a subsidiary of the NEB where the consideration for the disposal does not exceed £0.5 million.

# Appendix IX Joint Statement by L. Brezhnev, General Secretary, CPSU, and British Prime Minister, Kremlin, Moscow, 17 February 1975[1]

On 17 February three documents were signed by the Prime Minister and Mr Brezhnev, General Secretary of the Central Committee of the Communist Party of the Soviet Union: a Joint United Kingdom–Soviet Statement; a United Kingdom–Soviet Protocol on Consultations; and a Joint Anglo-Soviet Declaration on the Non-Proliferation of Nuclear Weapons. Three further documents were signed by the Prime Minister and Mr Kosygin, Chairman of the Council of Ministers of the USSR: an Agreement on Co-operation in the Field of Medicine and Public Health; a Long Term Programme for the Development of Economic and Industrial Co-operation; and a Programme for Scientific and Technological Co-operation. Texts of these documents follow below.

*Joint United Kingdom–Soviet Statement*

1. At the invitation of the Soviet Government, the Prime Minister of the United Kingdom of Great Britain and Northern Ireland, the Right Honourable Harold Wilson MP, accompanied by the Secretary of State for Foreign and Commonwealth Affairs, the Right Honourable James Callaghan MP, paid an official visit to the Soviet Union from 13 to 17 February 1975.

2. During their stay in the Soviet Union the Right Honourable Harold Wilson and his party, in addition to Moscow, also visited Leningrad.

3. The Prime Minister laid wreaths at the tomb of the Unknown Soldier in Moscow and at the Piskarevskoye Memorial Cemetery in Leningrad.

4. The Prime Minister and his party were everywhere accorded a warm welcome and cordial hospitality.

5. The Prime Minister and the Foreign and Commonwealth Secretary held a series of talks with L. I. Brezhnev, the General Secretary of the Central Committee of the Communist Party of the Soviet Union; A. N. Kosygin, Member of the Politburo of the Central Committee of the CPSU and Chairman of the Council of Ministers of the USSR; and A. A. Gromyko, Member of the Politburo of the Central Committee of the CPSU and Minister for Foreign Affairs of the USSR.

6. The following took part in the talks:

on the British side:

Sir John Hunt, Secretary to the Cabinet; Sir Terence Garvey, British Ambassador to the USSR; Sir John Killick, Deputy Under-Secretary at the Foreign and Commonwealth Office; Mr R. T. Armstrong, Principal Private Secretary to the Prime Minister; Mr P. S. Preston, Deputy Secretary at the Department of Trade; Mr J. T. W. Haines, Press Secretary to the Prime Minister; Mr J. A. Thomson and Mr M. S. Weir, Assistant Under-Secretaries at the Foreign and Commonwealth Office; Mr I. J. M. Sutherland, Minister at the British Embassy in Moscow, and Mr T. McNally, Political Adviser to the Foreign and Commonwealth Secretary, and other officials.

on the Soviet side:

L. V. Arkhipov, Deputy Chairman of the Council of Ministers of the USSR; M. R. Kuzmin, First Deputy Minister of Foreign Trade of the USSR;

[1] Extracts from Cmnd. 5924.

A. M. Aleksandrov and A. I. Blatov, Assistants to the General Secretary of the Central Committee of the CPSU; N. M. Lunkov, Ambassador of the USSR in London, and V. P. Suslov, Member of the Collegium of the Ministry of Foreign Affairs of the USSR.

7. During the talks, which were held in a businesslike and friendly atmosphere and in a spirit of mutual respect, questions of Anglo-Soviet relations and the prospects for their expansion in the political, trade, economic, cultural and other fields were discussed in detail. There was also a wide-ranging exchange of views on current international issues of mutual interest.

8. The United Kingdom and the Soviet Union took note of the important and positive changes in Europe and in international relations as a whole in recent years. They agreed that these developments had significantly improved the prospects for deepening détente in Europe. In these circumstances they resolved upon the systematic expansion of relations between the United Kingdom and the Soviet Union in all fields.

9. The talks reflected the mutual desire of the two sides to strengthen understanding, trust and co-operation between them. They agreed that the talks and negotiations which took place during the visit have marked the opening of a new phase in Anglo-Soviet relations and would make a positive contribution towards consolidating international peace and security, especially in Europe.

*Bilateral Relations*

10. The two sides emphasized the importance which they attach to the development of bilateral relations between Britain and the USSR. They noted with satisfaction the improvements achieved in recent times in relations between their two countries and agreed on practical steps to be taken with a view to promoting their further fruitful development.

11. They declared their adherence to the principles of peaceful co-existence, which means long-term, fruitful and mutually beneficial co-operation between states, irrespective of their political, economic and social systems, on the basis of full equality and mutual respect.

12. In the interests of deepening co-operation in the political field between the United Kingdom and the USSR, and conscious of their special responsibilities as permanent members of the United Nations Security Council, the two sides reaffirmed their resolve to hold regular exchanges of views at various levels on important issues of international and bilateral relations.

13. Guided by the desire to lay a stable and constructive foundation for Anglo-Soviet relations and acknowledging the responsibility of the United Kingdom and the Soviet Union for furthering the process of détente, the Right Honourable Harold Wilson, Prime Minister of the United Kingdom, and L. I. Brezhnev, General Secretary of the Central Committee of the CPSU, signed a Protocol on Consultations. The two sides expressed their conviction that the implementation of this Protocol would give a new impetus to the development of Anglo-Soviet co-operation in the political field. In this context, they stressed the special significance of meetings between the leaders of the two countries.

14. Having thoroughly reviewed economic questions, the two sides agreed that mutually beneficial commercial links are an important element in relations between the two countries. In this connection they noted the rôle of the Temporary Commercial Agreement of 16 February 1934 in the development of Anglo-Soviet relations and reaffirmed the importance of the Agreement on the Development of

Economic, Scientific, Technological and Industrial Co-operation signed in London on 6 May 1974. Two long-term Programmes giving practical effect to the Agreement of 1974, on economic and industrial co-operation and on scientific and technological co-operation respectively, were signed during the visit by the Right Honourable Harold Wilson, Prime Minister of the United Kingdom and A. N. Kosygin, Chairman of the Council of Ministers of the USSR. The two sides reaffirmed the importance of exchanging appropriate information on co-operation within the framework of the above mentioned Programmes.

15. The two sides commended the work done by the Permanent Anglo-Soviet Inter-Governmental Commission for Co-operation in the fields of Applied Science, Technology, Trade and Economic Relations which first met in London in January 1971. They expressed their hope that the fourth meeting of the Joint Commission to be held in Moscow in May of this year would promote further progress in the field of economic co-operation.

16. The two sides expressed their intention to make further efforts to increase the volume of trade in both directions on the basis of mutual benefit. They agreed to aim at achieving a substantial increase in the level of trade and a better balance and structure of trade over the next five years. In this connection they noted with satisfaction the expected increase in contracts for British machinery and equipment.

17. The two sides noted with satisfaction the recent conclusion of contracts for the supply by British firms of the latest technology and equipment for the chemical, petrochemical, automobile and light industries. A contract for the enrichment in the Soviet Union of uranium supplied by British customers was likewise welcomed.

18. The two sides agreed that there were good prospects for the early conclusion of a number of large scale contracts between the organizations concerned on a mutually advantageous basis. Particular note was taken of the promising proposals for co-operation involving Soviet organizations and enterprises and British companies in the development of natural resources including oil, the aviation industry, nuclear power, timber and woodworking, pulp and paper, ferrous and non-ferrous metallurgy, chemicals and petrochemicals, the transportation of natural gas and of ethylene, containerized transportation and textile and other light industries. At the same time traditional trade with smaller and medium firms would continue to expand.

19. The two sides agreed to examine the possibilities for the improvement of conditions for the work of the commercial representatives, organizations and companies concerned in London and Moscow.

20. Agreement was reached on credits for a 5-year period in recognition of the importance of finance in commercial and economic relations and of the need for both sides to extend to each other credits on the most favourable possible terms, subject to the laws and regulations in force in each country.

21. The special importance attached by both sides to the further development of scientific and technological co-operation was reaffirmed. The two sides resolved to continue to promote this co-operation through, in particular, the Agreement on the Development of Economic, Scientific, Technological and Industrial Co-operation; the Anglo-Soviet Inter-Governmental Commission for Co-operation in the fields of Applied Science, Technology, Trade and Economic Relations; and the Anglo-Soviet Agreement on Co-operation in the Fields of Science, Education and Culture. The two sides recognized that the long-term Programme on scientific and technological collaboration would make an important contribution in this respect.

22. The two sides noted with satisfaction the extent of co-operation between

Britain and the USSR in the field of nuclear energy, notably in contacts between the United Kingdom Atomic Energy Authority and the USSR State Committee for the Utilization of Atomic Energy and in the framework of the Anglo-Soviet Working Group on problems of electricity supply and transmission. The two sides also undertook to examine the possibilities for mutually profitable co-operation in the production of equipment for nuclear power stations.

23. The Prime Minister of the United Kingdom, the Right Honourable Harold Wilson, and the Chairman of the Council of Ministers of the USSR, A. N. Kosygin, signed an Agreement on Co-operation in the Field of Medicine and Public Health. The sides spoke also in favour of the further development of Anglo-Soviet co-operation in the fields of agriculture and protection of the environment.

24. The two sides emphasized the important rôle of cultural links between the people of the two countries as a means of promoting fuller mutual knowledge of achievements in literature, art and other fields of cultural activity. They noted in this context the exhibitions of paintings and other important cultural events which are to take place in Britain and the USSR and also the forthcoming signature of the next in the series of Anglo-Soviet Cultural Agreements covering the period 1975–77.

25. Guided by a desire to promote greater mutual understanding and trust, the two sides resolved to set up an Anglo-Soviet Round Table whose members would be distinguished representatives of public life, science, culture, commerce, the press, and other fields. The Royal Institute for International Affairs in Britain and the Institute for World Economy and International Affairs of the Academy of Sciences of the USSR have agreed to undertake the task of organizing the meetings of the Round Table. The first meeting will be held in Britain in 1975.

26. The two sides confirmed the importance which they attach to the development of contacts between the British Parliament and the Supreme Soviet of the USSR, and noted with satisfaction that a Delegation of the Supreme Soviet of the USSR will visit the United Kingdom later this year.

27. The two sides reviewed the possibilities of extending their contacts into other fields. In this connection they reached agreement on an exchange of visits between representatives of the Armed Forces.

*International Questions*

28. The United Kingdom and the Soviet Union noted with satisfaction the progress made in recent years in developing détente and peaceful co-operation between states irrespective of their political, economic and social systems. They agreed on the need to establish détente on a firm basis throughout the world, and pledged the efforts of their two Governments to this end.

29. The two sides are convinced that further progress in the improvement of the international situation demands active and purposeful efforts of all states. They emphasized their determination to ensure that favourable changes in the international situation become irreversible and that détente is extended to all areas of the world.

30. The two sides recognized the importance for the strengthening of universal peace of the agreements and understandings achieved between the USSR and the USA, including the agreements on the prevention of nuclear war and on the limitation of strategic arms.

31. The two sides noted with satisfaction the positive trends towards the establishment of relations of stable peace, good neighbourliness and co-operation in Europe. They emphasized the important rôle which the Conference on Security

and Co-operation in Europe was called upon to play in this process. The two sides stated that much progress had been made at the Conference. They are convinced that premises exist for completing the work of the Conference and for holding its third stage at the highest level in the near future.

32. Attaching great importance to the further strengthening of stability and security in Europe, the United Kingdom and the Soviet Union expressed themselves in favour of complementing measures of political détente with those of military détente. In this connection the two sides exchanged views concerning the negotiations on the Mutual Reduction of Forces and Armaments and Associated Measures in Central Europe. They recalled the agreed general objective to contribute to a more stable relationship and reaffirmed that the specific arrangements to be worked out should conform to the principle of undiminished security for each party.

33. In the course of an exchange of views on the Middle East the two sides expressed their deep concern at the dangerous situation in the area, and emphasized the necessity of achieving as soon as possible a just and lasting settlement, based on the implementation of the Resolutions of the United Nations Security Council. They confirmed their intention to make every effort to promote a solution of the cardinal questions involved in a just and lasting peace in this region, on the basis of Security Council Resolution No. 338, taking due account of the legitimate interests of all States and peoples of the region including the Arab people of Palestine, and with respect for the right of all States in the area to independent existence. The two sides considered that the Geneva Conference should play an important rôle in the establishment of a just and lasting peace in the Middle East and should resume its work at a very early date.

34. In connection with recent events in Cyprus, Britain and the Soviet Union reaffirmed their support for the principle of preserving the sovereignty, independence and territorial integrity of the Republic of Cyprus. They support the implementation of the relevant resolutions of the Security Council and the General Assembly of the United Nations on Cyprus. Britain and the Soviet Union recognize the one lawful government of Cyprus headed by President Makarios.

35. The two sides stated the necessity of strict observance by all its parties of the Paris Agreement on ending the war and restoring peace in Vietnam. They welcomed the concrete measures to implement the Agreement on restoring peace and achieving national accord in Laos and expressed themselves in favour of a just settlement of the Cambodian problem with full consideration for the national interests and legitimate rights of the people of Cambodia, without any outside interference.

36. The two sides consider that there are certain international economic problems in the solution of which they are both interested. They reached a mutual understanding on holding further exchanges of views on these questions at the appropriate level within the framework of the Protocol on Consultations.

37. In order to reaffirm the great importance which the two sides attach to the Treaty on the Non-Proliferation of Nuclear Weapons and to effective measures to control the spread of nuclear weapons and the means to make them, the Prime Minister of the United Kingdom, the Right Honourable Harold Wilson, and the General Secretary of the Central Committee of the CPSU, L. I. Brezhnev, signed a Declaration on the Non-Proliferation of Nuclear Weapons.

38. The United Kingdom and the Soviet Union are convinced that effective measures should be taken to end the arms race and to achieve general and complete

disarmament embracing both nuclear and conventional weapons under strict and effective international control. The two sides believe that the convocation of a World Disarmament Conference may contribute to the solution of the pressing problems of disarmament. They confirmed their intention of continuing their co-operation with the United Nations Ad Hoc Committee on the World Disarmament Conference.

39. The two sides expressed confidence that the exchange of instruments on ratification of the Convention on the Prohibition of the Development, Production and Stockpiling of Bacteriological (Biological) and Toxic Weapons and on their Destruction would take place very soon and that as a result the Convention would enter into force. The two sides are in favour of the earliest possible achievement of an international agreement on the prohibition of chemical weapons.

40. The two sides expressed themselves in favour of giving effect to the United Nations General Assembly resolution on the prohibition of action to influence the environment and climate for military and other purposes incompatible with the maintenance of international security, human well-being and health.

41. Attaching great importance to the Conference on the Law of the Sea, the two sides pronounced themselves in favour of adopting constructive decisions in that field on an international basis with due regard for the interests of all states. They will continue to work to this end. They acknowledged the value of the consultations held in the past between representatives of their two countries, and expressed the intention of continuing those consultations also in the future.

42. The two sides declared their determination to work for the strengthening of the United Nations and for promoting its effectiveness in the maintenance of universal peace and security on the basis of strict observance of the purposes and principles of the United Nations Charter. They support the work of the United Nations in promoting the consolidation of international détente, in strengthening international peace and security and in developing peaceful and fruitful co-operation.

43. The two sides shared the view that the meetings and talks held during the Prime Minister's visit have made an important contribution to the further development of relations between the United Kingdom and the Soviet Union and to the cause of international détente.

44. The Prime Minister of the United Kingdom, the Right Honourable Harold Wilson, invited L. I. Brezhnev, General Secretary of the Central Committee of the CPSU, A. N. Kosygin, Chairman of the Council of Ministers of the USSR, and A. A. Gromyko, Minister for Foreign Affairs of the USSR, to pay official visits to the United Kingdom. The invitations were accepted with gratitude.

Moscow, 17 February 1975

For the United Kingdom of Great Britain and Northern Ireland

H. WILSON
Prime Minister

For the Union of Soviet Socialist Republics

L. I. BREZHNEV
General Secretary of the Central Committee of the CPSU

# Appendix X Speech by General Secretary L. Brezhnev at luncheon in honour of Prime Minister Harold Wilson

Esteemed Mr Prime Minister and Mrs Wilson, Our esteemed guests, Comrades,

Permit me once again to greet you, Mr Wilson, and to express satisfaction at your visit. We are happy to have this opportunity to exchange opinions with you and Foreign Secretary Callaghan both on questions of the further development of Soviet–British relations and on several international problems.

Frankly speaking, the need for such an exchange of views is felt all the more strongly since there have been no sufficiently high-level contacts between the Soviet Union and Great Britain for already a fairly long time. It can even be said that in the last few years the development of mutually advantageous cooperation between our two countries has to a certain extent slowed down. Let us not now go into an analysis of the causes that led to such a situation. It is clear, however, that today we do have things to talk about.

In many parts of the world a struggle is at present under way between opposing trends – a line at international détente, the strengthening of peace and the development of cooperation among States, and a line at reviving the Cold War spirit, at a new whipping up of the arms race, and at interference in the affairs of other countries and peoples. But of decisive significance is, we feel, the profound and ever more clearly expressed will of the peoples – and, I emphasize, above all, of the peoples – for peace, and their determination to see to it that the tragedy of a new world war should never repeat itself.

Fully in keeping with these aspirations of the peoples are the significant positive changes that have taken place in recent years in international affairs, notably in relations between the Soviet Union and other Socialist countries, on the one hand, and States such as France, the Federal Republic of Germany and the United States, on the other. I should like to stress most vigorously, Mr Prime Minister, that the leaders of the Soviet Union are fully determined to do all in their power to impart an historically irreversible character not only to international détente as such, but also to a real turn towards the long-term, fruitful and mutually beneficial cooperation of States with different social systems on the basis of full equality and mutual respect. That is what we in the Soviet Union mean by peaceful coexistence. And it is towards that goal that the Soviet Union has always urged other States.

As I see it, Great Britain, too, could be a good partner of ours on this path of strengthening peace and peaceful cooperation. Her voice carries no small weight in world affairs. Not in all things and not at all times have our positions been similar, but surely we have no right to forget our record of fruitful cooperation. In particular, today, shortly before the thirtieth anniversary of the great Victory of the Powers of the anti-Hitler Coalition and the freedom-loving peoples over the Nazi aggressors and enslavers, there are grounds to recall that the Soviet Union and Great Britain have behind them the experience of a combat alliance in the fight for a just cause. You and I, Mr Wilson, like others of our generation, remember well enough that this was an alliance not only of Governments; it was also a fighting alliance of our armies and our peoples and a historic example of successful cooperation regardless of differences in social systems.

The present day of our Planet, on which we are all living as ever closer neighbours, is hallmarked by a struggle for dedication to the memory of those who gave their lives in the battle against aggression and for the right of people to live in conditions of peace, independence and liberty. It would, I suggest, be no exaggeration to say that never before have such vigorous efforts been made on a broad international scale to strengthen peace and peaceful cooperation among States. But there is still a lot to be done.

Take Europe, for instance. Here a good start has been made. The All-European Conference on Security and Cooperation is working, though not at a very fast pace. This forum of thirty-three European States with the additional participation of the United States and Canada – a forum unprecedented in the continent's history – is called upon to lay a durable foundation of peace and good-neighbourly cooperation on the soil of Europe for a long historical period. No small amount of work has already been done, but in our conviction far from all that is necessary is as yet being done. The immediate task now is to successfully and befittingly complete this great endeavour which, we are sure, can and must serve as the starting-point for a new, truly peaceful and constructive epoch in the life of Europe.

We believe that Great Britain could play no small a part in keeping the All-European Conference on a constructive course. The Soviet Union would welcome that.

The significance of the contribution made by any State and its leaders to the solution of the major tasks of building a lasting peace are, we believe, determined by the ability correctly to assess the historical scale of those tasks. Today important as never before is the knack of singling out the principal objectives whose achievement the peoples are looking forward to, and of separating those principal objectives from the superficial elements engendered by short-sighted political manoeuvring aimed at obtaining various momentary advantages for some participants in negotiations to the detriment of others.

This applies as well to the talks in Vienna on the reduction of forces and armaments in Central Europe. The persistent attempts of some countries there to lead matters towards obtaining one-sided advantages, attempts to 'outplay' the other side, are unfortunately still seriously impeding the progress of the Vienna talks.

The peoples are looking forward to the prompt embodiment of international détente into concrete deeds contributing to a better life for millions of people. Such deeds include curbing the arms race, cutting back the scale of the military preparations of States and of their military expenditures, and broadening peaceful economic and other kinds of cooperation between them. Today, given the serious economic difficulties besetting many Western countries, progress in these matters is, I believe, becoming an all the more pressing task in the eyes of public opinion.

As before, a paramount objective is the achievement of a peaceful settlement in the Middle East. The situation in that area remains explosive. And it cannot, indeed, be anything else so long as the aggressor holds the foreign land he has seized, so long as the rights of the peoples are flouted. The peoples of the Middle East need a just and lasting peace as much as the very air they breathe.

One sometimes hears arguments to the effect that a full peaceful settlement in the Middle East is hard to achieve and that, instead, one should be content in the next few years with partial arrangements.

What can be said on this score?

Naturally, partial measures, such as the withdrawal of the occupationists from this or that part of the captured Arab territory and its return to the Arabs, are in themselves useful, but only if they constitute steps towards the earliest possible real peaceful settlement and are not used as a pretext for freezing the situation as a whole, for delaying a peaceful settlement, and for weakening the unity of the Arab countries.

There are some who seem to want to offer the Arab peoples something like a
10*

soporific in the hope that they will calm down and forget about their demands for the restoration of justice and the complete elimination of the consequence of aggression. But a soporific knocks you out only for a short time, and then you wake up only to be faced with the same real life with all its problems.

Practical experience attests to this quite eloquently. It will be recalled that partial bilateral measures were already carried out in the Middle East. Have they eased tension there? Unfortunately, no. Have they given the peoples of the Middle East tranquillity? No, they have not. Have they lessened in any way the onerous and dangerous arms race in which the Middle East countries are involved? It is well known that they have not.

All this indicates that there is no substitute for a genuine and enduring peaceful settlement. And its postponement is inadmissible unless complete neglect is displayed for the destinies of the countries and peoples of the Middle East (naturally, including Israel, whose people can hardly be interested in living endlessly in a country converted into a military camp) and for the destinies of universal peace.

That is why the Soviet Union is resolutely in favour of the earliest possible resumption of the work of the Geneva Peace Conference. Of course, the voice of representatives of the Palestinian Arab people must be heard at the Conference on an equal footing with others, for the just solution of the Palestine problem is a key element of a lasting peaceful settlement.

In discussing ways to strengthen universal peace, mention cannot fail to be made of the ever-growing importance of preventing the further spread of nuclear weapons in the world, enhancing the effectiveness of the International Treaty on this subject, and increasing to the utmost the number of its participants.

In short, there are quite a few problems in the present-day world which cannot fail to preoccupy the peace-loving States and for whose solution it would undoubtedly be useful to pool the efforts of those States, including our two countries – the Soviet Union and Britain – and to improve our cooperation in foreign-policy matters, including regular consultations at various levels.

A no less urgent topic is, we feel, the question of further developing and deepening Soviet–British relations in the economic field. Here we can lean back on the already accumulated good experience. Economic ties between our two countries have been successfully developing for many years on the basis of equality and considerable mutual advantage. This has always been valued in the USSR – and not only for economic reasons. Soviet people invariably harbour feelings of comradeship and class solidarity towards the British working class. Our people remember that in the first and most difficult years of the Soviet State's existence the British proletariat came out against the imperialist intervention in the affairs of our country, proclaiming the slogan 'Hands off Soviet Russia!' The working people of the Soviet Union have always been in solidarity with the struggle of the working class and all working people of Great Britain for their rights and vital interests. And we are gratified to know that in the event of a further expansion of Soviet–British economic cooperation, there will be new job opportunities for thousands and thousands of workers in your country, and a new impetus for the development of her economy.

While positively evaluating the experience of the past, we believe at the same time, Mr Prime Minister, that the political climate and the technological and economic possibilities of our times are today inscribing into the agenda the question of the larger-scale and longer-term mutually profitable cooperation of our two countries in many economic spheres.

The realization of such cooperation could become one more example of the way in which the policy of peaceful coexistence is filled with specific material content and yields tangible benefit to millions of people.

Thus, we have no shortage of topics for discussion with the Prime Minister of Great Britain. The talks are already under way and I should like to propose a toast to their successful continuation and fruitful completion for both sides!

To the health of the Prime Minister and Mrs Wilson, Foreign Secretary Callaghan and all our British guests!

To the successful development of all-round friendly ties between the Soviet Union and Great Britain!

To a lasting world peace!

## Appendix XI Speech at Helsinki Conference on Security and Co-operation in Europe, 30 July 1975[1]

As the first speaker at this Conference, I should like to express the hope on behalf of all of us that in years to come the citizens of Europe and North America will look back at this meeting and regard it as a turning-point in our history, a turning-point not only in what we hope to achieve here, but also in marking the developments which have made our meeting possible.

In territorial coverage, in representation at top level of almost every State, large and small, it so far transcends any previous European meeting, that it makes the legendary Congress of Vienna of 1814 and the Congress of Berlin of 1878 seem like well-dressed tea parties.

On behalf of all of us I should like to express our thanks to President Kekkonen for his speech of welcome, but more than that for his hospitality and for the untiring efforts of his Government to ensure that our meeting is a success. I should also like to thank on behalf of all of us the Secretary-General of the United Nations for his address to us.

For this Conference fulfils some of the aims of those who created the United Nations. First, the virtual universality of European representation itself reflects the universality which is the hallmark of the United Nations, and which it is our duty to maintain, even of hostility and rancour.

But no less our meeting here of European and North American nations, thirty years after the United Nations Charter was proclaimed, inspired by the purposes and principles set out in that Charter.

At the end of a war involving every continent, the signatories of the Charter committed all nations, I quote:

To practise tolerance and live together in peace with one another as good neighbours,

and

To unite our strength to maintain international peace and security.

Similarly, the decisions of thirty years ago are put in a new setting, by our endorsement of the inviolability of frontiers, and the principle that changes in frontiers can be made in accordance with international law, by peaceful means, and by agreement.

We meet in the spirit of détente. It is only because that spirit has informed and inspired the preparatory work that it has been made possible for us to be here.

Détente is indivisible, as in the ultimate, freedom and peace itself are indivisible.

We meet here representing different social systems, different political systems. The nations represented here are, each of us severally, and through the powerful and deep-rooted alliances which bind many of us, we are all of us determined to the uttermost to defend not only our frontiers but our right to live under the political system each of us chooses for himself.

The preservation of the integrity of *each* of us is the key to the future of *all* of us.

Détente has become *possible* only because of that mutual determination.

And détente will be *maintained* only by the continued assertion of vigilance,

[1] Cmnd. 6197.

vigilance based on strength, vigilance based on solidarity. We who meet here today represent, in many cases, nations who were enemies in the most devastating war in history. For some, that war was itself the culmination of centuries of warfare between the nations involved.

And even after the war some of the nations here were ranged against one another on either side of what Winston Churchill characterized as the Iron Curtain, ranged on either side of the Cold War.

But today we are met on the basis of co-existence, a co-existence which we must all recognize depends on the vigilance and the solidarity to which I have referred.

I have sometimes found European statesmen chary of using the phrase 'peaceful co-existence' because it has been differently defined at different times by different leaders of nations.

I have no hesitation.

When I was the guest of Leonid Brezhnev and Alexei Kosygin in the Kremlin earlier this year I quoted there the wise words of my old chief and head of Government, Clem Attlee:

'The only alternative to co-existence is co-death.'

And Mr Brezhnev will, I hope, not object if I quote the words he used in this context. He said that the leaders of his country (and I quote) 'are fully determined to do all in their power to impart an historically irreversible character not only to international détente as such, but also to a real turn towards the long-term, fruitful and mutually beneficial co-operation of States with different social systems on the basis of full equality and mutual respect. That is what we in the Soviet Union mean by peaceful co-existence.'

For thirty years the differences which have divided us have seemed greater than the European heritage we hold in common. Yet it is upon that heritage that this Conference on Security and Co-operation in Europe has been built.

For two years our diplomatic representatives at Geneva have sought to put into words the means by which we can conduct our relationships in new and more civilized fashion, based on mutual respect, and understanding and tolerance. I do not pretend that the documents we are about to approve can, in themselves, diminish the tension and insecurity which have affected the peoples as well as the Governments of Europe since the end of the War. But they do represent more than good intentions, more than a desire to set our relations on a new course. They are a moral commitment to be ignored at our mutual peril, they are the start of a new chapter in the history of Europe. With the peoples of North America and the Soviet Union, we want to maintain the diversity of European civilization, but we want to end its fratricidal divisions and give it a new and better sense of direction.

It is right to say a word about the political developments which have made possible the preparation of this Final Act.

This Conference was preceded by the agreements reached in 1970 and 1972 between the Federal Republic of Germany and its Eastern neighbours.

Over a century the history of Europe has been intimately bound up with the history of Germany. Since the War the fate of Berlin has been, as it is and will continue to be, a touchstone of the state of relations in Europe. The Treaties, agreements and the arrangements between the Federal Republic of Germany, the German Democratic Republic, Poland, Czechoslovakia, and the four Powers in Germany have gone far to ease the situation in the heart of Europe. We played as the United Kingdom our full part in that process and we rejoice at the benefits it has brought.

These benefits must continue to be developed further after this Conference has been concluded. Subject to quadripartite rights and responsibilities, the

Government of the United Kingdom considers that the documents emerging from the Conference relate also to Berlin.

The Final Act of this Conference is not a treaty; nor is it a peace settlement. It does not, and it cannot, affect the status of present frontiers. It does not, and it cannot, in any way affect Four-Power rights and responsibilities relating to Berlin and to Germany as a whole. But it does contain a clear commitment about refraining from the threat or the use of force. Within the framework we are establishing, no excuse can henceforth be found for any participating State represented here today from attempting to prevent any other from exercising its sovereign rights, or to intervene in its internal affairs.

On the mutual honouring and observance of these undertakings, we shall be judged, all of us judged, each of us judged, by our own peoples, and by history.

Inevitably our discussions and decisions here must reflect the very thorough work done on the military aspects. The confidence-building measures; our modest arrangements for the exchange of observers at military manoeuvres, and for prior notification of these manoeuvres; the work so far done, but regrettably incomplete, on the notification of military movements. On this, we can only hope that when the discussion is resumed in Belgrade in 1977 we shall be able to make further progress.

Some of the Governments here represented are working for agreement in a still more vital area of military understanding, that of force reductions which are the subject of the negotiations in Vienna.

There are those who say that once the new political framework for our future relations has been established here, it will be easier to make progress in lowering the level of military confrontation and establishing that more stable relationship in Europe to which all governments participating in the Vienna negotiations are committed. Let us hope that is so. We for our part are determined to make a success of the Vienna negotiations, and hope that the energy which has been put into the conclusions of Geneva may now be put to equally good service by all concerned in Vienna.

Our work here will be judged not only by the spirit of 'Live and Let Live' which this Conference asserts. It will be judged by how that spirit is reflected in the lives of ordinary families, by such issues as the reunification of families, the marriages of citizens of different states, the greater possibilities of travel, by professional exchanges of all kinds, and by better working conditions for our journalists and businessmen.

Détente means little if it is not reflected in the daily lives of our peoples. And there is no reason why, in 1975, Europeans should not be allowed to marry whom they want, hear and read what they want, travel abroad when and where they want, meet whom they want. And to deny that proposition is a sign not of strength but of weakness.

The test will be how far what we have done becomes a reality, and this also will be one of the subjects for the 1977 assessment, no less than such issues as the military, economic and cultural provisions. From this Conference here in Helsinki onwards all these things become part of the permanent agenda of détente.

What we are deciding, then, as a new code of political and human relations within Europe, is of importance to all whom we here represent.

But in a wider sense, what we have achieved, and go on to consolidate, will be judged by history more by our success in extroverting our achievement to a wider world.

Many of us here are members of organizations, within Europe and also going much further afield.

Within Europe we have the European Economic Community whose nine member Governments have made a major contribution to the work of this Conference.

Some of our neighbours for their part belong to other organizations such as EFTA and Comecon, also powerfully represented here this week.

But in a broader world setting some here are members of the groupings of non-aligned nations. Some of us are members of the Commonwealth, which includes over thirty nations at every stage of economic development from the richest to the poorest, nations from every continent, nations whose shores are lapped by every one of the world's great oceans. Our achievements here will be diminished as a contribution to world history if what we have agreed here is not fruitful in enriching the lives of nations all over the world.

In the documents which we have approved we have taken a limited forward step on economic co-operation. We need to work more closely together – all of us – on economic co-operation world wide. This is a particular duty at a time when violent movements in oil prices and in other basic inescapable costs have shaken the economy of the world. They have shaken the structure of economically advanced nations, and brought about a massive increase in unemployment. But for countries who for years have lived on the very margin of starvation, the threat is not to men's jobs only, it is to the lives of hundreds of thousands of our fellow world citizens.

Our various intra-European groupings are tackling these problems within their own areas, and many of us are concerned with the efforts to find solutions world wide.

I am proud to feel that earlier this year the EEC promoted an international programme of benefit to forty-six developing countries in Africa, the Pacific and the Caribbean, and is now fully engaged in the energy and commodity dialogues. I should like to see the whole of Europe committed, and as far as this can be secured, committed with a common interest.

The British initiative on commodities, designed to help less developed countries, put forward at the Commonwealth Conference in May, is now being considered with other proposals in the preparatory work for the United Nations Special Session this autumn, to be followed next year at UNCTAD.

And in other ways what we have resolved in the work of CSCE should not be confined to this continent. For example, take freedom of movement of individuals and families – there has been welcome progress. But I hope that what we have each of us today committed ourselves to within Europe can apply also to those within our countries who want to go to start a new life outside Europe, whether in the Middle East or elsewhere.

Finally I want us all to seek to spread the concept of détente far more widely. If we are to be frank, détente in Europe, the détente which has been worked out in so statesmanlike a way between the world's two greatest Powers, that détente has been brought about and rests on the recognition of a balance of terror, above all in nuclear power.

The détente we assert should be matched by an equal determination to prevent the spread of that nuclear terror all over the world.

Three nations represented here are co-depositories of the Non-Proliferation Treaty. The great majority of countries here have adhered to that Treaty and in so doing have made a direct contribution towards creating the safer world we seek.

To those who have not so far adhered to the Treaty I should simply say that the proliferation of nuclear weapons threatens the security of us all. It is not a question that possession of such weapons confers any special status on the possessor – and it certainly confers awesome responsibilities. And it is certainly the profound hope of all nuclear weapon States here that this burden can eventually be shed through multi-lateral negotiations on nuclear disarmament in which of course it would be essential that China also take part.

Those of us who have these weapons or the capability of working towards them must accept a special responsibility.

Nuclear energy for peaceful purposes raises some different questions. This is a different, indeed welcome, proliferation, in that an invention deriving from man's ingenuity and resources can be directed to raising living standards all over the world. But even here we have to exert all our talents, all our caution, to see that this kind of nuclear peaceful proliferation does not imperil our efforts to create a safer world, or carry with it dangers of crossing the threshold from peaceful to warlike use of nuclear power. A universal system of international safeguards would help to keep us on the right side of the threshold.

We need to be particularly careful about the use of nuclear explosions for peaceful purposes and we are glad that the International Atomic Energy Agency has recently set up an advisory group on this important subject.

Upon those of us advanced in nuclear technology lies a paramount responsibility to ensure that the export of nuclear materials and technology is conducted under fair and totally effective safeguards to prevent their diversion to destructive purposes.

Of deepening concern in the world is the development of horror chemical and biological weapons. On this question Her Majesty's Government in the late 1960s took an initiative at the 18-Nation Geneva Conference. We are glad that the Biological Weapons Convention which emerged from that initiative came into force last March. But progress on chemical weapons has been very slow because of the serious and still intractable problem of verification. It is vital that any agreement that can be reached should be totally proof against evasion. I understand that at the Soviet–American talks in Moscow a year ago a joint initiative by those countries was foreshadowed, and I welcomed this.

In the wider context of disarmament, there is considerable support for a World Disarmament Conference. This could provide a forum which might help to speed the halting progress so far made. But, and I emphasize this, the prerequisite for such a conference is that it must be fully comprehensive, attended by *all* nuclear powers and that there must be full and adequate preparation through existing international machinery, strengthened as necessary for the purpose.

Mr President, détente, 'Live and Let Live', the acceptance of the principle that deep political and ideological differences do not mean that we have to live at war or even at enmity one with the other is at the heart of all our hopes for the future of Europe. All of us have the duty of proclaiming this same spirit in the United Nations, and in world-wide discussions on issues which not only divide nations, but threaten the peace of the world. For example, the Middle East, the divisions on race and colour in Africa, the strains of emergence from colonialism in different parts of the world.

What then is it we want to emerge from this Conference on Security and Co-operation in Europe?

Still more what do we want history to assess as our achievement?

I would put this answer in these words:

A Europe where its people practice tolerance, live together in peace with one another as good neighbours and unite our strength to maintain international peace and security.

Secondly, undertakings openly proclaimed, openly honoured, and in two years' time assessed, developed and built on at Belgrade.

Above all the assertion, in all our world relationships, that what we have together deemed as being good for us here, is good for the world; but not asserting this in words only but making it a reality by harnessing all the skill, all the influence, all the power and all the statesmanship of the nations meeting here today.

# Appendix XII Extracts from Final Speech to Labour Party Conference, October 1975[1]

The word 'Manifesto' is constantly heard these days, and that is right. No new Party grouping, over the whole spectrum of Party thinking, now considers itself respectable if it does not include the word 'Manifesto' in its title.

We are all Manifesto custodians now. Never has there been such unity in the history of the Party in supporting the Manifesto – or such diversity in its interpretation (*Laughter*).

As Leader of the majority group in Parliament, the MPs elected by your efforts and by a groundswell of national opinion last year, I have from 4 March 1974 onwards regarded myself as a full-time one-man Manifesto group (*Laughter*) . . .

(I then proceeded at breakneck speed, hardly pausing for breath, to list the measures passed in the Short Parliament, then to present a progress report on the October manifesto on Bills passed and Bills introduced.)

In the four and a half months in which the House was sitting during the Short Parliament of last year, 35 Bills became law, and I ask you to bear with me for a moment while I list them:

We passed the Trade Union and Labour Relations Act, preserved and extended existing unfair dismissals provisions and extended trade union immunities: the Health and Safety at Work Act setting up the Health and Safety Commission; the Prices Act which abolished the Pay Board, provided £500 million for food subsidies on key essential foodstuffs and strengthened the Price Code; we ended the sticky labels racket by prohibiting upward repricing of goods already on the shelves in the shops, and we restricted the frequency of implementation of price increases. In the National Insurance Act 1974 we fulfilled the Manifesto pledge to raise pensions to £10 for a single person and £16 for a couple; the Finance Act introduced major changes to eliminate tax dodgers. The Rent Act gave security of tenure to those in furnished accommodation. We doubled the Regional Employment Premium which the Conservatives were committed to abolish.

That was the Short Parliament. With a minority Labour Government (*Applause*).

Now the Manifesto on which we went to the country a year ago.

First, Bills which have already been placed on the Statute Book in the terms of the Manifesto:

Child Benefit, creating a new scheme of child credits; those are on the Statute Book; Finance (No. 1) introducing the Capital Transfer Tax; Finance (No. 2) tackling the lump; the Housing Rents and Subsidies Act, replacing the Tory Rent Act with a new financial system for public sector housing; the Offshore Petroleum Development (Scotland) Act nationalizing land for oil construction

[1] The Section on international affairs appears at the end of chapter 8, pp. 176–8.

sites; the Oil Taxation Act, fulfilling the Manifesto proposals for taxation of oil companies' profits on the North Sea; Pensioners' Payments; the Referendum Act fulfilling our pledge to give the British people the final say on membership of the EEC; the Social Security Benefits Act maintaining the real value of pensions and creating the new non-contributory invalidity benefit, invalid care allowances to help those families with disabled members, and increased family allowances; the Social Security Pensions Act totally reforming the whole system of state superannuation, and introducing the mobility allowance for the disabled. All those are on the Statute Book. I thought I would mention them just in case you might have forgotten any of them (*Applause*).

Now the Bills introduced, but not through all their Parliamentary stages:

The Community Land Bill, providing for the public ownership of development land; the Employment Protection Bill providing new rights for workers at work; the Industry Bill turning into legislative form the White Paper on which we fought the election, creating the National Enterprise Board and the system of Planning Agreements; the Petroleum and Submarine Pipelines Bill creating the British National Oil Corporation and providing new powers of control over the pace of depletion and for the provision of pipelines; the Scottish Development Agency and Welsh Development Agency legislation establishing these two important new institutions in Scotland and Wales; the Trade Union and Labour Relations (Amendment) Bill removing unacceptable Lords amendments forced into the previous year's Act in the conditions of our then minority Government; the socially redistributive budgets of November and April; the Sex Discrimination Bill asserting new rights for women, and creating the Equal Opportunities Commission. All these measures are before Parliament now.

I clearly cannot anticipate the Queen's Speech opening the second session of this Parliament, but a commitment has been given to the reintroduction of the Bill already published to take the aircraft and shipbuilding industries into public ownership; work is advanced – in some cases involving the drafting of the necessary legislation – on:

Devolution; ending the 11-plus; abolishing agricultural tied cottages; the Development Land Tax; the transfer of New Town housing assets to local authorities; liberalizing official secrets legislation; introducing an independent element into the procedure of complaints against the police; and a Race Relations Bill, to strengthen the existing legislation protecting minorities.

Work is also going on on legislation to phase out pay beds; to bring the ports into public ownership; to create the Cooperative Development Agency; on weights and measures legislation to provide for unit pricing.

Our outline proposals for a wealth tax have been published, and are being studied by a Parliamentary Select Committee in advance of the introduction of legislation.

The Government has announced its policy in respect of our pledge on industrial democracy and is setting up an enquiry to prepare the way for legislation.

That is a breathtaking list. It is a record of which the whole Party should be proud. But it is too easily forgotten, as many of our Party members may already have forgotten it.

It is a record made possible only by Ministers working full-time, MPs working full-time, and above all the Whips working full-time, all of them long into the night.

But it is made possible by something else too. The Manifesto we are fulfilling provided the best programme on which this Party has ever fought a General Election.

I reported on Portugal, our backing of Mario Soares – who addressed Conference later in the week – referring to the decision of the EEC Summit to give massive financial assistance provided democratic institutions were established,[1] to the meeting of Socialist leaders in Stockholm, following Helsinki,[2] and to the Downing Street meeting with him in September.

I reported on the Government's initiative at the Jamaica Commonwealth Conference.

Conference was taking an interest in the annual programme of meetings we had instituted between the Cabinet and the National Executive. Referring to the most recent, three weeks earlier, I said I had felt justified in asking NEC members, some with thirty years in Parliament, some with a record of political activity going back well before the War, if they could recall a time, and name the year, when relations with the United States were better; again, when relations with the Soviet Union were better; when relations with the Commonwealth were better; and when relations with Europe were better. Still more, I had asked the NEC if they could name a period when relations with America, with the Soviet Union, with the Commonwealth and with Europe were better than now – *and all at the same time*? No one had a date to suggest:

In my twenty-three years on the Executive this was the first time that we could record a measurable period of absolute silence on the Executive (*Laughter and applause*).

I put the same challenge to the Conference. Could any delegate name a period, a year even? No need to answer then and there – they could drop me a note. Not one did.

My third objective was to put into baulk the extremists, right and left, who were plaguing us. The left were not so much Communists as an assortment of left-wing deviationists, sailing under different and frequently-changed names. Had the different varieties been locked in a room without food or water until they produced an agreed policy statement, the mortality rate would have been high. All they could conceivably agree on would be the destruction of our present system of society, without any named positive replacement. But they had succeeded in devising wrecking techniques for use in individual constituencies, particularly those where the membership was small, and/or dominated by a small right-wing caucus,[3] sometimes but not always identifiable with the ruling group of the local council – or in a seat where an extreme right-wing MP held sway, confident that those who had selected him as candidate would not be ousted by a left-wing take-over. I was concerned also with a small group of hard-line right-wingers whose activities involved not only fighting the hoodlums but were directed also against moderate middle-of-the-roaders. This group had in fact tried a putsch with much Tory press support against me in the weeks before the February 1974 election: their strength

[1] See pp. 97 and 103 above.
[2] See pp. 175–6 above.
[3] This was no new development. After Labour's election in 1955 the NEC had set up an investigation into party organization under my chairmanship. We visited over 300 constituencies, and found a correlation between certain safe seats and infinitesimal membership. See the Report, printed with the 1955 Conference Report.

in the party was minimal and in more recent times has been deployed at the cost of tens of thousands of pounds in lawsuits against constituency parties. Hence,

This Party needs to protect itself against the activities of small groups of inflexible political persuasion, extreme so-called left (*Applause*), in a few cases extreme so-called moderates (*Applause*) having in common only their arrogant dogmatism. These groups, equally the multichromatic coalitionist fringe or groups specifically formed to fight other marauding groups, these are not what this Party is about (*Applause*). Infestation of this kind thrives only, and can thrive only, in minuscule local parties.

We have all talked at one time or another about City sharks who lie in wait until they can make a take-over bid for some small company which has some rich asset or large liquid funds.

But in our democracy, in our Party or any other, there is no richer asset than a seat with a five-figure majority. As Socialists we should do all in our power to control and sublimate predatory instincts in all situations.

However, when this happens, whether through laziness and apathy or by infiltration, often migratory infiltration – what in Yorkshire we used to call 'comers-in' (*Laughter*) – the result can too easily be groups of little exclusivities insisting on a monopoly of doctrine, thriving on noisy debate reflecting some esoteric theory which has nothing in common with a century of the political idealism and purpose of this Movement. Because what has proved possible is a take-over bid for a 20,000 majority seat based on an incursion of little more than a dozen.

Nor does the answer lie in the formation of the kind of anti-party group which has been disporting itself in Blackpool this weekend (*Applause*) leaking, as is their wont, their smears to an ever-ready Tory press. We have seen them at it before, a coup executed a few weeks before the last February election, a coup designed not to help the Labour Party, a coup designed to make it impossible for some of us to carry on.

The success of this Government depends on two things. First, the participation of the whole Movement in our programme and our Manifestos as in these recent years. Second, a determined Government, a determined Parliamentary Labour Party, such as we have today with well over 300 Labour members, there with the backing of 11.5 million Labour voters.

Can anyone in a broad democratic movement such as ours assert the claim that a man or a woman elected by 25,000 Labour voters one week, should be given his cards the following week by a small group of 50, who in themselves represent only 1 in 500 of the Labour voters who elected him and who only last year recommended such a man to the electorate? (*Applause.*)

We need bigger membership, a membership fully representative of our people. Even a Party with a thousand members might embody only 1 in 25 or 1 in 30 of those who voted Labour.

At local level – I make this appeal – while the record of some unions is good – we need much more popular trade union identification not only by the fact of affiliation but by active work and influence (*Applause*).

I am expressing here, of course, a personal view as Leader of the Party. But it is based on a little experience of having, for my sins, chaired the Organization Committee of the National Executive for longer than anyone else since the War.

But there is another consideration. I have led this Party, so far, for twelve and a half years, in unprecedented and difficult times for all of us.

During those twelve and a half years – and this is without precedent – I challenge anyone to dispute this – not one of the near 600 Labour Members of Parliament who have served in Parliament over these years has had the Party Whip withdrawn. I am proud of that. I am proud, too, that almost my first act on being elected Leader was to insist, against a more than resistant Shadow Cabinet, that the Whip be restored to six members of Parliament, one of whom is now in the Cabinet.[1] He replied to the economic debate yesterday, with the full acclamation of Conference (*Applause*).

I therefore have the right to ask who are these self-appointed Samurai who seek to assert a power of political life and death which the leadership of this Party and Whips' Office and the Organization Sub-Committee of the Labour Party have not in modern times sought to assert.

At this stage there was, as recorded in the Conference record, an 'interruption', a lone voice of protest from the gallery on my right. In a tone of reassurance I commented that I was not asking anyone to identify himself: 'it was a rhetorical question'.

As a Party we are committed to real industrial democracy. What we say should take place in industry, we cannot deny to our own Party members.

We demand more participation; if we mean what we say then democracy means the full participation of every Labour member in the biggest decision a constituency Party is asked to make – the decision who shall, or who shall not, represent them in Parliament.

Still more, when a candidate has received the stamp of electoral support, extremely grave cause is required, and the fullest participation of party democracy is needed, if the electorate is to be denied the right to re-elect him as an endorsed Labour candidate.

Our strength lies not in enforced uniformity of Party doctrine. It is based on tolerance and argument, on the ferment of political ideas and political passion – not regimentation – I do not want to lead a party of Zombies.

My fourth theme, a reprise of the November 1974 Central Hall Conference, was Labour as the natural party of government. If the Parliament elected in October 1974 ran its full course, Labour would have been in office for nearly $11\frac{1}{2}$ of those 15 years. For most of our 75 years we had been the party of protest, now

we have to ensure that simply because we are the Party of Government, we are still able to fulfil the role of protest. All of us, Ministers, Members of Parliament, constituency parties, affiliated organizations, Executive Conference, the wider Party.

All those who have reason to protest should recognize our Party as the natural voice to express that protest, for there is none other.

A considerable part of my speech of course dealt with economic issues, particularly inflation and unemployment. Inevitably a few paragraphs were devoted to our opponents – less than is usual in a Conference of either major party. The main theme here was the Conservatives' failure to spell out their alternative policy, particularly on finance. Their endless demand was to cut expenditure, but without saying what should be cut. On defence, and one or two other areas, they were

---

[1] Michael Foot. I had made an issue of the withdrawal of the Whips from him and the others at almost the first meeting of the Shadow Cabinet I had chaired in February 1963, facing as I was an almost unitedly hostile Parliamentary Committee.

demanding greatly increased expenditure. What I most enjoyed, as always, was taking them back to 1862 and Disraeli:

> Mere abstract and declaratory opinions in favour of reduction and retrench-
> ment are of no use whatsoever. I have so often maintained it in this House that
> I am almost ashamed to repeat it, but unfortunately it is not a principle which
> has yet sufficiently entered into public opinion – expenditure depends on policy.

My other reference to the Conservatives related to the poverty and public anonymity of their front-bench team. I challenged any hearer, including the skilled Parliamentary journalists sitting below, to write down the names of the incumbents of the twelve most senior 'shadow' posts, without resort to the reference books.

Lobby men afterwards admitted that not one of the many hundreds of press and broadcasting pundits could have done so.

# Appendix XIII Statement by the Prime Minister to the Cabinet, 16 March 1976, on his resignation

I have just returned from the Palace where I had an Audience of the Queen. I formally confirmed to her a decision of which I had apprised her early in December, that in March of this year I would intend to make way for a successor, and that I would resign as Prime Minister as soon as the Parliamentary Party had completed the necessary constitutional procedures for electing a new Leader.

In March 1974 I decided that I would remain in office for no more than two years. I have not wavered in this decision, and it is irrevocable. Indeed I had originally intended that it should take effect last September, but decided to defer it because of the paramount importance of ensuring the national acceptance and success of the counter-inflation policy the Government announced last July.

I must, of course, inform my colleagues of my reasons.

*First*, I have been Leader of this Party for over thirteen exciting and turbulent years – nearly eight of them in Government. My period as Prime Minister has been longer than that of any of my peacetime predecessors in this century. These years of office spanned a period when Britain, nationally and internationally, had to face storms and challenges without parallel in our peacetime history.

But it is not only those last thirteen years; in thirty-one years in Parliament I have been on one or other Front Bench for nearly thirty years – for almost eleven and a half years in Cabinet. No one should ask for more.

To have led four administrations, dedicated not only to solving the nation's economic problems but also to achieving a higher level of social justice and equality than our people have ever known, is a privilege conferred on very few men.

*Second*, I have a clear duty to the country and to the Party not to remain here so long that others are denied the chance to seek election to this post. This is the most experienced and talented team in this century, in my view transcending that of Campbell-Bannerman seventy years ago. I am proud of that. A leadership election will do good in showing the country the wealth of talent in our ranks . . .

The fact that I am leaving shortly after my sixtieth birthday has no bearing on the choice to be made. I have reached sixty after thirteen years' Party leadership, nearly eight of these in Downing Street. Some of my most distinguished predecessors were either just below or just over that age on becoming Prime Minister, including Clem Attlee, Winston Churchill, Harold Macmillan and Alec Douglas-Home in our own time. The fact that I began early and have borne the responsibility of this office for so long means that sixty is the right age for me to promulgate a change.

*Third*, it is my view that my successor should be in post now, to impose his or her style and to work out the strategy for the remaining years of this Parliament. But *I am certain that the new Administration will assert the same determination and dedication in our counter-inflation policies in this country, as we have unitedly shown to the world. Equally I am totally convinced that no conceivable reconstruction of the Cabinet could in any way lead to a weakening in our resolve to fulfil in full measure our commitment to our allies and partners overseas.*

*Fourth*, there *is* a danger, to which I have been alerted all my working life. It is that, in times of rapid change, you may be faced with a decision which, perhaps in different conditions, you have faced before. If, on the earlier occasion you considered and rejected a particular course of action, there *is* a tendency to say you have been into that, so that you do not give the fresh consideration the circumstances may require. I am determined not to succumb to this danger.

I want to make it quite clear, with the agreement of all my colleagues, that these reasons represent the total explanation of my decision. There are no impending problems or difficulties – economic or political – known to the Cabinet, which are not known to the country and which are not already the subject of the political discussion of our times.

Now I want to express my warm thanks to my colleagues, not only for their work and achievements, but for the fact that in all my four administrations these have been *happy* Cabinets. We have faced problems far more daunting than any Cabinet in our post-war history, and those problems have been met with more courage, more determination, more imagination and more comradeship and unity than by any Cabinet of which I have knowledge. I have in fact presided over 472 Cabinets and thousands of Cabinet Committees. I have answered more than 12,000 Parliamentary Questions.

I am proud of the achievements of these past two years.

We remember what we faced when we were recalled to office a little over two years ago. It was not only the economic paralysis. There was a widespread anxiety in the country that even the 'governability' of Britain was in doubt. It is not in doubt today, because the economic and social governance of Britain has been established on the basis of the consent of the people.

We have created a new relationship between Government and people to replace the clash and confrontation which two years ago almost brought this country to disaster.

This is a far more united and determined people now than for many years.

Our counter-inflation policies have been accepted by the great majority of the nation. Our counter-inflation target for the end of this year is now in sight of achievement.

In 1975 the current account deficit on our balance of payments was less than half the deficit in 1974, even though we have had to meet – and had to meet in a period of unprecedented world economic problems – the five-fold increase in the price of the oil we import.

The value of our exports is rising strongly – by 4 per cent in the last three months compared with the previous three months – and at a much faster rate than imports.

For two years we have had to face the consequences of world inflation and world unemployment. But now the economy is beginning to revive. Business confidence is higher than at any time since the autumn of 1973. There are growing signs that the rate of increase in unemployment is running at a very much smaller level than last year, particularly the last three months of last year.

We inherited a dangerously distorted and unbalanced economy. We are beginning to get it right.

For the first time, industrial problems are being tackled by relevant microeconomic action in place of an over-reliance on clumsy and often ineffective macro-economic lurches; through NEDC and direct action to restructure and modernize particular industries; through NEB and specific sectoral actions to strengthen our economic base, which is manufacturing industry.

We have embarked on the biggest programme of industrial training and retraining in our history.

We have carried through the greatest-ever improvements in the standards of pensioners and others dependent on the social services, particularly the disabled, previously so neglected.

We inherited the lowest housebuilding figures since the 1950s; we have restored the housing programme to over 300,000 houses a year.

In world affairs our relations with the United States, with European countries, East and West, *and* with the Commonwealth, are better than for many years. Our membership of the European Community has been confirmed. Our relations with the US were recently described by President Ford as being 'as good as they have ever been'.

Now, for the future.

Later this morning I will meet the Chairman of the Parliamentary Labour Party, and propose that he calls a special meeting of the Party this evening to put forward the Liaison Committee's suggestions for the leadership election, so that the nominations may be invited forthwith. I would hope that they may be able to devise procedures which enable full consideration to be combined with all reasonable speed – certainly more expeditious than the somewhat leisurely weekly procedures of the past.

I shall play no part in that election apart from casting my own vote by secret ballot. Nor will I seek to influence a single Member of the Party in his vote.

I shall remain in Parliament as long as my Constituency will put up with me. I have not been inactive on behalf of my constituents. I hope to see more of them and put in more time on their behalf. I am above all a Parliamentarian. I love Parliament and want to go on serving it and serving in it.

I shall not go into industry or take paid employment.

I shall not accept the headship or other office in any place of learning, apart from my present relationship with the University of Bradford. I may give occasional lectures here or abroad, as I have for many years, but not to the detriment of my Parliamentary work.

I want to say this to my successor, whoever he or she may be.

This is an office to cherish; stimulating and satisfying. You will never have a dull moment; you will never get bored. But it is a full-time calling. These are not the easy, spacious, socially-orientated days of some of my predecessors. Apart from quite generous holidays – when, thanks to modern communications, I have never been more than moments away from Downing Street – I have had to work seven days a week at least 12 to 14 hours a day. But the variety and interest – with, usually, at least 500 different documents or submissions to read in an average week-end after a busy week–means that you do not get bored; consequently, you do not get tired . . .

Every Prime Minister has his own style. But he must know all that is going on. Even if he were tempted to be remiss in this, the wide-open nature of Prime Minister's Questions – entirely different from that of any departmental Minister – requires familiarity with, and understanding of, the problems of every Department and every part of the country.

More than that, the price of an Administration's continuance and success is eternal vigilance – on duty or on call every minute of the day. Yet you must find time enough to stand back and think about the problems of the Administration, its purpose, its coordination and its longer-term strategy. Equally you have to watch for that cloud no bigger than a man's hand which may threaten not tomorrow's crisis, but perhaps next month's or next year's. In all this you have got to think and feel politically as well as in constitutional and administrative terms.

It is not only the job here in Westminster, Whitehall and Parliament. It is the job in the country. The leader of the Party, and no less the Prime Minister, has a duty to meet the people, to address political and other meetings. For 13 years I have averaged well over 100 a year, covering nearly every constituency, some of them many times.

You will be able to count on my full support, especially when the going is rough.

My advice and experience is available when you seek it: I do not intend to offer gratuitous advice.

I will give any help I can in any form you ask, inside the House, in the Parliamentary Party, and in the country, apart from accepting a Ministerial appointment.

In particular, I shall be guided by the letter and spirit of the undertaking which a pre-war predecessor gave when he stood down for a successor, who was in fact chosen – not elected as is our rule – 'Once I leave, I leave. I am not going to speak to the man on the bridge, and I am not going to spit on the deck.'

I am confident that this brief election period will be comradely and not divisive.

In this period every Minister will be expected to put his full effort into his Departmental and Cabinet duties. I will, of course, remain in full charge of the Administration until the electoral process is completed, exercising all the rights and duties of a Prime Minister to take any action that is needed.

I am confident that a new Prime Minister in taking over will enjoy from his Cabinet the same loyalty, support, understanding and even, when required, forgiveness, that it has been my privilege to enjoy.

My only advice to him and the Cabinet he forms – and I am sure this advice is not necessary – is to get out into the country, meet the people, tell them, explain to them, listen to them; and above all remember the Party is the Party in the country – not the Palace of Westminster, not Smith Square.

In return I would ask the Party everywhere – and I hope that our press friends, all of whom I forgive, will allow me to say this to them as well – that in all circumstances all concerned will comply with the spirit of the Speaker's Petition to the Queen on behalf of the Commons when a new Parliament meets: 'that the most favourable construction may be placed on all your proceedings'.

# INDEX

# Index

307

Offshore Petroleum Development Act, 123

Offshore Supplies Office, 34, 49

oil crisis (November 1973–February 1974), 2, 4, 13, 15, 16, 22–4, 25, 26, 86, 152–3, 161, 233

oil prices, 22–8 *passim*, 86, 110, 112, 152–3, 161, 185, 202, 228

Oil Taxation Bill, 42, 133–4, 135

Olszowski, Stefan, 57

O'Malley, Brian, 125

Open University, 18

Opposition parties, financial assistance to, 15, 133

Organization for Economic Co-operation and Development (OECD), 110, 185, 186

Organization of Petroleum Exporting Countries (OPEC), 23, 39, 135, 153

Orkney and Shetland, 108

Orme, Stanley, 73, 74, 75, 125, 128

Ortoli, M., President of EEC Commission, 64, 92, 93, 101, 102, 201, 202, 215

Ottawa, Wilson visits, 152

Outer Continental Independence Agency, 187

Overseas Bankers' Club, Wilson speaks at, 220

Paisley, Rev Ian, 74, 77

Pakenham, Lord, 17

Palestine Liberation Organization (PLO), 159

Palme, Olof, 175, 176, 214

Palmerston, Lord, 236

Panov, Valery and Galina, 57–8

Papua New Guinea, 181

Paris, Summit Conference, 55; Wilson visits, 56

Parliamentary and Scientific Committee, Wilson speaks at, 220, 224

pay-beds, 190–92

pay restraint, *see* prices and incomes policy

Peart, Frederick, 17, 21, 56, 103, 104, 124

Peat, Marwick, Mitchell, 136–7

pensions, 14, 25, 44, 122, 126–8, 146–8; Civil Service, 222

Perkins, 57

Peterson, Colin, 224

Petroleum and Submarine Pipelines Bill, 42, 123, 134

Peugeot, 141, 150, 200n

Pinnock, Frank, 157n

Pitt, William (The Younger), 66

'planning agreements', 29, 31, 33–6, 37, 123, 138, 140–41

Plant, Cyril, 222

Poland, 57, 165, 166, 172, 181

'political advisers', 19

Pompidou, Georges, 3, 11, 50, 56, 152

ports, 31, 35, 122

Portugal, 97, 103, 157, 164, 166, 168–72, 173, 176, 181, 182, 214; *Republica*, 170; Portuguese Socialist Party, 170, 171; Committee of Friendship and Solidarity with Democracy and Socialism in Portugal, 176, 182

Post Office, 148, 189

Powell, Enoch, 121, 235

Prentice, Reginald, 21, 103

press, 224–6, 228–9; Royal Commission, 229, 235; and Wilson resignation, 229, 232–4; and Wilson's successor, 233; and Labour prime minister, 234

Press Council, 225

Prevention of Terrorism (Temporary Provision) Act (1974), 210

Price Commission, 112

prices and incomes policy, 14, 15, 16, 24, 29, 42–3, 87, 111–13, 115, 119–21, 227, 237, 269–72; statutory controls, 3, 4–5, 42; Prices and Incomes Board, 251, 253; *Guardian* report, 251–4

privacy, right of, 224–5, 226, 228–9

Product and Process Development Scheme, 151

Privy Purse, 131

property boom, 2, 24, 43

Property Development Tax, 26

Public Accounts Committee, 200, 223; Report on North Sea oil, 38–40, 133

public expenditure, cuts, 25, 26; programme (1976–7), 229–31

public ownership, *see* nationalization

Public Sector Borrowing Requirement, 25, 26, 27